STRIKERS, HOBBLERS, CONCHIES AND REDS

Dave Backwith, Roger Ball, Stephen E. Hunt, Mike Richardson

•

Strikers, Hobblers, Conchies and Reds

A Radical History of Bristol 1880-1939

BREVIARY STUFF PUBLICATIONS
2014

First published 2014 by Breviary Stuff Publications,
BCM Breviary Stuff, London WC1N 3XX
www.breviarystuff.org.uk

A CIP record for this book is available from
The British Library

ISBN: 978-0-9929466-0-9

Contents

Illustrations

Acknowledgements

This book is essentially the result of a happy meeting of minds in 2005, which led to the formation of the Bristol Radical History Group. Early inspiration and assistance came from many sources, especially Ian Bone, Christina Heatherton, Peter Linebaugh and Marcus Rediker. Our activities were initially realised through the social networks surrounding the Easton Cowboys and Cowgirls Sports Club. We salute the cricketers, footballers, artists, performers, techies, publicans, ranters, ravers, Cancan dancers, stoners and other ne'r do wells who have given their labour for free in helping us along the way.

Most of the essays in this book have appeared in one form or another as part of the Bristol Radical Pamphleteer series. The authors Steve Hunt, Michael Richardson, Roger Ball and Dave Backwith would like to thank a number of people for providing help in their production. Our research efforts over the years have been greatly assisted by Dawn Dyer and her colleagues at the Bristol Central Reference Library, the staff at the Bristol Record Office and the University of West of England Library. Others have provided specific aid in the research including Georges Rey, David Sachs, Stuart E. Cox, Jim McNeil, Mark Steeds and Mel Plumer. Most of the visual sources, including maps, were discovered, photographed or created by Richard Grove. Sheila Rowbotham provided detailed comments, criticisms and helped edit Chapters 2, 3, 4 and 6. The diligent proof readers include Mark Ellingsen (Chapter 1), Stephen E. Hunt (Chapters 2, 3 & 4), Will Simpson (Chapters 5 & 8), Sheila Rowbotham and Rich Grove (Chapter 6) and John Roberts (Chapter 7). Our excellent graphic designer and techie, Richard Grove, fashioned all of the Bristol Radical Pamphleteer series and created the cover of this book. Paul Mangan of Breviary Stuff Publications has been helpful throughout the production process and we thank him for his patience.

Finally, we would like to thank our partners, families, housemates and friends for putting up with it all at one time or another.

Abbreviations

ASLEF	Associated Society of Locomotive Engineers and Firemen
ASRS	Amalgamated Society of Railway Servants
BCRL	Bristol Central Reference Library
BELP	Bristol East Labour Party
BEN	*Bristol Evening News*
BEP	*Bristol Evening Post*
BEW	*Bristol Evening World*
BM	*Bristol Mercury*
BMDP	*Bristol Mercury and Daily Post*
BRHG	Bristol Radical History Group
BRO	Bristol Record Office
BSP	British Socialist Party
BSS	Bristol Socialist Society
BTIA	Bristol Timber Importers Association
BTM	*Bristol Times and Mirror*
BUA	Bristol Unemployed Association
CC	*Clifton Chronicle*
CO	conscientious objector
COMINTERN	Communist (Third) International
CP/CPGB	Communist Party of Great Britain
DPP	Director of Public Prosecutions
DWRGLU	Dock, Wharf, Riverside and General Labourers' Union of Great Britain and Ireland
DWRGWU	Dock, Wharf, Riverside and General Workers' Union of Great Britain and Ireland
DWRU	Dock, Wharf, Riverside and General Workers' Union (Bristol)
GCTPA	Garden Cities and Town Planning Association
GRWU	General Railway Workers' Union
GWGLU	Gas Workers and General Labourers' Union
GWR	Great Western Railway
GWRC	Great Western Railway Company
ILP	Independent Labour Party
ITGWU	Irish Transport and General Workers Union
IUDA	Industrial Union of Direct Actionists
LBIF	London Building Industries' Federation
LRC	Labour Representation Committee
MFGB	Miners' Federation of Great Britain
MP	Member of Parliament
NAC	National Administrative Council (of the NUWM)
NFWW	National Federation of Women Workers
NSFU	National Sailors and Firemen's Union
NTWF	National Transport Workers' Federation
NUR	National Union of Railwaymen

NUWM	National Unemployed Workers' Movement
OGPU	Joint State Political Directorate (secret police of the Soviet Union 1922-1934)
PAC	Public Assistance Committee
SDF	Social Democratic Federation
TNA	The National Archive
TUC	Trades Union Congress
UAB	Unemployed Assistance Board
UIBs	Unemployment Insurance Benefits
UPSS	United Pointmen's and Signalmen's Society
WC	Watch Committee
WDP	*Western Daily Press*
WWI	World War I
WWII	World War II
YMCA	Young Men's Christian Association

Contributors

Dave Backwith is course leader for the MA Social Work at Anglia Ruskin University (Chelmsford). His PhD was on the politics of council housing in Bristol and Sheffield between the wars. His current research interests include poverty and social work.

Roger Ball is one of the founders of Bristol Radical History Group which developed out of the Easton Cowboys and Cowgirls Sports Club in 2005. As a result of this historical turn, he received his PhD from the University of the West of England in 2012 with a thesis entitled *Violent Urban Disturbance in England 1980-81*. As an independent researcher, Roger produced the first quantitative analysis of the August 2011 'riots', publishing articles in *Radical Statistics* and *Aufheben*, and speaking widely in the UK and US. He currently divides his time between his day-job as an aerospace engineer and historical research into urban 'riots' in Bristol and strikes, mutinies and refusals in the British armed forces during World War One.

Stephen E. Hunt is a writer, librarian, activist and radical historian. His PhD in English Literature was awarded for a research thesis from the University of the West of England on Romantic ecology. He continues to take an ecocritical approach to the Romantic era and its ongoing legacy. Within this field, particular interests include human well-being and the natural environment, great apes, garden cities, eco-anarchism and the 1970s ecology movement. He has written for many publications including *Capitalism Nature Socialism*, *Green Letters*, *Freedom* and *Environment and History*. Tangent Books published Stephen's latest book *The Revolutionary Urbanism of Street Farm: Eco-Anarchism, Architecture and Alternative Technology in the 1970s* in 2014. Contact Stephen at streetfarm@phonecoop.coop.

Mike Richardson is a Visiting Fellow at the University of the West of England. His recent co-authored books, which chronicles workers' resistance to changing patterns of exploitation, include *Partnership and the High Performance Workplace: Work and Employment Relations in the Aerospace Industry* (Palgrave, 2005); *The Reality of Partnership at Work* (Palgrave, 2008); *We Sell Our Time No More: Workers' struggles against lean production in the British car industry* (Pluto, 2009). He has also one the co-editors of *Flexibility at Work. Critical Developments in the International Automobile Industry* (Palgrave Macmillan, 2008), and co-editor with P. Nicholls of *A Business and Labour History of Britain: Case Studies of Britain in the Nineteenth and Twentieth Centuries* (Palgrave Macmillan, 2011). Contact Mike at michael964@blueyonder.co.uk.

Introduction

Bristol

In the 1970s and '80s, a revival of interest emerged in researching Bristol's vigorous radical past, reflected in the publications of the Bristol branch of the Historical Association and Bristol Broadsides.[1] This revival has continued, echoed in the more recent historical studies that have advanced the work of filling in Bristol's remarkable past — especially the involvement of the Bristol women's movement in the nineteenth century in anti-slavery campaigns, social reform, and the struggle for the emancipation of women, developing into the suffrage movement[2] — but gaps in our knowledge still exist. This collection of essays traces, in Bristol and the surrounding area from the late nineteenth century through to the 1930s, the relationship between labour struggles and the new ideas and practice of general unionism, socialism and anarchism.

Bristol's prosperity in the nineteenth and twentieth centuries had been, to a significant extent, built on its share of the triangular slave trade between West Africa, England, America and the West Indies. This prosperity, however, was enjoyed only by the few. The merchant community, an elite and secretive body represented by the Society of Merchant Venturers, including West India merchants and planters, flourished on the back of this vile trade. Industrialists, such as the Wills' family, had made their fortune from importing and processing tobacco leaves obtained from slave plantations. Similarly, the Fry's dynasty had imported cocoa, sugar and molasses from America and the West Indies to convert into beverages and chocolate, first for medicinal purposes, then as a delicacy for the wealthy, before production costs were driven down to such an extent it became an affordable 'luxury' for the masses.[3]

---

1   See for instance, D. Large and R. Whitfield, *The Bristol Trades Council 1873-1973* (Bristol branch of the Historical Association, 1973); B. Atkinson, *Trade Unions in Bristol* (Bristol Branch of the Historical Association, 1982); I. Bild (ed.), *Bristol's Other History* (Bristol: Bristol Broadsides, 1983); I. Bild (ed.), *Placards and Pin Money* (Bristol Broadsides, 1983).

2   See E. Malos, 'Bristol Women in Action (1839-1919)' in *Bristol's Other History* I. Bild (ed.) (Bristol: Bristol Broadsides, 1983); M. Dresser and P. Ollerenshaw (eds.), *The Making of Modern Bristol*, (Redcliffe Press, 1996), in particular June Hannam's chapter, "An Enlarged Sphere of Usefulness': The Bristol Women's Movement, c.1860-1914'; L. Boyce, *The Bristol Suffragettes* (Silverwood Books, 2013) and also Madge Dresser's (ed.) forthcoming book *Women in Bristol, 1400-2000: Making the City*.

3   W. Minchinton, 'The Port of Bristol in the Eighteenth Century' in *Bristol in the Eighteenth Century* P. McGrath (ed.) (Newton Abbot: David and Charles, 1972); P. McGrath, *The Merchant Venturers of Bristol: a History of the Society of Merchant Venturers of the City of Bristol from its Origin to the Present Day* (Greensboro, NC, USA: American Society of Civil Engineers, 1975); S. Diaper, 'J.S. Fry and Sons: Growth and Decline in the Chocolate Industry, 1753-1918' in

The share of Bristol's emerging working class in the wealth they helped to create was, however, minimal. Work in mining, construction, manufacturing and transport and communication industries was poorly paid, especially for women, and often carried out in harsh and unhealthy working conditions. Moreover, on leaving work after long arduous day, many would return to their living quarters in central Bristol that often comprised just 'one small room to a family in an ill conditioned badly drained house'.[4] Unsurprisingly, herded together in such crowded, smelly, disease-ridden homes the mortality rate in Bristol was the third highest in the country.[5]

The shared misery of workers in the first half of the nineteenth century began to bring about the awakening of class consciousness. As Edward Thompson put it in his ground-breaking book, *The Making of the English Working Class*, working class presence in the 1830s was at a level across England significantly high enough to produce 'a consciousness of the identity of the interests of the working class, or 'productive classes' as against those of other classes'.[6]

However, after 1848, with the collapse of the Chartist movement, which was never that strong in Bristol, a period of political indifference set in. The working class, largely deprived of the franchise (only 6.8% of the population in Bristol had a right to vote in Parliamentary elections in 1865, which rose to 12.1% after the 1867 Reform Act) turned to trade unionism to fight for a decent wage. But as a first resort many muddled headed union leaders held out the hand of friendship to employers opting for arbitration to settle disputes and avoid strikes. In any event trade union membership was small especially for unskilled workers in precarious employment.

Improvements in the social environment of Bristol's working class rested on the Municipal Council or 'Corporation' whose functions increased significantly in the latter half of the nineteenth century. Although by the 1880s this development resulted in improvements in the water supply and sewage disposal, which had made a significant contribution to lowering the mortality rates,[7] impoverished, overcrowded and squalid locales, such as the Dings, St Philip's, St Jude's, Barton Hill and Hotwells, continued to provide the only 'affordable' accommodation for significant sections of the working class, particularly for those that were unemployed or in casual work.

Disaffection with this state of affairs bubbled beneath the surface. A 20,000 strong demonstration took place on Brandon Hill in January 1880 that stimulated local Liberals, fearing social unrest, to take some action. An inquiry into 'Homes of the Bristol Poor' was initiated and a series of articles in the *Bristol Mercury*

Studies in the Business History of Bristol, C. Harvey and J. Press (eds.) (Bristol Academic Press, 1988); B. W. E. Alford, *W. D. & H. O. Wills and the Development of the U.K Tobacco Industry, 1786–1965* (London: Methuen, 1973).

4   D. Large, *The Municipal Government of Bristol 1851-1901* (Bristol Record Society, 1999), p. 102.

5   Ibid.

6   E. P. Thompson, *The Making of the English Working Class* (Penguin, 1982, first published by Victor Gollancz, 1963), p. 888.

7   I. Archer, S. Jordan, K. Ramsey, *Abstract of Bristol Historical Statistics part 4: Health Statistics 1838-1985* (University of the West of England, 1997).

was published between November 1883 and May 1885 tracking the findings. However, some observers commented that 'the active state of the public conscience would soon pass away, leaving things much as they were before.'[8] This prediction turned out to have some substance. According to the local press, in May 1885 the full report, published in March, had not received the attention it deserved 'owing to the pressure of grave political anxieties' including concern about the growing expenditure of the Council from ratepayers.

By the late 1880s Britain had begun to pull out of the Great Depression that had blighted the country since 1870, and Bristol, which in many ways can be considered as a microcosm of the national economy, with its diverse range of traditional and new industries, entered a period of economic recovery. However, the improvement in employment prospects acted as a catalyst to release the pent up anger associated with years of unemployment, poor living conditions and low wages, with a sudden and surprising intensity.

Given that Bristol's economic and social development over the last century or so followed a similar course to that of Britain as a whole makes it a particularly useful case study. The stage is now set for the essays that follow, but before we move on to briefly outline their content, it is worthwhile to present some of the relevant data available on population and employment in Bristol. The number of inhabitants, within the 1835 boundaries of Bristol, grew from 125,146 in 1841, 221,578 in 1891, 357,114 in 1911, to 397,012 in 1931 and those economically active increased from 47,590 in 1841, 101,769 in 1891, 163,612 in 1911, to 188,461 in 1931.[9] Reasonably accurate unemployment statistics are only available from 1922 when unemployment in Bristol stood at 17,834, approximately 10.2% of the workforce. In December 1930, those out of work peaked at 26,398, about 14% of the workforce.

Content

This collection of essays begins with the hitherto neglected history of *Anarchism in Bristol and the West Country*[10]. Chapter One looks at the gradual emergence of anarchism as a distinct political and cultural current within the wider labour movement from the late nineteenth century onwards. A trouble-making crew of West Country anarchists increasingly represented an uncompromising resistance to both state and capital, seeking to encourage workers to act in solidarity as a class for themselves and to seize economic power through syndicalist agitation leading to workers' control of the means of production. The Socialist League publication *Commonweal*, avowedly 'A Revolutionary Journal of Anarchist-Communism' during the early 1890s, enthusiastically reported on militant

---

8   *BM*, 20 December 1884.

9   P. Ollerenshaw and P. Wardley, 'Economic Growth and the Business Community in Bristol since 1840' in Dresser and Ollerenshaw (eds.), *The Making of Modern Bristol*, p. 126.

10   Samson Bryher's three-part book *An Account of the Labour and Socialist movement in Bristol: Describing its Early Beginnings, Struggles and Growth* (1931) provides a comprehensive and detailed history of the Bristol Socialist Society and Trade Union movement from the 1870s to 1920s. No similar contemporary work addresses the Anarchist movement in Bristol in the period.

resistance by strikers, their supporters and wider working-class solidarity networks, including such struggles as Bristol's great labour revolt, the Radstock miners' strike and the Southampton dockers' dispute. Beyond such economic struggles, however, anarchists sought — and of course still seek — wider social emancipation from the shackles of religion, imperialism, patriarchy and militarism.

In the early twentieth century we find that several internationally influential anarchists had West Country connections – the best-selling, though now largely forgotten, editor of *The Anarchist* George Barrett, Emma Goldman, the novelist John Cowper Powys and the indefatigable rebel Guy Aldred. There is also the untold story of anarchists who found themselves in West Country gaols and labour camps due to their internationalist resistance to the First World War. Often receiving harsher treatment than religious and pacifist conscientious objectors, a handful of unpublished letters to loved ones and comrades at *Freedom* magazine reveal a small but overlooked episode in uncompromising anti-militarism.

Chapter Two, *Pirates to Proletarians*, charts the experiences, in the nineteenth century, of Bristol's river pilots, and their assistants, in their struggle to defend their jobs and their traditional way of working, as steam power emerged to replace sail. Their relationship with the ship-owners, masters and city authorities was a complex one, which broke down periodically into open conflict. They lived almost exclusively in Crockerne Pill, a small village, five miles from Bristol, situated on the south side of the river Avon. Pill people exhibited a lack of deference and were looked upon by the Bristol authorities, and many town-dwellers, as disorderly and difficult. As the nineteenth century progressed, however, the realization took hold that the interests of the pilots and watermen of Pill had much in common with trade unionists in Bristol and the wider labour movement. This chapter acts as a case study demonstrating the effects upon and reactions of groups of workers whose traditional status and customary practices were being undermined by the rapid industrialisation of the nineteenth century.

Chapter Three, *The Bristol Strike Wave of 1889-1890: Part One: Days of Hope*, examines the support given by Bristol socialists to the rise of 'New Unionism' as worker militancy in Bristol exploded between September and December 1889. Drawing on many new sources it presents a detailed picture of strikes in the city during this period. A notable feature of these disputes was that as well as involving non-craft male workers, such as dock labourers, women workers also participated in significant numbers. Moreover, two middle class women, Miriam Daniell and Helena Born, played a leading role in the Strike Organisation Committee set up to support the strikers. Formerly members of the Bristol Women's Liberal Association, by the autumn of 1889 they had become active in the Bristol Socialist Society; and it was the involvement and influence of this organisation in the events of the upsurge of workers' militancy that added to the concern of employers and the city's ruling elite.

Chapter Four, *The Bristol Strike Wave of 1889-1890: Part Two: Days of Doubt*, charts the occurrences of industrial conflict in Bristol between January and August 1890, starting with the lockout of boot and shoe workers, and addresses the challenges faced by workers, and union and socialist organisers. These challenges included the continuation of the struggle over how to best defend women workers, as differences were apparent between those who advocated separate unions for women and stressed welfare over militancy, and those who agitated for an alternative model of unionism open to women and men willing to fight for their cause. Another key challenge examined, and one that expressed creeping apprehension, is how the Bristol labour movement responded to the Bristol Chamber of Commerce in sponsoring a Board of Arbitration and Conciliation. While the fervent hopes of the Bristol socialists aroused by the 1889-90 strike wave were not to be realised, Bristol's working class had appeared on the political, economic and social agenda as a force not to be ignored.

Chapter Five, *The Origins and an Account of Black Friday: 23rd December 1892*, explores the employers counter-offensive of 1892-93, which was aimed at rolling back the recent gains made by Bristolian workers. Although the autumn of 1892 centred on disputes initiated by the employers and involving dockers, miners, confectionery and chemical workers, the primary targets of the owners were the new unions forged in the strike waves of 1889-90. Aided by their dual-membership in the local council and judiciary, the Bristol bourgeoisie and their agents sought to intimidate strikers using lock-outs, violent policing, fines and imprisonment. Instead they were faced with an increasingly confident and popular movement of strikers and their supporters who took to the streets in their thousands. The relations of force that lay between the working-class movement and its bourgeois opponents became brutally explicit (and iconic) on 'Black Friday' (December 23rd 1892) when the local state employed police and cavalry units to break up a pre-Christmas lantern parade to collect money for strikers and their families.

At this point the reader can take a well-earned break during the *Intermezzo*, by venturing into the coffee taverns of Victorian Bristol. It was in these institutions that Socialists, Anarchists and Trade Unionists read their 'seditious' publications, discussed politics and met to organise strike committees and campaigns. These cultural spaces provided an environment which encouraged freedom of thought and debate and were also open, significantly, to single women.

Having downed our coffees we resume our story in Chapter Six, with *Bristol and the Labour Unrest of 1910-14*, which studies Bristol's experience of industrial strife between 1910 and the outbreak of the First World War, in August 1914. Britain, during this period, witnessed a significant increase in unofficial strike activity, as significant sections of the trade union rank-and-file began to express their frustration at the lack of progress made in their struggle for better working conditions and a new social order. Strikes reached levels not seen since the 'new unionism' upsurge of 1889-92. Workers unrest combined with clashes over Home Rule for Ireland, and the militant tactics of suffrage campaigners, which added to the problems of the ruling class. Confronted by these parallel rebellions the ruling class feared their convergence and some warned of the danger of revolution. Rather than focus on some of Bristol's famous union leaders, such as Ben Tillett and Ernest Bevin, this account scrutinises the events from the union rank-and-file perspective.

Chapter Seven explores cultural aspects of Bristolian history from below, with the essay *Yesterday's To-morrow* revealing the profound, yet now largely forgotten, influence of the garden-city movement in defining the urban morphology of the estates around Bristol's residential periphery. As we learn from the popularity of psycho-geography[11] and its contribution to radical history in recent decades, attention to such phenomena as patterns of settlement, sites of celebration and struggle and ecology has the potential to transform our experience of moving through, and being in, a particular environment. In this way a social history from below not only reveals the glaring mismatch of the mansion and the tenement but also explores the perhaps more subtly contested versions of social and economic forces at play in the presence and governance of the sports ground, the allotment, the cinema and the pub. It aspires therefore to encourage understanding of the enduring paradigms of hierarchy and authoritarianism and their underlying mechanisms of social control as well as open up more clearly to the imagination possibilities for authentic transformation and liberation. Such an attunement calls for watchfulness not just of the attractive formalist characteristics of a garden-suburb house and garden which may be similar in Sea Mills, Knowle West or Speedwell, but the less tangible influences of capital flows and social power that determine the conditions of life alongside bricks and mortar.

The banking crisis of 2008 and the following deep recession experienced by the world economy has led to mass unemployment and poverty in the U.K. Massive public sector cuts along with huge financial bonuses for the wealthy have exacerbated the systemic divisions between 'rich and poor' which lie at the heart of the neo-liberal economy. It thus seemed apt for our narrative to conclude with Chapter Eight, *Bread or Batons? Unemployed Workers' Struggles in Bristol in the 1930s*, which looks back at Bristol in the period of the last 'great depression'. There are numerous parallels with our recent history, from cuts in poor relief and public services, a collaborationist and emasculated Labour opposition, to the brutal policing of demonstrations and a corrupt and reactionary media.

Chapter Eight is divided into four sections; the first and second look respectively at the state of political economy from a national and Bristolian perspective in the 1930s. The third section considers what happened on the streets of Bristol principally in 1932. We look in detail at the demonstrations, the reaction of the police and protesters and the organisation of the principal players including crucially the National Unemployed Workers' Movement (NUWM), the

---

11 Psycho-geography was a term popularised by the Situationist International in the 1950s and was described by their leading theoretician Guy Debord as 'the study of the precise laws and specific effects of the geographical environment, consciously organized or not, on the emotions and behaviour of individuals' G. Debord, 'Introduction to a Critique of Urban Geography', in *Situationist International Anthology*, (ed.) K. Knabb (Berkeley, CA: Bureau of Public Secrets, 1981), p. 5.

main organisation opposing unemployment and the 'cuts'. The last section consists of an analysis of the reaction of the state to the protests of the unemployed, the changing police tactics they employed to 'deal with them' and the gains made by the NUWM.

Before we leave you to peruse these essays, as 'good' historians we are going to have a chat about our approaches and methodology, especially where they differ from conventional practice.

History from below

The researchers and writers that have contributed to this book would certainly consider themselves as practitioners of 'history from below', 'peoples' history' or the more benign 'social history'.[12] 'History from below' is an interesting expression as it carries several potential meanings which illuminate the focus, practice and dynamic of this form of enquiry. First, it locates the object of study as the non-elite; the exploited groups or classes in a social order. It also suggests a point of perspective, that is, history viewed from the subordinate position, rather than from above. However, rather than the passive 'of below' which implies merely a study of these classes by external experts, we have the active 'from below', which denotes that history is being made by these classes rather than merely being done to them. Lastly, it considers the position of the observer (in this case the historian), suggesting that history being researched and produced from below may be qualitatively different to that created from above. This *above*, may be a description of an elite, but it could easily be applied to institutions from which the majority are excluded.

Using the approach of 'history from below' in studying formal non-governmental organisations such as trade unions, political parties or campaigns is often difficult purely on the basis of inconsistent archiving and sometimes the paucity of sources. Also, until fairly recently (with the rapid expansion of the internet), access to the means of communication has been deeply unequal, with most of the mass media sources not only neglecting the voices of the majority but being actively biased in favour of the owning classes. To compound this issue, an even more challenging problem arises when we consider the actions of informal groupings, such as crowds, social networks or flexible and impermanent organisational forms ranging from strike committees, flying pickets and so-called 'gangs' to radical history groups! These bodies are notoriously lacking in 'hard' information and often suffer from the very fact that communication is often verbal and mostly unrecorded. These difficulties are exacerbated once again when we add to these scenarios the signifiers radical and/or illegal which by their very nature encourage clandestine behaviours and veiled organisational forms.[13]

---

12   The term 'History from Below' was originally coined by the French Annales school of history; 'It is their description of an approach to subjects previously considered historically unimportant, an attempt to surpass history as simply a story of kings, great men and their wars'; A. Isles and T. Roberts, *All Knees and Elbows of Susceptibility and Refusal: Reading History From Below* (Mute Books, The Strickland Distribution, Transmission Gallery, 2012) p. 9.

13   E. P. Thompson for example argued that the paucity of sources concerning the organisational forms and anatomy of the Luddite movement was neither evidence for its non-existence nor lack of organisation. Instead this 'suspicious' absence

So how do we research these problematic forms? Typically, proponents of supposed top-down 'objective history' begin by collecting the usually plentiful official data and then construct an argument explaining the basis for some decision made by 'great men'. In the case of our 'history from below' researchers have to sometimes reverse this process purely because we lack these evidential building blocks. So historians from below often start from the outcome of a social movement, such as a mass protest, an unofficial strike or a 'riot', and then hunt backwards in time for primary sources which provide evidence for the causes, subsequent organisational forms, decision-making and mobilisation processes which facilitated these events. Without this reversal, the tendency is for 'objective historians' to infer that as they can find no formal or official evidence prior to an event that it was completely spontaneous and there was no organisation, rationale or process behind it or even during it. This false causality often leaves us in ridiculous situations.

By way of example, in many studies of the 1831 'riots' in Bristol, the lack of antecedent evidence led many historians to relegate these events to irrationality produced by 'crowd hysteria', 'intoxication' or just plain 'madness'. In fact, a cursory examination of the buildings looted and torched by the rioters suggests conscious and selective destruction of symbolic targets across the city associated with the mercantile and business classes, the clergy and the system of incarceration by the local and national state.[14] So the 'rioters' of 1831 certainly left us concrete clues as to their final agenda, but perhaps not the hard-copy evidence of the communication, mobilisation and organisational processes which led them to that outcome. However, it would be certainly foolish to assume that there were *none* of these processes underway prior to or during the conflagration of 1831.

In the essays in this collection, we are faced with numerous examples of outcomes which lack significant documentary evidence for their origins and dynamics. Let us take a look at some of these interesting examples, the questions they raise and consider what sources of evidence are available to us.

Outcomes

In the late 1880s, membership of the General Unions in Bristol rose rapidly, particularly during the strike wave of 1889/90. The actual processes for this increase in participation are unclear; that is, was it facilitated by discussion or peer pressure in social networks within the home, community or the workplace, driven by 'socialist propaganda' or did a rudimentary class consciousness develop

---

of information and the 'wariness of working class commentators [lent] weight to the probable existence of an 'effective Luddite underground". Ibid., p. 101.

14   Issues concerning the analysis of the 1831 'riots' are discussed in the article *'1831 And All That'* at
http://www.brh.org.uk/site/articles/1831-and-all-that/. Also one source S. Thomas, *The Bristol Riots* (Bristol Branch of the Historical Association, Bristol University, Reprint 1999) explains the 'riots' as a direct attack on the Corporation, made up of wealthy merchants, industrialists and the gentry, who 'ran' the city. However, the publishers were at pains to warn readers that 'she [Susan Thomas] presents an interpretation which differs from the one usually given' and the 'publication of a pamphlet by the Bristol Branch of the Historical Association does not imply the Branch's approval of the opinions expressed within it'. It is interesting, over 150 years after the event, how contentious the history remains.

in the heat of the battle? These deeper questions are difficult to answer, though quantitative data for membership of the various unions is available to us.

A number of significant industrial disputes charted in the essays in this book begin through 'unofficial' solidarity actions, often breaking through problematic trade, regional and gender divides. In twenty-first century Britain such actions are extremely rare. It is often argued that the Tory anti-union legislation introduced in the 1980s (and supported by 'New Labour' in the decades after) has been the death knell for 'solidarity actions' of this sort. However, the employment of conspiracy to intimidate and protection of property laws to arrest, charge and hand out punitive sentences to pickets in the strike waves of 1889-93 and 1910-14 suggests that similar if not more draconian anti-union legislation was in action in the Victorian and Edwardian periods. So what was driving the solidarity which extended Bristolian hands to help Newport dockers, Glaswegian seamen and striking 'Sweet Girls'? Was it born of ideological influences from the burgeoning syndicalist movement or something deeper, related to organic class consciousness? Is perhaps syndicalist ideology merely a reflection and development of processes that already existed within the working class?

Equally, there are plentiful examples of self-organised activities by strikers outside of official 'union' control, including mass protests at the workplace, daily intimidation of scabs, mass blockades of 'blackleg' labour, 'blacked' commodities,[15] sabotage and selective attacks upon the police force. Many of these collective events do not seem to include solely strikers, but also friends and families; men, women and children from their communities. As historians it may be fairly easy to isolate evidence showing support for strikers from formal bodies such as the Trades Council or the Socialist Society, but what of these informal groups? How and why were they motivated to show solidarity with strikers or the unemployed, despite divisions around gender, age and waged and unwaged labour? Was the pre-WWI Bristolian working class less fragmented, more politicised and ultimately more effective as a result of these 'community' interventions?

Many of the solidarity actions and self-organised activities of strikers and their associated community and social networks were not approved of and certainly not officially sanctioned by their respective trade union leaderships. As a result in the following pages you will hear dissenting rank-and-file voices at numerous mass meetings. From dockers calling for the strike-breaker-in-chief to be done away with, to seamen angrily rejecting 'cosy' agreements with their employers brokered by union leaders and miners forcing their union agent out of the chair and replacing him with one of their own. Dissent followed by action was certainly a significant feature of relations between the rank-and-file and collaborationist or faint-hearted union leaders in the pre-WWI period studied in this book.

Despite the supposed obsolescence of the pre-industrial 'mob' in the modern

---

15   'Blacking' goods is the practice of refusing to move or handle commodities which are associated with an ongoing industrial dispute.

period the 'Bristolian crowd' makes its appearance at several points in this text, notably in the narratives of 'Black Friday' in 1892 and 'Bread or Batons?' in 1931-2. Although ostensibly separated from demonstrations of strikers or the unemployed, the 'Bristol crowd' appears variously as curious onlookers, an aggressive police-baiting 'mob', a mass 'flying wedge' crashing through police lines on 'Black Friday' in 1892 and 'rioting' in the city centre in 1932. Despite the valiant efforts of historians such as George Rudé,[16] the 'crowd' in the modern period is still tainted with irrationality, backwardness and lumpen-like behaviours. Essentially, for many historians (on the left and right), the 'crowd' cannot be trusted, precisely because it cannot be pinned down organisationally or ideologically. However, research in Bristol has shown us that this autonomous yet heterogeneous body, often neglected by historians, seemed to appear on the streets whenever working-class movements became mass and visible phenomena in the period. Unlike the 1790s, this was no reactionary 'Church and King mob' but generally aligned itself 'on the day' with the strikers and socialists pre-WWI and in the 1930s with the communist led National Unemployed Workers' Movement. So who made up the 'Bristolian crowds' and why did these people apparently support the 'Reds' in their struggles against the local and national state over access to the city's streets?

Evidence

As we have seen, all of these examples of outcomes in this text present questions which relate to their origins, the communication and mobilisation processes which brought them into being and, crucially, the collective mentalities of those involved. In searching backwards from their point of appearance we try to gather evidence that allows us to momentarily glimpse into the minds of those involved at the informal as well as formal level. In some cases we can obtain direct evidence, however these sources are rare, typically mere fragments, but sometimes diamonds. Take, for example, in this book, the 'inflammatory handbill' circulated amongst striking miners in 1912 which exhorted them to 'Fight for yourselves: your masters hate you: they would shoot you down like rabbits, but they need your labour....win, win, win', the unruly dockers' union branches whose resolutions included *not* increasing the salaries of full-time officials, demanding sympathy strikes with the miners, support for the suffragettes and declarations of neutrality on the eve of the First World War.[17] Add to this the fly posters for the 'Monstre Meeting' on 'Black Friday' which claimed 'Away with Politics, Labour to the Front' and after the debacle, the bills that unashamedly described the events as a 'Police Riot'.[18] Dealing with these kinds of fragmentary primary sources was described thus by one practitioner of 'History from Below':

---

16 G. Rudé, *The Crowd in History: A study of popular disturbances in France and England, 1730-1848* (London: Serif, 1995).

17 See Chapter 6.

18 See Chapter 5, *Figs. 1* and *9*.

> There is the great, brown, slow-moving strandless river of Everything, and then there is its tiny flotsam that has ended up in the record office you are working in. Your craft is to conjure a social system from a nutmeg grater...[19]

However, there are other evidential sources which can be used in an indirect way to aid the 'nutmeg grater' approach to determining collective mentality, though the researcher has to review them critically and/or apply them in an innovative manner.

Mass circulation newspapers are often regarded as problematic by social historians, as within the modern era, they are ultimately managed by bourgeois proprietors and despite their supposed differing political positions generally fall within controlled frameworks of debate. Although they obviously contain useful objective information, they also involve omissions, distortions, selectivity and fairly sophisticated propaganda techniques developed during the last century.[20] In contrast the newspapers of the late nineteenth and early twentieth centuries appear at least to carry a level of innocence, in that the reporting of strikes, protests and disturbances is often literally from journalists on the spot, (unlike today, where many journalists are at pains to leave the internet café or are so over-worked they are desk-bound), and typically detailed and comprehensive. Cross-referencing these sources tends to weed out obviously biased reporting and demonstrated the veracity of eye-witness reports. It was primarily from a close reading of this media that the anatomy of demonstrations and protests in this book were unravelled.

The fact that many of the events recorded in these chapters involved contestation with the state leads us to police and court records, the province of many historians of protest and social crime.[21] These often readily available sources are by their very nature contentious and it is surprising that historians often use them uncritically. Despite the supposed neutrality of law under modern bourgeois democracy, merely studying the conviction rates of police officers for murder in contemporary Britain starkly demonstrates the disequilibrium of power.[22] It is this environment, massively weighted for the state and against the civilian suspect and further exacerbated by relationships of class, ethnicity, sex and sexuality that the historical researcher has to trawl for evidence of motive and mentality amongst the subordinate.

Most of those who have been in trouble with the law for political reasons know that the introduction of such motives into any stage of the police or

---

19   Carolyn Steedman quoted in Isles & Roberts, *All Knees and Elbows*, p. 117.

20   Consider, by way of example, the reporting of the Hillsborough football disaster which despite being witnessed by tens of thousands of fans, was massively distorted by several newspapers in collusion with local politicians and senior policemen.

21   *Social crime* can be described as 'criminality as rebellion, resistance or collective survival strategies in poor communities' http://www.bunker8.pwp.blueyonder.co.uk/misc/socrime.html.

22   Despite nearly 1,500 deaths in police custody since 1990 none of the British constabulary has ever been successfully convicted of an offence. This figure up to April 2014 is derived from a breakdown of 'deaths in police custody (or following other forms of contact with the police, including pursuits and road traffic incidents)' from http://www.inquest.org.uk/statistics/deaths-in-police-custody

judicial process is a risky business. In practice, it is effectively a self-admission of pre-meditation and consciousness and is often interpreted by the bench as contestation with the state. In the eighteenth and nineteenth century in Britain this could get you hanged or transported and in the twentieth a longer custodial sentence plus the added benefits of 'blacklisting'.[23] As a result, taking an explicit political stand is often the province of those who are protected by large organisations, can afford better lawyers or are of independent means. It is no surprise that for the majority this is not an option; so searching for overt political motives in court records is immediately compromised on the basis of class-ethnicity paradigms related to being 'street-wise' in dealings with the law. In fact, better to be drunk than political, hysterical than conscious, stupid than intelligent and sheep rather than ring-leaders; that is, if you want to survive the judicial experience. These inherent problems with police and court records can lead the uncritical historian into mistaken assumptions concerning a lack of political consciousness amongst the accused, reduction of actions to mere 'criminality' or even to the 'outside agitator' theory (beloved by our rulers) that the 'mad were leading the stupid'.

The temporal proximity of events studied in this book is obviously important as it determines the possible existence of oral history sources, which became more widely available with the advent of magnetic tape recording in the 1940s and by the 1960s had become established practice amongst historians. These sources are important as in general they are physically unmediated, that is, the subject speaks directly, rather than being interpreted or filtered by journalists. The study of the unemployed workers' demonstrations in 1931-32 in Chapter Eight is the only piece of research in this book where such oral evidence was available. However, the interviews provide a fascinating insight into the anatomy of the protests, despite the fact that some of the recordings had only been archived in order to capture local dialects for posterity![24] Oral history is also vital in judging the motives and mentalities of at least a sample of actors in these historical events. Similar unmediated sources include letters and diaries, which are often readily available for the 'great men' in biographical form but are far harder to come across for the subordinate or subaltern. One recent exciting development aided by the rise of the internet has been the proliferation of studies into 'family history', which bodes well for the uncovering of hitherto hidden sources of this form.

Finally, during our public engagements (history walks and talks) concerning some of the subjects in this book, Bristol Radical History Group discovered residual currents of subterranean history amongst the audience. For example, several participants in a history walk retracing the unemployed demonstrations of 1932, recounted stories passed down from their grandparents concerning the

---

23 'Blacklisting' is the organised practice of excluding political dissidents and trade unionists from access to work or positions of authority within the private or public sector. This historically widespread practice continues today in the U.K.; see for example: http://www.bbc.co.uk/news/uk-scotland-26570977.

24 Interview with Bill Curtis, 11 Nov. 1998. British Library Shelf Mark C900/00510 http://sounds.bl.uk/Accents-and-dialects/Millenium-memory-bank/021M-C0900X00510X-2600V1.

hated 'means test' and their involvement in the violent protests. Others proudly stated they were relatives of socialist organisers from the period and provided anecdotal accounts. The important political events studied in this book may have been belittled or ignored in 'official' records but they remain a vibrant collective memory in many Bristolian family networks to this very day.

1

Anarchism in Bristol and the West Country: 1880-1939

•

Stephen E. Hunt

The prehistory of anarchism ended, and therefore the history of anarchism starts, when Pierre-Joseph Proudhon proclaimed himself as an anarchist in a positive sense during the 1840s. It was not until the 1880s however, that an explicitly anarchist movement appeared and started to flourish in England. By the second half of the nineteenth century, the preconditions for an identifiable and self-aware labour movement had been met in the West Country, together with other anti-hierarchical trends such as feminism, anti-racism and freethinking. By the 1880s there was an energetic home-grown labour and socialist movement in Bristol that attracted, and was nurtured by, reformists and revolutionaries of all persuasions. Our story is that of anarchism's emergence as a distinct current within and beyond the labour movement.

We must be wary of thinking about the Victorian socialist movement in terms of present political affiliations and divisions. Working-class activism was of necessity extra-Parliamentary in the context of a political system that only gradually granted adult suffrage to men in extensions to the franchise in 1867, 1885 and 1918. Women, as is well known, didn't fully attain suffrage until as late as 1929. The Chartist mass movement of the 1830s-1840s was by far the most prominent campaign for political reform during the early Victorian era. A widespread movement that consciously identified itself as socialist only developed in the wake of Chartism. The organised labour movement therefore, indirectly lobbying for political reform, concentrated its efforts in attracting the sympathies of Liberal and Radical candidates. The eventual foundation of the Independent Labour Party was not until 1893 and the Labour Party in 1900. Extra-parliamentary approaches to change were through trade-union activism or direct action in the fields, factories or on the streets. Bristol can boast the origin of the earliest trade unions set up to represent the interests of women as both the National Union of Working Women, begun in 1874, and the Women's Protective and Provident Association started by Emma Paterson in 1875, were founded in the city.[1]

---

1   Nigel Costley, *West Country Rebels* (London: Breviary Stuff, 2012), p. 124. See Chapters 3 and 4 in this book for a

15

From the 1880s onwards, three main socialist groupings were established in England. The Socialist League was a heterodox mix of libertarian and utopian socialists associated with William Morris. The constitutionalist Fabian Society (in its early days a branch of an association glorying in the title of the Fellowship of the New Life) was initially unaligned until it divided from the anarchists in 1886 and evolved into the forum for gradualist, reformist social democratic opinion that it remains today.[2] Finally, there was H. M. Hyndman's smaller Social Democratic Federation, with its commitment to Marxist 'scientific' socialism. However, these groupings were not, at first, mutually antagonistic and different currents of thought would coexist within local socialist groups without contradiction, despite energetic internal debates. The Bristol Socialist Society, for example, was a model of unity in diversity before the emergence of distinct, and sometimes warring, political factions. An influential socialist such as Edward Carpenter (we'll meet him again shortly), could, and did, sustain involvement with all three groupings and hobnob effortlessly in their overlapping circles.

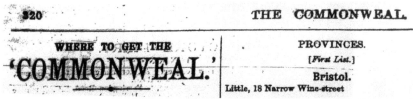

By the 1880s, 18 Narrow Wine Street was a regular outlet for radical literature such as *Commonweal* and *Justice* in Bristol (the proprietors being W. H. Morrish and later M. A. Little).

Nevertheless, fundamentally different approaches to the rocky road to socialism were to become increasingly apparent later in the nineteenth century, when significant divisions emerged in the labour movement. Bristolians of a radical persuasion could buy papers where political debates raged, such as the Socialist League's *Commonweal*, increasingly sympathetic to anarchist ideas, or the Social Democratic Federation's *Justice*, increasingly hostile to anarchism, from the shop of W. H. Morrish in Narrow Wine Street, Bristol.[3] The role of parliamentary representation was a key issue. Furthermore, for those who favoured revolutionary strategies over constitutional ones there was the rift between those with Marxist leanings, who wished to seize the state apparatus in order to implement a 'Dictatorship of the Proletariat', and those who preferred to destroy state authority outright, a mutual antagonism that resulted in the exclusion of anarchist and anarcho-syndicalist groupings from the Second International in Paris in 1889. Such international schisms were increasingly reflected in the movement at home. It is those associated with the explicitly anarchist current already present within the socialist movement by the late 1880s that are of interest here.

---

discussion of women's unions in Bristol and the, at times, antagonistic relations between them.

2   Dona Torr, *Tom Mann and his Times*, Vol. 1 (1856-1890) (London: Lawrence and Wishart, 1956), p. 266.

3   The proprietor was later Mary Ann Little, newsagent and stationer (J. Wright & Co.'s (Mathew's) *Bristol and Clifton Directory, 1889*, p. 254). Narrow Wine Street, situated in central Bristol, was destroyed during the Blitz.

Edward Carpenter and the Bristol Circle

Though not a Bristolian by birth or residence, Edward Carpenter (1844-1929) was an extraordinary radical and agitator who did much to nurture the socialist movement in Bristol and who was willing to align himself with this anarchist current. Carpenter was a colourful character — his particular colours being, in present-day terms, red for socialism, green for environmental concern, pink for gay liberation, (a particularly dangerous cause in late Victorian times), and black for anarchism. Carpenter was the original crank, a vegetarian and the kind of 'bananas and sandals wearer' that George Orwell had in mind when he wrote scathingly: 'One sometimes gets the impression that the mere words "Socialism" and "Communism" draw towards them with magnetic force every fruit-juice drinker, nudist, sandal-wearer, sex-maniac, Quaker, "Nature Cure" quack, pacifist, and feminist in England'.[4] Well he wasn't a Quaker or pacifist, but seven out of nine isn't bad. In any case, E. F. Schumacher was later to reclaim the honour of cranks by pointing out that they are tiny devices that can bring about great revolutions. In his own time admirers regarded Carpenter as a visionary and seer; many of those who still take notice of his legacy share the opinion that his was an extremely progressive voice.

Carpenter rejoiced in the inclusiveness of the early socialist movement and throughout his involvement — which was to last some half a century — he was for the most part on comradely terms with those with whom he had ideological differences. He favoured reconciliation between social democratic, anarchist and Marxist opinion to avoid the kind of polarisation that could blunt its ability to confront the existing social order. However, Carpenter was also sharply aware that some of the primary tensions within socialism (and indeed within society at large) — between statism and libertarianism, centralisation and decentralisation, scientific versus utopian socialism, individual freedom and collectivism — must be rigorously examined and not papered over. Furthermore, he could not be neutral on such matters and, while he did not expect the immediate abolition of the state, his leanings were clearly with the anarchist rather than the Marxist side

---

4   George Orwell, *The Road to Wigan Pier* [1937] (Harmondsworth: Penguin, 1962), p. 152.

of the increasing divide, believing for example:

> The multiplication of officials... strangles the spontaneous vitality of the people; it creates a vast body of parasites, as bad as the dividend-drawing parasites of Commercialism; and betrays the public into the power of a class hostile to change and to progress.[5]

Carpenter favoured a form of socialism based upon workers' control and syndicalism rather than wholesale nationalisation as a means of revolutionary change. As we can see from above, he was extremely sceptical about what he regarded as state bureaucracy, being radically egalitarian in both a political and economic sense. He favoured a 'free communal society' as the final and finest socialist objective. Carpenter was a regular contributor to *Freedom*, the anarchist magazine started by Peter Kropotkin, Charlotte Wilson and others in 1886 (still published today).[6] Marie-Françoise Cachin writes that, while he did not share with Kropotkin the idea that the 'very existence of government [is] the sole cause of all social ills', Carpenter explicitly regarded himself as an anarchist in his aspirations, asserting in a note 'Self I hold to Anarchist Ideal – Spontaneous free Society'.[7] His astute viewpoint anticipated the shortcomings of the disastrous experiments under the name of state socialism and communism that were to disfigure the political history of the twentieth century.

According to Sheila Rowbotham, Carpenter's present-day biographer, his first links with Bristol came through William Harrison Riley (*c*.1835–1907) who he met in 1879.[8] Riley, Rowbotham records, was an all-round agitator for radical change — a Republican in the Chartist tradition who had met both Karl Marx and Walt Whitman. He was also an advocate of land nationalisation and had been involved with managing an ill-fated communal farm which was one of John Ruskin's Guild of St George initiatives during the 1870s. Riley edited the English section of the International Working Men's Association paper, until it ceased in 1875 — the last issue being *The Herald and Helpmate*, which was published in Phippen Street, Bristol,[9] where he also managed the Mutual Help Association[10]. Rowbotham tells us that Riley and his wife (name unknown) 'started a temperance cultural centre, open to both sexes, the Social Improvement Institute at 6 Brunswick Square, Bristol.'[11]

While Riley's residence in Bristol was brief, the Social Improvement Institute

5   Quoted from Carpenter's *Towards Industrial Freedom*, by Marie-Françoise Cachin, '"Non-Governmental Society": Edward Carpenter's Position in the British Socialist Movement', pp. 58-73 in *Edward Carpenter and Late Victorian Radicalism*, ed. Tony Brown (London: Frank Cass, 1990), p. 61.

6   Now an online rather than print publication as of 2014, see http://www.freedompress.org.uk

7   Cachin, '"Non-Governmental Society"', pp. 66-67.

8   Sheila Rowbotham, *Edward Carpenter: A Life of Love and Liberty* (London: Verso, 2008), pp. 139-140 and 162-165. Rowbotham calls him John Harrison Riley, but William Harrison Riley seems to have been his name.

9   Samson Bryher, *An Account of the Labour and Socialist Movement in Bristol: Describing its Early Beginnings, Struggles and Growth* (Bristol: reprinted from and published by the *Bristol Labour Weekly*, 1929), I, p. 13. Sally Mullen notes that the real name of the historian S. Bryher was Sam Bale in 'The Bristol Socialist Society 1885-1914', *Bristol's Other History*, ed. Ian Bild (Bristol: Bristol Broadsides, 1983), p. 46.

10 *Justice* (10 April 1924).

11 Sheila Rowbotham, *Edward Carpenter: A Life of Love and Liberty* (London: Verso, 2008), pp. 66-67.

that he established in 1875 became a magnet for radical and progressive politicos. It was through Riley that Carpenter met John Sharland and Robert Sharland, both members of the Social Improvement Institute, who helped to found the Bristol Socialist Society in 1885. Robert Sharland and his wife Annie in particular were to remain lifelong friends. Carpenter attended Annie's funeral and supported his friend in his bereavement. No doubt socialist means and ends were among the great debates that sustained their dialogue across the decades. Robert Sharland attended Carpenter's funeral in Guildford in 1929, commenting in his obituary:

> It has been suggested [...] that Carpenter was not a Social Democrat, and in a sense that is correct. His teaching savoured more of Anarchist-Communism, but that is akin to the *ideal* of many of us. He always took a keen and helping interest in all phases of the Socialist and Labour Movement, realising the success of these political and industrial efforts was an essential step to the higher state he ever visualised.[12]

Carpenter forged increasingly strong ties with Bristol socialist circles and actively nurtured the city's movement for radical change in ideological and practical terms. This involvement lasted from the 1880s until well into twentieth century. Carpenter seems to have been the chief coordinating link between Bristol and the wider socialist and anarchist movement in London and the north. Again it was Riley who provided the connection through which Carpenter became acquainted with the Sheffield anarchist brothers John and Robert Bingham.[13] Carpenter was also actively involved in defending the Walsall anarchists,[14] in whose cause he testified that he was himself an anarchist and appointed a friend from the Bristol Socialist Society, Hugh Holmes Gore, to present their legal defence.[15]

Carpenter visited Bristol on a regular basis to address Bristol Socialist Society lectures and became a familiar and popular figure among local socialists and trade unionists. He made a donation to the local branch of the Social Democratic Federation to set up a library, (the SDF librarian was the then St Paul's resident and future Labour Prime Minister, Ramsay Macdonald).[16] He never asked for any fee for speaking and was received with affection by the Bristolian audiences. Writing in his 1929 *Account of the Labour and Socialist Movement in Bristol*, Samson Bryher suggests that Carpenter's addresses provided 'the environment that shaped the intellectual and ethical outlook of the earliest Bristol socialists'.[17] As well as the Sharland family, he included among his circle of acquaintances in the city Robert Gilliard, Ben Tillett (leader of the Dockers' Union), Christian Socialist Robert Weare, Cecil Reddie, and Fabians such as Katharine St John Conway, Enid Stacy and Gertrude Dix.

---

12   Bristol Reference Library manuscript B19561. Obituary of Edward Carpenter. *Social Democrat* (August 1929), p. 7.

13   Rowbotham, *Edward Carpenter*, p. 68.

14   See Chapter 6 in John Quail, *The Slow Burning Fuse: The Lost History of the British Anarchists* (London: Paladin, 1978).

15   Rowbotham, *Edward Carpenter*, p. 166.

16   Bryher, *Account of the Labour and Socialist Movement in Bristol*, I, pp. 30-31.

17   Ibid., p. 20.

Enid Stacy was a long-term member of the Independent Labour Party but her vision of democracy was imbued with Carpenter's principles, not of passive representative government. In 'Democracy' an essay published in *The Clarion* in 1894 when a large proportion of adults — non-propertied men as well as women — did not have the vote, Stacy proved herself fully aware of the limitations of representative democracy, and far-sighted enough to insist upon support for autonomous political activity, when she concluded,

Edward Carpenter,
from *The Clarion* (1
December 1894)

Can we over-estimate the power of these great party agencies for making political democracy useless as far as the attainment of real freedom and happiness is concerned? The best method of fighting these agencies is by building up a strong organisation of our own — an organisation in which each member shall take an active interest and part, in which the funds are provided and controlled by ourselves; a party which each member must take a pride in making stronger by his own individual effort, in which the officers shall be delegates and not masters. Towards building up an organisation of this kind our efforts must now be directed — an organisation of self-restrained, self-reliant men and women, with eyes clear enough to read the signs of the times and the necessity for change, and with wills firm and steady enough to do their own work for themselves.[18]

Carpenter also first met William Morris through their mutual connections to the Social Democratic Federation in 1883 and they continued to communicate regularly through their involvement with the Socialist League. Morris was one of the most popular and appealing socialists of the late nineteenth century, known for his charisma and integrity. Supporting a thoroughgoing social revolution, Morris's libertarian vision of socialism was enticing and compelling. In his most famous novel *News from Nowhere* (1891), in which the Houses of Parliament are famously recycled as a dung store, he presented a humane visionary utopia. While Morris explicitly was not an anarchist, there was much common ground and it is rare to find an anarchist who knows of Morris and doesn't admire him. He was a principal author of the *Manifesto of the Socialist League* (1885) that saw socialism chiefly brought about by the extra-Parliamentary means of education, agitation and organisation. When he took part in debates about (what was already) the thorny question of socialism through parliamentary representation during the 1880s, he largely supported anti-parliamentary strategies, being extremely sceptical about the development of state socialism.[19]

Morris spoke on 'Art and Labour' in a lecture room in the City Museum on 3rd March 1885, outlining a creed that characteristically combined social justice, aesthetics and human happiness. He spoke for the working classes' need

---

18   Enid Stacy, 'Democracy', *The Clarion* (28 July 1894).
19   Quail, *Slow Burning Fuse*, pp. 31, 37-38.

to enjoy 'a pleasant house in a pleasant place', 'education', and 'leisure' in a socialist society — 'that is universal co-operation in place of competition or universal war', looking forward to a time 'when the words rich and poor that have so long cursed the world shall have no meaning; when we shall all be friends and good fellows united in that community of happy, reasonable, honoured labour, which alone can produce genuine art or the pleasure of life'. While Morris commanded enormous respect from ordinary Bristolians in the audience, the editor of the *Bristol Evening News* predictably dismissed his talk as 'pernicious nonsense'.[20]

WILLIAM MORRIS.

William Morris, from
The Clarion (6 May
1893)

In the same spirit as this occasion, Robert Weare, Robert Gilliard and other local socialists established a Bristol Sunday Society as a part of the drive towards working-class self-education and mutual improvement. They aimed to promote the study of science and literature by inviting speakers of national and international renown to the city. Once more it is likely to have been through Carpenter's connections that they were able to secure a visit from Peter Kropotkin, surely the most famous Victorian anarchist, both at that time and today. Kropotkin was the invited speaker at an early meeting in 1889, held at St James' Hall in Cumberland Street. A notice in *The Commonweal* records that Kropotkin was delivering a series of lectures on 'Social Evolution' in London at this time, taking an historical overview of models of social organisation up to an exposition of modern socialism, anarchy and free communism, so it is likely that social organisation also formed the content of his talk in Bristol.[21] In 1890 he gave a second lecture as part of what John Quail records was his 'heavy schedule' of talks throughout England that year.[22]

It seems Kropotkin took an interest in West Country events. He cited fraternal generosity in Somerset as an example of solidarity among workers during strikes — clear evidence, he believed, of mutual aid in practice:

> The Radstock miners, favoured with larger kitchen-gardens [...] invited
> four hundred Bristol miners to take their share of cabbage and potatoes,
> and so on.[23]

The Radstock miners had been an indomitable force in the protracted strike that raged through the summer of 1889 when more than 3,000 had come out from the collieries to strike. *The Commonweal*, the paper of the Socialist League, reported that the summer was particularly 'hot for the scabs' due to the solidarity

---

20 An account of the event, including a summary of Morris's speech is in Bryher, *Account of the Labour and Socialist Movement in Bristol*, I, pp. 26-28.

21 *The Commonweal* (27 April 1889), p. 133.

22 Quail, *Slow Burning Fuse*, p. 94.

23 Peter Kropotkin, *Mutual Aid: A Factor of Evolution* [1902] (London: Freedom Press, 1993), p. 213.

of the Somerset women:

> ... the few people who went to work on the first day after the general
> cessation of work, seem to become the special charge of the fair sex, and
> they accompany some of these brave fellows to and from their work, and
> what with the beating of trays and bread tins and such like, produce a
> combination of sounds not in strict accordance with the rules of harmony,
> while occasionally above the din would be heard a shrill voice calling out
> 'blackleg'. The end of it all, of course, was that twenty-three women and
> boys were summoned for 'intimidation'. The appearance of all who were
> summoned was more than ordinarily respectable, and most of the women
> carried babies![24]

The casserolistas who orchestrated this rough music were bound over by the
local magistrates. A follow-up report welcomed the call of the secretary of the
Lancashire Miners' Federation to support the striking miners in Lancashire and
Radstock in order to also secure the advance of miners in Bristol, the Forest of
Dean and elsewhere, *The Commonweal* adding 'let us also remember that the
cause of the workers throughout the world is also one, and cannot be broken'.[25]
Such calls for solidarity and the kind of mutual aid that Kropotkin admired,
were successful, resulting in the effective ostracism of blackleg labour in the
local community and financial support from miners in other areas, including the
Welsh miners (who themselves often had 'very great difficulty in making both
ends meet'),[26] leading to eventual victory in the form of a significant
improvement in pay for the Somerset miners.[27]

The Bristol Sunday Society events went from strength to strength. *Clarion*
correspondent 'Leonard' reported in 1893 that they could boast six outdoor
meetings every Sunday with an average of four speakers at each.[28] They reached
up to 1,700 attendees at a new venue — the Empire Theatre, Old Market Street
— by the 1890s. They were still continuing, although a diminished force, during
the late 1920s.[29]

Carpenter developed particularly close friendships with Helena Born (1860-
1901) and Miriam Daniell (1861-1894), who also eventually took up the
anarchist faith. After spending her childhood in Devon and Taunton, Helena
Born moved to Bristol. She became interested in politics, met her lifelong
comrade Miriam Daniell and together they became active members of the
Bristol Women's Liberal Association. However, radicalised by experience, they
came to sympathise with the struggles of the city's striking workers and switched
allegiance to the growing socialist movement. As a practical demonstration of
solidarity, Born and Daniell moved from well-to-do Clifton to be nearer to the
frontline of the heated industrial disputes in St Philips.[30] They became prominent

---

24 *The Commonweal* (20 July 1889), p. 230.

25 *The Commonweal* (3 August 1889), p. 246.

26 *The Commonweal* (24 August 1889), p. 270.

27 *The Commonweal* (5 October 1889), p. 318.

28 *The Clarion* (9 December 1893).

29 Bryher, *Account of the Labour and Socialist Movement in Bristol*, II, p. 30.

30 For a full account of Daniell and Born's roles in the city's labour struggles in the late 1880s, see Chapters 3 and 4 in this

within the Bristol Socialist Society during the 1880s, delivering several lectures on such progressive and varied topics as 'Cosmopolitanism not Patriotism' (Daniell), 'Why women should organise' (Born), 'Evolution of women' (Daniell) and 'Nilhilism' (Daniell).[31] Helena Tufts' biographical account of Helena Born, written in 1902, paints a picture of her inseparable partnership with Miriam Daniell, both being committed to art and literature, advanced and interlinked causes from freethinking to vegetarianism, humanitarianism to simple living. Their dedication to simple living did not prevent them from living life to the absolute full. Tufts describes the practical anti-capitalist philosophy underpinning their preference for simple living:

> In ministering to artificial tastes, silly fashions, and unsocial customs, the labor of a considerable portion of the producing classes was utterly wasted; hence the producers themselves were exhausting their energies to supply the multitudinous demands of the idle rich, while unable to secure for themselves a sufficiency of wholesome sustenance.[32]

Born and Daniell synthesised their efforts for transformation in all aspects of their lives, uniting lifestyle change with workplace struggle. When floods hit some of the poorest areas of Bristol they were keen to work without condescension to help those affected. They aimed to offer support in a spirit of mutual aid rather than bestowing charity from above. Similarly, as industrial conflict spread, they threw themselves into the cause, supporting striking dockers, taking up honorary offices in the Gasworkers and General Labourers' Union and agitating for improvements in the conditions of homeworking seamstresses. Above all they gained enough experience and confidence to organise alongside the cotton operatives of Barton Hill in their protracted but successful strike during Bristol's great winter of discontent in 1889. A report on the Bristol Labour Revolt published in *The Commonweal* cites Born in this role:

> We have received an urgent appeal from our Bristol comrades for subscriptions for the women who are out at the cotton-factory. Subscriptions may be sent to: Helena Born, secretary, British Workman Coffee House, New Street, St. Judes, Bristol. These poor girls are subjected to the usual sweating and vexatious fines. It is a case which the Women's Trade Union Committee should surely take up.[33]

The home of the two friends, Born and Daniell, shared with a Scottish socialist named Robert Allan Nicol, at 9 Louisa Street became an important hub for the socialist movement in East Bristol during the 1880s. One member that knew them well wrote:

> There never was such an institution as the Bristol Socialist Society. Whitman sings beautifully of loving comrades, but his verses do not begin

book.

31   Bryher, *Account of the Labour and Socialist Movement in Bristol*, II, p. 7.

32   Helen Tufts, 'Biographical Introduction' to Helena Born, Helen Tufts (ed.), *Whitman's Ideal Democracy and other Writings*, (Boston, MA.: Everett Press, 1902), p. xiv.

33   *The Commonweal* (9 November 1889), p. 358.

to touch upon the real delight of the actual bliss of comradeship in practice.[34]

Later Daniell, Born and Nicol moved to Boston, Massachusetts.[35] They were frequent contributors to Benjamin Tucker's individualist anarchist paper *Liberty* and learned typesetting in its offices. Another influence upon Born's transition to a specifically anarchist variant of socialism was surely her study with Patrick Geddes, an influential forerunner of twentieth-century green thought, when she returned to this side of the Atlantic in 1892. Back in the United States the following year, Born joined Daniell in a small utopian community in the Sierra Nevada, California. This was again at Robert Allan Nicol's invitation, who appears to have had relationships with Miriam Daniell, Gertrude Dix and at least a flirtation with Edward Carpenter.[36] The experimental community was to be short-lived as Miriam Daniell died in 1894. Helena Born became a member of an anarchist group in Boston, Massachusetts and lover of William Bailie, a Manchester-born anarchist writer and contributor to *Liberty*.[37] It is unclear at what point Born came to advocate anarchism, although its principles were already familiar to her through the friendship she and Daniell shared with Carpenter in Bristol. Helena Born is believed to have been influenced in her anarchist beliefs through reading Herbert Spencer and Henry David Thoreau. Tufts writes:

> To the end of her life Helena accepted the name of 'socialist,' taking the term in its widest sense; but socialism, as it worked through customary channels, had less and less of her sympathy. A disinclination to sacrifice individuality to a system that was confirmed by the invaluable experience of a practical life, and in after-years she grew into the principles of philosophical anarchism.[38]

Gertrude Dix

Gertrude Mary Dix (1867-1950), daughter of Bristolian hymnist William Chatterton Dix, like Born and Daniell, witnessed and participated in the Bristol Labour Revolt of 1889. As a 'New Woman' of the 1890s, Gertrude Dix relocated to London where she wrote two novels *The Girl on the Farm* (1895) and *The Image Breakers* (1900). It is in *The Image Breakers* in particular that she explored the political milieu of socialism and anarchism, 'New Lifers' and sexual politics she had experienced in Bristol. A friend of Edward Carpenter at this time, she shared many of his ideas and was likewise a Fabian, but it seems her primary political affiliation was to Christian Socialism. As we have seen, Rowbotham records that the close ring of comrades centred around Miriam

---

34 Tufts, 'Biographical Introduction' to *Whitman's Ideal Democracy*, p. xvi.

35 See also Chapters 3 and 4 in this book. Bristol-based socialist feminist Sheila Rowbotham has researched this close-knit radical circle for a book provisionally called *Rebel Crossing*, which is forthcoming at the time of writing.

36 Rowbotham, *Edward Carpenter*, p. 203.

37 *Encyclopedia of Political Anarchy*, ed. by Kathyn Gay and Martin K. Gay (Santa Barbara, Calif.: ABC-CLIO, 1999), p. 35.

38 Tufts, 'Biographical Introduction' to *Whitman's Ideal Democracy*, p. xxxi.

Daniell also encircled a triangle of connections.[39] Miriam Daniell's partner was Robert Allan Nicol, until she died tragically young in 1894. Dix eventually also migrated to the United States where she later married Nicol (perhaps as many as fifteen years after they had first met in Bristol) and lived in California for the rest of her life.[40] Diana Maltz notes Dix's continued admiration of Edward Carpenter's ideas, since she distributed his works among her circle of friends in her new Californian home.[41] The Dix connection to Bristol, however, has not been entirely lost as a direct relative of Gertrude Dix, Vanessa Stevenson (thought to be her first cousin twice removed) still lives in the city today.[42]

The Image Breakers (1900) is set in the context of the late nineteenth-century socialist and anarchist movement. Events take place in London and the English city of Burminster which, with its trams, arcades, quays and socialist coffee taverns, seems uncannily like the Bristol of the 1890s.

The narrative of *The Image Breakers* unfolds from the point of view of two 'new women', Leslie Ardent and Rosalind Dangerfield, and tells us much about the dilemmas they face in trying to break out of their gilt cages, the conventional fate of middle-class Victorian wives expected to play the role of the angel in the home. Both resolutely struggle in their relationships for freedom to love beyond the shackles of matrimony, fearing the captive state in which they would have to 'look at the world through front-parlour windows'.[43] However, they find that the necessity to sell their labour as wage-slaves for the market also places crushing constraints upon their liberty, autonomy and well-being as economic independence proves to be an elusive goal.

At the outset the youthful and progressive Leslie Ardent sets out to meet Charles Whiston, a young firebrand anarchist, out of devotion to her admired and adored friend Rosalind Dangerfield, a woman of revolutionary passion in the unenviable position of being married to Herbert Dangerfield, a former socialist now become wealthy mill-owner and local mayor. Rosalind and Leslie have agreed to arrange a temporary safehouse for Charles for the sake of 'The Cause'. Disappointingly neither of the two anarchist men in the novel are fully developed characters. Charles conforms to the stereotype of the late nineteenth-century anarchist as dynamitard, responding to Leslie's comment about the city looking 'beautiful' in the early light:

> Beautiful! My God! Strange to see beauty in a hell of capitalism like that, where men slave and sweat among the most hideous surroundings! Beautiful! I can't see myself where the beauty comes in. I wonder how

---

39 Rowbotham, *Edward Carpenter*, p. 203.

40 Helena Tufts account of Helena Born and Miriam Daniell states that they joined Nicol in California. The marriage of Gertrude Dix to Robert Allan Nicol took place at Placer, California in April 1903. See https://familysearch.org/pal:/MM9.1.1/KZ3K-24W [accessed 2 April 2013].

41 Diana Maltz, 'Ardent Service: Female Eroticism and New Life Ethics in Gertrude Dix's The Image Breakers (1900)', *Journal of Victorian Culture* 17.2 (2012): 161.

42 Sheila Rowbotham's forthcoming book *Rebel Crossing* will explore the relationships between the Daniell, Born, Nicol and Dix circle in detail.

43 Gertrude Dix, *The Image Breakers* (New York: Frederick A. Stokes, 1900), p. 231.

many tons of Dynamite it would take to lay it in ruins.[44]

The steadfast but ineffectual and paranoid Charles thus represents the trend toward 'propaganda by the deed', against the ruling class, a position popularised in Western Europe out of desperation provoked by the slaughter, imprisonment and transportation of thousands of radicals following the collapse of the Paris Commune. By contrast, his comrade, Justin Ferrar, represents a 'moral force' approach. Justin, the novel's revolutionary and messianic theoretician, though dedicated to humanity in the abstract is, ironically, often oblivious to those around him. In this way the intense emotional counterpointing of the main characters is underpinned by distinct political and philosophical approaches. While little is known about Dix, *The Image Breakers* is thought to have a strong autobiographical element and the way that she animates the social circles of Burminster suggests that it is an intelligent insider's account. Although the biographical details about her life are speculative, Judy Greenway writes:

> Dix had firsthand knowledge of the utopian politics of the day. She was active in labour politics in Bristol, and knew the Rossettis in their *Torch* days [a publication subtitled 'A Revolutionary Journal of Anarchist Communism', edited by the Rossetti sisters, Helen and Olive], possibly while she was working as a governess to Sydney Olivier's children...[45]

Her involvement with Bristol socialism and support for strikers is born out by Bryher's reference to Gertrude Dix as 'worthy of special mention' alongside Enid Stacy, apparently as a public speaker.[46] It follows that the strike at Sampson's Sweet Factory in Chapter II is extremely likely to have been based upon the strike of the 'sweet girls' which lasted for more than twenty weeks at Sanders' Sweet Factory in Redcliffe, Bristol from 1892/93.[47] Enid Stacy was for a time the Honorary Secretary of the Bristol Strike Committee which supported the 115 'sweet girls' involved in the dispute.[48] Bryher's linkage of the two women in this context suggests that Dix also actively rallied support for the strikers.

Leslie Ardent, who as her name suggests, is passionate in her support of the socialist cause, is invited to a meeting in Burminster:

> A young man named Jameson [...] informed her that a special committee had been formed to consider the case of the employees in a sweet factory who had just come out on strike. Invited to attend it, she went with him through one of the meanest parts of the town to the coffee-tavern in

---

44 Ibid., p. 9.

45 Judy Greenway, 'No Place for Women? Anti-Utopianism and the Utopian Politics of the 1890s', *Geografiska Annaler*. Series B, Human Geography, Vol. 84, No. 3-4, Online: http://www.jstor.org/stable/3554316 [accessed 20 Jan 2010], p. 205.

46 Bryher, *Account of the Labour and Socialist Movement in Bristol*, II, p. 22.

47 This strike is described in Chapter 5 of this book. See also Sally Mullen, 'Sweet Girls and Deal-Runners', in *Placards and Pin Money*, ed. by Ian Bild (Bristol: Bristol Broadsides, 1986), pp. 112-126; and Bryher, *Account of the Labour and Socialist Movement in Bristol*, II, pp. 33-41. The link with Bristol in *The Image Breakers* is corroborated by a mention of a hatters' strike (p. 20) — hatters' had also been among the workers involved in the industrial unrest known as the Bristol Labour Revolt in 1889.

48 [anon] 'Confectioners' Strike at Bristol', *The Clarion*, 10 December 1892, p. 7.

which it was to be held. Arrived at their destination, they passed through a swing-door into a blue-washed coffee-room, with a long counter stretched across it, of which little more than the tops of its metal urns were visible.

CONFECTIONERS' STRIKE AT BRISTOL.

A correspondent calls our attention to the fact that this strike is still in existence. There are 115 girls involved, and their case has been taken up by the local Trades Council—sufficient to indicate that the girls are in the right. Help is urgently needed. Subscriptions may be sent to Enid Stacy, hon. secretary of the Strike Commtttee, British Workman, New-street, Bristol.

Confectioners' Strike at Bristol, *The Clarion* (10 December 1892)

It is likely that this location was The British Workman, a coffee tavern built in New Street, St Judes, the venue for meetings of the strike committee set up to support the confectionery workers and its postal address. The dispute attained national importance. As W. J. Petherick (Stacy's successor as Honorary Secretary) records in *The Clarion*, it duly attracted the attention and support of Ben Tillett, Will Thorne and M'Carthy (probably Tom McCarthy, Secretary of the stevedores' union).[49] As such the 'sweet girls' dispute in Bristol — together with the 1890 strike of women workers at the Barratt's sweet factory in London[50] — was a manifestation of the rise of New Unionism at this time, signifying growing class consciousness and a break with male-dominated craft unions as women outside of traditional skilled industries took to the streets to fight for better conditions alongside male comrades.

'Utopian' experiments in *The Image Breakers* are unsuccessful. Leslie travels to join Rosalind and Justin on a land colony, only to discover when she arrives that the project has already collapsed — it was dependent on a 'progressive' landowner who became unwilling to accommodate them when he found their 'free love' arrangements a step too far. This provides a pattern for the rest of the novel. Several of the male radicals prove to be egotistical demagogues in public, and chauvinists in private. Socialist and anarchist principles, (and certainly several of those who purport to practice them), are examined critically and often found wanting and satirised; the *status quo* of capitalism and the class system, however, are certainly not endorsed either.

Sally Ledger suggests that, given Dix's involvement with the Bristol socialists and friendship with Edward Carpenter, it is 'reasonable to surmise that Dix is in dialogue, in her portrayal of utopian socialism, with Carpenter's ideas'.[51]

---

49   W. J. Petherick, 'The Confectioners' Strike at Bristol', *The Clarion* (24 December 1892).

50   Lindsey German and John Rees, *A People's History of London* (London: Verso, 2012), p. 149.

51   Sally Ledger, *The New Woman: Fiction and Feminism at the fin de siècle* (Manchester: Manchester University Press, 1997), p. 57.

Carpenter describes Dix as being turned out 'in ballet costume knickers'.[52] Clothes and appearance are a recurrent feature of *The Image Breakers*; in the decade of rational dress what women, and men, wore was particularly significant. As new women, Leslie and Rosalind are subject to the tyranny of public opinion and expectations of female propriety. Thrown giddily into a world of intellectual ideas and radical action, Leslie's new connections present an exhilarating contrast to her life with older relatives in a stultifying home and a narrow-minded, censorious village. Rosalind mocks the local norms, in which wearing bare feet in sandals would be viewed as controversial and improper: 'My dear child, it is a crime to let one's feet feel the dew and sun. That in itself would be enough to scandalize a whole countryside'.[53] We have already seen that the simple act of wearing sandals was a subversive and political code, associated with Carpenter and 1890s rational dress and still disparaged as such by Orwell decades later. Clothes, then, were just one signifier in a culture war between radically different worldviews, statements of belief in themselves and part of a wider conversation about class and gender.

'Pleasure and Propaganda'

Activists such as Carpenter, Born and Daniell were involved with socialist politics of a kind that were not preoccupied with local government and parliamentary concerns. Theirs was a grass-roots struggle for justice and liberation in social, cultural and personal life and took a holistic view of progress for humanity and the planet in general. The idea that 'the personal is political'

---

52   In a letter from Carpenter to George Hukin, October 8, 1895, quoted by Rowbotham, *Edward Carpenter*, p. 234.

53   Dix, *Image Breakers*, p. 5.

was already alive during the nineteenth century it seems, even if the slogan appeared much later, (it is usually attributed to the 1960s feminist Carol Hanisch). Carpenter termed this cultural dimension to the late Victorian and early twentieth-century socialist movement the 'Larger socialism'.[54] This transcended party politics, touching upon humanity's whole social being, including our environmental, aesthetic and spiritual existence.

VIVE LA COMMUNE !
A CARTOON BY WALTER CRANE.
PRINTED ON FINE PAPER, FOR FRAMING.
Size, 14 inches by 10.
Price Twopence.
Commonweal Office, 13 Farringdon Rd., London, E.C.

Artwork by Walter Crane, from *The Commonweal* (9 March 1889)

We've already seen that industrial action and educational lectures were central to the struggle for a social revolution. Music, literature and art added sound, texture and colour. In 1888 Carpenter helped to arrange and compile the first English collection of rousing socialist anthems with John and Robert Sharland.[55] The *Chants of Labour* was published with a cover by Walter Crane (1845-1915), an artist who also has links with Bristol — some of his last work can still be seen in the painted lunettes of 1913 at the Royal West of England Academy of Arts in Whiteladies Road. It included other contributions from lyrical locals, such as John Gregory, bootmaker, poet and stalwart of the Bristol Socialist Society. Oscar Wilde, who had decidedly anarchistic leanings (see 'The Soul of Man Under Socialism'), reviewed the *Chants of Labour* in an article called 'Poetical Socialists' in the *Pall Mall Gazette*. He was pleased by the variety of the contributions, showing that 'Socialism is not going to allow herself to be trammelled by any hard-and-fast creed or to be stereotyped into an iron formula' and also quipping 'to make men Socialists is nothing, but to make Socialism human is a great thing'. Wilde reassures us that 'it is evident from Mr Carpenter's book that should the Revolution ever break out in England we shall have no inarticulate roar, but rather pleasant glees and graceful part-songs.'[56]

As a musician Carpenter also knew the Bristolian clergyman and Christian

---

54   Rowbotham, *Edward Carpenter*, p. 315.
55   Ibid., p. 112.
56   All quotations are from 'Poetical Socialists' in *Oscar Wilde: Selected Journalism*. ed. Anya Clayworth (Oxford: Oxford University Press, 2004), pp. 33-6.

Socialist Charles Marson, who collected folk songs in Somerset with Cecil Sharp.[57] Carpenter came to know and strike up a long-term friendship with the musician Rutland Boughton, who was influenced by the ideas of this 'larger socialism' epitomised in Carpenter and Morris's writings. Boughton was actively involved in the local Clarion Clubs and lived at Glastonbury during the early twentieth century. He set up his first festival of classical music in Glastonbury Assembly Rooms in 1914. Although it was a modest affair it was still necessary to defend the event from puritanical locals who feared its 'satanic influences'.[58] The first of many which were to develop into increasingly extravagant pageants of operatic and theatrical performance, it later continued in similar events at Bath and Stroud. He also founded the Festival Players who were eventually based in Bristol. In John Cowper Powys's *A Glastonbury Romance* (1932), Boughton was the inspiration for the pageants that made up the final action and his presence in part accounted for the socialist elements in this epic novel which also features a character called Paul Trent who Powys calls a 'philosophical anarchist'. Powys was himself an anarchist of sorts, as well as being, alongside Thomas Hardy, one of the greatest novelists of the West Country (indeed to my mind, simply one of the greatest novelists). Boughton also adapted several of Carpenter's poems, such as 'The Lake of Beauty', to musical compositions. As a communist, he was eventually removed from the Festival's Board in 1926 when he staged a production in contemporary dress — a topical gesture of solidarity with striking miners at time of the General Strike. Michael Hurd writes that he caused a scandal by presenting 'Christ being born in a miner's cottage and Herod as a top-hatted capitalist'.[59]

Following early Romantic concerns about industrialism's destructive impact on the natural world through to Ruskin, Morris and Carpenter, there was a significant green, environmental wing to this 'larger socialism'. Astonishingly, an experiment in back-to-the-land anarchist communism of the 1890s continues to the present day near Stroud. Samuel Bracher, a Gloucester journalist, first set up the Whiteway Colony on Tolstoyan principles in 1898.[60] Early members of the colony, Aylmer Maude (1858-1938) and Louise Maude (1855-1939), were friends of the novelist and Christian anarchist Leo Tolstoy, and translators of his work. In *Alternative Communities in Nineteenth Century England*, Dennis Hardy describes the radically progressive and experimental nature of the colony. He records that early libertarian residents ceremonially burned the land deeds, opposed private property, supported gender equality (favouring 'free union rather than State marriage') and pacifism, and took up vegetarianism.[61] Despite considerable compromise and dilution of the principles of the pioneers, Home Office officials still viewed the Colony as sufficiently objectionable and subversive

57 Rowbotham, *Edward Carpenter*, p. 298.

58 Patrick Benham, *The Avalonians* (Glastonbury: Gothic Image, 2006), p. 175.

59 Michael Hurd (1983), sleeve notes to *The Immortal Hour*, performed by the Geoffrey Mitchell Choir and the English Chamber Orchestra and conducted by Alan G. Melville (London: Hyperion Records, 1998).

60 See Quail, *Slow Burning Fuse*, pp. 228-9 and Peter Gould, *Early Green Politics: Back to Nature, Back to the Land, and Socialism in Britain 1880-1900* (Brighton: Harvester Press, 1988), p. 53.

61 Dennis Hardy, *Alternative Communities in Nineteenth Century England* (London: Longman, 1979), pp. 200-1.

to try to infiltrate it with the objective of closing it down on the grounds of what they regarded as sexual immorality during the 1920s.[62] They failed. One-time *Freedom* editor Tom Keell and his partner Lilian Wolfe moved to the Whiteway Colony from 1928 to 1932 and continued a newsletter edition of *Freedom* from there during one of its periodic editorial splits.[63] They published fifteen issues of *Freedom Bulletin* from a former carpentry shop at the Colony.[64] Joy Thacker, Whiteway resident and historian, records that Lilian Wolfe divided her energies between Sunshine Stores, Whiteway's healthfood outlet in Stroud, and *Freedom* until 1943 when she moved back to London and devoted much of her remaining twenty-five years to helping with *Freedom*'s production in London.[65] Nick Heath also cites the involvement of Mat Kavanagh and his wife Leah in the Whiteway Colony.[66] Later in the 1930s ten men exiled from the Spanish Civil War were given refuge at the Whiteway Colony.[67]

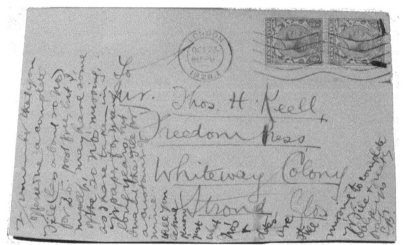

Postcard from Sam Brook of Welwyn Garden City to Tom Keell at Whiteway Colony, near Stroud (23 October 1928). Manuscript in *Freedom* Archive 460, International Institute of Social History, Amsterdam.

The 1890s also saw the foundation of *The Clarion*, a weekly newspaper that was to have a huge influence on the propagation of socialism. 'Leonard' the *Clarion*'s local correspondent boasted that the advance of socialism in Bristol was a particular achievement given the apparent hostility of some of the locals:

> In times past, this city has been conspicuous, among other things, for its

---

62 *Utopia Britannica: British Utopian Experiments 1325–1945*, 'One Hundred Years of Anarchy' [online] [accessed on 25 October 2013].

63 Quail, *Slow Burning Fuse*, pp. 305-6.

64 Joy Thacker, *Whiteway Colony: The Social History of a Tolstoyan Community* (Stroud: Alan Sutton, 1993), p. 82.

65 Ibid., p. 84. Sunshine Health, one of Britain's oldest health shops, is still at 25 Church Street, Stroud.

66 Libcom.org website. Nick Heath, 'Kavanagh, Mat (1876-1954)', [online]: https://libcom.org/history/kavanagh-mat-1876-1954 [accessed 17 May 2014].

67 Thacker, *Whiteway Colony*, pp. 132-35.

hypocrisy, and a wave of pious horror passed over the Bristol when first 'those wicked paid-agitators' unfurled the crimson cloth on the Sabbath. But in spite of the evil wishes of the 'respectable' and sanctimonious humbugs who denounced our gatherings, Socialism has triumphed, and become a very important factor in the politics of the city.[68]

A regular programme of meetings was scheduled to build support for Labour and Socialist representation on local governing bodies. Based on a strategy to build socialism by being sociable, Clarion clubs were also set up to organise convivial jollies involving activities such as drama, rambling, handicrafts and, above all, cycling. Their favourite slogan was 'Fellowship is Life'. The Clarion movement predated the foundation of the Independent Labour Party and was a meeting ground for leftists of all varieties, remaining strictly non-aligned — 'it promulgated no particular type of Socialism and resolutely declined to discuss the differences of S.D.F., Fabians or I.L.P. viewpoints.'[69] With a nod to Kropotkin and Morris, by 1914 the National Clarion Cycling Club's objectives were simply: 'Mutual aid, good fellowship and the propagation of Socialism as advocated by the Clarion'.[70] With their commitment to loose, autonomous structures and resistance to centralisation and factious politicing,[71] it is difficult to imagine their uncompromising libertarian spirit finding a place in the present-day Labour Party. In keeping with Robert Blatchford's *Merrie England* (1893), Clarion supporters celebrated singing and picnicking in the countryside as essential to a healthy quality of life. Needless to say, the West Country became a hotbed of Clarion activity, with Clarion Cyclists and the Rambling and Propaganda Society in Bristol and Clarion tours across Somerset and Dorset. Bryher gives a colourful description of local 'Clarionette' outings that combined pleasure and purpose similar to today's Critical Mass:

> Frequently a hundred or more members and friends, with their wives and children, attended. Miles of country lanes and fields were traversed, tea being partaken of at a pre-arranged beauty spot, after which games were participated in. On many occasions Will Sharland's choir delighted all by rendering of part songs and glees, and the walk home in the evening was

68   Leonard, 'Local Notes' report for the Bristol area, *The Clarion* (9 December 1893).

69   Bryher, *Account of the Labour and Socialist Movement in Bristol*, II, p. 75.

70   Denis Pye, *Fellowship is Life: The Story of the Clarion Cycling Club*, 2nd ed. (Bolton: Clarion Publishing, 2004), p. 26.

71   Ibid., pp. 20-22.

enlivened by the singing of Socialist songs. The actual propaganda was in practice less than anticipated, but always a quantity of Socialist literature was distributed amongst the villagers, and there was never a jaunt without a paste pot and brush handy with which to affix Socialist mottoes and texts to gateposts, stiles and the like. It was a practice of the B.S.S. at this time to quote such lines as 'The paradise of the rich is the hell of the poor'; 'Socialism means peace, Competition means war,' on all its posters and handbills, and these were cut off for the purpose. Vandalism, perhaps, but the object was to save human bodies and minds that were being sacrificed daily to the gods of mammon and capitalism.[72]

FOR TRANSMISSION ABROAD   SATURDAY, MAY 11, 1895.   Sent Prepaid to any Address for 1½d. p or 1s. 8d. per quarter; paid in adve

A century later, the Clarion Cyclist Club, founded in 1895, is still in existence with the West Country being represented with a Dorset section.[73] It was not all picnics and choirs however. The police, local authorities and hostile landowning interests frequently banned and disrupted the progress of the famous Clarion travelling horse-drawn vans. After the second annual women's Clarion van tour started from Bristol in 1897, police broke up a meeting in nearby Thornbury, leading to several arrests.[74]

For younger socialists, a Boy's Socialist Club was set up in Bristol in 1894, offering opportunities for literature and nature study as well as rambling and sports. This was eventually joined by the Sunday Socialist School, which was also open to girls, in 1898.[75]

Another instance of the potential for social improvement through extending the healthy and liberating benefits of the natural environment was the access struggle of the Bristol and District Footpaths Preservation Society in

---

72   Bryher, *Account of the Labour and Socialist Movement in Bristol*, II, p. 68.

73   See: http://www.clarioncc.org/. Something of the Clarion spirit also lives on in the present-day socialist walking and climbing group, Red Rope: http://www.redrope.org.uk/.

74   Pye, *Fellowship is Life*, p. 40.

75   Bryher, *Account of the Labour and Socialist Movement in Bristol*, II, p. 54.

1891.[76] This anticipated the direct action of radical ramblers who challenged the exclusion of the public from the countryside by private landowners in the twentieth century. Likewise environmental improvement inspired Bristolian reformers Elizabeth Sturge (1850-1944) and Eliza Walker Dunbar (1845-1925) when they planned a garden suburb in Shirehampton in 1907, encouraged by Ebenezer Howard's visit to Bristol, the following year. Carpenter, Kropotkin and Morris all strongly influenced Howard in his role as the 'inventor' and most energetic proponent of garden cities.[77] Such radical green strands aspired to a thorough transformation of the conditions of life, bringing about a finer realization of the human self — aspirations marginalized a century later in the recession racked, polluted West Country of the present day.

The Rise of Industrial Unionism and Syndicalism

In the Nineteenth Century the high-tide mark of industrial struggle in Bristol and Southampton in particular was from 1889 to 1892. An ebullient reporter for *The Commonweal* writes of the 'Great Revolt of Labour at Bristol' that they were 'beginning to almost despair of the provinces' until Bristol bucked the trend and:

> [...] surged up into enthusiastic rebellion on Tuesday October 22nd. That all has not been well at that seaport in the west of England has indeed been evident for some time. The crowd who, when the gas-men struck, barricaded the bridges and drove back the blacklegs with volleys of stones, would hardly have acted with such vigour and determination had they not also suffered from bitter wrongs. So, when the deal-runners struck they found plenty of imitators — the dock-labourers, corn-porters, carters, cotton-hands, wharfingers, swayers, haulers, scavengers, and warehouse-porters, all abandoning their work and parading the streets by thousands. The strike spread like an epidemic, and it seemed at one time as if the whole town would be out. What has been the consequence? Why, alarmed at the spreading revolt, and dreading something more serious than a mere cessation of work, if the strikers became hungry, the masters have in many cases given in.[78]

The report also concludes with satisfaction that the 'bright example' set in Bristol was a victory won before arrival of Tillett, Mann and Thorne, who appeared on the scene to find that 'the greater part of the battle had been won without their aid — won by the people's own courage and determination.'[79]

A similarly militant uprising took place in Southampton in September 1890 as striking dockers attracted 'immense crowds' of supporters in their dispute, repelling blacklegs and culminating in direct conflict with soldiers of the Yorkshire regiment. By now the revolutionary anarchist wing of the Socialist League was in the ascendant. The League's paper *The Commonweal* reported:

---

76   Ibid., p. 31.
77   See Chapter 7 of this book.
78   *The Commonweal* (2 November 1889), p. 350.
79   Ibid.

[...] the military were called in by the mayor, and there was desperate fighting, the troops charging the people with the bayonet. The crowd then marched round and smashed the mayor's windows. No blacklegs have yet arrived. The people of Southampton are showing a splendid spirit, and we hope they will continue their courageous fight against blacklegs and sweating.[80]

The next day, D. J. Nicoll was jubilant, reporting in *The Commonweal* that the escalating tumult even caused fearful capitalists to drop prices at the London Stock Exchange and the Paris Bourse after

[...] two gunboats are sent for — possibly with a view of affording a chance of escaping by water to the mayor, should the insurrection prove too strong and the commune be proclaimed.[81]

Nicoll, editor of *The Commonweal* in its most explicitly anarchist phase, continued,

[...] suppose an Anarchist revolt had really taken place and the dockers had taken possession of the docks and the factories, while the shipping and railways had been seized by the rest of the people, who at the same time had made a free distribution of tea, meat, bread, clothes, and groceries among the poor of the town; suppose even the insurrection had been crushed, — how much more should we have heard of 'smashing the unions' from the gentlemen of the middle classes? I believe they would even prefer the 'tyranny' of the unions to a miniature social revolution, which certainly would not stop at Southampton, but spread like a prairie fire through the length and breadth of the country.[82]

F. Kitz, present at Southampton, joined Nicoll in condemning Tom McCarthy, the stevedores' leader, in particular for a call to 'obey the law' and betraying the workers in their conflict. Kitz's concluding words made clear his fear that New Unionism needed to be defended from emerging leaders who could dilute the movement and follow the path of the old labour aristocracy:

I heard the epithets of 'loafers' and 'tramps' applied to those outside the New Unionism by the suddenly made Aristocrats of Labour. It is a fatal mistake. The propertied classes are preparing for a mighty struggle, in which the Southampton scenes are but an episode. The marching and countermarching, the proclamations in the name of our Sovereign Lady the Queen to keep the peace, etc are but the pattering raindrops before the storm. It is not the time to use harsh words in regard to paupers and tramps, who, after all, are what Society makes them; and least of all should the men in command of the forces of Labour join in the abuse of the residuum. If on no higher ground than policy, it is a tactical mistake to turn the unorganised mass into a reactionary force at the possible disposable of the enemy.[83]

---

80 *The Commonweal* (13 September 1890), p. 294.

81 J. D. Nicoll, 'The Great Strike at Southampton', *The Commonweal* (20 September 1890), p. 297.

82 Ibid.

83 F. Kitz, 'At Southampton', *The Commonweal* (20 September 1890), p. 298.

The major flashpoint at Southampton was recalled in *The Commonweal*'s 'An Address to the Army', (by now avowedly 'A Revolutionary Journal of Anarchist Communism'), the following year:

> Recently in Scotland, at Motherwell, at Liverpool, Southampton, Leeds and Bradford the services of the soldiery in whose hands this may fall – were utilised to put down the meetings of working men and women who are attempting to protest against the miserable wages paid, and the horrible conditions under which many of them lived.[84]

A REVOLUTIONARY JOURNAL OF

Anarchist Communism.

[VOL. 7.—No. 265.]   SATURDAY. MAY 30, 1891.   [WEEKLY: ONE PENNY.]

Such uprisings had been on the minds of Miriam Daniell and Robert Allan Nicol when they collaborated on a pamphlet called 'The New Trade Unionism', printed at the Oddfellows' Hall, Rupert Street, Bristol in 1890. The pamphlet is a commentary published in the heat of the 'Bristol Labour Revolt' by two activists directly involved in the events described.[85] The seismic importance of the shift towards militant labour activity, or at least as it seemed to those involved at the time, is demonstrated by the resounding opening declaration:

> Nothing has created greater astonishment in England of late than the phenomenal unrest which has pervaded all classes, and which, like the rumblings of an earthquake premonitory to some convulsion which will change the configuration of the earth's surface, has preceded the rise of the New Trade Unionism, and presages undoubtedly stranger altercations yet.[86]

What was new about New Trade Unionism was its aspiration to build a united front of workers in dispute with their employers, across sector and across workplace rank or grade, as can be seen by the wide range of workers taking action during the Bristol Labour Revolt. This was a challenge to the old unions

---

84   'An Address to the Army', *The Commonweal* (11 July 1891), p. 73. In 1892 'An Address to the Army' was later published as a leaflet, in which form it was seized during a police raid in which printing equipment and other literature was confiscated and the editor, D. J. Nicoll, arrested and held in Holloway Prison. *The Commonweal* (23 April 1892), [2].

85   Miriam Daniell and Robert Allan Nicol, *The New Trade Unionism: Its Relation to the Old; and the Conditions of its Success* (Bristol: A. Jenkins, MDCCCXC). The pamphlet also makes reference to the Bingham case, criticising the presiding judge's prejudice in the trial of John Bingham, a Sheffield anarchist (p. 7).

86   Ibid., p. 5.

who had been accused of sustaining practices that would ensure their monopoly of skills could advance the interests of a particular sector and level of skill — thereby a developing a so-called 'labour aristocracy' — with no attempt to improve conditions for the working class as a whole. By contrast new unionists sought to build up militant solidarity among workers. This also involved the inclusion of women workers increasingly willing to unionise and take industrial action. As previously noted, the foundation of the National Union of Working Women in Bristol in 1874 was another first for the city.[87] By the early twentieth century new unionist strategies evolved into syndicalist aspirations to build toward a general strike, able to establish workers' control of industry and to directly challenge capitalist control of the means of production. Daniell and Nicol were quick to recognise this 'evolution of labour to its emancipation', through the potential of the new unions to coordinate and organise both skilled and unskilled workers.[88] If workers could concentrate their combined social power, they could force a radical redistribution of wealth. At least at this stage in their thinking, Daniell and Nicol hoped this would realise the kind of elemental Christian socialism that Tolstoy came to favour, bringing about a society without organised religion, sharing the fruits of labour and the earth according to principles of 'love' not private profit.[89]

BEN TILLETT.

Ben Tillett, from *The Clarion* (12 March 1892)

During the 'Bristol Labour Revolt' there was a strong axis of support between the dockers of London and Bristol. Bristolian Ben Tillett (1860-1943) was a prominent figure in the local and national trade union movement. An early member of the Bristol Socialist Society, he retained his strong connections with the city after moving to London when he became leader of the Docks, Wharf, Riverside and General Labourers' Union which was eventually to amalgamate into the Transport and General Workers' Union. Tillett's triumphant return came in 1889 when, along with Tom Mann and Will Thorne, he took time away from the bitter London Dock Strike to support the industrial dispute raging back in Bristol. During the Bristol rising, workers from several sectors, including cotton operatives, dockers, gas workers, iron workers, united in joint action precipitating waves of coordinated strikes. The show of strength was to reap dividends in the form of concessions such as the key — and symbolic — demand for an eight-hour day and in raising class consciousness by bringing workers together in a wave of new unionism. The well organized Bristol workers continued to take militant action, provoking the state to take increasingly violent measures, culminating in an attack by a military attachment

---

87   Elizabeth Crawford, *The Women's Suffrage Movement in Britain and Ireland: A Regional Survey* (Abingdon: Routledge, 2006), p. 130.

88   Daniell and Nicol, *New Trade Unionism*, p. 8.

89   Ibid., p. 14.

of dragoons and police on a jeering crowd of 20,000 in the Horsefair in 1892. Fifty-seven verified injuries were sustained on what became known as 'Black Friday'.[90] In the controversial aftermath of 'Black Friday', Tillett was prosecuted for 'Incitement to Riot', eventually being found 'Not Guilty' by a London jury.[91]

On the radical edge of the labour movement, Tillett was to move a resolution in favour of the Walsall anarchists at the 1896 Trades Union Congress which was backed with an overwhelming majority.[92] However, by the early twentieth century some revolutionaries came to regard him as a figure of compromise and a careerist who had lost touch with grass-roots militancy. John Quail records that James Harrigan, a radical shoemaker who was perhaps one of the first home-grown English anarchists, is said to have encountered Ben Tillett, the future Dockers' leader, while taking on some additional casual work unpacking tea chests on the docks. He remarked: 'there was nothing he regretted more for he hated the political charlatans who used the workers' movement to make a career for themselves'.[93]

Of the three leading unionists who spoke in support of the Bristol workers in 1889, Tom Mann in particular continued to advocate militant unionism and participate in the syndicalist struggles of the early twentieth century. The syndicalist sympathisers of Tom Mann and Guy Bowman were inspired by the example and strength of the Industrial Workers of the World in the United States.[94] Tom Mann was not an anarchist, although his extra-Parliamentary support for revolutionary class war drew many anarcho-syndicalists to support the industrial union activity he inspired.[95] While he eventually set up the Communist Party of Great Britain in the heady aftermath of the 1917 Russian Revolution, Mann tried to build a broad-based labour movement, both fighting for the inclusion of anti-Parliamentarians and anarchists in the debates of the International Socialist Congress and forming alliances with the constitutional labour politicians and mainstream trade unionists, feeling that diverse strategies would advance socialism.[96] Mann developed a pivotal role within radical circles. His tenancy of a London pub from 1898 to 1901 performed a similar role to Carpenter's centre of operations at the more austere community at Millthorpe. It enabled him to open up a space for discussion and the dissemination of ideas, helping to encourage a 'larger socialism' to flourish. Speakers in The Enterprise pub included those venerable 'asylum seeking' anarchists Peter Kropotkin, Errico Malatesta and Louise Michel, veteran of the Paris Commune.[97] Mann family connections with Bristol were replenished when Tom Mann's granddaughter spoke in April 2010 at the memorial in Castle Park, commemorating

---

90   See Chapter 5 in this book.

91   Details from Bryher, *Account of the Labour and Socialist Movement in Bristol*, II, pp. 16-49.

92   Quail, *Slow Burning Fuse*, p. 202.

93   Ibid., p. 50.

94   Peter Marshall, *Demanding the Impossible: A History of Anarchism*, (London: Fontana/Harper Collins, 1993), p. 491.

95   Quail, *Slow Burning Fuse*, pp. 261-65.

96   Tom Mann, *Tom Mann's Memoirs* [1923], with a preface by Ken Coates (London: Macgibbon and Kee, 1967), p. 104.

97   *Tom Mann: Social and Economic Writings: A pre-Syndicalist selection*, edited and introduced by John Laurent (Nottingham: Spokesman, 1988), p. 17.

local members of the International Brigaders who died fighting fascism in the Spanish Civil War.[98]

In their struggle for workers' control of industry, watchwords in the Syndicalist paper *The Transport Worker* were 'Industrial Solidarity' and 'No Room for Sectionalism'.[99] The syndicalist contagion of the early Twentieth Century soon spread to the West Country.[100] By 1907 there were a number of regional branches federated as the Industrial Union of Direct Actionists. Anarchist Guy Aldred founded the IUDA to overcome the shortcomings of mainstream trade unions with leaders who were seen to capitulate and compromise the cause of their members and to advance only sectional interests.[101] Perhaps improbably, one branch of the IUDA was located in Weston-Super-Mare.[102] In 1911 the Liverpool General Transport Strike, an unofficial but extremely widespread strike of seamen joined by railway and other transport workers, escalated with the support of sympathy wildcat strikes on the part of the dockers. Winston Churchill, as Home Secretary in Asquith's Liberal Government, sent gunships and soldiers to Merseyside as police and strikebreakers fought with strikers and sympathetic Liverpudlians. The dispute spread from Liverpool to actions in other areas, including Bristol which was a centre of resistance at the beginning of the strike.[103] The struggle in the West Country came to a head at Portishead where more than a thousand workers attacked a working signalbox and tore up railway lines and the telegraph system, coming into conflict with the police and local military detachments.[104] Bob Holton records that there was a powerful rank-and-file syndicalist presence within the British Socialist Party, which included a branch which named itself the 'Bristol West Syndicalist BSP'.[105] In 1913 there was an ambitious attempt to hold an international conference to coordinate industrial unionist and syndicalist trade unionists across Europe and beyond. The 1913 London Congress was attended by E. Howell of the Bristol Operative Bricklayers and Ben Tillett (no longer actively involved in Bristolian industrial politics).[106] Militant industrial agitation markedly went on hold during the war years, although both Bristol and Bath were affected by the women bus and tram workers' celebrated, though often forgotten, wildcat strike for a pay increase and equal pay with men towards the end of the War in 1918.[107] It seems likely that if the General Strike had taken

---

98   'Remembering Bristol Men Killed in Spanish Civil War', Bristol Post (5 April 2010) [online]: http://www.bristolpost.co.uk/Remembering-Bristol-men-killed-Spanish-Civil-War/story-11231397-detail/story.html [accessed 26 January 2014].

99   *Tom Mann's Memoirs*, pp. 224-27.

100 See Chapter 6 in this book.

101 Bob Holton, *British Syndicalism 1900-1914: Myths and Realities* (London: Pluto, 1976), p. 46.

102 Quail, *Slow Burning Fuse*, p. 248.

103 Holton, *British Syndicalism*, p. 104.

104 SelfEd Collective, *History of Anarcho-Syndicalism*, Unit 6: 'Revolutionary Syndicalism in Britain and Ireland 1910-1917', p. 12. Available online at: http://www.selfed.org.uk/docs/units/2001/pdfs/06.pdf [accessed 10 Apr 2010].

105 Holton, *British Syndicalism*, p. 180.

106 Wayne Westergard-Thorpe, 'Towards a Syndicalist International: The 1913 London Congress' in *International Review of Social History* 23 (1978): 54, 70.

107 Libcom.org website. Ken Weller, 'The London Transport Women Workers' Strike 1918', [online]:

place during the phase of militant union activity and syndicalism before the First World War rather than in 1926 the impact would have been more far-reaching.

Keeping the Lamps on in Europe: Anarchist Resistance to Militarism in the First World War

The First World War comes down to us in a caliginous mist of trench-warfare and barbed wire; dead, mutilated and shell-shocked troops commemorated in fields of blood-red poppies. The 'Great War' is familiar today through the words of the War poets, documentaries incorporating footage from the first extensively filmed war and Armistice Day parades. We are aware too that the ghastly sequence of events of 1914-18 seemed to continue, influencing the unfolding of the twentieth-century's remaining, and even more murderous, years. The modern states that emerged continued to boost the colossal death toll through the mass deaths of the totalitarian fascist and Stalinist regimes, the Holocaust and the Second World War, being the most fatal conflict in human history. In the ruthless power struggles between states and would-be states since 1945, in excess of fifty million people have died, (the majority of them civilians), in more than two hundred conflicts.

As a defining conflict, the First World War raised fundamental questions for the anarchist movement. Why were large numbers of working-class people in countries with advanced, internationalist labour movements seemingly ready to jettison their principles and common interests and go to war? Why were prominent anarchists such as Peter Kropotkin and Jean Grave supporting the Allies against the Central Powers? Other anarchists and socialists spent months in prisons and detention camps — several of them in the West Country — for war resistance. Today, with these outcomes in mind, we can look back on WWI with the massive benefit of hindsight. This does not in itself make the issues of the conflict any less controversial.[108]

Both at the outbreak of the war and as the campaign became prolonged, in the West Country, as elsewhere, there was significant anti-militarist discontent including widespread conscientious objection and agitation against conscription. In 1916, for example, twenty-eight Bristolian men were listed as being imprisoned for their opposition to military service. Most were initially held in Horfield Gaol, at least until their courts-martial, after which they were transferred to serve their sentences in prisons or work camps for hard labour across the West Country — Dorchester, Exeter, Devonport, Portsmouth, Gloucester, Shepton Mallet — and beyond.[109] The story of conscientious

---

https://libcom.org/history/london-transport-women-workers-strike-1918 [accessed 17 May 2014].

108 Unsurprisingly, pints were spluttered when Ian Bone, well-known anarchist and one-time editor of *The Bristolian*, blogged that anarchists should wear red poppies with pride for Remembrance Sunday. Ian Bone, 'Remembrance Sunday November 8th' [online]: http://ianbone.wordpress.com/2009/10/27/remembrance-sunday-november-8th/ [accessed 27 October 2013].

109 Joint Advisory Committee for Conscientious Objectors, *What Every Bristol Man Should Know* (Bristol: Joint Advisory Committee for Conscientious Objectors, 1916) [Bristol Reference Library: History VI B32051]; Mabel C. Tothill, *Toleration or Persecution* (Bristol: Joint Advisory Committee for Conscientious Objectors, 1916). Other conscientious

objection (inherently anti-authoritarian) has often been told, with the Peace Pledge Union recording that around 16,000 conscripts formally registered as conscientious objectors (COs) in WWI. Recognition of conscientious objection was granted in tribunals in a minority of cases and was often dependent upon a minister of religion's testament as to an individual's previous attendance in a place of worship and conduct, which amounted to a substantial obstacle to those who opposed war because of socialist or other secular beliefs. Only 400 men were granted total exemption.[110]

As we might expect, veteran unaligned socialists such as Edward Carpenter continued to argue that the roots of war lay in nationalism and capitalist expansion. At the height of hostilities in 1915, Carpenter put forward the idea of creating 'a United States of Europe', a proposal Winston Churchill later suggested after World War II.[111] In his anti-war pamphlet, 'Never Again' (1916), Carpenter, still in contact with the Sharlands in Bristol, put forward a characteristically hopeful, utopian vision. He contrasted the irrational slaughter of war with the tremendous benefits to be gained if humanity were to succeed in harnessing our ingenuity and reaching a higher potential by redeploying its economic capacity away from military conflict and towards satisfying authentic social needs. In a description of which William Morris would have approved, Carpenter contemplated the creative power of unalienated, aesthetically pleasing and socially useful production:

> It will only come with the determination of the workers (that is, of everybody) to produce things useful, profitable, and beautiful, in free and rational co-operation — things useful because deliberately made for use, things profitable for all because not made for the gain of the few, and things beautiful because of the joy and gladness wrought into their very production.

> Simultaneously with this peeling of the Old, and disclosure of the New, will of necessity appear — indeed it is taking shape already — the blossom of international solidarity and federation — the common cause of Humanity and Labour liberated over the world.[112]

By the early twentieth century, however, a new generation of anarchist militants and anti-parliamentarians had emerged. With reference to James Tochatti and two later anarchist writers and orators, George Barrett and Guy Alfred Aldred, and several anti-war detainees, it is timely to briefly reclaim some overlooked history; the presence of anarchist resistance, rooted in internationalism and anti-capitalism, to the First World War in the West Country.

---

objectors were held in the West Country in prison or undertook hard labour at Dartmoor and Taunton.

110 See Peace Pledge Union, *Refusing to Kill: Conscientious Objection and Human Rights in the First World War* (London: Peace Pledge Union, 2006), p. 42.

111 In *The Healing of Nations*. See Chushichi Tsuzuki, 'Carpenter, Edward (1844-1929)', entry in the *Oxford Dictionary of National Biography* [online]: http://www.oxforddnb.com/view/article/32300?docPos=1 [accessed 29 December 2013].

112 Edward Carpenter, *Never Again: A Protest and a Warning Addressed to the Peoples of Europe* (Manchester: National Labour Press, 1916), p. 11.

George Barrett's Forgotten Bestseller

George Barrett (born George Powell Ballard; 1888-1917) was born in Ledbury but moved to Bristol when he came of age.[113] He provides a link between the Bristol Socialist Society and the militant agitation of this period. He married Edith Oxley, daughter of prominent Bristol Christian socialist, W. R. Oxley. Quail records that Barrett's first political involvement with the Bristol Socialist Society initiated his later efforts as an anarchist soapbox speaker and pamphleteer. Barrett seems to have resigned from the Society around 1908 however, due to his differences of opinion brought about by his anarchist politics which disturbed the group's 'otherwise peaceful routine'.[114]

Barrett moved away from the West Country to Glasgow and London, becoming a key activist within the Glasgow Anarchist Group and an editor of a weekly paper called *The Anarchist* between 1912 and 1913.[115] Although now largely forgotten, even by the anarchist movement, he was a popular propagandist for the cause. He undertook energetic lecture tours throughout England, Scotland and Wales. These tours also enabled him to maintain links with the West Country, for example speaking in nearby Cardiff in early January 1912 before moving onto Bristol where he spoke for several nights in succession on such topics as 'Recent Strikes' and 'Anarchy and Progress', and continuing his schedule in Stroud.[116] Speaking in 1913, he states that he thought that the anarchist groups of 'South Wales and Bristol are the most active of all, perhaps'. He continued to visit Bristol after the outbreak of war, which was now the focus of his attentions. A report in *Freedom* in September 1914 suggests that a visit from Barrett helped to raise the spirits of the local anti-militarist anarchists who held regular meetings in Ashton Avenue:

> It is good to be able at last to report group activity in this city. Each Sunday since the commencement of the war, comrades Porter, Hall and Plattin have endeavoured to turn the patriotic sentiments of the 'man in the street' into a more healthy direction than the subsidised Press would have them take, exposing the warmongers and the 'patriotism' of the armaments and dynamite manufacturers and food merchants. We have had, of course, considerable interruption from the Jingoes, and our literature sales have not been very encouraging. On the 16th, we were fortunate in having a visit from our comrade George Barrett, who in a quarter of an hour's earnest talk with the crowd (the first in the open air since his long illness) completely silenced the Jingoes, and evoked

---

113 The few details of Barrett's life available are provided by S. E. Parker, 'George Barrett – A Biographical Note', *The Raven* 12 (Oct-Dec 1990), pp. 335-338.

114 Quail, *Slow Burning Fuse*, p. 274, quoting *Freedom* for February 1908.

115 Ibid., p. 276.

116 Report in *Freedom: A Journal of Anarchist Communism* Vol. XXVI. No. 273 (January 1912), p. 7. A report for the following month indicates that other Freedom Group lecturers in Bristol around this time were trade unionist and anarcho-syndicalist John Turner (1864-1934), C. Brewer, A. Despres and the influential Irish anarchist Mat Kavanagh (1876-1954). Report in *Freedom: A Journal of Anarchist Communism* Vol. XXVI. No. 274 (February 1912), p. 15.

applause from the more thoughtful of his audience.[117]

Paying tribute to 'Objections to Anarchism' as 'one of the first, and best, anarchist pamphlets I ever read', Colin Ward much admired Barrett as a forceful debater and exponent of anarchist ideas and for his ability to take arguments back to first principles and apply them to real world scenarios.[118] Some of Barrett's attacks upon capitalist society would equally hold true today, for example the following from his 1915 pamphlet, 'The Anarchist Revolution':

> Millions are on the verge of starvation, hundreds of thousands are spending their lives in producing instruments for the destruction of human life, and millions again are wasting their existence in a dull tragedy of monotony.[119]

Writing three years before the outbreak of the First World War, Barrett was already rehearsing some of the arguments that he was to put forward in his war-time agitation. He observed that in some areas there was already a sporadic conflict, a class conflict, underway on the streets. In the insightful and, probably in the view of the authorities, inciting essay, 'Anarchy and the Labour War', penned in 1911, he angrily challenges and reverses the governing capitalist class's customary adoption of a high moral ground:

> They say anarchy means blood-shed and brute force, & at the same time they get ready then paid men armed with thick sticks & revolvers & swords & guns with which to fight the workers.
> <u>Capitalism means bloodshed & brute force or as the only alternative the absolute submission of the workers.</u>[120]

This was not just hyperbolic propaganda, Home Secretary Winston Churchill had recently presided over industrial conflict in which police (from Bristol and Gloucester) and troops were sent to confront strikers in the Tonypandy Riots of 1910. In the Llanelli Railway Strike the following year troops were deployed again, this time with fatal consequences. A strike wave erupted in June 1911 following national industrial action that started in Liverpool and Southampton, culminating in the extensive deployment of troops (resulting in a docker being shot dead in Liverpool) and even gunboats on Merseyside.[121]

The foreboding prospect of conflict between competing nations was already widely anticipated at this time. Barrett wrote in the hope that the working class would recognise their international commonalty as a class for itself:

---

117 'Bristol Group's Activity', *Freedom: A Journal of Anarchist Communism* Vol. XXVIII. No. 305 (September 1914), p. 72. The speaker the following week, presumably also making the case against the War, was cited as 'comrade Gosling, late of the Royal Navy, and now of the Bricklayers' Union'.

118 Colin Ward, 'George Barrett's Answers', *The Raven* 12 (Oct.-Dec. 1990), p. 333.

119 George Barrett, *The Anarchist Revolution* (London: Freedom Press, 1915), p. 2.

120 By an Anarchist, [George Ballad ('Barrett')], *Anarchy and the Labour War*, Manuscript: Freedom Archive 457, International Institute of Social History, Amsterdam, p. 1 [published as pamphlet and in *Freedom* 269 (September 1911), pp. 69-70].

121 BBC Liverpool, 'Liverpool's Fatal 1911 Riot's Remembered': http://www.bbc.co.uk/news/uk-england-merseyside-14529243 [Accessed 15 December 2013].

No fight put up by the Capitalists of one country against the Capitalists of another has ever been half so important as the fight that is being carried on the streets of our great cities today. It is a part of that great war by which the workers of all nations shall rid themselves of the powerful class which lives at their expense. Shall for the first time enjoy the fruits of their labor & finally throwing off the power of their masters shall come out of the last form of slavery into Freedom.[122]

In his conclusion to 'Anarchy and the Labour War', Barrett declares,

Workers! Friends! Comrades! Your power is unlimited. You are the creative force behind all history. Down with your slums and open wide your castle gates. The wealth of the world is yours. You are the inheritors of the invention and genius of the past. Fight on! Powerless, muddleheaded politicians alone stand in your way. This fight for our freedom is the only meaning of our existence. Come up to the front rank of human progress & even now breathe the life-giving air of the Social Revolution.[123]

Barrett's pamphlet, 'The Last War', written at the outbreak of the First World War in 1914, deals most directly with the implications of the impending hostilities. It was published by the Bristol Workers' Freedom Group, based at 19 The Haymarket, Bristol.[124] There were a number of Workers' Freedom Groups set up at this time to promote anarchist-communism. Nick Heath notes that these groups were particularly strong in Swansea, Abertillery and other parts of South Wales, thus corroborating Barrett's suggestion that anarchism had active support in South Wales and Bristol.[125] The reach of 'The Last War' went far beyond Bristol or Barrett's base in Glasgow, however, as it reputedly sold as many as 10, 000 copies before it was banned.[126]

In 'The Last War', against the background of WWI, Barrett sets out core aspects of his argument for revolutionary anarchism, the bloodbath of war itself making the strongest case for the necessity for an alternative to the *status quo*. Barrett's argumentative force no doubt accounts for the success and impact of 'The Last War' which makes the case for internationalism against patriotism, class consciousness developed through the recognition of common interests on the part of ordinary people and the necessity for personal and collective responsibility, while, all importantly, expressing utopian hopes with intimations of positive anarchism as a manifestation of humanity's spiritual evolution and

---

122 By an Anarchist, [George Ballad ('Barrett')], *Anarchy and the Labour War*, Manuscript: *Freedom* Archive 457, International Institute of Social History, Amsterdam, p. 4.

123 Ibid., p. 11.

124 This was the address of Jack Flynn the newsagent, an outlet for radical literature and a venue for socialist and anarchist meetings during the early twentieth century. W. R. Fowler, 5 Sherborne Road, Yeovil was the other listed outlet for *Freedom* in the West Country at this time.

125 libcom.org website. Nick Heath, 'Anarchists Against World War One: Two Little Known Events – Abertillery and Stockport', [online]: http://libcom.org/history/anarchists-against-world-war-one-two-little-known-events-abertillery-stockport [accessed 27 October 2013].

126 Libcom.org website, [Nick Heath], 'Barrett, George 1888-1917', [online]: http://libcom.org/history/barrett-george-1888-1917 [accessed 29 October 2013].

THE LAST WAR

By. Geo. Barrett

THE Journalist, the Military Expert, the Politician, the Clergyman & the Labour Leader, have all given us their views on the war. The workers, who feed and clothe them, have a different outlook. This pamphlet sets forth their view of the matter.

PRICE :: :: ONE PENNY

destiny.

Barrett quickly sets out to deconstruct patriotism as grounded in an accident of chance as to which nation a person happens to be born into and therefore making an 'ill guide to reason'. He calls upon his readers to transcend the narrow sectional interests defined by nationality:

> We who are not politicians, or kings, or czars, or Kaisers; we who serve in the shops, who work in the factories, drive the trams – and, in a word, make and distribute all that is necessary for life; we surely have a very different view of things from those who have organised this war and who call us to fight it.[127]

Barrett makes a passionate case for the necessity for revolutionaries to embrace internationalism and unite against all ruling classes if any real progress towards human liberation is to be made. He posits a radically different, subversive sense of the term 'patriotic' suggesting 'a new sense' of the idea, which would reverse

---

127 George Barrett, *The Last War: A Collection of Three Essays by George Barrett* (Sheffield: Pirate Press, 1990), 'The Last War', p. 4.

45

the terms of the debate. He urges workers to insist that if the rich 'master-class' really believe that workers' 'love of country' is a fine thing, it logically follows that workers should possess what is familiar and dear to them about their country by bringing about the real 'conquest of England by the English people', thus enabling them to control its wealth.[128] For free men and women there is no conflict between their local interests and the struggle for humankind at the global level; both are complementary parts of the project to build 'a rich and beautiful community'.[129]

Barrett's approach also indicates that, had he lived, his anti-militarist sentiments would, without contradiction, have led him to support armed struggle rather than pacifism against Nazism and Fascism during the Spanish Civil War and World World Two, in as far as they could be conceived as people's wars for liberation. 'We have a treaty to keep,' writes Barrett,

> … it has been signed by the blood of our comrades in every nation of the world, for there is not one of the governments but it has shown itself ready and over anxious to shoot down the workers directly they begin to think of recapturing the land that has been taken away from them.[130]

That Barrett had in mind the potential for the brutal repression of workers in any of the belligerents' streets and factories, including England is suggested by his reference to 'huge military camps' set up in Liverpool and London to quell unrest before the war.[131] In his autobiographical account of his role in WWI, *Goodbye to all that* (1929), Robert Graves for all his proclamations of socialism and a hearty scepticism about the military conflict learned from first-hand experience, recounts an argument with the philosopher Bertrand Russell, (an active opponent of the war), who asked,

> "Tell me, if a company of your men were brought along to break a strike of munition makers, and the munition makers refused to go back to work, would you order the men to fire?"

> "Yes, if everything else failed. It would be no worse than shooting Germans really."

> He asked in surprise: "Would they obey you?"

> "They loath munition-workers, and would be only too glad of a chance to shoot a few. They think they're all skrim-shankers."

> "But they realize that the war's all wicked nonsense?"

> "Yes, as well as I do."
> He could not understand my attitude.[132]

The context of this reported exchange makes Graves' remarks more than

---

128 Ibid., p. 6.
129 Ibid., p. 19.
130 Ibid., p. 7.
131 Ibid., p. 14.
132 Robert Graves, *Goodbye to all that* [1929], rev. ed. (Harmondsworth: Penguin, 1960), pp. 204-205.

rhetorical. The inflexible code of Graves and his troops to stand firm and not flinch from their allotted roles, overrides any other consideration, even when undertaking actions that clearly breach other ethical codes and contradict other aspects of his world-view (and they have the insight to recognise such contradictions). The implication of Graves' defence, as I interpret it, is grounded in the insistence that the virtue of never breaking rank must be upheld beyond all else, even in the kind of extreme scenario that Russell describes.

Barrett would have no truck at all with Graves's mentality and, both during and after the conflict, many would disagree with the logic of such a 'socialist'. Barrett argued passionately for a sharply contrasting and contesting notion of solidarity. Barrett insisted that class consciousness is essential if workers are to avoid divisions and attain the kind of global solidarity necessary to decommission the social structures and physical apparatus of war. The lack of a strong world-view forming a viable alternative to patriotic and religious sensibilities, argues Barrett, makes ordinary working people susceptible to the ideas of others and led into conflicts against their better natures and own best interests. Instead it is necessary to change the paradigm if there is really to be a war to end all wars. For Barrett, the 'last war' is

> [...] the international war in which the workers of all lands shall be united against the invaders — the rich who have seized the land and lived on the labour of the poor.[133]

The last war, then, is not a battlefield conflict but one ordinary people wage to take control of the land and means of production with a final objective to attain 'universal peace'.[134] Barrett makes his case with clarity, personal address and common sense, creating a vision of hope while never underestimating the magnitude of the struggle for change and a time when

> Men and women will be free, united by the common purpose of building up a rich and beautiful community, in which they shall have their place and play their part.[135]

'The Last War' is clear and succinctly argued and its basic premises hold true. The small number of other essays that Barrett wrote share a similar combination of keen reasoning and rhetorical flourish. 'The First Person' written in 1916, during the bleak throes of the middle years of the First World War, and, as it turned out, in the last months of Barrett's life, pursues a unanswerable logic of personal and collective responsibility against bad faith (self-deception) and false consciousness (failure to recognise the collective power of ordinary people as a class).

In 1916, the last year of his short life, Barrett was one of the signatories of a statement by internationalist anarchists who condemned Peter Kropotkin's support for the Allied Cause in the First World War. As late as 1914 Kropotkin

---

133 George Barrett, *The Last War: A Collection of Three Essays by George Barrett* (Sheffield: Pirate Press, 1990), 'The Last War', p. 10.

134 Ibid., p. 4.

135 Ibid., p. 19.

had vehemently attacked the institution of war as an inevitable outcome of statism and capitalism. In a Freedom Press pamphlet, entitled 'Wars and Capitalism', he described the role of international finance in shaping policy and public opinion to its own interests:

> The economical forces which could produce harmony and well-being, and give a fresh impulse to libertarian civilisation if they had free play in society, — these forces, being directed by the State, that is to say, by an organisation specially developed to enrich the rich and to absorb all modern progress in order to benefit privileged classes — these same forces become an instrument of oppression, of monopolists, and endless wars.[136]

Yet his long-standing hostility towards the German state in particular, which appeared to extend to the German people, and his contrasting support for the French Republic, ensured that his sympathies came to be defined by national sympathies rather than internationalist principles. To the consternation of his anarchist comrades, therefore, at the outbreak of the War, Kropotkin was unequivocal in its support of the Allied armies of Britain, France and Russia, a position that in his own mind required little adjustment of his ostensibly internationalist principles. Furthermore, in early 1916 Kropotkin and Jean Grave drafted, and were the most well known signatories to, the so-called Manifesto of the Sixteen, which took a pro-war stance, unambiguously advocating support for the Allied Cause against Germany and the Central Powers.[137] Kropotkin, horrified by the slaughter of the Paris Communards following the Prussian victory over France in 1871 and fearful of the rise of Prussian militarism, believed that the defeat of the Kaiser's regime was essential if libertarian politics were to make progress in Europe and the world.

Kropotkin's approach was based on closely related premises: that it would be expedient to support the states of Britain and France, more liberal despite their imperialism, capitalism and nationalism, since they represented the lesser evil and that abandoning the weapon of international solidarity in the short term would make political progress easier once the Kaiser had been defeated; that German political culture was inherently belligerent and that the defeat of the German armed forces would bring about a permanent neutralisation of Prussian militarism and open the future to liberation in Europe. Kropotkin's belief that a strategic long game, in which the short-term means of supporting the patriotic war of the capitalist Allied states was necessary, if regrettable, and justified because it served ostensibly anarchist ends was not vindicated by the historic outcomes of the conflict. Despite the logic underpinning Kropotkin's position that appealed to several anarchists, (although always a minority), none of these premises were born out by the eventual Allied victory and subsequent world history. The notion that racial chauvinism was inherently German, moreover,

---

136 Peter Kropotkin, *Wars and Capitalism* (London: Freedom Press, 1916).

137 See George Woodcock and Ivan Avakumović, *The Anarchist Prince: A Biographical Study of Peter Kropotkin* (London: T. V. Boardman, 1950), pp. 373-387, for an account of the controversy around Kropotkin's attitude to the First World War.

was flawed, given that rudimentary eugenic theories were by no means confined to Germany. With hindsight we know that the eventual defeat of Germany subsequently led to the emergence of such ideas in Nazism, their most virulently racist form, but we can only speculate as to the outcome for Europe and the world of the counter-factual scenario of an Allied defeat in 1914.

For his critics a particularly exasperating aspect of Kropotkin's stance was the fact that it entailed an alliance of Britain and France with Czarist Russia, for Barrett 'the most brutally reactionary government in Europe'.[138] (Kropotkin knew this well from bitter experience but believed that an alliance would moderate the character of the Russia state). Barrett's involvement in the debate, however, was to be foreshortened. Describing Barrett as 'the brilliant young editor of the Glasgow Anarchist', George Woodcock and Ivan Avakumović recount a letter to Tom Keell in which Kropotkin expresses concern for Barrett's health as early as 1914, when he was already suffering from tuberculosis. Barrett was to die of the disease aged just 29 years, in Torquay in 1917.

James Tochatti takes on the Jingo-Patriots

In addition to George Barrett's energetic opposition to war and conscription, Scottish anarchist James Tochatti spoke in Bristol in 1912 and again in 1914.[139] *Freedom* carried a short report of Tochatti's lecture 'The Attitude of Revolutionists towards the War', delivered on 12th October 1914, at the Kingsley Hall in Old Market. Tochatti saved the day when he stepped in to speak after George Barrett was forced to cancel due his ongoing ill health:

> Tochatti opened by explaining the psychology of the war, pointing out the damnable effects of the Jingo war press, with their faked or one-sided stories of brutality, cowardice, or heroism. He also pointed out what a powerful factor the religious superstition played in inculcating habits of unquestioning obedience and submission to authority, and emphasised the need of secular education, and a strong atheistic propaganda. He practically ignored all the diplomatic jugglery that is supposed to have brought about this war, and pointed out the real causes – trade, power, profits, etc. He said that the only way to prevent these disasters to humanity was by realising the Anarchist Communist ideal.
>
> At the close of his well-reasoned and interesting address, we anticipated he would be bombarded with antagonistic questions, but to our surprise most of the questioners were practically in agreement with the lecturer. The most interesting question was: What would be the lecturer's attitude in case of invasion by a foreign Power? Tochatti pointed out that even Anarchists were human, and the best of us are little more than savage brutes when blood has been spilled. He would resist, as would the whole population were they armed. There would then be little fear of a German conquest. But that is just what all Governments fear – the arming of the people; they know only too well that that would mean the end of their enslavement of the masses. An armed and freedom-

---

138 Barrett, *Last War*, p. 8.

139 Reported in *Freedom*. See Libcom: http://libcom.org/history/tochatti-james-1852-1928 [accessed 20 April 2010].

loving people would free themselves alike from English as from foreign rulers, landlords, and monopolists. Remember the massacre of the Communards![140]

Guy Aldred: Minister of the Gospel of Revolt

Guy Aldred (1886-1963) is most prominent of the British anarchists who actively campaigned against participation in the First World War. Aldred was a contemporary of Barrett, though much longer lived, also gravitating to anarchist circles in Glasgow. He opposed Barrett in Glasgow, apparently due to his long running quarrel with the Freedom Collective with which Barrett was associated, forming the rival Glasgow Communist Group.[141] A tireless propagandist, Aldred publicised a broad range of topics, (not least, it seems, himself), including sexual liberation and equality, freethinking, anti-capitalism and industrial militancy, and support for teetotalism and anti-nicotinism, right up to his death in the 1960s. In a flyer advocating his services as a speaker, Aldred asked that requests for lectures should be addressed to 'Guy A. Aldred, Minister of the Gospel of Revolt'.[142]

Aldred believed that any authentic resolution of military conflict was impossible without identifying and attacking its root causes in nationalism and capitalist expansionism. Aldred trenchantly set out his arguments against war in *At Grips with War* (1929), a book of the interwar period written in the light of his experiences of resistance in WWI. Again in common with Barrett, Aldred's anti-war sentiments were grounded not in pacifism but in class consciousness and internationalism. Aldred's programme for tackling the root causes of war rests in removing the old enemies of humankind:

> One cannot seek a genuine reduction of armaments without challenging the very foundations of bourgeois society. One cannot believe in Mammon without worshipping at the altars of Moloch. The wages-system is one of militarism. Profits imply markets and pseudo-patriotisms. Exploitation demands cannon-fodder and destruction. Accordingly, the Anti-Parliamentarian declares that the only answer to Capitalist Imperialism is World Communism, Cosmopolitan Working Class Republicanism.
> All nationalisms must go.
> All patriotisms must go.
> All alienisms and antagonistic sovereignties must go.
> Passports must vanish.
> Political society must be liquidated.
> The world must become a single nation, a single brotherhood, merging or retaining its several languages, but moved by a common economic impulse and social integrity.

---

140 'Propaganda Notes', *Freedom: A Journal of Anarchist Communism* Vol. XXVIII. No. 307 (November 1914), p. 83.

141 Nicolas Walter, 'Guy A. Aldred, 1886-1963' [1981], in David Goodway (ed.), *Damned Fools in Utopia and Other Writings on Anarchism and War Resistance* (Oakland, Calif.: PM Press, 2011), p. 248.

142 Publicity flyer on Guy A. Aldred (accompanying a letter to Tom Keell dated 1907). Manuscript in *Freedom* Archive 439, International Institute of Social History, Amsterdam.

Sovereignty must belong to each individual. Allegiance must be recaptured from states, churches, and creeds, and returned to each individual's own conscience. Society must be a merging of desires, not a dictatorship of subjection.[143]

Something similar actually happened in 1905 when the working classes of Sweden and Norway neutralised potential conflict by refusing to engage in armed hostilities. For Aldred, therefore, mass disobedience and fraternisation was not a utopian pipedream, since the Scandinavians had provided a strong and very recent precedent of the possibilities of such a strategy:

> Early in August 1914, the Syndicalists of France united with the Social Democrats of Germany to deluge Europe with proletarian blood. ...
>
> What induced the 3,317,271 organised workers of Germany to attack cheerfully their affiliated 1,064,413 brothers of France? ... Why could they not have done as the Swedish and Norwegian armies did in 1905-6 when ordered to fight each other – have fraternised and so forced peace on their respective governments without a shot being fired? Three months later, British and German soldiers were fraternising in the trenches. Amidst the horrors of the battlefield, they were trusting their lives on agreed "off times" to friendly understandings.[144]

The labour movement again mobilised to prevent the invasion of Allied Forces aiming to overthrow the Soviet government in the wake of the Russian Revolution.

Aldred was forthright in his opposition to the First World War, his resistance being more than theoretical. He delivered campaigning speeches and condemned the conflict in both the mainstream media and anarchist publications, such as *The Voice of Labour*, during the early years. He maintained indefatigable resistance to the war throughout, editing and contributing to the *Spur*, (with his partner Rose Witcop), a one-off paper called *War News* and a prisoners' paper called *Granite Echo*.[145] When conscription was introduced in 1916 he was arrested and court-martialled. Aldred was first court-martialled in May 1916 for not carrying out military service and a second time in June 1916 at the Fovant camp near Salisbury, Wiltshire, when he received nine months' hard labour for refusing to parade.[146] While awaiting his court-martial at Fovant he wrote a poem called 'A Meditation', that concluded with the lines,

> May no worldly ambition
> no temptation in this wilderness of understanding
> lead me to serve the enemy of man,
> the principle of power and domination.[147]

---

143 Guy A. Aldred, *At Grips with War* (Glasgow: Bakunin Press, 1929), p. 15.

144 Ibid., pp. 31-32.

145 Walter, 'Guy Aldred', pp. 248-249. Another clandestine prison newspaper which Aldred may have seen was the celebrated *Winchester Whisperer*, written on toilet paper by war resisters during WWI.

146 Information on Aldred's war experiences are detailed at the following: Glasgow Caledonian University, Radical Glasgow webpages, 'Guy Aldred': http://www.gcu.ac.uk/radicalglasgow/chapters/aldred.html [accessed 25 November 2013].

147 Annarky's Blog, 'Enemy of God and Foe of Kings':

Aldred spent most of July and August of 1916 in Winchester Prison. He continued to face courts-martial and detentions, including some time in Exeter Military Camp, throughout the rest of the war until as late as 1919.

Fraternally yours: Anarchist Conscientious Objectors

Guy Aldred was just one of a number of anarchists who were imprisoned in detention camps for resisting conscription during the First World War. Several letters to the editors of *Freedom* magazine from anarchist war resisters survive and are held in the *Freedom* Archive at the International Institute for Social History in Amsterdam. These letters were penned during 1916, the year that conscription was introduced in Britain following the passage of the Military Service Act. Mostly written in haste by young men, they provide rare but brief glimpses of the concerns of grass-roots anarchists who are not speechmakers or authors, providing fragments of snatched conversations from a hidden history overheard. In taking a personal stand against the war they found themselves in extraordinary circumstances where their political convictions were tested to the utmost; they were forced to make life and death decisions, tested in the crucible of a real global cataclysm.

We will look at seven letters from correspondents who were incarcerated in the West Country. Written in detention from various guardrooms, the letters are prosaic, with sentences that are themselves, understandably, sometimes guarded in nature, their writers mindful because they are well aware that such communications will almost certainly be scanned by the authorities. It is also worth bearing in mind that the letters date from 1916, that is, in the early days after conscription was introduced, and often pre-date, or were written around the time of tribunals or courts-martial. Reported sentences of hard labour were, therefore, periods that may well have been subsequently extended or repeated if the prisoner concerned continued to refuse to 'recant' and undertake military service.

What were their concerns? The letters are firstly an opportunity to communicate the practical details of the detainees' particular cases and courts-martial to those outside. They often comment upon the treatment they are receiving and express sentiments regarding their family, friends and comrades in the movement. In this respect it is noteworthy in terms of their motivation and commitment that they are choosing to prioritise their (no doubt restricted) opportunities to write letters to contact the anarchist paper *Freedom*, often requesting the editors to pass on information to their families. Beyond this, in more expansive and reflective passages, the question is raised as to how far anarchism functioned as a kind of secular faith, inspiring them, like their religious counterparts, to take an ethical stand against war. The letters convey a need to rationalise the decision to become a conscientious objector, to share with other like-minded comrades in a situation where they might be otherwise

---

http://radicalglasgowblog.blogspot.co.uk/2013/04/enemy-of-god-and-foe-of-kings.html [accessed 29 December 2013].

isolated, perhaps seeking corroboration or even reassurance for their stance among respected and like-minded peers. Their defiance reflects an explicit identification with a wider struggle rooted in anarchist politics of refusal and resistance. In some instances there is deliberation about how far to go in making individual sacrifices when acting in isolation. The need to share thoughts and to think out a position lends an occasional confessional tone to some of the correspondence.

Four of the letters are from detainees who were held, like Aldred, at the military camp at Fovant, Salisbury.

A brief note from anarchist conscientious objector J. F. Hall to Tom Keell, dated 8th June 1916, reports 'a little better treatment' following the 'brutal treatment' that he, and at least one other detainee, had recently received. This unspecified treatment was evidently sufficiently severe that the case was due to be raised in Parliament. Family concerns are also uppermost in Hall's thoughts, as he requests financial mutual aid:

> The young Lady tells me that mother is having a strugle [sic] to live so if you can will you send her a little out of the fund as I dont like to hear of her going short.[148]

He also requests Keell to 'remember me to all the comrades.'

P. F. Meacham reported his defiant stance against the court-martial process in a letter to his 'dear comrade', an unknown recipient called Miss E. J. Wilkinson, apparently another editor of *Freedom* at that time. The letter was written in response to a previous (presumably long lost) letter from Wilkinson which had been opened by the authorities. Written in instalments from the Fovant camp over two days, 9th-10th August 1916, Meacham announces his intention to make, and then confirms that he made, the following statement at his court-martial which he quotes in full:

> I challenge your claim to try me by Court Martial, or, any other court whatsoever, in so much that I have ~~signed~~ swore no oath of allegiance, and have signed no papers of any kind for service in any branch of the British Army. Therefore on this ground I decline to plead either Guilty or Not Guilty, and shall not examine any of the witnesses this court may call, no matter whom they may be. This is all I wish to say on the matter. And I have no further interest in the proceedings.

Meacham's statement was promptly 'ruled out of order', leaving him contemptuous of the court-martial proceedings:

> Disgusting exhibition of cant and hypocrisy. Outside building were men and implements intended for warfare. Inside were the officers commanding the men, being sworn in on what they claim to be the message of the Prince of Peace, The Bible. An absolute farce. No equal at all. I have a more bitter hatred & disgust for militarism than I have ever had before.

---

148 Letter from J. F. Hall to Tom Keell, Fovant Camp, Salisbury (8 June 1916). Manuscript in *Freedom* Archive 458, International Institute of Social History, Amsterdam.

Meacham's conclusion is sanguine:

> I have been sentenced to 112 days hard labour. Shall do sentence quite
> cheerfully. Hope "Freedom" & "The Voice of Labour" will be kept
> going. With best wishes to all comrades till we meet again.[149]

Both *Freedom* and *The Voice of Labour* were suppressed under the Defence of
the Realm Act 1914.

Fred H. Lellow took an equally pragmatic attitude in some brief lines to
Lilian Wolfe, penned at Fovant on 15th August 1916. As in Meacham's case, the
outcome of Lellow's court-martial was 112 days of hard labour, (commuted
from six months). He writes,

> I am feeling quite well & in the best of spirits. Please thank T.K. [Tom
> Keell] for his letter-card. I have been unable to reply to it. You will soon
> have T.K. back with you again would like to have been there when he was
> released to grip his hand and congratulate him but that is impossible all
> the while "My King & Country Needs Me!" [150]

A. Foyle (almost certainly Alfred William Foyle) wrote a hurried and equally
defiant 'scribble' to Lilian Wolfe on 4th September 1916, updating her on his
situation and wishing her 'Good luck to you and the comrades of the movement'.
He requests Wolfe to assure his family, and particularly his grandmother, that he
is 'alright' and writes:

> Just a line to let you know that I have not given in and that further I am in
> the best of spirit and I mean to face the fight right to the finish whatever it
> may be.[151]

Foyle wrote his letter on patriotic headed notepaper from the YMCA, defacing
the header by crossing out the legend 'For God, For King & For Country' and
replacing it with 'For Freedom'. The conclusion of the letter is not available.
Foyle recounts his position as an absolutist Conscientious Objector, upholding
total non-cooperation, refusing to sign police papers, wear khaki, (he was
forcibly undressed and made to wear the uniform), go on parade or clean the
camp canteen.

As a consequence he was to face a court-martial at the time of writing. Apart
from getting his civilian clothes torn off by 'a bully of a sergeant', Foyle has no
complaints to make about his treatment at the hands of the authorities at that
time.

A fascinating and revealing letter of 18th September 1916 from another

---

149 Letter from P. F. Meacham to E. J. Wilkinson, Fovant Camp, Salisbury (9 August 1916). Manuscript in ibid.

150 Letter from Fred H. Lellow to Lilian Wolfe, Fovant Camp, Salisbury (15 August 1916). Manuscript in ibid. The co-
editors of *Freedom*, Tom Keell and Lilian Wolfe, were both imprisoned for war resistance in 1916. Letters were written
to Wolfe after her earlier release while Keell remained in Pentonville Prison from June to September 1916. It seems,
therefore, that Lellow's congratulations were premature since Keell may not have been released until the following
month.

151 Letter from Alfred William Foyle to Lilian Wolfe, Fovant Camp, Salisbury (4 September 1916). Manuscript in ibid.

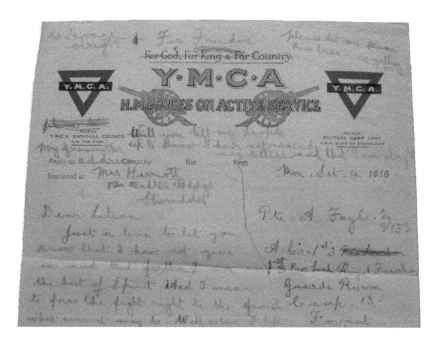

absolutist detainee named Alfred Comm to the recently released Tom Keell, refers to four anarchist conscientious objectors, (including himself), at the Hazeley Down Camp near Winchester, Hampshire at that time. Comm is testing the bounds of resistance:

> What I am writing you for really is to ask you from your experience how far it is possible to refuse orders in prison. For I do not intend to have anything to do with alternative service and it seems the logical policy is to refuse orders in prison. But if it mean that they may keep you in prison until you do obey, it seems hardly worth the candle.[152]

Faced with the contradiction of sacrificing freedom in the cause of freedom, Comm sought out the opinion of Keell, who may have risked compromising his own precarious liberty had he responded to advocate complete non-cooperation. Comm has won a small victory in gaining the right to a lacto-vegetarian diet while in detention. He expressed concern for the isolation of a close comrade with whom he had previously lived before their separation to be detained in different parts of southern England. In common with fellow correspondents Meacham and Chapman, Comm refers to reading anarchist literature — in this case the *The Ego and His Own* — while explicitly affirming the influence of Max Stirner's book by writing 'That is the philosophy on which I base my resistance'. Comm's letter to Keell has a confessional tone as he weighs the ethical challenges of the situation that confronts him. This is particularly evident in the concluding lines in which Comm considers the limits of his individual resistance:

---

152 Letter from Alfred Comm to Tom Keell, Hazeley Down Camp, Winchester (18 September 1916). Manuscript in ibid.

> But I am afraid I shall have to respect the legal formulae & go through the thing [illegible]. I am not quite reckless enough to flout them entirely and be "impossible." I suppose this is a confession of weakness. You see, as soon as one starts arguing with them, one concedes something. One should be deaf, dumb and silly.

W. Brown was possibly one of the other anarchist conscientious objectors to whom Comm refers to as being held at the Hazeley Down Camp. His undated letter is written to his wife in London. Clearly aware that his letter is likely to be read by his guards, Brown warns her not to mention names in her response and it is evident that his main intention is communicate with his circle of comrades who he is forbidden to address directly. Unlike the other correspondents, therefore, Brown does not write to the *Freedom* editors, (although he does refer to 'Miss Wolfe'), nor does he explicitly identify himself as an anarchist, making his stand rather in the name of 'socialism and conscience' and linking himself most closely with the No-Conscription Fellowship, which, linked to the Independent Labour Party, was the main organisation for conscientious objection and resistance to the war in the absence of opposition from the mainstream labour movement. The presence of Brown's letter among others held in the *Freedom* archive links him to the anarchist movement. In his mention of Foyle, he seems to have been referring to Alfred William Foyle, a detainee, who as we have seen, wrote to Lilian Wolfe in September 1916.

The details of the letters from Foyle and Brown can be contextualised through a newspaper cutting from the *Daily Express*, also held in the *Freedom* archive. This reports a police and military raid on a garden party held in Bow, London and organised by Lilian Wolfe to raise money for *The Voice of Labour* paper. This was a significant solidarity event to sustain the paper, which had reportedly been 'twice suppressed by the police', attended, we are told, by 67 men — all of whom 'avowed themselves to be revolutionists' — and 100-150 women. 27 of the men, including William Brown and our previous correspondent, Alfred William Foyle, (described as a 23-year-old fitter), were detained as unable to prove their exemption from military service. In court the 24-year old Brown is reported to have said that he stated, 'he would not shoot down his fellow workers "be they German, French or English"'.[153] This was reiterated in a follow-up report on the arrest of the so-called 'shirkers' in the *Daily Express* the next day, which reported Foyle's statement that 'he did not recognise the military machine'.[154]

The light-hearted nature of the lines to his wife reflects Brown's given profession as comedian. Brown's letter is also perhaps exaggeratedly positive in its reassurances and sentiments, in part a cloak, I surmise, to convey the underlying message of resistance at its core:

> They have tried every possible way to get me to obey orders, but I have

---

153 'Garden Party Raid. Absentees Under Military Service Act Charged'. Newspaper clipping from the Daily Express (28 August 1916). Manuscript in ibid.

154 'Shirkers Caught at a Party. Revolutionists Sent into the Army'. Newspaper clipping from the *Daily Express* (29 August 1916). Manuscript in ibid.

refused point-blank (with tolerance and with civility).[155]

In H. Chapman's brief note to Keell, written from detention in Newton Abbot, Devon, on 14th December 1916, we learn that Mr Meacham — almost certainly P. F. Meacham — has also been transferred from Fovant to the same camp by this date. In keeping with Meacham's sentiments, Chapman's request indicates the same desire to continue the struggle by reading and circulating anarchist literature while imprisoned:

> I have no money to pay for them [two copies of Satire]. After we have "Crushed Germany" money will be no object.[156]

The small anarchist circle based around *Freedom* magazine therefore operated a support network for mutual aid in difficult times. Several correspondents report that they were being treated well, with Foyle finding the 'fellows mostly decent', that 'the grub is good' and even that the officers were attentive. Comm also acknowledged that he was 'Being treated well so far', while comedian William Brown's unfailing cheerfulness is perhaps intended as a morale boost for his wife and written previous to his forthcoming court-martial. By contrast both Lellows and Meacham faced 112 days hard labour, the latter in particular complaining of suffering confinement in a detention room with 90° temperature, while Hall, as we have seen, alluded to having received 'brutal treatment'.

Some of the grievances expressed by the anarchist detainees are in keeping with the Joint Committee for Conscientious Objectors' formal complaint regarding the treatment of conscientious objectors held in Bristol's Horfield Prison, which raised the following issues:

1. Solitary confinement of Conscientious Objectors in a narrow cell.
2. Bread and water dietary.
3. Forcible clothing in khaki.
4. The removal of a Bible found in the possession of any Objector, and the refusal to allow the use of Bibles to those who desired them.
5. Refusal to allow the Objectors to see or to communicate with friends.[157]

There is no conclusive evidence in the tiny sample of correspondents in the West Country as to whether socialist or anarchist conscientious objectors may have been treated any more or less harshly than others. What is certain, however, it that absolutist COs who refused alternative service and any cooperation, challenging the state most directly, were subjected to the most punitive regime as a consequence.

Stanley Oxley, a Bristolian conscientious objector who certainly seems to have been a socialist and may well have had sympathies with anarchism, faced particularly punitive treatment. Oxley was an outright resister, refusing from the outset either to respond to call-up papers or to voluntarily attend a tribunal to

---

155 Letter from William Brown to Mrs. W. Brown, Hazeley Camp, Winchester (c. 1916). Manuscript in ibid.

156 Letter from H. Chapman to Tom Keell, Newton Abbot (14 December 1916). Manuscript in ibid.

157 Joint Advisory Committee for Conscientious Objectors, *Conscientious Objectors at Horfield* (Bristol: Joint Advisory Committee for Conscientious Objectors, [c.1916-c.1917]) [Bristol Reference Library: History VI B32050], p. 1.

register as a CO. Three men forcibly took his own clothes from him in line with the third objection above. He was also cited as an instance of the fifth grievance on the list since his father complained that he had paid repeated visits to see his son, which on each occasion was refused with the promise that he could see him on the next visit until he was finally told that his son had been 'sent away'.[158] The father in question was almost certainly W. R. Oxley, the prominent Bristolian socialist, father of Edith Oxley and father-in-law to George Barrett.[159] Stanley Oxley's sentence of 21 months' hard labour was at the upper end of sentences meted out to Bristolian conscientious objectors cited by Mabel Tothill, Honorary Secretary of Bristol's Joint Advisory Committee for Conscientious Objectors.[160] The treatment of Stanley Oxley of Ashley Road, Bristol, was sufficiently conspicuous in its severity, being court-martialled at Horfield and then twice subsequently at Portsmouth, for the case to be raised in the House of Commons.[161] He appears to have been a particularly formidable and articulate opponent of conscription and the British state, concluding in a celebrated statement on the occasion of his court-martial at Chiseldon, Wiltshire on 26th April 1916:

> I can bring nothing to oppose your violence, in it you are entirely victorious. You can bring nothing to oppose my reason, in it I am entirely victorious. I stand opposed to you. I cannot hope to defeat the British Army. You cannot hope to defeat my reason.[162]

A handwritten agents' and subscribers' book for the anarchist paper *Freedom* from this period includes an entry for a Stanley Oxley, now living at Mead Way in Sea Mills, Bristol. It seems reasonable to speculate, though this is admittedly not conclusive proof, that this is one and the same person as the conscientious objector.[163]

Unlike Oxley, who defiantly awaited his call-up papers and confronted the conscription process head-on, other Bristolian war resisters went into hiding as a tactic to avoid military service. According to a report in the *Glasgow Herald*, two Bristolians were among six men captured in the Carsphairn Hills, in Kirkcudbrightshire. 29-year old William Dancy Wall from Bristol and 21-year old William Borthwick Livingstone of Southville, Bristol, both clerks, were in hiding with their comrades before being arrested for apparently attempting to avoid military service following a 'wild chase' across the hills. Initially suspected to be German spies, the reporter writes of the fugitives that,

> From the fact that all the men wore red ribbons in their coats, and that

---

158 Joint Advisory Committee for Conscientious Objectors, *Conscientious Objectors at Horfield*, p. 1.

159 There is a family photograph of W. R. Oxley, his (unnamed) wife, his daughter Edith Oxley and son Stanley Oxley in Bryher, *An Account of the Labour and Socialist Movement in Bristol*, II, p. 21. W. R. Oxley died shortly after the end of the war in 1920.

160 Tothill, *Toleration or Persecution*, p. 1.

161 Hansard HC Deb 2 August 1916, vol. 85, cols. 282-83.

162 Peace Pledge Union, *Refusing to Kill*, p. 30.

163 List of *Freedom* agents, August 1916 – [1920s]. Manuscript in *Freedom* Archive 407, International Institute of Social History, Amsterdam.

they sang 'The Red Flag,' it is conjectured that they are Socialists and were seeking to escape military service.[164]

For groups like Bristol's Joint Advisory Committee for Conscientious Objectors, it was often difficult to make the case for the better treatment of conscientious objectors when thousands were already losing their lives at Ypres and in the Somme.[165] In the context of a prevailing climate in which the capitalist press dubbed conscientious objectors 'shirkers', 'cranks' and 'pasty faces', it was not easy to elicit popular sympathy; on occasion they were even subject to violent attacks. Yet, as the No-Conscription Fellowship and other critics pointed out, for the state to force its citizens to wear khaki uniform, to suppress the reading of the Bible and other literature, then further to deliberately alienate them by preventing communication with other prisoners, friends and family, was to attack their identities and, as such, to undermine an ostensible purpose of the war to uphold the values of 'freeborn Englishmen' against autocratic Kaiserism.[166] In any case conscientious objectors were not so much isolated victims of the state, but rather positive agents who, through small personal decisions, were undertaking acts of individual refusal and solidarity that demonstrated the regenerative power of disobedience. Such intentional acts of mental courage on the part of COs reflected their desire to uphold human values in the face of the insanity of war. At a time of extreme global crisis, like other conscientious objectors, the tiny number of anarchist contrarians and refuseniks attempted to uphold their ethical principles by responding to the war machine with, at turns, cheerfulness and civility, stoicism and mockery, rage and humour. They attempted to fill the pacifist vacuum of the absence of violence by resisting militarism strategically with positive alternatives of workers' solidarity rooted in syndicalism and internationalism. They were engaged in a desperate struggle, hoping to keep the lamps on in Europe for social liberation. Steeped in the class conflict of everyday life their fight was in the streets, factories and countryside rather than the battlefield — they envisaged an alternative war on capitalism and its endemic militarism, hierarchy, poverty, jingoism, injustice, alienation and imperialism; a war that might *really* end all future wars.

Inter-War Years

I can say without fear of contradiction that the 1920s were not a highpoint for anarchism. Even *Freedom* ceased regular publication for most of the decade.

Nevertheless the flame of revolution was not completely extinguished and an alternative politics of resistance to capitalism was consolidated by this time even if it was smouldering beneath the surface rather than blazing on the streets.

---

164 'Mysterious Camp. Police Chase in Carspharain Hills'. Newspaper clipping from *Glasgow Herald* (18 April 1916). Manuscript in *Freedom* Archive 458, International Institute of Social History, Amsterdam.

165 Many conscientious objectors were violently abused and received harsh punitive treatment with the result that 73 died in WWI. See Peace Pledge Union, *Refusing to Kill*, chapter 4.

166 *The Tribunal* (6 July 1916), for example, the No-Conscription Fellowship paper published to support conscientious objectors, attacked the Army's 'domination over civil rights and religious freedom' (6 July 1916), p. 1. Manuscript in *Freedom* Archive 458, International Institute of Social History, Amsterdam.

Bristol's Horsefair once accommodated an outlet popularly known as the 'Bomb Shop'. Today it's the address of Marks and Spencers, a front for the sale of fair-trade coffee, coats, hats and knickers, rather than a front for subversive literature. It seems that Jack Flynn's bookshop was the haunt of various varieties of socialist, anarchist and communist, a place where unemployed workers could sneak a look at *The Daily Worker* for free and local politicos would pass the time in heated debates in the backroom. According to Sally Mullen the shop was associated with the production of 'Socialist bombs' in 1896, pithy socialist verses printed on single sheets for propaganda purposes. It seems to have stocked cigarettes, second-hand books, and a range of leftist literature from all socialist persuasions, including anarchist, and to have continued through to the 1930s.[167]

The famous Russian-American anarchist, Emma Goldman, stayed in Redland and lectured in Bristol in 1925.[168] Her autobiography, *Living My Life*, suggests that her visit to England at this time was unsuccessful and dismal. Her talks in Bristol in May 1925 included 'Labour under the Dictatorship in Russia' at the YMCA and on 'Heroic Women of the Russian Revolution' at the Folk House, Park Street.[169] Speaking to small audiences, she struggled to cover her expenses. Goldman wrote that the three weeks experience in Bristol was not a happy one: 'The fogs and wet remained faithful and wandered through my system at their own sweet will. I was laid up with chills and fever', leaving her glad to receive an invitation to join friends in the warmer climes of Nice.[170] However, she gave several more lectures on Russian drama in Bristol and Bath later in the autumn and spring.

One of the highlights of her time in England was to visit Edward Carpenter, then in his eighties, in order to meet 'the great libertarian' and get him to write an introduction to a new edition of her former lover Alexander Berkman's *Prison Letters*.[171]

Since the First World War she had also been a long-term friend and correspondent of John Cowper Powys, closely associated with Dorset. When Goldman was living in England again in 1936 both she and Powys referred to each other in terms of warm mutual respect. Powys told Goldman he believed all Americans of a certain generation 'remember your name from their childhood — one of the *great names of history* along with Kropotkin & Bakunin and Tolstoy — as a champion of human and individual liberty on moral spiritual & philosophical lines.[172] Powys continued to be deeply distrustful of the

---

167 Sally Mullen, 'The Bristol Socialist Society 1885-1914' in *Bristol's Other History*, ed. by Ian Bild (Bristol: Bristol Broadsides, 1983), p. 42; Angela Tuckett, *The People's Theatre in Bristol 1930-45*, Our History pamphlet 72 (London: History Group of the Communist Party, [1979]). In 1927 Douglas Hyde mistakenly went down to buy a bomb to explode in protest at the execution of anarchists Sacco and Vanzetti *I Believed: The Autobiography of a Former British Communist* (Melbourne: William Heinemann, 1951), p. 4.

168 Letters of Emma Goldman and James Colton, http://libcom.org/history/letters-emma-goldman-james-colton [accessed 20 April 2010].

169 According to 'Chronology of Emma Goldman' website: http://anarcho.tripod.com/emma3.html [accessed 12 July 2010].

170 Emma Goldman, *Living My Life* [1931] in 2 vols. (New York: Dover, 1970), II. p. 981.

171 Rowbotham, *Edward Carpenter*, p. 428.

172 John Cowper Powys to Emma Goldman, 9 February 1936, quoted by David Goodway in *The Powys Review* (1984-85) 15.IV.iii.

Communist Party and Stalinism throughout the Second World War, confiding to Louis Wilkinson his fears that 'the OGPU & Gestapo are so much the same' and writing in another letter that:

> If you really want individual liberty I tell ye it's the Anarchists who're the boys! And why did the Spanish Revolution fail? Because these Stalinites & their amiable No. 1-ites deliberately sabotaged the Spanish popular cause and the Barcelona Anarchists. Here on this point, honey, I *know* I am right. O why haven't I old Emma [Goldman] at my side to put you *wise* on Stalin & the Communist Party! I tell you, with Emma's help for 2 years I got every week, in English, the Anarchist Bulletin from Catalonia, & what was it full of? The treacherous, pig-headed, *wicked* deeds of the Communistic Party! Every week it showed how the Party – & think of submitting to "the *Party*" – hated the Anarchists & *preferred* that Franco would win. Good God! is *that* intellect, is that Liberty?[173]

Both Goldman and Powys had (much less directly) supported the Republican cause during the Spanish Revolution of that year. In February 1937 Goldman and Ethel Edith Mannin (1900-1985), the Irish novelist and anarchist, spoke on the Spanish conflict in Bristol as International Antifascist Solidarity representatives.[174]

Parting shots

So the West Country has its own chapter in the rarely told story of English anarchism. Bristol in particular, as the south's second largest city, reaped the benefits of technological advance but equally bore the scars of the Industrial Revolution's early years. The negative aspects quickly became clear to the Romantic movement, with its hostility to the ideology of industrial capitalism, objecting, for example, to the destruction of the natural environment and the consequences of rapid urbanisation, which for many people brought with it loss of economic autonomy, impoverishment and social dislocation. By the eighteenth century's close, debates about the class system, the slave trade, the role of religion and the position of women were already raging in the coffee houses and public meeting places of Bristol and beyond. The machine breakers and Swing rioters of Wiltshire and Dorset and the tumultuous Kingswood miners were as quick as their Luddite brothers and sisters in the North to realise that the new industrial and technological order was not for their benefit.[175]

With a more rapid communications infrastructure the West Country was a crossroads for ideas, in easy reach of the metropolis, Wales and the Midlands and the point of contact with Celtic Cornwall. It was on the itinerary of radicals who would include not only Bristol but often Bath and many of the smaller

---

173 *Letters of John Cowper Powys to Louis Wilkinson 1935-1956* (London: Macdonald, 1958), (4 February 1942), 104 and (15 June 1942), p. 111.

174 'Chronology of Emma Goldman' website: http://anarcho.tripod.com/emma3.html [accessed 12 July 2010].

175 See BRHG pamphlets, Roger Ball, *Tolpuddle And Swing - The Flea And The Elephant'* (Bristol: Bristol Radical History Group, 2010) and Steve Mills, *A Barbarous And Ungovernable People - A Short History Of The Miners Of The Kingswood Forest* (Bristol: Bristol Radical History Group, 2010).

market towns and even villages in their tour circuit, as they directly addressed mass assemblies of a discontented population. Large attributes the pioneering of the 'use of the mass platform as an agitational device to attack the establishment' to the West Country's own Henry 'Orator' Hunt.[176] The developing railway network made it easier for radicals such as Carpenter to alight upon the flower of socialist discontent and flit between the circles of the north and south, cross-fertilizing them with subversive ideas.

These factors fomented a tradition of radicalism that developed from the Chartist, socialist and suffrage movements of the Victorian and Edwardian periods. Varieties of an explicitly anarchist sensibility had already appeared by the late nineteenth and early twentieth century, at once inspired by the energies of such mobilizations, and reacting to their shortcomings. Numerically small, perhaps, and often isolated, these anarchistic voices, were nevertheless in their own way significant due to the passion of their resistance, pushing the imaginative limits of the possibilities for social transformation, always seeking to kindle a new world from the dead wood of the old. As we have seen, anarchistic sensibilities took a range of forms, such as philosophical musings on the character of a perfect human society, a belief that evolution not religion could be the ultimate path to the paradise of a self-managed and socially just heaven on earth, industrial unionist and syndicalist struggles for a general strike to destroy the class system, war resistance or early environmentalist yearnings to live in harmony with the natural world. Using extra-parliamentary strategies, anarchists contributed to the larger culture of socialism, aware of a rich tradition of dissent, taking direct action in the here-and-now and attempting to unite ends and means to prefigure the kind of society that they wished to create in the future.

The Victorian labour movement mostly took a parliamentary route that found its expression in the Labour Party. Today, however, many of the principles that the earlier socialists held dear are more likely to be found in the anarchist movement than in the parliamentary Labour Party — preferring co-operation and 'commonweal' or community ownership over capitalism and market forces, hostility to the royal family, supporting working people not the bosses in workplace struggles. The local Labour Party no longer marks royal jubilees with publications like the Bristol Socialist Society's *Jubilee Humbug*, written in honour of Queen Victoria's great day in 1897! Ruskin, Carpenter and Morris's passion to protect historic buildings and the natural environment are likely to chime with the anarchists, libertarian socialists and greens who in recent years have fought to protect Twyford Down, Solsbury Hill and Wells from road developments, Golden Hill and Stokes Croft from Tesco's and the Edwardian swimming pool in Gloucester Road, Bristol from closure and abandonment. Anarchists have consistently opposed patriotism, racism and militarism. They have upheld Kropotkin's principle of mutual aid and the old radical watchwords such as 'educate, agitate and organise' or 'liberty, equality and fraterntity'. While in the late nineteenth century different currents of socialism were able to work together in loose associations such as the Bristol Socialist Society and the

---

176 Large, *Radicalism in Bristol in the Nineteenth Century*, p. 3.

Clarion movement, by the early twentieth century wider schisms were evident. The Bristol communist, Angela Tuckett, found increasing disunity and divisions between the ILP, SDF and anarchists, especially in their responses to the Boer War. As antagonistic positions became entrenched they 'were all divided on aims and tactics and often confused the two'.[177] Consequently, the anarchist movement found itself at an extremely low ebb by the 1920s, only to rally with the resurgence of revolutionary politics during the 'Hungry Thirties' and the inspiration of the Spanish Revolution.

---

177 Tuckett, *People's Theatre in Bristol*, p. 3.

A view of Pill from the Avon Bank in 1913.

2

Pirates to Proletarians

The Experience of the Pilots and Watermen of Crockerne Pill in the Nineteenth Century

•

Mike Richardson

Introduction

Crockerne Pill (henceforth Pill) is a small village standing on the south side of the River Avon five miles from Bristol. Its location ensured that the livelihoods of its inhabitants depended directly or indirectly on the sea. And because it was near the river mouth, Pill held a strategic position, which enabled local seafarers to guide vessels through the treacherous shoals and currents of the river up to the Port of Bristol. From the fifteenth to the nineteenth century Bristol was a major trading city and the prosperity of the people of Pill thus depended on its links to the port.

During the sixteenth and seventeenth centuries the boundaries between legitimate trade and illegal dealings through smuggling or even piracy were semi-permeable. Moreover, the economic interrelationship between Pill and Bristol penetrated the illegitimate commercial transaction as well as those that were above board. During the sixteenth century Bristol city merchants were actually financing and organizing much of the smuggling. The anchorage at Hung Road, Pill became one of the key inlets off the Bristol Channel for loading goods for export, which were described as 'uncustomed' — not having paid custom duties.[1]

However differing standards prevailed and, while the wealthy men who provided the finance could take cover, the penalties for those apprehended actually doing the smuggling and piracy were brutal and severe. In July 1577, three of the four pirates caught pillaging the *Dungarven*, a small sailing ship anchored at Pill, were taken to the Port of Bristol and hung

> by their feet from the bridge opposite Prince Street, Bristol, at low tide,
> and if they did not first die of apoplexy they were doomed to watch their

---

1   E. T. Jones, 'Illicit Business: Accounting for Smuggling in Mid-Sixteenth-Century Bristol', The *Economic History Review*, New Series, Vol. 54, No. 1 (Feb., 2001), pp. 17-38; C. Hill, *Reformation to Industrial Revolution: A Social and Economic History of Britain 1530-1780* (London: Weidenfeld & Nicolson, 1967), p. 59.

death slowly approaching with the rising water.[2]

A story like this presents a grim image, which catches the accretion of antipathy that continued to affect relations between Pill and Bristol well into the nineteenth century. So, while the fortunes of Pill were locked into the maritime commerce of the Port of Bristol, the relationship, from the perspective of the people of Pill, appeared to be as unequal, loaded and frequently unjust.

In 1611, Bristol Corporation gave the Society of Merchant Venturers (henceforth the Society), which was made up of a combination of influential traders, the right to collect wharfage fees, charges for the use and upkeep of the wharves in the city's port. As an integral part of this economically beneficial arrangement, the Corporation charged the managing and regulation of licensed pilots to the Society.[3] Hence, it was in the Society's interest to see that the system of pilotage ran smoothly and effectively, and patronage was employed to ensure good working relations with the pilots. The Society would confer rights of pilotage to Pill men who then had a monopoly over guiding vessels coming in and out of Bristol docks. On the recommendation of the Society, they even received superannuation if they were regarded as too old to work.[4]

At the beginning of the nineteenth century trade in other English ports, particularly Liverpool, quickened and Bristol lost its position as the second most important trading port in England, triggering a debate on how it could reverse its fortunes. New commercial interests wedded to unrestrained market values challenged both the older regulatory ethos of the Society and the 'privileged' position of the Pill pilots over traffic in the Bristol Channel.

In 1823 the proprietor of *Felix Farley's Bristol Journal*, John Mathew Gutch, writing under the pseudonym of 'Cosmo', expressed in the strongest possible terms both his hatred of Pill river pilots and his opposition to the use of compulsory pilotage in the perilous waters of the Bristol Channel, between Barnstaple and Gloucester:

> "[As] Trustees for Charitable uses, your Society [of Merchant Venturers] has fulfilled its functions most honourably", but "I ask again, where is the monument, the inscription, or record of your fame? Is it in the nest of Pirates, I had almost called them, instead of Pilots, which navigates our rivers? Where is the reformation to be seen, which you have effected in the behaviour of this lawless, profligate race of our fellow subjects? Have you evinced any public spirit in proposing, or have you yet even designed

---

2   Anon. 'Notes on the History of the Pilotage Service', Bristol Central Library, p. 1. C. Wells, *A Short History of the Port of Bristol* (Bristol: J. W. Arrowsmith, 1909), p. 394; *See* also John Latimer, *Sixteenth Century Bristol* (Bristol: J. W. Arrowsmith, 1908), p. 63.

3   H. Bush (1828), *Bristol Town Duties - A collection of original and interesting documents*, British History online, Chapter 4, *Wharfage, Cranage and Pilotage*, p. 18, http://www.british-history.ac.uk/report.aspx?compid=108166, accessed 20 July 2012; J. Rich, *The Bristol Pilots: A Treatise on the Bristol Pilots, from Their Origination, to Their Amalgamation: Including a List of Pilots" Names, Dates and Some of the Boats, for Almost 500 Years*, (Pill, England: Atlantis 33, 1996), pp. 100-101; P. McGrath, *The Merchant Venturers of Bristol: a History of the Society of Merchant Venturers of the City of Bristol from its Origin to the Present Day* (Greensboro, NC, USA: American Society of Civil Engineers, 1975), p. 313.

4   W. Minchinton, 'The Port of Bristol in the Eighteenth Century' in P. McGrath (ed.), *Bristol in the Eighteenth Century* (Newton Abbot, England: David and Charles, 1972), p. 135.

to think of establishing steam vessels for towing our ships up and down the Avon and the Channel, instead of perpetuating the original sin of licensing more Pill Pilots? Look at the Clyde and the Mersey! Are the Merchants of Glasgow and Liverpool left at the mercy of such a set of extortioners…?"[5]

His letter, which appeared in *Felix Farley's Bristol Journal*, reflected the hostility among some masters, ship owners and traders to compulsory pilotage, and associated work. Anger over this matter was directed at the Bristol Corporation and the Society.

Before the Bristol Corporation had first authorized the Society to manage and appoint pilots in the early seventeenth century, pilotage was only chargeable between the Port of Bristol and the mouth of the River Avon at King Road. The Society, however, was concerned by the high incident of accidents to ships as they passed through the Bristol Channel to King Road, attributing these largely to unskilled pilotage. Hence, in 1752, the Society agreed to give a gratuity to Bristol pilots to encourage them to invest in larger boats capable of meeting inward bound ships as far westward as Lundy Island, approximately 90 miles from Pill. By this strategy the Society aimed at reducing the number of ships foundering in the Bristol Channel, with the attendant loss of cargo and sometimes lives. The gratuity gave pilots the opportunity to receive a payment — the tariff was set by the Society — for guiding ships through the Channel, which was to be paid over and above the established fees for navigating vessels to and from the city's port to King Road. There was one caveat, however; pilots could not force their services on incoming vessels. They had to have consent from the person commanding such vessels.[6]

It was this stipulation that proved at times to be contentious. For hundreds of years, Pill pilots had been using their knowledge and skills to navigate the tricky waters of the Bristol Channel. However, some ship captains, sailing to and from the Port of Bristol, had been reluctant to pay for experienced pilots and either employed unauthorized, lesser-experienced ones, or on occasions piloted their own ships. Increasingly, Bristol pilots, having invested in larger boats to extend

---

5   *Cosmo's Letters Part 2*, Bristol, 1823, published by J. M. Gutch, Bristol Central Library; Also cited in McGrath, *The Merchant Venturers of Bristol*, p. 316.

6   Bush (1828), *Bristol Town Duties*, Chapter 4, p. 19; Undated petition, cited in Rich, *The Bristol Pilots*, pp. 58-62; McGrath, *The Merchant Venturers of Bristol*, p. 313.

their area of operation, felt it was their right to insist on piloting any ship in the Channel that was bound for the Port of Bristol. This situation became serious enough by the mid-eighteenth century for pilots to petition the Society to intervene and put a stop to the use of unskilled and unlicensed pilots:

> To the Worshipful the Master, Wardens[,] Assistants and Commonalty of the Society of Merchants Adventurers within the City of Bristol.
>
> The humble Petition of the Pilots of Crockham [sic] Pill in the County of Somerset
>
> Sheweth — That your Petitioners have laboured under the greatest disadvantage in our calling or business thro' a sett [sic] of people who call themselves Deputy's [sic], who takes the liberty of boarding merchants vessels to take no pilot but themselves, and upon our boarding such vessels they threaten to throw us overboard, and by that means hinder us of our proper rights...
>
> That your Petitioners humbly prays your Worships will not permit or suffer any person that is not qualified by a Branch to pilot or conduct any vessel coast-ways or foreign bound to the Port of Bristol or going therefrom.[7]

The Bristol Channel Pilotage Act of 1807 addressed this issue. By Royal Assent, compulsory pilotage was formalized and Bristol was given the sole right of pilotage upon the whole of the Bristol Channel, effectively limiting pilotage to Bristol men. Bristol's control extended to Lundy Island, 90 miles west of Bristol, which was much resented by other Channel ports.

Following the passing of the 1807 Act, the Bristol Corporation allocated the total responsibility of command over inspection, regulation and appointment of pilots to the Society of Merchant Venturers.[8] Thus this institution held control over shipping traffic heading to or returning from the Port of Bristol. The 1807 Act also served to strengthen the monopoly over pilotage held by the seafarers of Pill, where most of Bristol's licensed pilots lived. Ship captains had little choice over the pilots they engaged. They felt that they were open to having to pay extortionate rates, despite price regulation administered by the Society.

Pill's licensed pilots benefited from this outcome and, along with the growth in trade, it led to a significant expansion in the volume of their work. The number of registered pilots' cutters (known as skiffs, between 40 to 50 feet in length) increased from 12 in 1795 to 45 in 1863. Over the same period, crew numbers rose from 25 to 74.[9] However, pilots were to become increasingly dependent on the Bristol authorities for the protection of their livelihoods.

---

7   Undated petition, probably 1756, cited in Rich, *The Bristol Pilots*, pp. 58-59.

8   Bush (1828), *Bristol Town Duties*, p. 18; McGrath, *The Merchant Venturers of Bristol*, p. 313. Also see *Bye-Laws, Rules & Orders, for the Conduct, Management & Government of all Pilots and others within the Port of Bristol* (Bristol: Bryan, 1809), Bristol Central Library.

9   G. Farr, 'Bristol Channel pilotage: historical notes on its administration and craft', *Mariner's Mirror*, XXXIX (1953), pp. 28-44; Rich, *The Bristol Pilots*; P. J. Stuckey, *The Sailing Boats of the Bristol Channel* (Newton Abbot, England: David and Charles, 1977).

Economic integration was thus being overlaid by the social and political links.

The potential to break the pilots' monopoly beckoned when steam-powered tugs became available in the 1820s. The navigation of ships no longer had to be dependent on wind and tides, calling into question the importance of pilotage.[10] Moreover, the hobblers, men (and, on occasions, women) who hauled the ships from Pill to the city docks, realized that the employment of steam tugs would most likely put a significant number of them out of work. Bristol's resistance to their introduction, however, served to heighten the ship owners' anger and frustration. While Pill pilots viewed the advent of steam as a threat to their livelihoods, ship owners were keen to exploit its potential. They saw the existence of compulsory pilotage as the barrier to achieving that end and their vexation was directed at Pill pilots.

Enmity towards, and fear of, the watermen of Pill was not new. The economic fortunes of Pill in the eighteenth and nineteenth centuries depended to a large extent on earnings from work associated with seafaring. The people of Pill resented any outside interference to the way in which they worked and lived, showing hostility to anyone that threatened their way of life. Outsiders entering Pill often did so with some trepidation. In the 1740s, Charlotte Charke, an actress and noted transvestite, briefly ran a small pastry cook's shop in Pill. In her autobiography, she described the place as 'not unpleasant, if it were inhabited by any other kind of people than the savages who infest it, and are only, in outward form, distinguishable from beasts of prey.'[11] She was not alone in holding this view. In 1755, the founder of Methodism, John Wesley, recorded in his journal: 'I rode over to Pill, a place famous from generation to generation ... for stupid, brutal, abandoned wickedness.'[12]

The establishment in 1757 of the first Methodist church in Pill was a move to redeem the 'abandoned' ones. Even press-gangs displayed caution in roaming over Pill, as the villagers were 'a trifle too rough' and not afraid to use 'fist and club'.[13] However, regardless of strong resistance, press gangs, during the Napoleonic Wars, did successfully seize local recruits for military service, resulting in a depleted number of men available for pilotage work. On 14 May 1803, an incident occurred, as a result of this shortage, which illustrated the strength of feeling of the Pill community when it came to protecting their work and way of life. A vessel, aptly named the *Sturdy Beggar*, sought to negotiate its way along the River Avon to the city docks 'without tow-boats (presumably through lack of hands)'. In response 'a mob at Pill assailed with a shower of stones the people on the deck wounding many. Men in three boats boarded the vessel and prevented her from proceeding to Bristol.'[14]

10   H. Hignett, 'Pilotage History', *The Pilot: The Official Journal of the United Kingdom Maritime Pilots' Association* (*UKMPA*), No. 278, July 2004, p. 2.

11   C. Charke, *A Narrative of the Life of Mrs Charlotte Charke, written by herself* (London: Whittaker, Treacher and Arnot, 1755), p. 136.

12   *John Wesley's Journal*, 3 October 1755.

13   J. R. Hutchinson, *The Press-Gang Afloat and Ashore*, (Montana, USA: Kessinger Publishing, 2004, first published in New York: Dutton & Co, 1914), p. 70.

14   E. Thomas, *Shirehampton Story*, (Avonmouth, Bristol: Ethel Thomas, 1983), p. 86. Thomas named the vessel involved in

Pill pilots competed fiercely but fairly among themselves to secure the right to direct a ship through the hazardous waters of the Bristol Channel. Their experience was essential to providing the safe passage of incoming (and outgoing) vessels through the channel with its large tidal range of 46 feet, strong currents, and shifting sand banks. Crewed by a pilot, a boatman (known as a westernman or westwardman) and an apprentice (boy), sailing cutters, built for speed, sought inward bound vessels. Each cutter (skiff) was marked with a number allocated by the Haven Master. The first cutter to hail a ship secured the right of pilotage and could guide the vessel to stretches of the river where ships could anchor, at King Road, at the mouth of the Avon, or a little further up river at Hung Road, Pill. Large ships would then sometimes elect to transfer their cargoes to lighters, flat-bottomed small barges, used to transport goods to their final destination, otherwise they would be pulled, like the smaller ships, either by rowing boats, or hauled by horses and men on the towpath up the winding river, to the city docks.[15] The five-mile haul was difficult and arduous but this individualistic struggle for existence was tempered by informal relationships of community-based mutual support. When faced with a large-scale threat, both fostered new forms of collective action to sustain the traditional way of life of the Pill pilots.

Emerging Class Struggle

Harsh laws forbade workers' combinations and strikes in the first quarter of the nineteenth century; the Combination Acts of 1799 and 1800 were an attempt to curtail the growth of trade unionism. In 1812, the hobblers of Pill struck work. Seemingly, this was either brave or foolhardy, as this was a time when machine breaking (Luddism) was at its peak in Yorkshire, Lancashire, Leicestershire and Derbyshire, and a law had been passed that allowed the courts to sentence to death anyone convicted of such action. Although the State was prepared to come down heavily on anything it regarded as rebellious, seemingly strikes did not fall into this category as punishment for workers who withdrew their labour was comparatively light — up to three months imprisonment or two months hard labour — although still dreadful for those affected.[16]

The boundary between legal and illegal resistance was permeable; as Eric Hobsbawm has described, resentment and resistance often resulted in 'collective action by riot' in this period.[17] To bring about the maximum disruption to the Port of Bristol, during the 1812 strike, hobblers hauled pilots' boats ashore, which the Society of Merchant Venturers deemed as 'violent and illegal proceedings'. Although no criminal proceedings were brought against the men

the incident as the *Study Beggar* but it was in fact the *Sturdy Beggar*, see the original source F. J. Nicholls and J. Taylor, *Bristol Past and Present* (Bristol: Arrowsmith, 1882).

15 Rich, *The Bristol Pilots*; P. J. Stuckey, *The Sailing Boats of the Bristol Channel*; A. Collins, 'River and Harbour Pilotage in the UK', www.mariners-1.co.uk/UKPilots.html, accessed 8 August 2012.

16 K. Laybourn, *A History of British Trade Unionism c.1770–1990*, (Stroud, England: Alan Sutton, 1992), p. 17.

17 E. J. Hobsbawm, *Labouring Men: Studies in the History of Labour*, (London: Weidenfeld and Nicolson, 1968), p. 7.

concerned, the Society refused to consider the hobbler's call for higher wages.[18] Pilots were responsible for paying their crews and for towing arrangements in the river, which placed them at the centre of this dispute, yet the Society refused to intervene.[19] The dispute simmered on into 1813 when it became clear that the Society had to do something if only to find ways to protect pilots from illegal obstruction. It met with the Corporation and came up with a solution that involved the establishment of regulations in respect to relations between pilots and watermen.[20] Rather than enforce a settlement, the Society and the Corporation chose to assuage the parties concerned, possibly because of the fall in income revenues from wharfage duties as a result of the impasse.

Pilot boats in Pill harbour (date unknown).

This non-confrontational stance was adopted in relation to disciplinary hearings concerning Bristol pilots. For instance, in July 1816 the pilot John Browne was brought before the Society's Parliament to answer the charge of abusive language made against a ship's lieutenant. It was recommended that he should receive a month's suspension but he apologized and escaped with a warning.[21] It was this attitude that seemed to rile John Gutch, the proprietor of *Felix Farley's Bristol Journal*. He felt that the pilots were a law unto themselves. In support of this claim he described an incident that occurred in 1822. A captain of a steam packet observing a vessel at Pill

> likely to lose the tide, took it in tow; for which act of kindness and consideration, he received a letter from *his own brother*, a Pill Pilot, that if he ever did such as act again, his life would be in danger.[22]

18   McGrath, *The Merchant Venturers of Bristol*, p. 319.

19   G. Farr, 'Bristol Channel pilotage', p. 42.

20   McGrath, *The Merchant Venturers of Bristol*, p. 319.

21   The Society of Merchant Venturers' Hall Book, 11 and 15 July 1816, Microfilm, Bristol Central Library.

22   *Cosmo's Letters Part 2*, Bristol, 1823, published by J. M. Gutch.

Divisions between the Representatives of Capital

John Gutch initiated the formation of the Bristol Chamber of Commerce (BCC) in January 1823 to combat the Corporation's resistance to the call for a reduction in wharfage duties, and the removal of other impediments to trade and commerce, including compulsory pilotage.[23] In respect to pilotage and associated work, a Board of Directors Report to a special meeting of the Chamber, held on 2 January 1824, called into question the expedient social relationships that existed between the Corporation, the Society of Merchant Venturers, and Pill pilots and watermen by attempting to disturb or to bring about a qualitative change in these relationships. It denounced what it perceived as the excessive use of labour in bringing vessels to and from the city docks, concluding that the employment of steam tugs would do much to resolve this issue:

> [T]he great expence [*sic*] incurred in bringing a vessel to and from Kingroad and the Floating Harbour of Bristol, we believe is not equalled at any other port in the kingdom. Sufficient horses are frequently employed from the Mouth of the River to the Dock gates, to render it quite unnecessary that so many as 30, 40, and frequently 50 men and boys of the most indolent character, with four or five boats, should be added to the expence [*sic*]; the greater part of them in many cases rendering the ship no service whatever, indeed many of them being very old men and boys, they are incapable of doing the duty of able men, if required. We trust, however, now that steam-boats are introduced into this Port, that, following the example of Liverpool, Newcastle, &c. they will be employed in towing ships up and down this River, whereby the heavy charge for horses, men and boats, will be much diminished.[24]

Pilot boats leaving Pill harbour in about 1900.

For its part, the Corporation took exception to the manner in which the Chamber, a cross-party body of merchants and manufacturers, attempted to

---

23 *Cosmo's Letters Part 1 and 2*, Bristol, 1823, published by J. M. Gutch; Bristol Chamber of Commerce Minutes, 1 January 1823, BRO.

24 Bristol Chamber of Commerce, 'Report of the Board of Directors', 2 January 1924.

intervene. What mattered most to the Corporation was the preservation of its rights; it did not take kindly to anyone who challenged its authority. Moreover it feared that the introduction of steam tugs would reduce the number of pilots and watermen required, and put a strain on existing social relationships between the Corporation, the Society of Merchant Venturers and Pill seafarers. The Corporation did not want the responsibility of paying outdoor relief[25] to those thrown out of work, which would fall on the local parish; in the case of the Pill men this would have been the parish of Easton-in-Gordano.[26] The fostering of trade was a secondary concern to the Corporation, an attitude which many local merchants and manufacturers deplored.[27]

The implications of the pressure applied by the Chamber of Commerce on the Corporation to employ steam tugs and open up pilotage to competition were not lost on Pill pilots and watermen. Recognizing that they shared a common plight with all pilots, they initially responded to this attack on their rights, livelihood, customs and culture, rooted in a pre-industrial Britain, by calling on the organizational and financial support of the Friendly Society of Licensed Pilots. This organization submitted to the Society of Merchant Venturers a 'printed copy of certain articles'. The content of these articles is unknown but the Society found them 'in some respects objectionable' and forwarded them for the Corporation to scrutinize.[28] This Pilots' organization is not mentioned again, however the episodic formation of collective organizations was not unusual during this period.

The Pill Friendly Society, established in December 1822, provided an alternative local source of financial and moral support. Like other friendly societies during this period it was conservative in nature and, while it had the potential to generate trust and solidarity, its objective was to encourage self-help and individualism.[29] The lack of information on this organization, however, prevents any meaningful assessment. In all probability it had outlived its usefulness by 1875 when it was dissolved.[30]

Friction in the interactional relations between the local parties reflected the struggle for supremacy taking place between the old and new forms of capitalist control mechanisms throughout the country. In 1824, after years of campaigning, radical MPs managed to push the repeal of the Combination Acts through Parliament. One of the arguments that persuaded Parliament was that the Acts of 1799 and 1800 had done more to sustain rather than suppress trade unionism and collective solidarity. By lifting the ban some radical reformers believed and hoped that trade unionism would more likely founder than flourish.

---

25   A system of funds or food given to the impotent poor — the sick, elderly, those unable to work — who were to be helped via outdoor relief without demanding they stay in a workhouse, which was 'Indoor Relief'.

26   'Impediments to the Trade of Bristol', *BM*, 20 April 1822. When Christ Church was built in 1861, Pill became a separate ecclesiastical Parish detached from the civil Parish of Easton-in-Gordano.

27   G. Bush, *Bristol and its Municipal Government 1820-1851*, (Bristol: Bristol Record Society, 1976), p. 46.

28   Merchant Hall Books, No. 15, 6 February 1824, p. 360, cited in J. Rich, *The Bristol Pilots*.

29   See M. Gorsky, 'Mutual aid and civil society: friendly societies in nineteenth-century Bristol' in *Urban History*, 25,3 (1998): 303-304.

30   *A list of Friendly Societies or other Institutions*, Returns to an address of the Honorable House of Commons, 25 May 1824, p. 16; *London Gazette*, 23 April 1875.

They were to be disappointed. Despite the fact that that the 1825 Combination Act severely limited workers' rights, such as the ability to strike, the changed legal and political environment led to an increase in collective action.[31] *Felix Farley's Bristol Journal* blamed the development of the 'spirit of combination' on Owenism and its 'doctrine now so industriously propagated that the profit of the capitalist is the idle man's share of the industrious man's earnings.'[32] Owenites believed that trade unions could be used as vehicle for bringing about a 'New Moral World' based on cooperative production.

In 1825, Pill pilots and watermen may or may not have been aware of Owenism, but they reacted swiftly against wage cuts that were imposed after pressure was brought to bear concerning pilotage rates on the Bristol Corporation by the Bristol Chamber of Commerce, the organization that Gutch helped to establish. In December 1824, the Corporation repealed a bye-law, passed in 1813, that

> ordained, constituted, and provided, that every Man employed on board, or for hauling or towing any Ship or Vessel, and mooring or unmooring, from Bathurst Basin, or Cumberland Basin [Basins adjoining the City of Bristol's main harbour] to Kingroad and Portishead [mouth of the river Avon where it meets the Severn Estuary], or either of them, and from other places to Cumberland Road or Bathurst Basin, shall receive and be entitled unto Three shillings and Nine-pence per Man and no more.[33]

This by-law was immediately reintroduced with just one amendment and made public in the first week of February 1825. The entitlement for pilotage and associated work was reduced to 'Three Shillings per Man and no more.'[34]

On hearing the news, Pill watermen protested by stopping three inward-bound vessels and forcibly removing their pilots. The Society of Merchant Venturers intervened to calm the situation.[35] Whilst the men were reprimanded for their actions, they convinced the Society that the reduction in their wages was unjust. On the recommendation of the Society, the Corporation repealed the bye-law it had passed only a couple of weeks before, the effect of which was to restore the watermen's wages back to their previous level of three shillings and nine-pence.[36] This incident, however, led commentators to predict that such disruptive action would 'induce our merchants to turn their attention to the establishment of Steam-Boats, for towing vessels in the river.'[37]

Resistance to the Use of Steam Tugs

However, in the late 1820s and early 1830s, the political and economic and

---

31   Laybourn, *A History of British Trade Unionism c.1770-1990*, pp. 20-22.

32   *Felix Farley's Bristol Journal*, 29 October, 1825, cited in I. J. Prothero, *Artisans and Politics in Early Nineteenth-Century London: John Gast and His Times* (Folkestone: Dawson, 1978), p. 161.

33   Cited in *BM*, 7 February 1825.

34   Ibid.

35   *BM*, 14 February 1825.

36   McGrath, *The Merchant Venturers of Bristol*, p. 320.

37   *BM*, 14 February 1825.

social situation was still not a favourable environment for operators to risk investing in steam tugs. Harvest failure and the increase in unemployment in 1829-30 triggered rebellions from below in the form of the Swing Riots; and the initial failure of the House of Lords to support the second Parliamentary Reform Bill resulted in major disturbances in several cities, the largest and most violent of which occurred at Bristol, in September 1831. The rioters' 'targets were the wealthy members of the Corporation who undemocratically ruled the city, the religious hierarchy and the prisons' regarded as unjust and repressive.[38] Such was the mood of the poor and disenfranchised in Bristol.

In this atmosphere, it is little wonder that the Corporation, which continued to hold on to its monopoly over pilotage, characterized by one opponent in August 1833 as 'plunder',[39] showed little interest in promoting the use of steam tugs. However, matters came to a head over this issue in 1836. On 8 February, between 25 and 30 Pill men attacked the crew of the steam tug *Fury* when it was anchored at Portishead, touting for the business of towing vessels to and from King Road and the Port of Bristol. *The Times* characterized this attack as a 'RIOT' and the *Bristol Mercury* called it a 'DISGRACEFUL OUTRAGE AND PIRACY'.[40] Brought in from Newcastle, the *Fury* was the first steam tug in Bristol to be commissioned with the specific purpose of driving down the cost of pilotage and associated work. It posed a more serious threat to Pill watermen than the occasional use of steam packets had presented.

The *Fury* was part-owned by Mark Whitwill (senior) of the ship broking company Whitwill and King, whose premises in Queens Square had been ransacked in the 1831 Bristol Riots. He was on board at the time of the attack with another part-owner of the boat, William Leedham. Armed with pistols, the assailants fired shots; one of them narrowly missed the master of the ship but it was alleged that Whitwill was the intended target. After a struggle, the crew consisting of the master, the engineer and five sailors, together with Leedham and Whitwell, were forced into a rowing boat and set adrift. The assailants then attempted to scuttle the *Fury*, but in their hurry to get away succeeded only in casting it adrift. The tug was recovered the next day with the paddles torn off and the engine damaged.[41]

Some of the attackers, knowing that they could be identified, fled to Ireland. Leedham had recognized one of them who, with another man, had on the previous evening threatened him saying that 'he hoped to have my heart for supper and to see my head upon a pole parading about Pill.'[42] Despite the fact a

---

38   R. Wilson and C. Heatherton, 'Lore Turned Upside Down', *Mute Magazine*, 8 February 2007 (Metamute.org accessed 27 August 2012). See also Terry Jenkins, *Bristol Borough: The History of Parliament: the House of Commons 1820-1832*, ed. D.R. Fisher, Cambridge University Press, 2009,
http://www.historyofparliamentonline.org/volume/1820-1832/constituencies/bristol [accessed 27 August 2012].

39   A. Burgess, 'Letters on the Trade of Bristol: The causes of its decline and means of its revival', published in *BM*, 10 August 1833.

40   *The Times*, 12 February 1836; *BM*, 13 February 1836.

41   Merchant Hall Books, 10 February 1836; *BM*, 13 February 1836; *The Times*, 12 February, 1836; W. G. Neale, *At the Port of Bristol, Vol. 1: Members and Problems 1848-1899*, (Bristol: Port of Bristol Authority, 1968), pp. 192-3.

42   *BM*, 13 February 1836. It is likely that newspaper misspelt the name Rumley. The 1841 census recorded that there was a family living in Pill of a similar name, Rumney.

reward of fifty guineas was offered by the Society of Merchant Venturers for the apprehension of the assailants, only four — John Rumley, Charles Rumley, William Sully and William Buck — were identified.[43] Remarkably, it seems that 'the rioters went unpunished'.[44] Nevertheless, this attempt to halt the introduction of steam tugs into Bristol failed. Within a month Leedham was advertising his steam tug service in the local press.[45]

The *Mayflower* steam tug was built in 1861. It is now moored in Bristol harbour by the M Shed.
It is seen here on the Sharpness Canal at Frampton-on-Severn.

The replacement of sail and human power was not straightforward. Steam navigation was still in its infancy and required to be cradled. Demand for the old traditional method of pilotage therefore continued, as did the Corporation's control over pilotage which, despite 'agreeing to appoint two more Bristol Pilots to reside at or near Newport',[46] was reaffirmed in an Act of 1836. Even when steamboats were used, sometimes masters of these vessels had to call on watermen for assistance. For instance, on the evening of 5 March 1836, the ship *Elizabeth,* from Mauritius, was taken in tow at King Road by a steam packet. On heading towards Bristol, gale force winds sprang up and a second steamboat was employed. The gale increased in intensity and 'twelve horses were attached, with which they got her [*Elizabeth*] so far as the Hotwells, when about a hundred men laid hold of ropes from the ship' and returned her to King Road to await more clement weather.[47]

Increasingly, though, steamboats were called upon to tow vessels to and from the mouth of the Avon to the Port of Bristol. By 1840, George Lunell and Company, Hotwells, Bristol, had built and brought into operation eight steam

---

43 *BM,* 20 February 1836.

44 W. G. Neale, *At the Port of Bristol, Vol. 1: Members and Problems 1848-1899,* p. 193.

45 *BM,* 19 March 1836.

46 McGrath, *The Merchant Venturers of Bristol,* p. 317.

47 *BM,* 12 March 1836.

tugs.[48] Even in normal weather conditions trouble could arise, for steam engines were susceptible to explosions. For instance, in 1840 the *Tiger* steam tug burst her boiler as she was attempting to refloat a ship that had run aground in the River Avon: 'The explosion was tremendous and created great consternation amongst the bystanders, who were numerous, and also alarmed the residents of Clifton.'[49]

A steam tug towing a steamer under Clifton Suspension Bridge in around 1890.

The first steam tug to appear, the *Fury*, met a dramatic end. In 1859, minutes after arriving at the mouth of the Avon by King Road, the boiler exploded, hurling her funnel into the air. The damaged incurred caused her to sink almost immediately. The engineer James Jones and the fireman John Case, both residents of Pill, were working below deck and were probably killed by the force of the explosion. In any event they went down with the tug and their bodies were never recovered; another crew member, John Smith, died of his injuries a few days later.[50] Pill families had always faced the prospect, and sometimes the reality, of losing their loved ones in the course of seafaring work, and the introduction of steam tugs did little to alleviate this stark fact.

By the mid-1840s, the need for hobblers to tow or haul boats to and from Pill to Bristol had reduced significantly. However, a few new jobs became available and Pill men were employed, like Jones, Case and Smith on the *Fury*, as engineers and fireman aboard steam tugs. Pilots too were still in demand, although they had to learn new skills in order to familiarize themselves with the navigation systems of steam tugs. The new steam tugs were not always an improvement in terms of design. In November 1851, the newly built *Demerara* was grounded under the watchful eyes of thousands of spectators. In part this

---

48 *BM*, 20 June 1840.
49 *BM*, 14 August 1841.
50 *BM*, 24 September 1859.

mishap was blamed on the pilot who rejected the suggestion of the ship's captain that 'he had better slacken the speed' as the vessel approached a sharp double bend in the river about half-a-mile from the dock-gates. However, the cause of the accident was also attributed to the fact that the design of the tug was not 'one adapted especially to the navigation of the Avon', the length of the vessel being nearly twice that of other tugs operating on the river.[51]

Not only did the introduction of steam tugs present new challenges to Pill men, during the 1850s their increased use, along with the growth of trade in Bristol Channel ports, encouraged the Bristol Chamber of Commerce to continue its pressure on the Corporation to relinquish their monopoly position over pilotage. The combination of economic and political forces was to prove the greatest threat to Pill pilots.

LAUNCH OF THE "DEMERARA" ROYAL MAIL STEAM-SHIP, AT BRISTOL

The *Demerara*'s launch in Bristol on 27 September 1851.

The 1861 Bristol Channel Pilotage Act

In July 1861, continued lobbying by the town councils of the ports of Gloucester, Cardiff and Newport eventually succeeded in the passing of the Bristol Channel Pilotage Act, despite opposition from the Bristol Corporation. This enabled each of these ports to have the right to appoint their own pilotage Boards. As a result,

> Pilotage Commissioners were constituted for these Ports with powers to licence [*sic*] Pilots for non-compulsory Pilotage of ships in the Bristol Channel and River Severn bound for these Ports, each Port having a defined area of jurisdiction.[52]

Bristol pilots' rights were preserved. Moreover, they were given the opportunity 'to be examined with reference to other [Bristol Channel] ports, and if they passed, to leave the right to them, and have priority over any one else with the

---

51 *BM*, 15 November 1851.

52 W. A. Stone, *A History of Gloucester Harbour Trustees: Part 1 1890-1966*, p. 3.
    http://www.gloucesterharbourtrustees.org.uk [accessed 14 September 2012].

The *Demerara* ran aground at Horseshoe Bend on 10 November 1851.

respect to pilotage of these places.'[53]

As the Pilotage Bill was passing through Parliament, the Bristol Corporation removed control over pilotage from the Society of Merchant Venturers, which had held it for 249 years, and handed it over to the Docks Committee.[54] Two years later, in 1863, this Committee would express concern about the decline in the income of pilots since the passing of the Act. Earnings had fallen to a little more than half what they had been before, resulting in destitution for many of the men and their families. Competition among pilots had also increased. One recommendation coming from the Committee was that pilots should be discouraged from introducing their children to the profession.[55]

Life was changing in Pill. In 1861, Christ Church was built and Pill became a separate ecclesiastical Parish detached from the civil Parish of Easton-in-Gordano.[56] It was not long before the railway came to the village; Pill station opening in 1867. Many houses were demolished to make way for the line, which was built on a brick viaduct (seven piers and six arches) nearly 100 yards long with foundations in one place laid to a depth of thirty feet.[57] The process of construction aroused some opposition, but nonetheless provided a lift to the local economy. Moreover, the arrival of the navvies introduced a notoriously rowdy group of newcomers, some of whom set up home with local women, possibly helping to reverse the decline in population. The only data available relates to the wider Easton-in-Gordano area and shows that, after a decrease during 1841 to 1861, the population increased by nearly 11% between 1861 and 1871, rising at the even greater rate of 19% between 1871 and 1881.[58]

---

53   *BM*, 27 July 1861.

54   McGrath, *The Merchant Venturers of Bristol*, pp. 317-18.

55   *BM*, 3 October 1863.

56   http://www.pillchurches.org.uk accessed 15 September 2012; West of England Baptist Association,
       http://www.webassoc.org.uk/ChurchDetail.aspx?id=77 (accessed 15 September 2012).

57   *BM*, 15 April 1865.

58   J. Rich, 'The Parish of Easton-in-Gordano', http://www.easton-in-gordano.org.uk/Pages/History.html (accessed 14

By the 1870s it is possible to detect the emergence of a cultural demarcation in the village. Some pilot families sought respectability by elevating their social standing through the church. An illustration of this development can be found in the history of Pill Methodist Church. In 1872, seat rent securing a family pew within the church at one shilling a quarter was paid by several pilot families including Mrs R. Case (4 seats), Mrs Ray (6 seats), Mrs Selway (4 seats), Thomas Ray (2 seats) and E. Rowland (2 seats). Free seats and seats for children were also available. Attendance at its Sunday school increased from 50 in 1867 to 120 in 1884.[59]

Yet, throughout the nineteenth century Pill was also well-known for its high

Pill Pilots, *c.* 1880.

September 2012).

59   S. C. Tidwell, *Pill Methodist Church 1757-1982*, (Bristol: Pamphlet, July 1982), Bristol Central Library, Pill Library and BRO.

density of public houses (12 pubs and five beer retailers in 1871).[60] The prevalence of heavy drinking, and a desire to help the poor, brought the Salvation Army to the village in 1886.[61] As elsewhere, in the Parish of Easton-in-Gordano there were regular calls for outdoor relief from families unable to purchase basic provisions, such as bread and potatoes. In return they were expected to carry out some form of supervised work.[62] A Seamen's Mission was operating from around the mid-1870s, supplying free meals to the 'deserving poor' at Christmas; as many as fifty men and their families fell into this category in 1882.[63]

However, the most significant transformation in the lives of Pill inhabitants occurred because of the deterioration in the relationship between on the one side, the Docks Committee and the Corporation, and on the other the pilots and watermen of Pill. A trade union for pilots would emerge out of this discord. In the late 1870s, a major disagreement, in which the Bristol Trades Council was called upon to assist, arose over the treatment of a suspended pilot from Pill. In the course of the dispute a wider issue arose when a local ship owner made a concerted attack on the traditional way in which pilots competed for work. The Pill pilots retaliated and the consequent rise in militancy led to the eventual formation of a pilots' association.

A Case of Injustice

Relations between pilots and the Docks Committee worsened following a disciplinary hearing in 1877, which resulted in Edward Canby having his pilot's licence revoked for life. His comrades felt this to be an overly harsh decision, which broke with precedents. Indeed this sentence would soon be retracted by the Docks Committee and replaced by a twelve-month suspension. However, at the behest of the Haven Master in December 1878, this retraction was overturned, and the lifetime ban was again imposed.[64] The *Bristol Mercury and Daily Post* reported in January 1879 that this about turn was perceived as a gross injustice and not only in Pill — Canby's punishment gained him sympathy from pilot bodies in England and from the general public.[65]

Canby's case proved to be of long-term significance. His 'crime' was an error in judgement in running the steamship *Cornwell* aground in the River Avon near the Suspension Bridge. No one was hurt and the ship received little damage. It was not unusual for pilots to have their operating licences suspended for periods of six or twelve months for incidents similar to the one in which Canby was involved. It was his first offence in twenty-two years as a pilot so the complete forfeiture of his licence had been widely regarded as extremely unjust; therefore

---

60   Matthews Street Directory, 1872.

61   http://www.pillchurches.org.uk (accessed 15 September 2012).

62   The total cost of outdoor relief to the Parish of Easton-in-Gordano for the half-year ending December 1871 was £336 11s 4d, *BM*, 9 March 1872.

63   *BMDP*, 20 January 1882.

64   *BMDP*, 2 January 1879.

65   *BMDP*, 20 and 24 January 1879.

it was not so surprising that this decision was to be modified. However, when the suspension period ended, in order to retrieve his licence Canby still needed the Haven Master to vouch that he was able to carry out his duties competently. It was to be on Canby's application to regain his pilot's licence that the Haven Master refused.

In December 1878, the Docks Committee backtracked, informing the Bristol Corporation that Canby's licence should not be restored. The *Bristol Mercury and Daily Post* quoted them as saying that this was because the grounding of the *Cornwell*

> was only the last of a series of offences, of which the list is now before the committee, and add that in their judgement the decision they first arrived at, in which the Haven Master concurred, viz., that Canby's license should be withdrawn, was the correct one, and that they were wrong in yielding to the representations made on his behalf, of which the result was the modified sentence that was reported to and approved by the Council.[66]

If an allegation was made against a Bristol pilot for a dereliction of duty, the procedure was that the pilotage fee would be withheld and only if the outcome of an inquiry exonerated the pilot would the fee be released. In the case of Canby, he had never had his pilotage fee withheld during his long service as a pilot on the Bristol Channel and River Avon. Given this unblemished record, it was incumbent on the Docks Committee to furnish details of the other offences Canby was alleged to have committed.[67] However, they declined.

The Committee's judgement, in reality, rested simply on the Haven Master's *opinion*. Campaigners for seamen's welfare protested; Roger Moore, brother-in-law of Samuel Plimsoll, the seamen's friend and the Honorary Secretary of the Local Plimsoll Committee,[68] declared,

> Never has a question of such vital importance previously arisen, to the pilots in particular and the public in general, by which the rights of English labour were assailed, consigning a respectable man to indigence and disgrace.[69]

Bristol Trades Council took up his case and, at its first meeting of 1879, passed a resolution to forward a memorial to Lord Sandon, President of the Board of Trade, calling for an independent inquiry 'with a view of reinstating Canby in his former position of pilot.'[70] While the Board of Trade looked into the matter it concluded that, having consulted with the Bristol Corporation and having heard that it was not a first offence, it 'would not move further on this

---

66   *BMDP*, 31 December 1878.

67   *BMDP*, 11 April 1879.

68   Samuel Plimsoll, born in Bristol in 1834, was elected as a Liberal MP for Derby in 1868. He campaigned vigorously against the overloading of merchant ships. He became known as the seamen's friend after a bill was passed in 1875 making it mandatory to mark a line on the hull of all cargo ships showing the depth to which they could be safely loaded.

69   *BMDP*, 20 January 1879.

70   *BMDP*, 3 January 1879.

matter.'[71] The campaign to get Canby's licence reinstated continued, though it would not be until December 1882 that the Docks Committee reconsidered its decision and recommended that Canby be licensed as a second-class pilot.[72]

The campaign had demonstrated a unity between the Bristol labour movement, Pill pilots and indeed seafarers around the country, which eventually resulted in a successful outcome. Something quite new had come about. However, it was the attack on the traditional way in which pilots worked that galvanised them into forming the Bristol Pilots' Association, a trade union in all but name.

The Emergence of the United Kingdom Pilots' Association

Towards the latter part of 1880, Mark Whitwill, second generation owner of Mark Whitwill & Son (ship-owners, importers, shipping-agents), whose father had been involved in the 'Fury' incident in 1836, selected four pilots, Richard Case (related to John Case who was killed in the 1859 steam tug explosion), Thomas Ellis, George Reed and John Berry, to have exclusive pilotage rights to steam vessels either owned or chartered by him. The Merchants' Shipping Act's provision for the first pilot to offer his services having an automatic entitlement to navigate a vessel in and out of the Port of Bristol had been overlaid by custom and practice. Whitwill felt himself strong enough to go against this system of selection; as a consequence a selected core of pilots were given the monopoly of the American steam traffic which comprised the lion's share of trade. This then condemned the remaining fifty pilots to pick up what business was left, which was insufficient to feed their families.[73]

Careful plotting by Whitwill, which included the sending of private signals to his favoured pilots and the transmission of secret instructions to ships' captains on where to pick up these pilots, gave every chance that his plan to monopolize pilotage for steamboats under his control would succeed. The Merchants' Shipping Act designated the colours that all pilots must fly. The chosen pilots made it easier for the American steamers to recognize them by painting the hulls of their skiffs in a distinctive manner, and, by means of floating lights, illuminating their vessel's identification number. However, Whitwill's practices were breaking the law. Special indicators infringed the Act. But until the situation was brought to the authorities' attention by the Pill seafarers' solicitor, Mr Waterhouse, no move was made against Whitwill's chosen pilots.[74]

On the 22 November the westwardmen of Pill wrote to Captain Parsons, R.N., the Haven Master for the Port of Bristol, giving notice of their intention to strike if Whitwill did not take immediate steps to discontinue the use of 'picked' pilots.[75] This did not happen and the strike commenced. Thirty-one skiffs were detained at Pill creek. Pilots, who were debarred from striking as part of their

---

71   *BMDP*, 28 March 1879.
72   *BMDP*, 2 December 1882.
73   *BMDP*, 24 November 1880.
74   *BMDP*, 25 November 1880.
75   Letter dated 22 November 1880 published in *BMDP*, 24 November 1880.

licensing conditions, could not operate without their westwardmen. The pilots, however, were fully behind the strikers for the obvious reason that it was their livelihoods that were at stake as well. However, they were at great pains to shed their disreputable reputation and took the decision, in an endeavour to win public support, to sanction the use of Newport and Cardiff men to pilot vessels, other than the steamboats, destined for the Port of Bristol through the Channel to the mouth of the River Avon. From here, as agreed, Bristol pilots took over navigational responsibility and accompanied ships up river to the city docks. The fees received for these services were shared out equally between all pilots and watermen, as there was simply not enough work to go round. While this was a co-operative and egalitarian move, it was to reduce the effect of the strike on Bristol's import and export trade.

In the meantime, there followed a series of public meetings, all held at Pill, in which decisions about tactics were based on how to advance the dispute lawfully and peacefully. To voice the strikers' grievances and lobby for support, it was agreed to send deputations to Bristol MPs, the Docks Committee and the Bristol Trades Council. The Reverend J. W. Lace, Anglican vicar of Christ Church, Pill, by publicly announcing his backing for the strike, boosted the strikers' case. It was further strengthened when John Berry, one of Whitwill's four selected pilots, announced that he was sorry for his actions and would no longer participate in Whitwill's attempt to break the traditional way in which pilots operated.

The Docks Committee received the Pill delegation on 29 November 1880, ostensibly giving them a favourable reception. On hearing the news that the Committee had acknowledged that Pill's watermen had indeed been treated unjustly and that Whitwill's chosen pilots, Case, Reed and Ellis would be summoned to the next meeting of the Committee and censured, the strikers and their supporters strode about, quietly confident of achieving a quick and favourable resolution to the dispute.

However, following this meeting, held on 6 December, there was silence. The failure of the Docks Committee to come up with a remedy, and indeed communicate the result of the disciplinary hearings in regard to Case, Reed and Ellis, fuelled resentment among the strikers and their supporters. The reception given to one of Whitwill's steamers on 8 December as it passed Pill creek reflected their feelings:

> [T]he inhabitants turned out *en masse*, and lined the banks of the river on the Pill side, and yelled and groaned and hissed to their hearts' content... the women and children being the most demonstrative. Captain Parsons, the haven-master, put in an appearance, accompanied by three members of the water police, and he was received with similar marks of unpopularity.[76]

In the afternoon the women and children paraded effigies of Case, Reed and Ellis around the village and burned them on a large bonfire on the banks of the

---

76   *BMDP*, 9 December 1880.

river.

The strikers' patience with the Docks Committee was exhausted. With the help of Waterhouse, the strikers' solicitor, a memorial was prepared, and sent later that day to the Board of Trade. It appealed to the Board to intervene and 'redress or remove' their grievances, which were outlined in the petition. Three days later Captain Parsons made the outcome of the Docks Committee meeting of the 6 December 1880 known to the strike committee. Whitwill's pilots, Case, Reed and Ellis had been warned about the unfair way in which they were treating

> the rest of their comrades, and informed them as to the measures they [Docks Committee] might have to recommend to the Council to take the by-law to put a stop to such practices if still continued.

The Pill seafarers regarded this as insufficient; they desired 'a settlement of the whole matter once and for all.'[77] Their case now rested on getting support from the Board of Trade.

At this point some exasperated Pill men decided that it was time to take direct action. Before the Board had got round to giving Pill's petition consideration, eleven pilots and westwardmen were charged for a breach of the 1875 Conspiracy and Protection of Property Act; and were indicted for a common law misdemeanour. The case centred on an incident involving Whitwill's man, Richard Case, and several strikers. At the outbreak of the strike, Case's skiff was one of the thirty-one confined at Pill creek. On the morning of the 8 December 1880, at high tide, with his son and two other boys, he made an attempt to release his skiff and put to sea. Seeing him evade one barrier, a rope attached to the pilot skiff (No. 19),[78] the strikers prevented him from leaving by stretching a second rope from one pilot boat (No. 9) to another (No. 15) across the mouth of the creek. Realising the futility of his efforts to pass, he left his skiff to seek assistance. He got into a rowing boat and crossed the river to the Haven Master's office at Shirehampton. He returned with Captain Parsons, the Haven Master, a police sergeant and two water-police to find that the rope had been slackened, but, as he tried again to escape from the creek his way was barred, on this occasion by a chain extending from the left hand bank of the creek to the fore of the pilot skiff (No. 26) and on the right hand bank to the aft. Parsons supported by the police demanded that the pilots, (the eleven men charged), gathered on board skiff (No. 26) remove the chain and let Case go about his legal business. Accompanied by a cacophony of jeers and shouts the pilots refused, and displayed their dissent by tightening the chain further. After twenty minutes or so the tide had fallen and the opportunity to put to sea had gone. Case had to give up. After consulting with Captain Parsons he obtained a summons from Bristol magistrates and the charge of obstructing a pilot was brought against William Cary (junior), John Berry, James Hazell, Thomas Dickins, Thomas Harris, Frederick Thomas, Thomas Ray, John Brookes,

---

77   *BMDP*, 13 December 1880.

78   Each boat was marked with a serial number to identify its owner.

THROWING MUD AT COMMANDER CAWLEY.

"It is time there were special measures adopted by the Council to deal with such men as Commander Cawley."—HERBERT ASHMAN.

"It is time we had more men like Commander Cawley in the Council to deal with shipping matters and those who are ignorant of them."—*Magpie.*

A cartoon from 1896 depicting George Cawley, who was the first president of the United Kingdom Pilots' Association. Herbert Ashman was Councillor for St Pauls and later Mayor of Bristol.

George Buck, James Buck and William Selway.[79]

The first charge against the eleven men was dismissed on the grounds that the 1875 Act did not apply to seamen or apprentices to seamen. On the second charge an agreement was reached between the parties that the defendants would 'enter into recognisances not to repeat any unlawful act and to keep the peace towards him [Case].'[80] It took much persuasion by Waterhouse to get the defendants to agree to this, as it was seen as a moral victory for Case. Yet Pill seafarers were now very much dependent on the Board of Trade to find in their favour, and Waterhouse was confident that it would do so.

He presided at the next meeting of Pill seafarers, held on the 16 December, and recommended that the strike be terminated. J. F. Hopkins, Chairman of the Bristol Trades Council, W. Count, its secretary, and Roger Moore, representative of the Cardiff pilots, spoke in support. The Reverend Lace summed up the reasons for advocating a return to work when he addressed the meeting. He felt that the action taken was inspirational in that the strike, in asserting Pill seafarers' traditional rights, had shown the strength of feeling

---

79   The details of this account are drawn from the prosecution case for the complainant Richard Case. The defence did not challenge the accuracy, apart from some minor points, but it did deny that the action was a conspiracy or agreement between the defendants. *BMDP*, 16 December 1880.

80   *BMDP*, 16 December 1880.

running through the whole community, but, now that they had forcibly made their case, it was time for the Board of Trade and the Docks Committee to consider the question. Given this state of affairs he could no longer see the benefit of continuing the strike. Beneath the ethical rhetoric, however, an awkward reality lurked. Inadvertently, the strike had shown that the absence of pilot skiffs in the Channel had done little harm to trade coming in and out of Bristol. This was not lost on Whitwill's supporters and played into the hands of those people of influence who wanted to abolish compulsory pilotage. The meeting held on 16 December unanimously carried the proposition to resume normal working and take their boats to sea. It was agreed that the men who had to stay behind to give evidence in the court case against Richard Case were to be paid out of the earnings of the rest.[81]

The court hearing against Case, held on the 31 December, in respect to his alleged infringement of the Merchants' Shipping Act, turned out to be little more than a farce. He pleaded guilty to the charge that on the 7 July 1880 he displayed a flag that infringed the colour code and size dimension stipulated by the Merchants' Shipping Act. He was fined one shilling and costs. A period of fourteen days suspension from pilotage operations was also imposed.[82] This was just a token gesture. That several other alleged cases of infringement had not come before the courts was due to the procrastination of the Docks Committee in dealing with the complaints brought to its attention by Pill seafarers' solicitor. In reality the message to Whitwill and his pilots was that they could continue to monopolize the pilotage of American steam traffic.

From the perspective of the Pill seafarers, the law had proved a feeble protector. Many felt disillusioned about attaining justice through the legal system. Nevertheless, despite the setbacks, Pill men came out of this dispute unified and conscious that they required independent representation rather than continuing to rely on patronage as they had done in the past. They formed the Bristol Pilots' Association to represent both pilots (at twopence a week) and westwardmen (at a penny a week). J. F. Hopkins, chairman of the Bristol Trades Council, presided at the first meeting at which officers for the newly formed organisation were elected. When Hopkins referred to the Association as a trade union 'united to protect and not combined to injure' approving 'Hear, hears' echoed round the hall.[83] The union constituted a link between Pill and Bristol workers. However, Whitwill's stubborn resistance to opening up pilotage of his steamers to competition, continued and, on 3 March 1881, once again, disturbances in Pill broke out.

The hardships faced by the Pill seafarers' families had intensified, because Whitwill's chosen pilots were depriving them of work. In their desperation westwardmen and women from the community showed their condemnation by direct action of a time-honoured kind which predated modern unions. As Richard Arthur Case, the son of Richard Case, Whitwill's chosen pilot,

---

81   *BMDP*, 17 December 1880.

82   *BMDP*, 1 January 1881.

83   *BMDP*, 5 January 1881.

attempted to land a rowing boat at the landing slip on the north side of Pill creek, three westwardmen jumped on board. One of them struck Case on the head and attempted to throw him in the river. In the struggle Case managed to free himself and get away. He was chased up the slipway and on reaching the top was blocked by two women, Jane Summers and Emma Dickins, (wife of the westwardman Thomas Dickins), who tarred and floured him. It was an act of shaming and humiliating, characteristic of women's action in protests and disputes.[84] As he ran away a crowd of locals threw stones and mud at him.[85]

The Case family responded in kind. Later the same morning Richard Case (senior) landed at Pill Custom House near the creek. Frank Smith approached him. Case pulled out a revolver and said 'if you touch me, I'll blow your brains out.' Smith stepped to the side and Case walked on, revolver in hand, until he came across the redoubtable Emma Dickins with a tub of tar in her hand. He said to her 'If you do anything to me I'll shoot you'. He then pointed the gun at her and fired. The bullet passed close to her head. He was then seized, disarmed and tarred and feathered before being arrested. Brought before the Police court on the 10 March, Case claimed the gun went off accidently. The magistrates decided to commit him to trial, which took place in August at the Bristol Assize Court. The Judge said in summing up that

> [t]o think that in a civilised country a man was prepared to be persecuted and followed, and tarred and feathered without defending himself, would surely be to say it was an uncivilised and barbarous country, and these people ought to be thoroughly ashamed of themselves.

Unsurprisingly, the jury without due hesitation acquitted Case.[86] In contrast, Jane Summers and Emma Dickins were charged with assault along with three westwardmen, Frank, William and Sidney Smith. They were sentenced to fines of 40s each, and costs, or fourteen days' imprisonment, with hard labour. Waterhouse, their solicitor, assured the court that the fines imposed would be paid at once.[87]

In the meantime, Reverend Lace brokered a resolution to the dispute between Whitwill and the Pill seafarers. The principle of only using the three selected pilots was ostensibly broken. However, the steamboat captains would have the final say as to which pilot they wished to employ. In the words of the letter written by Whitwill to the Reverend Lace:

> I have now decided to allow such of my captains as have been long in my service and who know the pilots full liberty to take or refuse any men who may hail them to the westward of Lundy; but I shall give to those captains who have been more recently appointed hints as to the pilots to whom I object for any reason that may seem sufficient to myself.[88]

84 See E. P. Thompson, *Customs in Common* (London: Merlin, 1991), pp. 233-236.

85 *BMDP*, 10 March 1881.

86 *BMDP*, 8 August 1881.

87 *BMDP*, 10 March 1881.

88 Letter from Mark Whitwill to the Reverend J. W. Lace, dated 28 April 1881, published in *BMDP*, 2 May 1881.

Although Pill seafarers accepted this resolution as finally putting an end to the dispute, the concession made by Whitwill, in theory, still allowed him to employ pilots of his choosing. Indeed there is some evidence suggesting that this did happen.

On 7 September 1883, Charles Case was selected to take the large steamer, *Cousins Arbib*, from King Road to the city docks. After checking the depth of the loaded vessel in the water, the service of a second tug was called for. This request was met with a blanket refusal that well may have been to do with Case having been chosen ahead of the other pilots. After he consulted with the ship's captain it was decided to take the boat up river to the city docks with a single tug. This decision turned out to be unwise as the ship ran aground at Round Point, about half-a-mile from its destination. The newspaper report on the incident registered its concern about what it termed 'jealousy' over the selection of pilots, 'which for the best interests of the port requires an immediate remedying.'[89] It is interesting that Charles Case shares the same surname as the men that were tarred and feathered, although there is no specific evidence that this was the reason his selection provoked animosity. Nevertheless the Pill pilots, with an eye to the main chance, proffered their rescue services at a high rate, only to squabble among themselves until they were forced to reduce it.

During the 1880s, Pill pilots, while maintaining their tradition of individual competition for work, shifted away from defending their interests in isolation towards a more collectivist approach. In the process they connected to a wider labour movement beyond Pill. In October 1883, at a meeting in Bristol, the decision was made to form a national association of pilots. The Bristol Pilots' Association issued a statement outlining why it was wholeheartedly in support of this decision:

> For some months past there has been amongst the pilots of the Bristol Channel a movement, silently but surely progressing, towards the formation of a union upon the Trades Union principle. The movement has originated through the amount of harassing piecemeal legislation taking place — the attempts to curtail their pilotage districts, to reduce their fees, and sundry other subjects.[90]

The United Kingdom Pilots' Association held its inaugural conference on 11 June 1884 in the Athenæum Hall, Bristol. Captain Henry Langdon of the Bristol Pilots' Association became its secretary.[91] He was in contact with William Morris's Socialist League, which supported the pilots. In October 1885, he wrote to the League thanking them for their 'sympathetic expressions, favourable to the Pilots (*sic*) exertions for relief from the thraldom in which they are now enveloped.' He went on to remark that capitalists 'grind down their employees'.[92]

---

89   *BMDP*, 10 September 1883.

90   *BMDP*, 5 November 1883.

91   Hignett, *Pilotage History*, p. 4; *BMDP*, 12 June 1884.

92   Letter dated 23 October 1885, from H. Langdon, United Kingdom Pilots Association, Bristol to H. Halliday Sparling, Secretary of the Socialist League, held at the International Institute of Social History, Amsterdam. Sparling was the son-

The Pill seafarers had travelled a long stormy voyage; from being pirates they had become proletarians.[93]

in-law of William Morris (1834-1896), artist, writer and revolutionary socialist.

93 For information on Pill pilots after the formation of the United Kingdom Pilots' Association see J. Rich, *The Bristol Pilots*, pp. 100-101; Also see Ray Buck's memories of his time as a Pill pilot in the twentieth century. http://www.lifestoriesandmemories.co.uk/37/1/story/Ray-Buck.asp [accessed 14 September 2012].

3

The Bristol Strike Wave of 1889-1890: Socialists, New Unionists and New Women

Part One: Days of Hope

•

Mike Richardson

1

Bristol is rarely seen as a city with a history of militant labour disputes. However, in the early 1870s, a period when the economy was booming, there had been widespread union activity which reached out to semi-skilled and unskilled men. Progress was to be short-lived for it proved difficult to hold onto members once improvements in pay and conditions had been achieved.[1] Over a decade of depression would follow. During the 1870s and 1880s, men's wages in Bristol were on average lower in comparison to other towns and cities in England;[2] and, as elsewhere, advances in technology reshaped the way people worked. The introduction of machinery, such as the Goodyear chain-stitching machine in Bristol's boot and shoe factories in the 1870s, led to the deskilling of some craft work;[3] the shift from wind to steam power demanded dock workers turnaround ships quicker than before;[4] and in 1879 the new gas works built in Stapleton, Bristol, utilised the latest gas retorts which, given their increased demand for fuel, compelled stokers to work harder.[5] However, a decade of relatively peaceful labour relations was maintained before the next wave of sustained industrial rebellion took off in autumn 1889.

Rumblings of discontent were already evident during the summer of 1889 among miners and gasworkers. Coal workers organised and formed the Bristol Miners' Association. They joined the miners' national campaign to secure a

---

1   B. Atkinson, *Trade Unions in Bristol*, Bristol Branch of the Historical Association (Bristol: The University, 1982), p. 6.

2   B. W. E. Alford, 'The Economic Development of Bristol in the Nineteenth Century: An Enigma?' in P. McGrath and J. Cannon (eds.), *Essays in Bristol and Gloucestershire History* (Bristol: Bristol and Gloucestershire Archaeological Society, 1976), p. 275.

3   J. Press, 'G. B. Britton and Footwear Manufacturing in Bristol and Kingswood, 1870-1973' in C. Harvey and J. Press (eds.), *Studies in the Business History of Bristol* (Bristol: Bristol Academic Press, 1988), p. 216.

4   R. Price, *Labour in British Society* (Beckenham, Kent: Croom Helm, 1988), p. 115.

5   Ibid.; *BM*, 27 March 1879.

substantial pay increase, which, after a succession of strikes, was achieved. Bristol gasworkers organised too, as relationships between them and the directors of the Bristol United Gas Light Company began to break down. But the high point came between October and December 1889 and affected a wide range of industries, from cotton to cocoa. Semi-skilled and unskilled workers, including a significant number of women, were involved. Previous attempts had been made to organise women in separate unions from the mid 1870s but this was to be the first time that Bristol women workers would be able to join a general union on an equal footing to men. Thus, though organisation outside the skilled crafts was not entirely unprecedented, the late 1880s and early 1890s saw a level of industrial militancy on a scale that Bristol had never experienced before.

The upsurge in resistance was part of a wider picture. In early July 1888 the East London matchwomen, employed at Bryant and May's factory, walked off the job in protest at the dismissal of one of their female colleagues for what they believed to have been a 'trumped-up' charge. Feeling she had been targeted, the matchwomen then extended their demands to include improvements in conditions of employment and sought support for their cause through repeated processions to parliament.[6]

Ben Tillet

The terrible consequences of phosphorous necrosis of the jaw (phossy jaw), caused by the phosphorous in matches, aroused widespread sympathy. The matchwomen's case was publicised by the prominent women's rights campaigner Annie Besant through the London socialist movement. Besant was well known in Bristol radical circles, as well as among educated middle class women concerned to improve working women's conditions; and the matchworkers' rebellion would find echoes in the city.[7]

The matchwomen's success would provide an inspirational example for thousands of East End Dockers to follow. In the middle of August 1889, a dispute that started over the hourly rate paid for unloading of the ship The *Lady Armstrong* at the South-West India Docks developed into a full-scale strike, which quickly spread to other London ports. The dockers extended their demands calling for six pence an hour (the dockers' tanner) for day workers and eight pence per hour overtime. They also demanded minimum work periods of four hours and union

---

6   L. Raw, *Striking a Light: The Bryant and May Matchwomen and their Place in History* (London: Continuum, 2009) pp. 131-4.

7   Ibid., pp. 96-127.

recognition. In order to gain community support, daily processions were organised. In mid September 1889, during the fifth week of the strike, with public opinion mounting against the employers, the dockers' key demands were conceded. After their victory, thousands of dockers joined the newly formed Dock, Work, Riverside and General Labourers' Union. Ben Tillett, a Christian socialist, was elected as the union's first General Secretary.[8] Tillett had a particular connection to Bristol. He had been born in the city but ran away as a child, eventually settling in London. The dockers' victory in September 1889, and Tillett's role in it, would, in turn, provide the momentum for dock labourers in Bristol to take strike action.

John Gregory

The matchwomen's and the dockers' strikes revealed the importance of community support, while the formation, in March 1889, of the Gasworkers and General Labourers' Union (later the National Union of Gasworkers and General Labourers of Great Britain and Ireland), marked the emergence of a new kind of trade unionism influenced by left-wing socialists. This 'New Unionism' presented political and social as well as economic demands, such as campaigning for the eight-hour day. Moreover, it reached out beyond skilled craftsmen to recruit non-craft workers, including women.

The matchwomen, the dockers and the gasworkers presented alternative ways of organising workers, lessons that were taken up by two key groupings in Bristol. The Bristol Trades Council, formed in 1873, brought together trade unionists in a range of industries across the city and included several figures with considerable experience, including Robert Tovey, from the Clothiers' Cutters' Association, who was to become Bristol's first Labour councillor, and John Gregory, the socialist shoemaker poet who, in 1874, had become the first Bristol Secretary of Amalgamated Boot and Shoe Riveters' and Finishers' Society.[9] While the Trades Council could offer organisational support, it was a male-dominated body, weak in numbers, with its roots in the craft artisanal traditions of the Bristol working class.[10] It was galvanised by a more recent grouping, the Bristol Socialist Society, established in 1885. The Bristol socialists included both working class and middle class critics of the capitalist system, including women, and were prepared to back the claims of women workers.

8   Ibid., pp. 163-9.

9   G. Sables, 'John Gregory and William Morris: Two Socialist Poets' in *William Morris Society Newsletter*, Summer, 2008, p. 17.

10   D. Large and R. Whitfield, *The Bristol Trades Council 1873-1973*, (Bristol: Bristol Branch of the Historical Association, 1973).

In part, the industrial unrest in Bristol during 1889 and 1890 grew out of a long-term national economic recession which dated back to the early 1870s. The picture is a complex one, however. Workers fortunate enough to experience continuous employment had seen real wages (wages recalculated to take into account inflation) grow steadily from the late 1860s, with a few blips in the late 1870s and early 1880s, and increase rapidly from 1884 to 1890.[11] However, unemployment based on the only data available (trade union records) reached a high level and it was this that led to discontent. While Bristol benefited from economic diversity in the last quarter of the nineteenth century, it was still vulnerable to the vagaries of the national and international economy. There is no breakdown of the unemployment figures for Bristol but hardship is evident; in January 1880, an estimated 20,000 unemployed men and women gathered on Brandon Hill overlooking the City of Bristol to protest about their situation.[12] A Bristol Trades Council report in March 1884 also highlighted the problem of unemployment:

> We cannot but admire the patient endurance of those of our fellow-citizens who would gladly work but cannot find employment, and are with their families literally starving.[13]

Moreover, in the period 1881-1891, the number of economically active people in the city fell from 117,508 to 101,769.[14] A collective awareness of injustice arising from the economic and social relationship between capital and labour had begun to emerge in the 1880s. This would crystallize in the union organising in the late 1880s, which became known as New Unionism.[15] In October 1889 the *Labour Elector* hailed the 'wave of enthusiasm in the cause of [New] Unionism', which had first been seen in London, sweep across Bristol.[16] It was a dramatic break with Bristol's previous pattern of industrial relations.

While the economic recession may well have been a key explanatory factor for the relatively low levels of industrial conflict between 1874 and 1888, another factor was the paternalistic style of management. Successful industrialists in Bristol tended to be non-conformists and politically active Liberal philanthropic reformers. They favoured a paternalistic style of management. And yet, despite their reputation as 'model' employers, their companies were to be as hard hit by the 1889-90 strikes as any others. The impact of the strikes was not simply economic; the combination of material unrest with socialist ideas and militant

11   D. H. Aldcroft and H. W. Richardson, *The British Economy 1870-1939*, (London: Macmillan, 1969), pp. 4-5.

12   *BM*, 29 January 1880.

13   Bristol Trades Council Report, year ending 31 March 1884, John Wall Papers, BRO.

14   Minimum age of those economically active was five years in 1881 and ten years in 1891. Source: P. Ollerenshaw and P. Wardley, 'Economic Growth and the Business Community in Bristol since 1840' in M. Dresser and P. Ollerenshaw (eds.), *The Making of Modern Bristol*, (Bristol: Redcliffe Press, 1996), p. 126.

15   See Y. Kapp, *The Air of Freedom: The Birth of the New Unionism*, (London: Lawrence and Wishart, 1989); J. Lovell, 'British Trade Unions 1875-1933' in L. Clarkson (ed.) *British Trade Union and Labour History: A Compendium* (Atlantic Highlands, New Jersey, USA: Humanities Press International, 1990) pp. 84-93; A. E. P. Duffy, 'New Unionism in Britain, 1889-1890: A Reappraisal', *The Economic History Review*, Vol. 14, No. 2 (1961): 306-319.

16   *Labour Elector*, 26 October 1889, cited in E. J. Hobsbawm (ed.), *Labour's Turning Point: Nineteenth Century Vol. III 1880-1900*, (London: Lawrence and Wishart, 1948) p. 86.

forms of organising, upset the political and religious elite's hegemonic control over the Bristol working class and led sections of the middle class to question the economic and social order.

The dissidents confronted a powerful establishment. Before 1880, Bristol had been a predominately Liberal city. However, after this date the Conservatives mounted an effective challenge and parliamentary seats were shared more or less equally between the two parties until the 1906 election. Moreover, the Conservatives held dominance over the local Bristol Council Chamber throughout the nineteenth century, and as a consequence, the city did not adopt the raft of municipal social reforms introduced by some other cities, such as Birmingham.[17] The exceptions to this were the municipal ownership of Bristol Docks and, later in the 1880s, the electricity supply.[18]

Religion continued to exercise considerable influence in Bristol from the mid-nineteenth century to the 1880s.[19] In 1851, church attendance was 56.7% and considerably higher than other large cities in England.[20] This figure, moreover, was maintained well into the 1880s. Both the Anglican and non-conformist churches exercised control not only directly upon their congregations but also through an extensive network of charitable projects which reached into the poorer areas.

The extraordinary militancy which erupted in 1889 took this complacent paternalistic establishment by surprise. Samson Bryher, the author of *An Account of the Bristol Labour and Socialist Movement in Bristol* (1929), depicts the city as 'a seething centre of revolt'.[21] Yet the course and extent of Bristol New Unionism, along with the role, as organisers, of both working class and middle class socialists, and the prominence of women among them, has received relatively little subsequent scrutiny.[22]

17   S. Jordan, K. Ramsey and M. Woollard, *Abstract of Bristol Historical Statistics, Part 3: Political Representation and Bristol's Elections 1700-1997* (Series Editor Peter Wardley, Bristol Historical Databases Project, Faculty of Humanities, University of the West of England, 1997), p. xiv.

18   K. Kelly, 'The Port of Bristol 1919-1939: A Study of a Municipally Owned Port', (unpublished PhD, University of the West of England, 1999); P. Lamb, *Electricity in Bristol 1863-1948*, (Bristol: Bristol Branch of the Historical Association, 1981), p. 3.

19   B. Atkinson, 'The Bristol Labour Movement 1868-1906', (D.Phil., Oxford University, 1969), p. 99.

20   Ibid., p. 26.

21   S. Bryher, *An Account of the Labour and Socialist Movement in Bristol*, (Bristol: 1929), II, p.16.

22   Key texts are Bryher, *An Account of the Labour and Socialist Movement in Bristol*; Atkinson, 'The Bristol Labour Movement 1868-1906'; B. Atkinson, *Trade unions in Bristol*; Ellen Malos, 'Bristol Women in Action, 1839-1919: The right to vote and the need to earn a living' in I. Bild (ed.), *Bristol's Other History*, (Bristol: Bristol Broadsides (Co-Op), 1983). The following publications also refer to the strikes: M. Richardson, *Trade Unionism and Industrial Conflict in Bristol: An Historical Study*, (University of the West of England, 2000); K. Kelly and M. Richardson, 'The Shaping of the Bristol Labour Movement, 1885-1985', Dresser and Ollerenshaw, in Dresser and Ollerenshaw (eds.), *The Making of Modern Bristol*; S. Rowbotham and J. Weeks, *Socialism and the New Life: The Personal and Sexual Politics of Edward Carpenter and Havelock Ellis*, (London: Pluto, 1977) pp. 65-72; S. Rowbotham, *Edward Carpenter: A Life of Liberty and Love*, (London: Verso, 2008), pp. 126-7, 134-5, 203; J. Hannam, "An Enlarged Sphere of Usefulness'; The Bristol Women's Movement, c.1860-1914' in Dresser and Ollerenshaw (eds.), *The Making of Modern Bristol*.

2

A notable feature of the Bristol strikes was the involvement of women workers and the leading part played by two middle class women, Miriam Daniell and Helena Born. When they became actively involved in the Bristol Socialist Society and supported the strikers in the autumn of 1889, they antagonised many of their former associates in Liberal and non-conformist religious circles. Their engagement in New Unionism and socialism would transform their lives.

Elizabeth Miriam Daniell

Elizabeth Miriam Daniell (née Wheeler) was born in Clifton, Bristol in 1861, the daughter of Catherine Anne Wheeler and Robert R. Wheeler, a grocer in Portland Street, Clifton Village. She was baptised on 30 March, 1875, at Pembroke Congregational Church, Oakfield Road, Clifton. Her home, a comfortable dwelling for the well-to-do, was close by. She lived with her parents, brothers and sister. Her father, and her brother Herbert, were active members of Pembroke Church; Robert serving on its committee from 1867-1888 and Herbert in the 1880s and early '90s.[23] By the nineteenth century, Congregationalism had shed its radical dissenting origins, however Congregationalists retained their emphasis upon democratic organisation within the church which connected them to Unitarians. There was also a stress on the example of Christ living a humble life among ordinary people.[24]

On 13 July, 1881, aged 20, Miriam married Edward Tuckett Daniell who was 27 years of age. Edward was a solicitor and was in partnership with his elder brother, James Livett Daniell. Both were active in the Liberal Party and supported women's suffrage. Miriam moved up the social scale through this marriage into the professional middle class. Edward lived about half-a-mile away from Miriam, very close to Clifton Downs.[25] After their marriage they moved to Ashley Down, on the other side of Bristol, only to return a few years later to the affluent triangle of Bristol suburbs, Clifton, Redland and Cotham.

Like her younger sister Mary, Daniell was artistic and studied at the Bristol School of Art in Queen's Road, Clifton, obtaining, in 1885, a second grade government prize and certificate for her work.[26] The Bristol School of Art was far from being a radical institution. Male and female students were taught separately and kept apart. Local dignitaries such as Lewis Fry MP (of the Fry's

23   Pembroke Congregational Church, Oakfield Road, Clifton – Roll of church members, BRO.

24   K. S. Inglis, *Churches and the Working Classes in Victorian England* (London: Routledge, 1963), pp. 100-115.

25   Details obtained from their marriage certificate. Miriam's address before she married was 15 Hanbury Road, Clifton. Edward's address was 5 Downfield Road, Clifton.

26   *BM*, 23 March 1885.

Quaker family) and George Alfred Wills (of W. D. and H. O. Wills' Tobacco Company) were patrons of the school; in 1886, the former was president of the school and the latter sat on its committee. The teaching of fine art was traditional, such as drawing flowers, foliage and landscape, and modelling from drawing or nature.[27] Nevertheless, in 1885 radical ideas about the role of art were being propounded in Bristol. In March, William Morris, artist, poet and socialist, delivered a lecture entitled 'Art and Labour' at the Bristol Museum, a few hundred yards from the Art School.[28] He appealed to the middle class section of his audience, many of whom were from Clifton:

> Throw in your lot with the workers. So doing you will be part of a great army which must triumph, and be helping to bring about the day when the words rich and poor that have so long cursed the world shall have no meaning; when we shall all be friends and good fellows united in that community of happy, reasonable, honoured labour, which alone can produce genuine art or the pleasures of life.[29]

While there is no explicit evidence that Daniell attended Morris's lecture we know she moved among Clifton artists and musicians.[30]

A year after Daniell had gained her art certificate she was taken ill. She underwent an operation and was advised to refrain from sexual intercourse and thereafter slept in a separate room from her husband. She travelled to Edinburgh in 1886 to convalesce and returned there on a number of occasions over the next few years. It was here that she became acquainted with Robert Allan Nicol, a medical student, who later was to become her lover.[31] He had a thirst for knowledge that extended beyond his medical degree studies. A letter written by him to the writer on evolution and town planning, Patrick Geddes, indicates that during his time as a medical student he also studied European history, under Geddes' tutelage.[32] Later in life he told his daughter, Amaryllis, that in his youth he was 'a close companion' of Patrick Geddes.[33] The unconventional Geddes, who flirted with anarchism and socialism, taught in the University Extension movement and supported the higher education of women and social reform.[34] Nicol was younger than Daniell; however, there was an obvious affinity. Robert Gilliard, Bristol Socialist Society member, described the rebellious and sometimes unpredictable side to their characters:

> They were fiery enthusiasts (in the best sense) whose vital forces could not be suppressed, could not help but come out in full blaze. They had no

27 Bristol School of Art Minute Book, 1871-1902, BRO.

28 Bryher, *Labour and Socialist Movement in Bristol*, I, p. 26.

29 Ibid.

30 H. Tufts, 'biographical introduction' in H. Born, *Whitman's Ideal Democracy and other Writings* (Boston, USA: Everett Press, 1902), p. xiii.

31 *BM*, 1 May 1894; *The Standard*, 1 May 1894.

32 Correspondence from R. A. Nicol to P. Geddes, 9 March 1886, National Library of Scotland (Ms. 10524 f. 82), Edinburgh: I am grateful to Georges Rey, (Georges Rey Private Collection) for this reference.

33 Correspondence from R. A. Nicol to his daughter Amaryllis, 2 June 1953. I am indebted to Sheila Rowbotham for providing me with this reference from her notes.

34 H. E. Meller, *Patrick Geddes: Social Evolutionist and City Planner* (London: Routledge, 1990), p. 97.

power in themselves to adopt with any continuity, quiet and plodding grooves — They were as true as steel to the cause but had a tendency to drift off into new, bold, and untried projects in it. They feared nothing![35]

Gilliard went on to say how Daniell's friend, Helena Born, had a modulating influence upon them.

[She] was just the soul needed as a companion and sister for them — she herself was no less determined than they, no less self sacrificing (as I view it she was self-abnegating more than they) her ideal, and desire to reach it, was as high & strong (I should say stronger than theirs).[36]

Helena Born

Born's early life is recounted by Helen Tufts, her close American friend, in *Whitman's Ideal Democracy and other Writings*.[37] Born in Devon on 11 May 1861, Tufts relates how Mary Helena Born was educated at a day-school in Hatherleigh, near Oakhampton and later at an academy in Taunton where she acquired an interest in mathematics, science, economics and literature. Denied college training, she moved with her family to Bristol. When her mother died, she did what was probably expected of her, which was to take over as her father's housekeeper at their home in Whiteladies Road, Clifton, just around the corner from the Unitarian Church she attended in Oakfield Road. In the church Born began to overcome, what Tufts notes as, her 'extreme diffidence'.[38] The Unitarians were not only democratic in their approach to church governance, they based their doctrine on reason, enlightenment and virtuous living. Traditionally, new members, known as hearers, underwent a period of instruction before being accepted as full members of the church, at which point they were encouraged to fully participate in discussion arising out of lectures, usually given by the resident minister.[39] Bristol Unitarians during the 1870s and 1880s were interested in social and political reform. For instance, in early January 1879, the Reverend William Hargrave, whose preaching Born enjoyed,[40] lectured at Oakfield Road Unitarian Church on 'National Insurance; a cheap, practical, and popular means

35   Robert Gilliard, letter written on behalf of the Bristol Socialist Society, to Helen Tufts, 9 May 1901, Tamiment Library / Wagner Archives, New York. I am grateful to Sheila Rowbotham for providing me with this reference from her notes.

36   Ibid.

37   H. Tufts, 'biographical introduction', p. xii.

38   Ibid.

39   R. J. Saywell, 'The Unitarian Meeting 1691-1774' in *Notes on Bristol History* No. 8 (University of Bristol, 1968).

40   Tufts, 'biographical introduction', p. xii.

of abolishing poor rates'.[41] During the 1880s, similar topics would be considered by the debating society in an anteroom adjoining the church. Born contributed to these debates, played the piano and sang in the church choir. She particularly admired Stopford Wentworth Brooke, the minister at her church during 1884-86,[42] who was an active Liberal. She was, moreover, influenced by freethinkers, such as the secularist Charles Bradlaugh[43] and became active in the Bristol Women's Liberal Association in the 1880s, serving on its executive, and addressing meetings. Daniell was also a member of this Association.

In March 1889, Born and Daniell, along with other middle class philanthropists, threw themselves into helping people affected by the severe flooding of 8 and 9 March 1889, which hit the low-lying working class districts of Bristol. Especially badly hit were the areas around Baptist Mills, St Judes, St Philips and Broadmead.[44] On 14 March, Daniell sent a letter from her home at Hampton Park, Redland, to the local newspaper appealing for donations of clothes to assist those affected by the floods.[45] Her husband and his brother donated money to the relief fund.[46] Protests followed, 'against the criminal apathy of the Town Council'.[47] The floods created a public outcry, Liberals, socialists and ministers of religion were active in calling public meetings urging the council to carry out the necessary work to the drainage system to ensure that such devastation would not occur again. An informal coalition of progressives, galvanised by the floods, began to form. Tufts considered this direct experience of working class hardship to have been decisive in radicalising Born and Daniell.[48] By 1889 both women would be associated with the Bristol Socialist Society.

3

The Bristol Socialist Society had been founded by a small group of committed individuals who had participated in radical reform groups active in Bristol in the early 1880s. Disappointed by the lack of attention given by the Bristol Radical Reform Association[49] to the economic and social problems faced by the working class, dissenters established a Pioneer Class in November 1883 'for the discussion of democratic and social reform schemes, and the mutual

---

41 *BM*, 4 January 1879.

42 Tufts, 'biographical introduction', p. xii.

43 Ibid, p. xii; Helena Born's scrap books, 1870-1892, Tamiment Library/Wagner Archives, New York. I am indebted to Sheila Rowbotham for providing me with this reference from her notes.

44 Authorities were well aware that these areas were prone to flooding. A report by Mr Howard, the former engineer to the Docks Committee, had recommended in 1882 that work should be urgently carried out to alleviate the problem. J. Latimer, *The Annals of Bristol in the Nineteenth Century: 1887-1900* (Bristol: George's sons, 1902).

45 *WDP*, 14 March 1889.

46 *WDP*, 13 March 1889.

47 *WDP*, 15 March 1889.

48 Tufts, 'biographical introduction', pp. xiv-xv.

49 Interestingly, Reverend Hargrave — Minister at the Unitarian Church, Oakfield Road, frequented by Helena Born — delivered a lecture entitled 'class prejudices' to this association in January 1884, *BM*, 10 January 1884.

improvement of all its members.'[50] Within a few months, in February 1884, these discussions led by Robert Sharland, who, through his association with an early Christian socialist and Republican, William Harrison Riley, had become acquainted with the gay socialist writer Edward Carpenter,[51] resulted in him and fellow members of the Pioneer Class to dissolve their organisation in favour of instituting a Bristol branch of Hyndman's Democratic Federation, which was later to become the Social Democratic Federation.[52] The branch was active and set out their programme in a written address to 'Fellow Workers' in 1884. It declared that,

> The present must be superseded by a more righteous system of production and distribution of wealth, there should be collective ownership of land, machinery and all means of production and distribution, and all departments organised on cooperative principles, and worked for the people's benefit...[53]

And concluded with the plea,

> Rouse from your apathy and lend a helping hand to emancipate labour and work to make this truly OUR COUNTRY, with means of living sure, and having homes with pleasant surroundings for ourselves and children. EDUCATE! AGITATE! ORGANISE![54]

In March 1886, however, the Bristol branch officially split from the Social Democratic Federation — in the wake of the Social Democratic Federation scandal of accepting 'Tory Gold' to finance its General Election campaign in November 1885 — and became a branch of the short-lived Socialist Union led by H. Campbell, C. L. Fitzgerald and James Ramsay MacDonald.[55] In 1887, a minority concerned at the rise of unemployment reconstituted an SDF branch, but this would be disbanded in 1889.

The influences on the Bristol Socialist Society were eclectic. The socialist and sexual reformer Edward Carpenter was a frequent visitor to Bristol, often delivering lectures on socialism. He would become especially friendly with Robert Sharland, the Christian Socialist Robert Weare, and the Swedenborgian, Robert Gilliard. Gilliard was so impressed by a lecture delivered by Carpenter in 1885 that he joined the branch soon to be known as the Bristol Socialist Society.[56] Carpenter had been influenced by both German idealism and his own background in the Anglican Church. After losing his Christian faith he became interested in Eastern religious thinking and struggled to relate this with his belief in social change. His mind was open to new ideas and thus his views were

---

50 Bryher, *Labour and Socialist Movement in Bristol*, I, p.12.

51 See Rowbotham, *Edward Carpenter*, pp. 66-69.

52 See M. Crick, *A History of the Social Democratic Federation*, (Wakefield, Yorkshire, UK: Ryburn Publishing/Keele University Press, 1994), for insightful information on Hyndman and the Social Democratic Federation.

53 Written address from the Bristol Branch of the Democratic Federation to 'Fellow Workers', 1884, BRO.

54 Ibid.

55 Minutes of the Bristol Socialist Society, 4 March 1886. Ramsay MacDonald, later to become the first Labour Prime Minister, had been a member of the Bristol branch of the Social Democratic Federation in 1885.

56 Bryher, *Labour and Socialist Movement in Bristol*, I, p. 7.

continually evolving.[57] He was well respected by Bristol socialists and was to be a formative influence on the development of their brand of ethical socialism.

One of the strengths of the group was personal fellowship. Meetings were a joyful as well as a serious occasion. They usually started either with a glee from the musical Sharland brothers, Robert, Will, John, Jim and Tom, or with readings from poets, such as Walt Whitman, Percy Bysshe Shelley, Charles Kingsley or Gerald Massey, along with members' own compositions. A lecture or debate would follow and, if felt necessary, an appropriate resolution would be put to the meeting. Then they would close the meeting by singing socialist songs led by the Sharland brothers.

In the mid 1880s the Bristol Socialist Society embarked on a series of open-air public meetings. The first of these was addressed by the Socialist Union organiser, C. L. Fitzgerald.[58] At a second open-air meeting, held the following week, a resolution calling for the establishment of a labour registry office and useful public works was passed. A deputation delivered it to the City Mayor, Sir Charles Wathen, a Liberal Unionist. It read,

> That this meeting calls on the municipal authorities to open without delay a labour registry office for the city, and as soon as the numbers of the unemployed are accurately ascertained at once to open public works of such a nature as will permanently benefit the workers themselves and the community at large by reducing the rates which now press so heavily on the smaller ratepayers; the wages to be sufficient to enable the workers to live in comfort and decency.[59]

This resolution was met with derision by the Mayor who suggested to the Bristol Socialist Society deputation that 'the working men come down to the same level as the working men on the Continent, work more hours and for less pay.'[60]

By 1889, the year of the strike wave, the economy had improved and unemployment was down. A united Bristol Socialist Society welcomed all socialists into their fold, whether Marxist, Fabian, Christian or Secularist.[61] They worked closely with the Clifton and Bristol Christian Socialists, formed by two friends of Carpenter, E. D. Girdlestone, a member of the Land Nationalisation Society,[62] and a young solicitor, Hugh Holmes Gore, a High Anglican Church man. This organisation attracted other young Anglo-Catholics. Gertrude Dix, and Paul and Enid Stacy, who worshiped at All Saints Church in Clifton, were among the first to join; all three were later to become significant figures in the socialist movement.[63]

---

57   Rowbotham, *Edward Carpenter*, pp. 65-87.

58   *BM*, 5 April 1886.

59   *BM*, 7 April 1886.

60   Minutes of the Bristol Socialist Society, 15 April 1886.

61   Bryher, *Labour and Socialist Movement in Bristol*, II, p. 57.

62   *BM*, 2 February 1883; not to be confused with F. B. Girdlestone, secretary of the Docks' Committee and anti-trade unionist.

63   Bryher, *Labour and Socialist Movement in Bristol*, II, p. 21.

4

The autumn upsurge in militancy began in mid September 1889, with fifty-four men employed in the dipping department at the galvanising iron works of the 'benevolent' employer John Lysaght.[64] Following a meeting held under the presidency of Frank Rawle, a Lysaght's striker, and addressed by the vice-president of the Bristol Trades Council, Albert Vincent, and Hugh Holmes Gore, a majority of the men enrolled with the Gasworkers and General Labourers' Union.[65] The strike spread and within a few days the company acceded to the men's demand for an advance in wages. The Gasworkers and General Labourers' Union, sought to spread this success more widely to semi-skilled and unskilled men and women. On 21 September 1889, at a rally held to celebrate the victory of Lysaght's workers, James Vickery, the first chairman of the Bristol branch of the Gasworkers and General Labourers' Union, demanded, 'was there no Annie Besant in Bristol to fight the battle for the poor oppressed female workers of the city?'[66] Vickery's emotive call obscured over a decade of political wrangling and attempts to defend women at work.

In the 1870s protective laws had been the critical issue. When the Bristol National Union of Working Women was formed in 1874, like its sponsors, Emma Paterson's Women's Protective and Provident League, it held the view that legislation would be used to exclude women from working opportunities. It aimed 'to exercise a supervision over any acts which may injuriously affect the employment of women, and oppose any future legislation having the same tendency...'[67] However, after the Factories and Workshop Bill, which extended protection to women and children, became law in 1878, this position was revised. The group's emphasis moved towards attempting to make legislation work in the interests of women workers by organising women factory-inspectors who could make sure the laws were actually implemented;[68] although the controversy over whether protective legislation benefited or restricted women workers did not entirely dissipate.

In January 1875, the Bristol National Union of Working Women had been the first women's union to gain admittance to the Trades Union Congress (TUC). By 1881, the women middle class reformers in the Bristol National Union of Working Women were also to be found on the executive of the Bristol Association of Working Women. This Association included several middle class women reformers, including Agnes Beddoe, a Cliftonian woman, who was a leading member of the Bristol and West of England Society for Women's Suffrage, as well as the Bristol Women's Liberal Association. In May 1879 she

---

64 John Lysaght and Company's history proudly proclaims that it was one of those employers in Victorian times 'who were in advance of their time' providing amenities such as a sick club, company canteen and library: *The Lysaght Century, 1857-1957* (Bristol: J. Lysaght, 1957).

65 *BTM*, 17 September 1889; *WDP* 17 September 1889.

66 *WDP*, 23 September 1889.

67 S. Lewenhak, *Women and Trade Unions: An Outline History of Women in the British Trade Union Movement* (London: Ernest Benn, 1977), p. 71; *Daily News*, 1 September 1874.

68 See ibid., p. 76.

was presiding over a meeting of the Bristol National Union of Working Women and is also reported as chairing a meeting of the Bristol Association of Working Women in May 1881.[69] The women's trade unions and their middle class leaders inclined towards being supportive of women's welfare needs and keen to encourage harmonious relationships with employers. Formed because the craft unions often excluded women, they had had some support from 'old' craft unions but were also accused by male trade unionists of a lack of independence because they were subsidised by charitable donations.

Male trade unionists' attitude towards accepting women in the Bristol labour movement in the mid 1880s remained, at best, indifferent. In 1885, at the behest of the Bristol Trades Council, the Bristol and District Labour League had been established. To qualify for membership, however, you had to be a wage earning male – women were excluded. In 1886, the socialist Robert Gilliard, charged with drawing up a manifesto for the League, attempted to overturn this rule but the clause declaring that female workers could join was, following a vote, rejected and removed. The League therefore remained exclusively an all male club.[70] Separate trade union organising for women and men persisted. However, the rise of the Gasworkers and General Labourers' Union in 1889 was to present an alternative model of 'New Unionism' open to women and men alike.

This shift was beginning to occur nationally. The matchwomen had gained recognition through their strike in 1888 for the Union of Women Matchmakers,

Robert Allan Nicol

however, by the end of the year the new union had changed its name to the Matchmakers' Union and amended its rules in order to open up the union to both women and men.[71] The formation of the Gasworkers and General Labourers' Union, which actively encouraged women to join its organisation and where they enjoyed the same representational rights as the men, meant that by the time of the outbreak of industrial unrest in the autumn of 1889 in Bristol, a trade union actively encouraging both women and men to join its organisation was already in place. It was against this backdrop that Miriam Daniell, Helena Born and Robert Nicol, along with other socialists in Bristol, threw themselves into organising and agitating against the poor working conditions which prevailed, especially among women.

Just over a week after John Lysaght had capitulated to the demands of his employees, a strike broke out at Redcliff Crown galvanised iron works.[72]

---

69   *BM*, 2 May 1879 and 19 May 1881.

70   Bryher, *Labour and Socialist Movement in Bristol*, II, p.33.

71   S. Boston, *Women Workers and Trade Unions* (London: Lawrence and Wishart, 1987), pp. 47-51.

72   *WDP*, 30 September 1889.

Meetings, held at the British Workman Coffee House, situated in the working-class district of St Judes, were called to organise support for the strike.[73] At the first meeting, addressed by Albert Vincent, Frank Rawle, Robert Sharland and Miriam Daniell, it was agreed to set up a strike fund administered by a committee. Daniell was propelled into the position of treasurer and Born to that of secretary.[74] A demonstration was held on Saturday 5 October in support of the strikers, at which the banner of the Socialist Union was proudly paraded, displaying the slogan 'EDUCATE, AGITATE, ORGANISE'. This was followed by a meeting to distribute financial aid. Daniell dealt with all the urgent calls for help and organised the distribution of strike pay: 6s 3d for married men with 6d extra for each child; single men 5s and boys and women 3s 4d.[75] After the weekend, Mr Tinn, the iron works' proprietor, put forward an offer for his workforce to consider. A meeting was held on the following day addressed by a jubilant Daniell extolling the virtues of unity, men and women standing together against an unjust employer. The press reported that 'she was very glad to know that a settlement had been arranged and that the women were also going in again with an increase in wages. Their victory showed them how necessary it was to organise in such matters, and not fight separately.'[76]

Industrial conflict in the city spread rapidly. On 9 October, following meticulous preparation, Bristol gasworkers struck, demanding higher wages. Their grievances had reached a high point in the summer of 1889 when the Bristol United Gas Light Company decided to pay wages two days in arrears, which led the men to 'protest against the over-bearing and unjust attempt of the Directors to keep back a portion of their wages'.[77] The men formed the Bristol United Gaslight Company's Labour Union, which soon after, in July 1889, amalgamated with the London-based Gasworkers and General Labourers' Union. This development was a key factor in organising strike action in October. By then tension existing between the Bristol United Gas Light Company and their workers had reached breaking point. The company refused to give into the wage demands of its several hundred unionised workers. The strike was called when gas supplies to the city were low with only enough to last two days.[78] To fully exploit this situation, the union had organised a network of support which enabled it to repel strike-breakers brought into the city by train from Exeter, forcing the directors of the Company to settle on terms favourable to the strikers. Bristol Trades Council marked this success with a victory celebration attended by ten thousand people.[79] Atkinson notes how violent picketing, which marked this dispute, 'was possible only because the men had public sympathy, a

---

73   The British Workman Coffee House, New Street, St Judes, was owned by the Society of Friends (Quakers). It had multiple rooms including a large hall, kitchen, scullery and wash house.
74   *WDP*, 1, 2, 5 and 7 October 1889.
75   *WDP*, 7 October 1889.
76   *WDP*, 8 October 1889.
77   H. Nabb, *The Bristol Gas Industry 1815-1949*, (Bristol: Bristol Branch of the Historical Association, The University of Bristol, 1987), p. 27.
78   *Daily News*, 9 October 1890.
79   Atkinson, *Trade Unions in Bristol*, p. 9.

THE GAS STRIKE.

The gasworkers' strike of October 1889 satirised in *The Bristol Magpie*.

sympathy which was not shown in financial aid — there was not time for that — but in the attitude of the police.' He contrasts this with the action of an unsympathetic police force during later strikes in Bristol when between 1892 and 1893 police forcibly intervened to protect non-strikers.[80] Confidence was high in October 1889, poor pay and working conditions were starkly exposed

---

80   Atkinson, 'The Bristol Labour Movement 1868-1906', p. 208.

and long-held grievances surfaced, the unexpected militancy delivered a seismic shock to Bristol's paternalistic system of industrial relations.

Not long after Daniell assumed office as the treasurer of the Strike Committee, an episode occurred that would have a significant effect upon the direction of her life and the lives of Born and Nicol. On 19 October, a meeting was held at the British Workman Coffee House, where workers employed by the cocoa and chocolate making firm of J. S. Fry and Sons were addressed by trade union leaders, members of the Bristol Trades Council and the Bristol Socialist Society. Fry's workforce was not unionised and the objective of the meeting was to consider 'the desirability of organisation for the purposes of maintaining a fair standard of wage and honourable conditions of labour.'[81] Some of Fry's male workers were aggrieved at the unfair distribution of a recent pay award, while around 900 women and girls engaged in Fry's factories were discontented over the length of the working day and wanted shorter working hours. The meeting attracted a large audience. Albert Vincent chaired the meeting of the men and boys upstairs, and Miriam Daniell, who in such a short time had already established a commanding position in the Bristol labour movement, addressed the women and girls downstairs.[82]

The motion carried at the men's gathering read 'that the employees of Messrs Fry and Sons pledge themselves to form a branch of the General Labour Union of Great Britain and Ireland.'[83] Daniell informed her audience that a strike fund committee, originally set up to support workers at Redcliffe Crown galvanised iron works, had continued to carry out their operations in support of the gasworkers, and had been approached to chart grievances and discontentment at Fry's works. She said 'they had a just claim to be fairly and humanely treated, and the committee wanted to know the facts of their case and if found to be just they would endeavour to help them as they had helped women in other factories.'[84] The meeting finished with Daniell and Vincent urging the men and women present to organise, and to this end a group of Fry's employees was appointed to work with the Bristol Trades Council.[85] Prior to this meeting, Daniell and Nicol had compiled data drawn from Fry's workers that brought to light the poor working conditions that they laboured under.[86] Noting these were 'deplorable', they observed that within months of commencing employment at the chocolate factory girls could be seen to suffer 'from lassitude' and compared their circumstances to 'white slavery'. They asked pointedly whether 'rich Cliftonians, some of whom live on the labour of these girls, [would] allow their daughters to run such risks?'[87] This attack on the Liberal Quaker establishment struck a nerve; the accusation of 'white slavery' was a step too far. Daniell's

---

81   *WDP*, 21 October 1889.

82   Ibid.

83   Ibid.

84   Ibid.

85   *BTM*, 21 October 1889.

86   Miriam Daniell and Robert Allan Nicol, *The Truth about Chocolate Factories or Modern White Slavery*, (G.H. Wood Collection, Huddersfield University, 1889).

87   Ibid., p. 9.

THE LATE GASWORKERS' STRIKE AND OUR ORNAMENTAL POLICE.

The police response to the gasworkers' strike of October 1889 lampooned in *The Bristol Magpie*.

husband, Edward Tuckett Daniell, tried to stop the publication of these facts.

The action taken by Miriam Daniell's husband to stop publication triggered a dramatic response. She left him and her comfortable home and moved to a poor working class district, St Philips, in the heart of Bristol, taking Robert Nicol, who for the past three or four weeks had been living with the Daniell's at their Redland residence, and Helena Born with her.[88] She rejected her husband's offer of 'an allowance of a £1 a week while she was living in the slums, and more if she left that style of life.'[89] She would later condemn 'legalised marriage, which she considered lust and prostitution.'[90] In Bristol middle class society such a break was profoundly scandalous despite the presence of Helena Born. Bristol working class socialists were scrupulously respectable, however they approved of this move into a humble home away from the rich trappings of the Clifton elite. Ideas of the simple life, propounded by Edward Carpenter and the American transcendentalists, Ralph Waldo Emerson, Henry David Thoreau and Walt

---

88   *BM*, 1 May 1894.

89   *Reynolds's Newspaper*, Sunday, 6 May 1894.

90   *BM*, 1 May 1894.

Whitman were circulating in the socialist movement.[91] Daniell, Born and Nicol were living the 'new life'. Once they were living independently, Daniell and Nicol lost no time in publishing their report of working conditions at Fry's chocolate factory from their new address, 9 Louisa Street, St Philips, just half-a-mile from the British Workman Coffee House.

Miriam Daniell's defiance was extraordinary; she was confronting her husband, her family, as well as one of Bristol's leading employers. The family of J. S. Fry and Sons, a Quaker company, was highly respected by the liberal elite in Bristol, and the firm was viewed as a 'model' employer.[92] Atkinson accepts this benign image uncritically and points to good employee relations 'largely as a result of excellent management techniques, the family nature of the firms and the presence of many women in the labour force.'[93] Yet the fact that a group of workers were sufficiently dissatisfied to discuss forming a trade union to press for shorter hours and higher wages points to an undercurrent of resentment.

Fry's displayed sophistication with a rapid response to the local labour movement's attempt to organise the workforce. The company called a meeting on the evening of 22 October, on the firm's premises, announcing that day workers would receive an advance of 1s per week.[94] It did not concede, however, the demand for shorter hours for women and girls, or the boys' appeal for an increase in wages. The spokesman for J. S. Fry, George Buckland, delivered the message that employees were free to join a trade union if they so wished, but conveyed J. S. Fry's hope 'that the unity of spirit which now existed among the employees of Messrs Fry would never be severed by outsiders.'[95] Fry's tactics successfully divided the workforce. Long-serving employees were rolled out, emphasising the qualities of their employer and blaming the unrest on those employees who had been working for the company 'for less than six months.' The meeting finished with 'a vote of confidence in the three heads of the firm which was passed amid loud cheering.'[96] A few days later, another Bristol company, C. P. Thomas, soap makers, situated very close to Daniell, Born and Nicols' residence in Louisa Street, also avoided a strike by offering its workers a significant wage increase, as did the Bristol Wagon Works Company and several other establishments in the city.[97]

---

91 See M. Bevir regarding the influence of American Romanticism on British Socialism, 'British Socialism and American Romanticism', *The English Historical Review* Vol. 110, No. 438 (September, 1995): 878-901.

92 S. Diaper, 'J.S. Fry and Sons: Growth and Decline in the Chocolate Industry, 1753-1918' in C. Harvey and J. Press (eds) *Studies in the Business History of Bristol* (Bristol: Bristol Academic Press, 1988), p. 47.

93 Atkinson, 'The Bristol Labour Movement 1868-1906', p. 302.

94 In a footnote to their pamphlet, *The Truth about Chocolate Factories or Modern White Slavery,* Daniell and Nicol record that since it 'was printed, an advance of 1/- on all the men's wages has been granted, October 24th, 1889.'

95 *BTM*, 23 October 1889.

96 Ibid. That some of Fry's young workers would have been aware of, and may have been attracted to, the local labour movement campaigns was evident in the recollections, nearly 50 years later, of William Straker, who had entered the employment of J.S. Fry and Sons in 1882 at the age of fourteen. He recalled that one of his 'youthful interests was attending meetings of the old Bristol Socialist Society'. Later, with others, he established a union branch for confectionery workers, which was affiliated to the Dockers' Union, *BEP*, 9 May 1938; H. Meller, *Leisure and the Changing City, 1870-1914* (London: Routledge & Paul, 1976), p. 193.

97 *The Times*, 26 October 1889. Notably, the owner of C. P. Thomas was a benefactor of the Unitarian Church in Oakfield Road, Clifton, frequented by Helena Born; *Daily News*, 4 November 1889.

There was little time for members of the Bristol labour movement to dwell on either of these concessions or on the failure to organise Fry's workers for on 21 October 2,300 dock workers and, three days later, 1,700 cotton workers in Bristol struck work for better pay and conditions. Inspired by the East London 'dockers' tanner' strike, Bristol dock workers quickly extracted the same concession from their employers, but had to strike to secure enhanced overtime rates. The municipal ownership of the Port of Bristol put the city's dockers in a unique position. Bristol Corporation employed around a third of the total workforce,[98] while the Port was administered by a Docks Committee on behalf of 40 employers and enjoyed a significant amount of independence from the City Council.[99] Nonetheless, those dock workers who were qualified to vote would still indirectly influence council policy on employment relations by supporting candidates sympathetic to the labour cause in local municipal elections. Moreover, as Atkinson observes 'municipal ownership of the docks meant that in labour disputes the ratepayers stood to lose money', and therefore the Council was more likely to pursue a conciliatory policy in their employment relationship with dock workers.[100] Robert Tovey, Bristol's first Labour councillor, had been elected for St Paul's Ward in November 1887, and was appointed by the Council to serve on the Docks Committee, a position he retained until March 1891.[101]

Aware that dock work was of a casual nature, and that dockers would have experienced long periods without work, (some of them even driven to spending time in the local workhouse in the winter months), public opinion fell behind the strikers, and within a few days they secured a decisive victory.[102] On 26 October, a procession of 15,000 people, including striking cotton workers, marched to Clifton Downs to celebrate their, success with Ben Tillett, General Secretary of the Dock, Wharf, Riverside and General Labourers' Union, Tom Mann its President, and Will Thorne the General Secretary of the National Union of Gasworkers and General Labourers of Great Britain and Ireland.[103] Mann and Thorne were members of the Social Democratic Federation and, along with Tillett, strong advocates of the eight-hour day.

Immediately after victory celebrations on Clifton Downs, a meeting was held at the Castle Coffee Palace, Castle Street, Bristol, where, after addresses by Mann, Tillett, Thorne and others, the following resolution was unanimously adopted:

> That this meeting appoint a sub committee to render every possible assistance to the at present unorganized workers of Bristol including the obtaining of necessary offices the issue of circulars and posters and by

---

98 Atkinson, *Trade Unions in Bristol*, p. 9.

99 Kelly, 'The Port of Bristol 1919-1939: A Study of a Municipally Owned Port'.

100 Atkinson, 'The Bristol Labour Movement 1868-1906', p. 13.

101 W. G. Neale, *At the Port of Bristol: Volume One. Members and Problems 1848-1899* (Bristol: The Port of Bristol Authority, 1968), p. 171.

102 See letter from John White, District Secretary of Bristol Dockers' Union, with regard to the casual nature of dock work, published in the *BM*, 3 March 1890.

103 Atkinson, *Trade Unions in Bristol*, p. 9; Richardson, *Trade Unionism and Industrial Conflict*, p. 14.

every other way to assist the workers of both sexes.[104]

Twenty-four people were appointed to form this committee, which came to be known as the Strike Committee. It was comprised of several representatives from the Bristol Socialist Society, including Daniell, Born and Nicol.[105] On the following day the Strike Committee met at the Castle Coffee House where it was decided that an office 'for registration purposes' be established at the British Workman Coffee House for three months. The office was to open from 10am to 9pm. Nicol was appointed organising secretary at a salary of 30s per week. [106] The Strike Committee met six days a week until the end of November 1889; and it would be re-launched on a more permanent basis as the Workers' Organising Committee in January 1890. This is the name on the front cover of the bound copy of the minutes over October 1889 to July 1892.

5

The Strike Committee set about its work in October 1889 against a backdrop of escalating industrial disputes. The previous day *The Times* had reported that in Bristol workers' agitation for better pay and conditions was spreading across industry.

> In the morning work was generally resumed on the docks, but the dispute with the lightermen and bargemen was not settled until the evening, when the masters conceded the men's terms. ... About 200 warehousemen are still out. ... About 500 timber sawyers are out on strike for a reduction in working hours to 54. ... About 200 women employed by Hudden and Co., tobacco and cigar manufacturers, ceased working in the evening, piece-workers demanding an increase of 2d in the shilling, and day hands and advance of 1s. weekly. ... Nearly 100 scavengers employed by one contractor came out last night. A general strike is threatened in the boot and shoe trade, and the masters meet today.[107]

As well as collecting money for strikers and their families, the committee faced two pressing problems. The first dilemma arose over of how to resolve the difference of opinion that existed regarding which union the dock labourers and riverside workers should join; Dock, Wharf, Riverside and General Labourers' Union or the Gasworkers and General Labourers' Union.

The Strike Committee adopted a seemingly equivocal position on the question of which union the dock labourers should register with. It decided that unskilled labourers, male and female, including dock labourers, should be invited to enrol with the Gasworkers Union 'and that as soon as possible the Dockers be affiliated to their parent Society in London.'[108] Ben Tillett did not

---

104 Workers' Organising Committee Minutes, Oct. 1889-July 1890, Bristol, 26 October 1889.

105 Ibid. Helena Born still held executive office with the Bristol Women's Liberal Association while being active in the Bristol Socialist Society.

106 Workers' Organising Committee Minutes, 27 October 1889.

107 *The Times*, 26 October 1889.

108 Workers' Organising Committee Minutes, 27 October 1889.

accept this decision and within days he, together with John Fox, General Secretary of the Bristol, West of England and South Wales Trade and Provident Society, addressed a meeting of Bristol dockers on this question. At this meeting, Bristol dockers decided unanimously that they would immediately affiliate to, and become a branch of, the London-based Dock, Wharf, Riverside and General Labourers' Union.[109] This decision gave rise to 'considerable unpleasantness'. However, to avoid any discord, Will Thorne withdrew his union's claim on organising dock labourers, leaving the way clear for Ben Tillett's Union.[110]

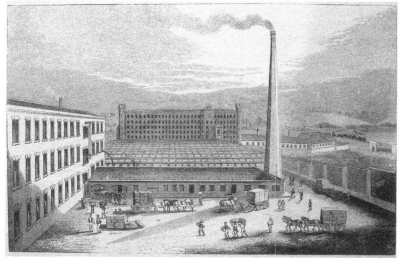

The Great Western Cotton Works

The second difficulty was how best to support the cotton workers (principally women) in their strike at the Great Western Cotton Mill, Barton Hill, who had been successfully organised into the cotton workers' Bristol branch of the Gasworkers and General Labourers' Union. The cotton workers' strike presented a stiffer challenge because of the obdurate position adopted by the management of the company. On 24 October, 1889, at 9am, Miriam Daniell had presented herself, together with a deputation of the workforce, at the Great Western Cotton Works and requested to see George Spafford, the Managing Director. He acceded but made it clear that 'he could not allow her to interfere between the management and the workpeople'.[111] On hearing the demands put forward by the deputation, of which the main claim was the return of the 10% wage cut applied by the company during a trade depression five years earlier, Spafford exclaimed that they were 'unreasonable', rejecting them out of hand. Accordingly, the deputation walked out taking the rest of the workforce with them. By 11am,

---

109   Ibid., 30 October 1889.
110   Ibid., 29 October 1889.
111   *WDP*, 25 October 1889.

1,700 workers had left the premises and paraded two miles from the factory in Barton Hill to the city centre to demonstrate their strength of feeling.[112]

At a meeting of the Strike Committee, held on 28 October, two days after the rally on Clifton Downs, some of its members expressed the view that the cotton operatives should be advised to reduce their demand for a 10% wage increase to 5%. Daniell thought this would be misguided, suggesting that more information was required in order to fully assess the situation. It was, therefore, decided to send Hugh Holmes Gore and Daniell, as a deputation, to visit the Managing Director of the Cotton Mill and see if he was willing to offer any concessions good enough to settle the strike. Francis Gilmore Barnett, a radical liberal, solicitor and the brother of Samuel Augustus Barnett, Canon of Westminster and social reformer, requested that as he was 'personally acquainted' with the Chairman of the Cotton Mill, Sir Joseph Weston, he would approach him, in his 'private capacity' to see what Weston's position was in regard to settling the dispute.[113]

A meeting was arranged and went ahead but the outcome was negative. Gore and Daniell immediately consulted as many of the Strike Committee as they could find, telling them that the only concessions Spafford was offering were in regard to the abolishment of fines in respect to bobbins and windows, access to doctor's records, and the revision of wages in one or two departments. Spafford threatened to close the mill if its employees refused to return to work at the old rate of wages.[114] Barnett reported that his private meeting with Weston served only to confirm Spafford's position. In face of this threat, the Strike Committee decided to assemble the cotton workers that day and advise them 'to go back to work at the old rate of pay subject to the slight concessions Mr Spafford had offered.'[115] This meeting went ahead within hours but on 'the question being put to the meeting they [cotton workers] almost unanimously decided not to go back.' The Strike Committee respected their decision and, for the purpose of raising funds for the strikers, put in place an *ad hoc* sub-committee comprising Miriam Daniell (Treasurer), Helena Born (Assistant Treasurer and Secretary), Gilmore Barnett, Frank Rawle, Robert Weare and Dan Irving.[116] Apart from Barnett, the whole of this sub-committee were members of the Bristol Socialist Society, although Irving also held membership of the Bristol Operatives' Liberal Association.[117]

Within forty-eight hours of the decision to continue the strike, a letter from Charles Helton Tuckett, who was related through marriage to Miriam Daniell, was published in the *Western Daily Press*, holding Daniell accountable for the strike.

---

112 Ibid.

113 Workers' Organising Committee Minutes, 28 October 1889.

114 Ibid., 29 October 1889.

115 Ibid.

116 Ibid. Dan Irving was elected to parliament, in the 1918 General Election, as a Labour MP.

117 Bristol Operatives' Liberal Association was founded in December 1867. Henry Rogers, a shoemaker, and later to become a Bristol Socialist Society member, was the driving force behind this association, Atkinson, 'The Bristol Labour Movement 1868-1906', p. 65.

> [T]here was not a sound of discontent at the cotton factory until the appearance of Mrs Miriam Daniell. The morning Mrs Daniell presented her demands all the girls had been at work as usual, and it was on receiving the reply from the manager that Mrs Daniell retorted "Then I will take them out to the last women." The men as might have been suspected followed in support of this woman.[118]

This brought an immediate response from Daniell: 'I deny utterly the truth of Charles Helton Tuckett's statement. ...The fact is I said to Mr Spafford that probably the girls would come out if their demands were not granted.' She went on to say that the girls 'came out of their own accord as a protest against the "starvation" wages they have been receiving.'[119] Spafford was reputed to have said 'that he would rather burn the mill rather than concede' to his workers' demands.[120]

It was becoming clear that the increasing volume of work taken on by the Strike Committee was falling heavily on the shoulders of Robert Nicol. In order to relieve the situation Vickery and Rawle were co-opted to work full-time with Nicol for one week, commencing 4 November; their wages were to be paid out of the strike funds.[121] Furthermore, the Strike Committee 'considered that for the many hours he [Nicol] was devoting to the duties [he] was very inadequately remunerated'. The Strike Committee decided, therefore, to increase his salary from 30s to £2 a week and that the office would close an hour earlier at 8pm.[122]

The Strike Committee, in the battle to get public opinion on its side, wrote to Reverend W. H. Skinner, Honorary Secretary of the Bristol Ministers Fraternal Society, asking him if he would receive a deputation and allow it to put the case for the striking cotton operatives.[123] Skinner agreed but when the deputation of three cotton workers, and Rawle, arrived at his house they were met by fourty non-conformist ministers who explained that they wanted to hear from both sides in this dispute:

> They [non-conformist ministers] appeared to sympathise with the strikers. ...They manifested considerable sympathy towards Mrs Daniell, with regard to Mr Spafford's statement that she had brought the Cotton workers out, and said they considered Mrs Daniell had done nothing else than an Englishwoman would do.[124]

However, this sympathy evaporated quickly. After taking a day's break in order to meet with the company and check the accounts, a small delegation, of ministers, led by Reverend Glover, returned to inform the Strike Committee that they should tell the strikers to drop their demands and return to work as, in their

---

118 *WDP*, 31 October 1889.

119 Ibid., 1 November 1889.

120 Correspondence from Miriam Daniell and Helena Born to the editor of the *Women's Union Journal*, published 15 November 1889, p. 89.

121 Workers' Organising Committee Minutes, 2 November 1889.

122 Ibid., 4 November 1889.

123 Ibid., 2 November 1889.

124 Ibid., 5 November 1889.

view, any advance in wages was unaffordable.[125] While the Committee disregarded this advice, the seeds of doubt already present were given some succour.[126] On the following morning, at a gathering of about 1,200 striking cotton workers, it was decided to send a request to the company directors asking them to receive a deputation of around thirty, on the following Monday. Meanwhile, the Strike Committee continued to give support and raise money not only for the cotton workers but also for other striking workers, including French polishers, brush makers, pipe makers, coal carriers, scavengers, box makers, cigar makers, animal charcoal and blue factory workers, and the 300 hatters employed at Howes. Born, Weare, Vickery and Rawle were appointed to distribute funds to the striking hatters, who were seeking a rearrangement of their working hours.[127] Moreover, final arrangements were being made for the labour demonstration that was scheduled to take place on the Saturday, and for a church parade on the Sunday. Preparation for the latter entailed contacting the police, who 'promised' to keep the details of the parade confidential.[128]

The idea of a church parade was put to the striking cotton workers on Friday, 8 November and several hundred, mainly women cotton operatives, volunteered to take part. The plan was to parade up to Clifton on Sunday morning, divide into groups and drop into a number of church services, peacefully and in silence, but with their strike banners on display. The plan went ahead. Around 400 strikers paraded to All Saints Church and 300 to Tyndale Baptist Chapel.

> Yesterday [Sunday] many hundreds of strikers walked in procession to Clifton and crowded two fashionable places of worship and made collections at the doors. At All Saints, the cathedral of Ritualism in Clifton, no reference was made to the unwonted advent of the cotton work girls in factory attire. At Tyndale Baptist Chapel the Reverend R. Glover spoke of the improvement in the working men's condition of late years.[129]

This was the same Reverend Glover who had led the deputation of non-conformist ministers in communicating to the Strike Committee that the strikers should drop their demand for advancement in pay and return to work. While church dignitaries remained opposed, this church parade form of petitioning was repeated over the following weeks and would prove effective in gaining support from members of the congregation. Two young, well-educated women, Katherine St John Conway and Enid Stacy, regulars at All Saints Church, were so moved by the appeal of the women that they went to the strike headquarters in St Judes to offer their services. Both joined the Bristol Socialist Society.[130] It

---

125 Ibid., 7 November 1889; *Daily News*, 9 November 1889.

126 Workers' Organising Committee Minutes, 6 November 1889. Gore raised the question as to whether the cotton workers should be balloted as to whether they were willing, in the light of the director's threat to close the mill, to return to work without an advance in wages. Dan Irving suggested the dispute should go to arbitration. These proposals, however, were rejected.

127 Ibid., 7 November 1889.

128 Ibid.

129 *Daily News*, 11 November 1889. See also *WDP*, 11 November 1889.

130 Bryher, *Labour and Socialist Movement in Bristol*, II, pp. 22, 29-30.

was Robert Weare who introduced Conway to Edward Carpenter's writings on socialism. Later she recalled,

> I came under Carpenter's influences as a morbid High Churchwoman with vague humanitarian impulses and the lead he gave me was literally from darkness and bondage out into life and liberty.[131]

Not long afterwards another High Anglican Church woman, Gertrude Dix, would put herself at the disposal of the Strike Committee. She was already active in the Clifton and Bristol Christian Socialist Society and, in 1891, joined the Bristol Socialist Society following the decision of the two organisations to merge their efforts in order to offer 'greater opportunities for usefulness.'[132] All three women became prominent figures in the British labour movement as speakers and writers. Dix wrote two novels, *The Girl from the Farm* (1895) and *The Image Breakers* (1900); the later drew loosely on some of the events she experienced as a socialist activist.[133]

The directors of the cotton works opened their doors to a delegation of workers on the following Tuesday, 12 November, only to tell them that the company's position had not changed and that they would not accede to the worker's demands. This message was conveyed back to the workforce. When a vote was taken as to whether they would return to work at the old rate of pay, the strikers, by a large majority, voted to stay out.[134] Bristol and Liverpool dockers refused to handle the cotton company's materials, and the strike continued for several more days. The Strike Committee desperately increased its fund-raising efforts. They were able to recruit a little help from outside their socialist network. Two non-conformist ministers, Reverend J. R. Graham and Reverend Thomas William Harvey, member of the Church Socialist League, and the first vicar of St Agnes, which was located in the heart of the inner city working class area of St Pauls, supported the strikers by arranging collections, as well as making personal donations to the strike fund. Harvey 'had a brief for a class not nearly enough considered by the Church — the intelligent artisan.'[135] Also contributing valuable assistance was Born's associate in the Women's Liberal Association, Anna Priestman, who opened a soup kitchen for the strikers and their families.[136]

Tensions rose, however, as the pressure increased on the cotton operatives to concede defeat. On the 22 November, the Committee Minutes record that the Reverend Harvey's brother-in-law, Reverend J. M. Wilson, headmaster of Clifton College,[137] sent an 'insulting' letter to Helena Born in her role as the

---

131 Quoted in Bevir, *British Socialism and American Romanticism*, p. 899.

132 E. D. Girdlestone, *Christian Socialism in England, The Dawn* (Andover-Harvard Theological Library, first published in Cambridge, Massachusetts: Progress Publishing Company, May 1890), p. 16.

133 See Chapter One. For an informative and fascinating account of Dix's life up to the First World War see S. Rowbotham, *Rebel Crossing* (London: Verso, forthcoming).

134 *Daily News*, 15 November 1889.

135 H. C. A. Colvile, *Thomas William Harvey, Prophet and Priest*, (Bristol: J. W. Arrowsmith, 1918), pp. 32, 64.

136 Workers' Organising Committee Minutes, 11 November 1889; Bryher, *Labour and Socialist Movement in Bristol*, II, p. 19.

137 Clifton College, an elite public school, was founded in 1862.

secretary of the Strike Committee.[138] Moreover, Wilson sent an open letter to striking cotton workers, published in the *Western Daily Press* and the *Bristol Mercury*, heavily criticising the committee, and telling the strikers that they had no choice but to return to work at the old rate of pay. The letter not only defended the directors' right to manage but said that workers should place unquestioning trust in them, because they were the only people who knew and understood the business, and that they had the employees' best interests at heart.

> You [employees] must leave the judgement of all such matters in the hands of the directors, and when, with full knowledge, with large experience, such men tell you that it is of necessity a choice between the present rate of wages or none you must accept their word...
>
> Believe me, it is safer to trust the word of RESPONSIBLE AND HONOURABLE MEN of the stamp of your directors than it is to any one else who is busying himself, or herself, in this matter. And you know it so. You cannot really believe all that is put before you in speeches, even though you may applaud it at the time. You must know that the directors are TRUSTED FOR THE MONEY which has been entrusted to them, and they have no right to defraud the shareholders of their just claims for interest.
>
> These are foolish people [organising committee] with WARM HEARTS AND WEAK HEADS who tell you that if you only hold out you will win... YOU HAVE BEEN MISLED, as all Bristol knows, not wilfully but in ignorance.[139]

Two days later, on the Sunday, 24 November, another church parade was held. The strikers marched to and presented themselves at churches in Clifton and Redland. At the Emmanuel Church, Clifton, the Reverend T. G. Luckock addressed the strikers directly, making his position clear in these words, 'Would those who gave them [strikers] advice give them work if they lost their present work by listening to their advice.' At the Trinity Wesleyan Chapel, Redland, the Reverend G. S. Weston suggested that the strikers read Wilson's letter published in the *Western Daily Press*.[140] It is little wonder that Daniell and Nicol, in a subsequent pamphlet on new trade unionism, would express bitterness against the leaders of Christianity,

> [T]he Church has failed to respond to the new movement, and where it has enunciated itself in regard to strikes it has been a Heavenly medium for a worldly voice pronouncing itself boldly on the side of the rich, instead of being, as it once used to be, an earthly medium for a Heavenly voice encouraging the oppressed poor and rebuking the wealthy. The exception of Cardinal Manning and a few others only prove the rule.[141]

---

138 Workers' Organising Committee Minutes, 22 November 1889.

139 Extracts from a open letter to striking cotton workers at Great Western Cotton Mill from Reverend J. M. Wilson, headmaster of Clifton College, published in the *WDP*, 22 November 1889.

140 *WDP*, 25 November 1889.

141 M. Daniell and R. A. Nicol, *The new trade unionism; its relation to the old; and the conditions of its success*, (Bristol: Pamphlet, 1890), p. 14, London School of Economics selected pamphlets. Cardinal Manning was sympathetic to the

Reverend Harvey also took this view. His was one of the few lone voices from the churches in Bristol that supported the labour cause. He 'threw himself into the movement with all his soul.'[142] In 1900, the Bristol Socialist Society in expressing its regret that Reverend Harvey was leaving the city paid, tribute to his contribution and 'the earnestness with which he has laboured and used his influence for the upraising and the bettering of the social life of the people'.[143]

The day after the cotton workers' church parade, the Strike Committee's response to Wilson's letter, written by Robert Weare, himself a Christian Socialist, was published. Weare denied that the Committee advised the cotton workers to strike, explaining that their demands were not 'suggested by the committee, but by the workpeople themselves.' Moreover, he stressed that three weeks previously, the Committee had recommended, as Wilson well knew, that the strikers should to return to work; advice that was given purely on the grounds of preventing any more suffering. But the strikers indicated that 'they would rather go to the Union [Workhouse], or to prison, or starve, than go back to work under the old conditions'. In answer to Wilson's contention, that shareholders must get a dividend of at least 5½%, Weare replied that the strikers 'now rise against it, and say it is no inexorable and divine law, but a transitory precept to which we no longer submit.'[144] The implications of the cotton workers' strike were beginning to go beyond protest against their immediate conditions and shifting towards a rejection of the profit system.

The day before Wilson sent his letter to the press, a deputation from the Strike Committee had gone to the cotton company directors, and, though the meeting had been previously scheduled, the directors pulled out and asked for the strikers' demands to be put in writing instead. The deputation compiled a written list of its demands, which, after authorisation from the Strike Committee, was presented to the company directors. On the morning of Tuesday, 26 November, after due deliberation, the company submitted their response. While reiterating it would not contemplate an advance in wages, the directors of the cotton works did concede many of the other demands made by the strikers; it was accepted that fines for damage, (other than wilful), to windows and payments for bobbins be abolished; that 'the engine be stopped at the proper time for meals, viz., 8.30am, 1pm, 5.30pm'; overtime for mechanics be paid at time-and-a-quarter; that a better quality cotton be used, (less breakages enabled windows to be opened to improve ventilation — temperatures could reach 100° Fahrenheit); and that none of the strikers would be dismissed or refused work. 'These replies were deemed satisfactory' and the Strike Committee decided to recommend acceptance of the company's commitments and that strikers be advised to return to work.[145]

---

dockers' cause. He was an important member of the Mansion House Committee that persuaded the employers to meet most of the dockers' demands.

142   Colvile, *Thomas William Harvey, Prophet and Priest*, p. 78.

143   Ibid., p. 84.

144   *WDP*, 25 November 1889.

145   Workers' Organising Committee Minutes, 26 November 1889.

The Reverend Trebilco, a Liberal radical, offered the Russell Town Congregational Chapel to the Strike Committee, as a large enough venue where they could report back to the cotton operatives the company's latest position. The meeting went ahead on Tuesday afternoon. Leaders of the Strike Committee, including Daniell and Born, were present, as was Clementina Black, a socialist from London, who was concerned about the low pay and bad conditions of women workers. She was there in her capacity as the honorary secretary of the Women's Trade Union Association. This was yet another attempt to organise women workers and had been created in October 1889 as a result of dissatisfaction with the existing organisation for women workers, by the Women's Trade Union and Provident League, the successor of Emma Paterson's Women's Protective and Provident League.[146] It was supported by the leading New Unionist, Tom Mann.

After an hour and a half's discussion the resolution to accept the company's terms and return to work was put to the meeting and was passed by a majority, although not without some rancour.[147] This result was seized upon by opponents of the strike, such as Emily Sturge, founder member of the Bristol Women's Liberal Association and a supporter, like Agnes Beddoe, of the Bristol Association of Working Women. In an address, entitled 'Women and the Labour Movement', delivered to the Bristol Women's Liberal Association at Redland Park Hall, Bristol on 16 December 1889, Sturge declared that if there had already been a women's union at the cotton works 'the employers might have been met, and a fair arrangement come to which would have prevented such a strike.'[148] The Bristol Women's Liberal Association and the Bristol Association of Working Women advocated women workers' organisation as a basis for industrial peace. They argued that the existence of unions made negotiations possible; seemingly intractable disputes might then be resolved by 'the peaceful work of Boards of Arbitration and Conciliation.'[149] Membership of the Bristol Women's Liberal Association and Bristol Association of Working Women overlapped, making for a cross-class engagement susceptible to the hegemony of the Bristol elite. Mary Talbot, General Secretary of the Bristol Association of Working Women, for instance, was the sister-in-law of the Reverend Wilson.[150] In *A Plea for Women's Trade Unions*, Talbot appealed to 'educated women' to set in motion union organising campaigns so that eventually, when membership levels were sufficient, working women could undertake this work themselves. Stressing the 'educative power of association', [151] Talbot saw involvement in trade unions in terms of moral uplift and collective self-help. By demonstrating the moral superiority of their members, they would, she believed, 'appeal to the

146 E. Mappen, *Helping Women at Work: The Women's Industrial Council 1889-1914* (London: Hutchinson, 1985) p. 13; L. Glage, *Clementina Black: A Study in Social History and Literature* (Heidelberg: Carl Winter, 1981), p. 35.

147 Workers' Organising Committee Minutes, 26 November 1889.

148 *WDP*, 17 December 1889.

149 M. Talbot, *A Plea for Women's Trade Unions*, (Bristol: Pamphlet, 1892), p. 6.

150 Ibid. In a second marriage, following the death of his first wife, Reverend Wilson married Mary's younger sister Georgina, *BM*, 27 March 1883.

151 Talbot, *A Plea for Women's Trade Unions*, p. 7.

hearts of those whose chief desire for women, is their moral and spiritual good.'[152] Echoing these sentiments, Talbot gave an example of one union woman's experience,

> I do wish you could see our young Union girls manage their own club. But to see them now, unless you had seen them two years ago, would only shew [sic] you half... they learned pride and self-respect through their Union. ... The self-respecting, intelligent girl at her club, will carry these qualities into her life in her home, in the street, in the workshop.[153]

Events in the autumn of 1889 were to reveal a very different source of education through action. Indeed once roused the cotton workers themselves would be the ones pushing for continuing resistance.

Initially, the strategy of organising women and men together seemed to be endorsed by the experiences of autumn 1889. Certain tensions did, however, remain. After the turmoil of the strike wave died down, these would begin to surface. Firstly, while the Bristol socialists accepted the need to organise women workers, they were not all fully committed to women's equality. Secondly, some of them shared with other socialists in the country at large a scepticism about the significance of trade union action, which was often dismissed as a form of economic reformism. Within a couple of days of the cotton operative's walk-out, the socialist James Watts Treasure, active in trade union organising groups, wrote, in a letter published in the *Western Daily Press*, that 'strikes will only make the condition more untenable for the unemployed.' He went on to argue that only a 'revolutionary change in society' could 'benefit all concerned.'[154] Thirdly, not all socialists were united; on pragmatic grounds Hugh Holmes Gore was reluctant to give his support to the Fry's workers because 'he felt he was not justified in asking terms the employers could not concede.'[155] Gore saw their demands as unrealistic.

6

The militant enthusiasm of the workers themselves was forcing the pace, yet they lacked the funds of established craft unions. The Strike Committee, and indeed the Bristol Socialist Society, thus found themselves responsible for many peoples' livelihoods. Strenuous efforts to raise funds were made but these were clearly stop-gap measures. It became evident that some alternative was imperative.

Arbitration of disputes was being mooted by Liberals and some employers in Bristol were prepared to cooperate. After the cotton strike was settled, an editorial in the *Western Daily Press* advocated the establishment of an 'Arbitration Council' to which future industrial disputes might be referred. By the end of November, Trade Union leaders, the Strike Committee, and the

---

152 Ibid., pp. 7, 10.
153 Ibid., p. 7
154 *WDP*, 26 October 1889.
155 Letter from Robert Weare published in the *WDP*, 25 October 1889.

Bristol Socialist Society, confident they could bargain from a position of strength, were also open to the idea.[156] The move towards arbitration coincided with an inter-union dispute after a strike by 7,000 dockers in Bristol, 460 in Sharpness and 1,000 in Gloucester demanding the elimination of foreign labour (i.e. seamen) in the loading and discharging of ships' cargoes. Their union, the London-based Dock, Wharf, Riverside and General Labourers' Union, failed to secure support from the Gasworkers and General Labourers' Union. Friction between the two unions still existed over the way in which Tillett had persuaded Bristol dock workers to leave the Gasworkers' Union and join his organisation,[157] and to compound the situation support was not forthcoming from National Amalgamated Sailors' and Firemen's Union either.[158] This weakened the position of the dockers' union and Bristol's Mayor was called in to mediate.[159] The strike was called off after five days. Nonetheless, the dockers secured a commitment that every endeavour would be made to eradicate the practice of using foreign labour, with a promise of a review after six months. The employers also pledged to move immediately towards the hiring of dock labour directly by the merchant or ship-owner, thereby cutting out the middleman. This was viewed as an important concession and this partial victory saw thousands of dockers celebrate the end of the strike with a procession through the streets of Bristol that finished on Clifton Downs, where they were addressed by Ben Tillett and other union leaders.[160]

Bristol socialists had been involved in yet another dispute that autumn. On 28 October 1889, 2,000 Bristol shoemakers had walked out on an unofficial strike demanding a 10% increase in pay. A meeting was held that evening at which union leaders persuaded strikers to return to work pending the outcome of negotiations, which were to be held later that week. At these negotiations, a temporary settlement was concluded comprising a 5% advance in wages, and a signed statement intimating that in the classification process — used to rate the order of difficulty in making different grades of boots and shoes — wages would correspond with that paid in the industry in Northampton for men's work and Leicester for women's work.[161] This agreement was made between the Bristol, West of England and South Wales Boot Manufacturers' Association, representing most but not all firms in Bristol, and the National Union of Boot Riveters and Finishers, representing men and women in the industry.

On 21 December, 1889, several weeks after the strike settlement, and following a breakdown in talks over the classification process, the manufacturers' association imposed a lockout.[162] W. J. Gale, its chairman, argued that 'classification should be a Bristol classification only' and the lockout was implemented due to the refusal of workers in the industry to consent to the

---

156 *WDP*, 28 November 1889.

157 Ibid., 29 November 1889.

158 Atkinson, 'The Bristol Labour Movement', p. 214.

159 *WDP*, 30 November 1889.

160 *Daily News*, 3 December 1889; *WDP*, 3 and 4 December 1889.

161 *Daily News*, 29 and 31 October 1889; *BM*, 2 January 1890.

162 *WDP*, 23, 24, 26 December 1889.

The police response to the gas workers' strike of October 1889 lampooned in *The Bristol Magpie*.

forming of a permanent Board of Arbitration. The Bristol socialist shoemaker, John Gregory, responded by stressing that the workers would only agree to this after the matter of classification was settled.[163] The boot and shoe workers belonged to the older craft unionist tradition and were as proud of their skills as

163 *Daily News,* 23 December 1889.

of their union. At a mass meeting of Bristol boot and shoe workers, held on 1 January 1890, William Inskip, General Secretary of the National Union of Boot Riveters and Finishers, assured those present that,

> He would remind the employers that they were not dealing with a body of unskilled workmen, but men who could pack their kits under their arms and get work in any town (loud applause). The men were supported by a combination which had withstood every attack, and the executive were never more united as to the necessity of a real advance in wages being forthcoming for a body of men than for the Bristol men (applause).[164]

The National Union of Boot Riveters and Finishers, and its Bristol branch, had been formed in 1874 as mechanisation (stitching and riveting) began to replace hand-craftwork in footwear production. John Gregory had been its first secretary. Factories were set up first in the centre of Bristol, and then in outlying districts, such as Kingswood, to house the innovative machines and closely supervise the work of machine operatives in order to secure maximum output. Nonetheless, up to the end of the nineteenth century key parts of the labour process still rested on outworkers, who completed the finishing of the footwear for low wages.[165]

By 1889, the union had become well-established at the larger concerns in Bristol, such as Derham Brothers, Brightman Brothers and Hutchins and May.[166] The national union had £22,000 available to assist those members involved in strikes or lock-outs, although its policy was 'to avoid strikes.'[167] Thus, the union was able to sustain its negotiating position without undue financial hardship to its members. It conducted the running of the dispute outside the purview of the Workers' Organising Committee.[168] However, the manufacturers' lockout affected around 8,000 boot and shoe workers, located at home or in small units. The vast majority were not union members, and included substantial numbers of women and children. Their desperate predicament meant extra funds had to be found. This brought the shoemakers into alliance with the New Unionists.

As 1889 drew to a close the Bristol socialists could look back on an extraordinary three months of industrial unrest. The turmoil raised hopes of a new era in labour relations in the city. Despite the problems faced by the cotton workers and the boot and shoe outworkers there had been dramatic successes. These, along with the experience of defying employers, had created a spirit of confidence among the Bristol working class, women as well as men, unskilled, semi-skilled and unorganised as well as skilled and organised.

'New Unionism' with its message of inclusion to all workers had arrived in Bristol. This new model of trade unionism would result in conflicts with existing

---

164 *BM*, 2 January 1890.

165 J. Press, 'G. B. Britton and Footwear Manufacturing in Bristol and Kingswood, 1870-1973' in Harvey and Press, *Studies in the Business History of Bristol*, pp. 213-18.

166 Ibid.

167 *BM*, interview with William Inskip, General Secretary of National Union of Boot Riveters and Finishers, 2 January 1890.

168 The Strike Committee had re-launched itself as the Workers' Organising Committee on 4 January 1890.

unions but what was also beginning to emerge was an interesting amalgam between 'new' and 'old' craft unions. This would be evident in the ongoing boot and shoe strike during the New Year.

How to organise the unorganised? How best to defend women workers and how to ensure that workers' interests were fairly represented on the Board of Arbitration and Conciliation were all issues with which the socialist organisers would continue to struggle over the course of 1890.

4

The Bristol Strike Wave of 1889-1890: Socialists, New Unionists and New Women

Part Two: Days of Doubt

•

Mike Richardson

1

The previous chapter, *Days of Hope*, described the series of unprecedented strikes and industrial unrest that began in September 1889 and continued until the end of the year. It addressed the experience of the Bristol's working class, women as well as men, and the ways in which Bristol socialists and trade unionists responded to what were unmistakably signs of serious discontent. The report of the Bristol Strike Committee published in March 1890, best sums up the feelings of labour activists at the time:

> The Bristol labour revolt against the tyranny of Capitalism was the logical outcome of the successful campaigns of the London gas stokers and dockers, and was the first utterance by the mass of the people of the socialistic truths, that "if any will not work neither shall he eat," and that the workers must have the full result of their labour. With very few exceptions the workers gained honourable victories, their demands being indisputably just, and merely a tithe of their rights. ... Compared with other cities in England which have passed through similar crises the Bristol record of strikes is a very hopeful one, and the Committee confidently affirms that the enlightened view held by the majority of working men and women of this city augur well for the labour movement of the West of England.[1]

This chapter charts the events and issues facing unions and socialist organisers, as employers, having recovered somewhat from the 'surprise' outburst of strikes in 1889, became better organised.

The successes achieved in the autumn of 1889 had begun to shift the scepticism within the Bristol Socialist Society towards strikes. Instead of focusing on propaganda and education about socialist ideas alone, they started to

---

[1]   The Bristol Strike Committee, Miriam Daniell, Treasurer, Helena Born, Secretary, *The People's Press,* 22 March 1890.

place a higher priority on support and agitation among workers. The lock-out in the boot and shoe industry pointed to the potential of a combination of skilled, organised workers with the unskilled and unorganised, using publicity, demonstrations and arbitration. It also encouraged forms of social unionism, with links to the wider community. Regular collections were organised by the National Union of Boot Riveters and Finishers to help outworkers, many of whom were women. Strike funds were distributed at St Agnes mission hall, which was kindly made available by the Reverend Harvey. The Union took up the tactic of regular processions, adopted in 1889 by the cotton workers. Headed by the women operatives, they attracted thousands as they passed through the principal streets of the city. One such procession of 1,500 workers, led by union officials, was actually restricted to non-unionists; they marched to the out-of-town boot and shoe manufacturing district of Kingswood and back via Hanham to the city.[2] Socialist, John Gregory played a leading part in his capacity as a member of the union, as did Albert Vincent.[3] And, on the evening of 12 January, at the culmination of a torchlight procession some 5,000 strong, Miriam Daniell, who had clearly become a local heroine, was greeted with 'loud cheers' when she addressed the crowd with the call for 'shorter hours of labour and more wages.' She declared that 'Eight hours a day was quite long enough to work. Capitalists must be content with less profit, and the workers must have more comfortable homes.'[4] Involvement in labour agitation meant members of the Socialist Society had gained a reputation as sympathisers and supporters locally. They brought the important issue of time into the dispute. Moreover, women were very active in this rebellion and Daniell had played a leading part.

In January 1890, the Boot and Shoe manufacturers' association finally agreed to the workers' demand that classification (the range of skill requirements in the making of boots and shoes) should be dealt with before proceeding to arbitration. After rejecting Bristol's Mayor, Charles Wathen — known in the labour movement as an anti-trade unionist — as an arbitrator, the union's choice was Moses Philip Manfield, a boot manufacturer from Nottingham, who would later become a Liberal MP. It was agreed that after the completion of the classification process, which determined how wage rates were set, he would make the final judgement on all the outstanding questions in dispute.[5] This process was concluded to the satisfaction of both parties, and Bristol's shoe operatives returned to work on 18 January. Soon after, a permanent Board of Arbitration was established for the Bristol boot trade. Setting the terms of arbitration thus became to be seen as an advance for the labour cause.

Arbitration was not new in fact,[6] but the surge in the number of labour disputes revitalised employers' interest in mediation and arbitration to resolve disputes, especially in cases where firms were represented by employer

---

2   *BM*, 9 January 1890.

3   See reports in the *BM*, 1-18 January 1890.

4   *BM*, 13 January 1890.

5   *BM*, 9 January 1890.

6   See J. H. Porter, 'Wage bargaining under conciliation agreements, 1860-1914', *Economic History Review* 23 (1970): 460-475.

organisations. Workers in diverse Bristol industries were thus able to compel employers to negotiate with their workforces rather than rely on either authoritarian or benevolent forms of paternalism. The Bristol Chamber of Commerce, following steps made by the Associated Chambers of Commerce to encourage the establishment of Boards of Conciliation and Arbitration across the country,[7] raised the prospect of forming a Bristol Board of Conciliation and Arbitration. However, it was to be June 1890, in a quite different climate of labour relations, before the first meeting was held between interested parties (employer and union representatives) to consider a draft scheme.[8]

2

In January the *ad hoc* Strike Committee was replaced by the Workers' Organising Committee. Many participants of the Strike Committee were elected as members of this new body and the Socialist Society again played a leading role. A set of objectives was framed and adopted that gave precedence to assisting, by all means possible, the organisation of workers into trade unions, 'to endeavour to bring about a federation of labour' and 'to promote lectures … on the Social question so far as it affected Capital and Labour.'[9] The socialists thus sought to broaden the disputes by placing them in a wider context.

The clothing trade was one of the largest employers of labour in Bristol, with a high proportion of women workers,[10] and the first target of the new committee that January was to take up the organisation of women tailoresses. It is notable that the Workers' Organising Committee brought together old and new unions in this campaign. On January 13, under the auspices of the Amalgamated Society of Tailors, the Clothiers' Cutters' Association, the Bristol District of the Gasworkers and General Labourers' Union, the Bristol Trades Council, and the Workers' Organising Committee, a meeting, specifically for tailoresses, was arranged and advertised through the distribution of a handbill. Thirty nine of the attendees at this meeting enrolled in a new tailoresses' union, provisionally hailed as the female branch of the National Union of Working Women of Great Britain and Ireland, Bristol District. Miriam Daniell and Helena Born were adopted as honorary secretaries, *pro tem*.[11] Following this meeting another handbill was distributed, informing readers of the place and opening hours where those wishing to join the union could enrol, and reasons why tailoresses should do so.[12]

The meeting caused a furore. First, William Taylor, of the firm Taylor, Tucker and Co., Broadmead, Bristol, challenged the claim made by Robert Tovey (Clothiers' Cutters' Association),[13] who presided over the meeting of

7   *BM*, 15 January 1890.

8   *BM*, 13 June 1890.

9   Workers' Organising Committee Minutes, 19 January 1890.

10 B. Atkinson, 'The Bristol Labour Movement 1868-1906' (D.Phil., Oxford University, 1969), p. 15.

11 Ibid.; *BM*, 14 January 1890.

12 Copy of this handbill, Tamiment Library/Wagner Archives, New York: I am grateful to Sheila Rowbotham for providing me with this reference.

13 Tovey had been the first Labour councillor to be elected in Bristol's St. Paul's Ward, 1887.

tailoresses, that in the past few decades there had been 'a progressive decrease' in the wages of clothing workers,[14] a debate that continued on the pages of the local press for weeks. Second, a contest materialised over which union the tailoresses should join. Mary Talbot, articulated, in a calm dignified letter to the local newspaper, betraying only the slightest hint of surprise or annoyance, the intentions of the Bristol Association of Working Women:

> Whilst wishing well to every sincere effort to improve the condition of working women, we, who are attached to the principles and working of the older trade union, believe that a union which does not offer benefits in sickness, etc., or when out of work (except on strike), has not in it the power to retain its members permanently. We therefore believe that there is still room for our effort to extend our union, and are prepared to work steadily to increase our members and to attract those who are not already enrolled in the new union.[15]

Robert Tovey

A public meeting of the Bristol Association of Working Women, which, like its sister body, the Women's Trade Union Provident League,[16] was still stressing welfare over militancy,[17] was convened on 28 January. Its purpose was to explain the objects of the association, and how it differed from the new union for tailoresses established two weeks previously. It placed the emphasis on Boards of Arbitration over organisation.[18]

In contrast, on behalf of the new tailoresses' union, Helena Born had taken on the task of searching out new recruits from home workers in the clothing industry scattered in and around Bristol. Helen Tufts described the arduous work that was undertaken by Born with great enthusiasm and determination:

> Week after week she labored [sic] hopefully in the good cause. From house to house she passed, striving to arouse interest in the union. It was no uncommon day's work for her to tramp thirty miles, scouring the country on her self-imposed mission.[19]

---

14   *BM*, 16 January 1890.

15   Letter from Mary Talbot published in *BM*, 17 January 1890.

16   See Chapter 3.

17   P. Levine, *Victorian Feminism 1850-1900* (London: Hutchinson Education, 1987), p. 113.

18   *BM*, 29 January 1890.

19   H. Tufts, 'biographical introduction' in H. Born, *Whitman's Ideal Democracy and other Writings* (Boston: Everett Press,

Dan Irving

After several meetings a set of rules were drawn up, printed and allocated to the membership of what came to be called the Bristol Tailoresses' branch of the Bristol District of the National Union of Gasworkers and General Labourers of Great Britain and Ireland. The District Secretary of the GWGLU was Robert Allan Nicol, who had proved himself as organising secretary of the Strike Committee, a role which had ceased at the end of November 1889.[20] However, the motivating force behind this particular organising project came from Helena Born and Robert Tovey. Born did the groundwork, toiling to recruit new members, many of whom were scattered, while Tovey took on the propaganda war in the local press, conflicting not only with the tailoresses' employer William Taylor, but also with Mary Talbot over whether the tailoresses should join the new union or the Bristol Association of Working Women. A proposal for a means of resolving this matter appeared in a letter to the local press from another stalwart of this association, Agnes Beddoe. She advocated the calling of a conference on the matter.[21] Talbot exclaimed in response that 'she should hail with joy any united conference.'[22] This suggestion was supported by Francis Gilmore Barnett who, acting as mediator, raised the issue with the Workers' Organising Committee. Daniell and Dan Irving were elected to represent the committee at such a conference, but there is no evidence that it ever took place.[23]

The organisation of women workers was notoriously difficult and disputes over how to best go about the task had occurred through the 1870s and '80s. In 1890 disagreement about the relationship of women to trade unions combined with conflict over two models of trade unionism. On 24 January an anonymous correspondent in the *Western Daily Press* presented this as a stark clash between the old and new unions:

> Of the simultaneous movements now going forward in Bristol one seems
> to spring out of fear for the necessity of constant strikes, the other out of

---

1902), p. xix.

20   The Rules of the Bristol Tailoresses' Branch of the Bristol District of the National Union of Gasworkers and General Labourers of Great Britain and Ireland, Tamiment Library/Wagner Archives, New York: I am grateful to Sheila Rowbotham for providing me with this reference.

21   *WDP*, 3 February 1890.

22   *Women's Penny Paper*, 8 February 1890.

23   Workers' Organising Committee minutes, 6 February 1890.

anticipation of increased mutual respect between employers and employed. The vital question is which will promote the aim that both have in view of the increased self-dependence of women and improvement in the condition of labour.[24]

This sharp polarisation between 'new' and 'old' trade unionism over-simplified a relationship which in Bristol was more complex. Indeed Robert Tovey, who had been active before 'New Unionism', berated this correspondent contending that his or her statement was 'unwarranted' and not based on facts. He then went on to accuse the Bristol Association of Working Women — that was in the process of reorganisation — of being disingenuous in advocating union independence and the self-dependence of women when it was accepting money from Cliftonians to pay expenses required for reorganisation and recruiting tailoresses.[25] Mary Talbot's rejoinder to this reiteration of the old taunt of middle-class intervention was to 'disclaim any notion of patronage or charitable assistance to the union by the request I have made to some Clifton friends for money to meet the initial expenses of re-organising our union.'[26]

Despite the free publicity the competing unions received in the local press, the series of public meetings, run independently by both sides, and the hard work put in by Born cold calling on tailoresses in their own homes, these efforts to organise tailoresses in sufficient numbers failed.[27] Born and Daniell were forced to admit defeat and the Bristol Association of Working Women would fare no better, by 1894 its total membership was a meagre 39.[28] Unlike the cotton workers, many of the 4,000 or so tailoresses were working at home and therefore isolated, which made it difficult to build links with co-workers. Moreover, women who could sew were never in short supply. Discouragingly the tailoresses proved too difficult to organise. Other concerns, however, were occupying the minds of the Workers' Organising Committee.

3

Early in 1890, a second strike broke out at John Lysaght's galvanising iron works. During the busy Christmas period the firm had hired extra hands to ensure that customers got their orders on time. After Christmas trade slackened and the company decided to shed some of its labour force. But instead of following the custom and practice of laying-off recently employed work hands it took the course of sacking some long-serving ones. One of the new hands retained was not a member of the union. On Monday morning, 20 January, a deputation prevailed on the factory manager, alleging that the firm's decision to discharge some of the older workers was because they 'had too much to say in

---

24 Anonymous Letter, *WDP*, 24 January 1890.

25 Ibid. Bristol Association of Working Women was in the process of rewriting its rules and re-registering the union under the 1871 Trade Union Act, in order to legitimise its activities and protect its funds.

26 Ibid., 25 January 1890.

27 Letter from Edward Watson, Fabian member of the Bristol Socialist Society, published in *BM*, 18 December 1890.

28 A. A. Bulley and M. Whitley, *Women's Work* (Montana, USA.: Kessinger Legacy Reprints, first published London: Methuen, 1894), p. 91.

the last strike',[29] demanding that the one non-union new hand be replaced with a long-standing union member. The firm rejected this call and later that day, after a meeting of the galvanisers' branch of the Gasworkers and General Labourers' Union, 350 workers employed in the galvanising shop at Lysaght's struck against the use of non-union labour. The following morning strikers attended a meeting at the British Workman Coffee House and drew up demands to be put to the company by a deputation in the afternoon.

The John Lysaght Limited Netham Ironworks in 1905.

Firstly, the strikers' called for the reinstatement of all the long-serving hands who had been sacked, along with assurances that the criterion for any future lay-offs would be based on selecting employees with the shortest length of service first. Their second stipulation was that all the men currently employed, and all future employees, must join the Gasworkers and General Labourers' Union. Effectively this was a demand for a closed shop. When a deputation delivered these demands to the company they were told in no uncertain terms that unless they returned to work their grievances would not be heard and the works would be closed. The company, moreover, maintained that the settlement terms of September 1889 strike stipulated that employment may be terminated only after a week's notice by either side.

Another meeting of the strikers was held that afternoon with Nicol and Daniell in attendance. In his role as District Secretary of the Gasworkers' and General Labour Union, Nicol agreed that the men should not have struck without giving a week's notice. 'He firmly believed that they ought to be fair in

---

29   *BM*, 22 January 1890.

this way'.[30] However, Frank Rawle, one of the strikers, disputed this, insisting 'that there was no agreement signed for a seven days' notice on either side'.[31] The strikers refused to return to work. Thereupon the company closed the works, this meant that with the exception of 50 men working in the spelter and roofing works, an arm of the business that was not involved in the dispute, the whole workforce was locked out.

Neither side would initiate talks. Demonstrations led by a Lysaght's brass band were mounted daily and regular meetings were held. At one of these gatherings, John White, Honorary Secretary of the Bristol branch of the Dockers' Union, suggested that the dispute be referred to arbitration, naming the Mayor as possible arbitrator. This proposition was rejected by the strikers at a specially convened meeting in the evening of Friday 24 January. At this meeting an *ad hoc* Strike Committee was established. Yet again Miriam Daniell and Helena Born were appointed financial secretaries with Robert Tovey, Treasurer, and Robert Allan Nicol, General Secretary.[32] Incredibly, Born still found time to wax and shine the floor of their house in Louisa Street in preparation for a visit from Edward Carpenter who was on a short stay in Bristol.[33] On Sunday Carpenter addressed around 250 Lysaghts' strikers at Shaftesbury Hall, St Philips, after they had attended a church service at Bristol Cathedral.[34] A few days later, before the company plans were disclosed, Robert Sharland issued a call to arms, urging the strikers 'to be united, and to resist any attempt to break up the union', while Nicol implored that 'they must not give in on any account'.[35]

Nevertheless, the union was the first to break; within a week or so it dropped its opposition to talks and called on the company to receive a deputation. This advance and subsequent ones were rebuffed. It soon became clear why. The company had taken advantage of the strike to initiate the modernisation of its galvanising plant. Over the course of a couple of weeks it dismantled the existing plant and began to reassemble it, introducing new methods of production. This new production process conveniently enabled the company to obtain a patent protection. Many of the old skills of work hands were made obsolete.[36] The company was learning quickly. It had devised an effective plan to defeat the union, and gain competitive advantage, by increasing control over the labour process. Under these new circumstances the galvaniser's branch of the Gasworkers and General Labourers' Union was impotent. Realising the difficult position it was now in, the galvaniser's branch turned to the Bristol Trades Council for help. The Trades Council wrote to the company requesting mediation as a way forward in resolving the dispute. The company politely refused.[37] It had already put into operation the hiring of new hands selected on

---

30   Ibid.
31   *BM*, 23 January 1890.
32   *BM*, 25 January 1890.
33   Tufts, op. cit. p. xvii.
34   *BM*, 27 January 1890.
35   *BM*, 30 January 1890.
36   *BM*, 10 February 1890.
37   *BM*, 15 February 1890.

the basis of what the company thought were the men 'best fitted to work on the new lines'.[38]

Resigned to defeat, strikers returned to work in large numbers; 240 were taken on, leaving around 100 without work. Rumours arose over an alleged maladministration of the strike fund, causing a rift between the men and the Strike Committee; Miriam Daniell was the main target of these allegations, which were made by Frank Rawle.[39] To satisfy any doubters, the audited accounts of the Galvanisers' Strike Committee were published in the local press.[40] The accusation was without substance, however the cloud of suspicion persisted in a climate of defeat. The cotton workers' branch of the Gasworkers and General Labourers' Union pressed for an inquiry into Rawle's complaint against 'a certain member of the committee' concerning financial irregularities, maintaining it was unfounded. The result of an inquiry did indeed find that his allegations were untrue, and Rawle was expelled from the Organising Committee in April 1890.[41]

There were a few other significant disputes in the first half of 1890, such as the strikes at Malago Vale Colliery,[42] the quarrymen's strike at Fishponds and Stapleton, and the associated strike of 90 masons and 100 mason's labourers at the extension works of the Bristol Lunatic Asylum at the end of March and early April.[43] The Workers' Organising Committee were heavily involved in supporting the mason's labourers; coordinating street collections and directing meetings. As well as supporting striking workers, members of the Committee struggled to think through the strategic direction of the Bristol Socialist Society in regard to New Unionism. It was becoming evident that the employers had become better organised, while the impact of picketing was being curtailed by the systematic intervention of the police and judiciary in industrial disputes.

4

During the Howe's hatters dispute (referred to in the previous chapter) three strikers had been gaoled for alleged intimidation. The Conspiracy and Protection of Property Act, 1875 made peaceful picketing legal but laid down strong penalties for intimidation, annoyance by violence or otherwise. This included, 'watching or besetting' of a person with the object of compelling him or her to refrain from doing anything which he or she has a legal right to do, such as taking part in a strike or lock-out.[44] Daniell was vexed by the interpretation of this law, stating publicly 'that if picketing was not legal it ought to be made so.'[45]

---

38 *BM*, 21 February 1890.

39 Ibid.

40 *BM*, 6 March 1890.

41 Workers' Organising Committee minutes, 20 April 1890.

42 *BM*, 25 April 1890.

43 Workers' Organising Committee minutes, 1, 16, 20 April 1890; *BM*, 29 March, 1, 5, 14, 15, 16, and 20 April 1890.

44 Conspiracy and Protection of Property Act 1875 (1875 Chapter 86), see M. Daniell and R. A. Nicol, *The new trade unionism; its relation to the old; and the conditions of its success* (Bristol: Pamphlet, 1890), p. 14, London School of Economics selected pamphlets, p. 7.

45 *BM*, 3 February 1890.

Activists in the Bristol labour movement agreed. Three hundred of them greeted the three former employees of Howes on their release from Horfield Prison, after serving one month's hard labour for alleged intimidation. They hoisted the freed men onto their shoulders and carried them to a waiting wagonette and led by brass bands paraded from the gaol down to the city, past the hat factory, finishing at the Ropewalk, St Judes, where a celebratory meeting was held.[46]

A dispute had arisen in January 1890 at the Bristol Flour and Bread Company, managed by Isaac Wilmot, Horsefair, Bristol, over his refusal to countenance an agreement drawn up by the representatives of the Master Bakers' Employers' Association and the Amalgamated Union of Operative Bakers and Confectioners that stipulated night work would be paid at the rate of time and a half. Picketing of the premises followed, which resulted in the issuing of multiple summonses against pickets, (two of whom were officials of the Baker's Union), for alleged intimidation.[47]

The case was heard by Justice Cave. He was cognisant of the feelings aroused when strikes occur and picketing takes place, and did not require 'that the men should plead guilty to watching or besetting' but was content that eight of the men before him had pleaded guilty to the 'act of disorderly following'.[48] However, a similar charge of intimidation against Bristol bakery workers was dropped, as in the judge's view — although eight of the accused had 'pleaded guilty to a conspiracy to follow in a disorderly manner,' — the men 'were desirous of carrying out the law of 1875'.[49] The interpretation of intimidation, like that of 'conspiracy' was always subject to both opinion and to political pressures. Justice Cave's conclusion showed that the judiciary was not a completely united body. Justice Cave was regarded by radical liberals as one of the few judges that 'by their union of dignity with courtesy, are among the remaining barriers against the roughness of the majority of Judges, whose private and public training, one would fancy, had been nearer to Billingsgate than to that culture to which they pretend.'[50] Similarly, Daniell and Nicol, in a pamphlet called *The new trade unionism; its relation to the old; and the conditions of its success*, concurred that 'fortunately' Justice Cave was 'an impartial judge' and 'provided in such cases [brought under the Conspiracy and Protection of Property Act 1875] there is a reasonable judge on the Bench, there is little fear of injustice being done.'[51] His judgement gave solace to Daniell, Born, Nicol and other Bristol socialists, at a time when their faith in the ability of the working class to bring about radical change was diminishing.

By March 1890, the Workers' Organising Committee faced the daunting

46 Ibid.

47 *BM*, 16 January 1890.

48 Bristol Spring Assizes, 28 March 1890, in Daniell and Nicol, *The new trade unionism; its relation to the old; and the conditions of its success*, pp. 16-20.

49 Bristol Spring Assizes, 28 March 1890, 'REGINA on the prosecution of WILMOTT v. WESTLAKE, AND OTHERS, Before Mr Justice CAVE and a Jury: Observations of the Learned Judge at the close of the proceedings' in Daniell and Nicol, *The new trade unionism; its relation to the old; and the conditions of its success*, Appendix, pp. 16-20.

50 *Reynolds's Newspaper*, 30 March 1890.

51 Daniell and Nicol, *The new trade unionism; its relation to the old; and the conditions of its success*, p. 7.

prospect of organising and maintaining strikers and of entanglement with the law. Prior to the eruption of strikes in September 1889, the Bristol Socialist Society had followed the Social Democratic Federation line in advocating a form of state socialism, with its backing for democratic reforms along the way. Its Marxism was, however, tempered by its independent brand of ethical socialism, 'the religion of love, and the right of all to a comfortable living and suitable conditions for the freedom and development of the "untold latencies" which lie fettered in humanity'.[52] Socialism in Bristol contained a utopian sense of alternative human relations as well as a more sober awareness of the need to awaken the masses through education. Like the Social Democratic Federation, Bristol socialists saw this as being brought to workers by class conscious socialist activists and by the promotion of a socialist programme. Participating in local and national elections provided an opportunity to do this. However, the Bristol socialists were determined not to lower their socialist goals to the level of municipal or parliamentary politics. They took a similar attitude towards what they considered to be the self-serving interests of trade unions. When the strike wave was at its height this wariness had lessoned, however, by the early months of 1890 doubts had set in.

Bristol employers showed guile, intervening quickly to divide workers, taking intractable stances when they could and then conceding to arbitration which they sought to control as best they could. The tumultuous period between September and December 1889 had seemed to augur a crisis for capitalism; it refuelled a more chiliastic interpretation of socialism by which social revolution appeared as not only inevitable but imminent. Early in 1890, it was already becoming evident that this was not the case, at least for the then foreseeable future.

The momentous victories secured in 1889 proved to be short-lived. Instead of spear-heading revolution, trade unions in Bristol, new as well as old, were drawn into arbitration and mediation, as a way in which to resolve disputes peacefully and establish or maintain a union presence. This was not necessarily a complete retreat. As Vic Allen has observed, for 'the acceptance of arbitration by employers was ... an acknowledgement that independent persons could sit in judgement on what hitherto had been regarded as the private preserve of employers'.[53] Some of the Bristol socialists, while refocusing on their policy of making socialists through socialist agitation, were pulled pragmatically in this direction and turned towards aligning themselves with this change in trade union policy. They would respond by putting on hold their hopes of extensive social change through workers' action, forming instead closer alliances with radical liberals. Socialist leaders within trade unions worked to establish a working arrangement with the Bristol Chamber of Commerce, in an attempt to establish a Bristol Board of Conciliation and Arbitration.

---

52   Ibid., p. 11.

53   V. L. Allen, 'The Origins of Industrial Conciliation and Arbitration', *International Review of Social History* Vol. 9:2 (1964): 241.

5

For fiery enthusiasts like Daniell and Nicol however, the combination of industrial defeats and participation on arbitration boards was soul destroying. They started to question the significance of so much endeavour, viewing the strike wave 'as merely a big incident in the labour war.'[54] In their pamphlet on trade unionism they struggled to explain why the militant upsurge had been frustrated, concluding that in the face of the employers' counter-offensive a one-dimensional materialistic trade unionism could not sustain the gains that had been made, let alone bring about social change. They pronounced,

> [It] has been sadly shown of late by the many disastrous strikes witnessed in the past six months ... that the futility of organisation not founded on any great spiritual idea has been fully proved.[55]

Not only had strike activity in pursuit of higher wages encountered daunting setbacks, Daniel and Nicol felt that organised labour had no soul. Their mood of disillusionment was accentuated by several instances of rivalry between different sections of workers, which had impeded the development of solidarity across the labour movement. In March 1890, trade union officials were involved in a physical fight. John White, honorary secretary of the Bristol branch of the Dockers' Union, was found guilty of unlawfully wounding James Fitzpatrick, secretary of the Bristol branch of the National Amalgamated Sailors' and Firemen's Union, by thrashing him with a stick so severely it broke in two. The dispute between them was over a project initiated by White to establish a sailors' branch of his union.[56] Little sense of unity was evident that March, let alone a common objective to initiate transformational social change.

Daniell and Nicol, however, refused to be completely pessimistic, maintaining that a turn to spirituality was beginning to give power to the people to

> work out their own salvation ... and the Way is not through Christ's blood or His suffering, but by sufferings and sacrifices such as he accomplished for humanity — at last we shall have come within the measurable distance of the greatest Union of all — the union of the Souls of Mankind in a perfect Love, out of which will emanate perfect and eternal Peace, which will express itself not in religious traces or in lethargy, but in active, beautiful, and simple service, sacrifice and life.[57]

This transcendental approach moved away from emphasis upon working class struggle which had featured in the autumn of 1889. It was acceptable among the Bristol socialists who were close to Edward Carpenter, like Robert Weare and Robert Gilliard. However, it did not solve the practical problem of how to improve living and employment conditions for the working class.

---

54 Daniell and Nicol, *The new trade unionism; its relation to the old; and the conditions of its success*, p. 13.

55 Ibid., p. 12.

56 *BM*, 27 March 1890.

57 Daniell and Nicol, *The new trade unionism; its relation to the old; and the conditions of its success*, p. 15.

Divisions surfaced in March 1890, over the socialists' relation to the Liberal Party. Several members retained connections. Helena Born had never fully disassociated herself from the Bristol Women's Liberal Association. She was reappointed on its executive in January 1890.[58] Dan Irving also had not completely severed his links with radical Liberals. That March a spat between Irving and Edward Watson, a trainee solicitor at Gore's legal practice, and a Bristol Socialist Society member, over whether placing pressure on the Liberals would produce gains for the working class, was openly debated in the letter pages of the local press. Watson argued that workers should have nothing to do with the Liberal Party. In contrast, Irving contended that working within the Liberal Party 'under the banner of "New Radicalism," which is already Socialistic in its tendencies', was the only vehicle through which workers' aspirations, such as eight-hour day and land nationalisation, could be realistically achieved. Irving went on to say that

> In these Democratic times, when such vast political power rests in the hands of the people, it is idle to put responsibility upon leaders; it is "paying too much attention to a name" to blame parties. The greater part of the responsibility for the continuation of the present political and social condition of the workers must rest with themselves. [59]

Edward Watson

However, Watson and Irving were united in the view that progressive change could only be achieved through securing a voice in Parliament and that the state could moderate class conflict by passing political and social reforms in the interests of workers. The difference between them was largely over who were Irving's 'sterling men' that would fight for the workers' cause and bring about a Socialistic society if elected to Parliament? Irving thought that given that there was not an independently organised Socialist or Labour Party then these 'sterling men' would come from the radical ranks of the Liberal Party.[60] Watson had argued in the letters page a few days before that 'the sooner Liberalism and Labour separate the better for labour.' He went on to say that Socialists must 'recruit, recruit, recruit, and as soon as we have a fit eleven, send them to the wickets.'[61]

This disagreement notwithstanding, later both Irving and Watson, along with

---

58   *BM*, 24 January 1890.
59   *BM*, 18 March 1890.
60   Ibid.
61   *BM*, 13 March 1890.

Born, and Nicol, opted to serve on the Bristol Committee for the promotion of better housing for the poor.[62] And significantly, Irving, Watson, Daniell, Nicol, Gertrude Dix and Born worked in partnership with other trade union representatives, including Mary Talbot, the Bristol Trades Council, and the Bristol Chamber of Commerce, to discuss a draft scheme for a Board of Conciliation and Arbitration.[63] This ironic legacy of the strike upsurge would culminate in the creation of a Board, in October 1890, for voluntary use in the settlement of labour disputes arising in Bristol and surrounding districts.[64] While Dan Irving put his hat in the ring in the vote for labour representatives to serve on the Board, he was not elected. Labour representation was taken up almost exclusively by members of the old male craft unions, John Fox, Trade and Provident Society, Henry Jolliffe, Carpenters and Joiners' Society, T. J. Dancey, National Amalgamated Sailors' and Firemen's Union, A. J. Tarr, Engineers' Society. The only exceptions were J. Vickery, from the Gasworkers and General Labourers' Union, and F. Paul, from the Bristol Association of Working Women.[65]

In April 1890, the Bristol Socialists, in the activities of the Workers' Organising Committee, put most of their energy into preparing for the first Bristol May Day demonstration. Reflecting new union policy of making alliances with 'progressives', in order to broaden the base of the movement for the eight hour day,[66] local Liberal dignitaries, Lewis Fry MP for Bristol North, Handel Cossham MP for Bristol East[67] and Charles Townsend, a Liberal parliamentary candidate, were invited to attend the demonstration. All three declined. The latter replied indicating that he was against protective legislation but,

> I am in most sympathy with the movement for an eight-hour day, but I cannot see my way to legislation which would absolutely prohibit men in all trades from working longer than this if they wished to do so. In the case of underground miners and other dangerous occupations I should support a bill for the restriction of the hours of labour.[68]

J. H. Perry, the secretary of the Bristol Women's Liberal Association, and Mary Talbot, secretary of Bristol Association of Working Women, were also invited to attend. Talbot accepted and asked if she could bring the Bristol Association of Working Women's banner to the event. This was agreed. At the last minute the date of the demonstration was moved forward from the Sunday to the Saturday in response to non-conformist religious objections to a Sunday meeting. In doing so the demonstration committee was able to accommodate Eleanor Marx-Aveling, who was unable to come on the Sunday, as a key

---

62   *BM*, 30 June 1890.

63   *BM*, 13, 14 June 1890.

64   Rules of the Bristol Conciliation and Arbitration Board, for the Adjustment of Disputes between Capital and Labour, Established 1890, BRO.

65   *BM*, 28 August 1890.

66   D. Bateman, 'The First Bristol May-Day, 1890: Eleanor Marx-Aveling on the Downs', unpublished paper, no date, p. 18.

67   Handel Cossham replied on 22 April, the day before he died, declining the invitation.

68   Samson Bryher, *An Account of the Labour and Socialist Movement in Bristol* (1929), II, p. 25.

speaker.[69]

Compared with previous demonstrations in the City, the turnout of around 2,500 was small. They assembled in the open space either side of the Ropewalk, which was the official starting point. The route of the procession took them right through the central areas of Bristol: Old Market, Castle Street, Wine Street, Drawbridge, Park Street, up to Whiteladies Road, finishing on Clifton Downs with a mass meeting.[70] Bringing up the rear of the procession were the Bristol Socialists, carrying 'a massive and impressive red banner made by Miriam Daniell.'[71] As the procession passed through the city, Henry Stacy, Paul and Enid's artist father, quipped, 'There goes the procession, winding its way like a serpent through the narrow streets, but the sting is in its tail!'[72] Even though it was no longer clear quite what the sting could achieve, this demonstration's significance lay in bringing together sections of left and right persuasions of the labour movement in Bristol in a show of solidarity. Two platforms had been erected on the Downs. On the first platform Tom McCarthy, from the London Dockers' Union, moved that in order to help mitigate unemployment Bristol workers should call for legislation to limit the hours of labour to eight per day, or forty-eight hours per week.[73] In supporting this resolution, Eleanor Marx-Aveling said that an 'eight hours' system would not settle the question between capital and labour, but it would be the first great step in that direction.' She went on to call for the establishment of a Labour Party, 'and not merely have a Labour candidate who would go at the tail of the Liberal or Tory Party. They must have a Labour programme, and to that programme their candidate must be pledged.'[74]

Though this idea of Labour representation would be significant in the future, immediately the strength of her call was undermined when, on the second platform, Robert Tovey disclosed that owing to the ill-health of William Whitefield, the local miners' leader, the decision had been made to drop him as the Labour candidate for the forthcoming by-election in Bristol East, called due to the death of the sitting Liberal Gladstonian MP, Handel Cossham. Shortly after Tovey's contribution, Hugh Holmes Gore stepped up to the platform and alleged that Whitefield was not given the support he deserved. Sir Joseph Weston, Chairman of the Great Western Cotton Works, was the Liberal Gladstonian candidate for this seat. Gore raged that Weston 'had kept down the wages of his working men and by their labours he had become more than rich, while they were just where they were 30 or 40 years ago, and they would remain such until they returned to Parliament a working man.' Then, to the astonishment of Tovey, he went on to call for the return of the Conservative candidate Jason Inskip.[75]

At an emergency meeting of the Election Committee held the next day at 9

---

69   Workers' Organising Committee minutes, 21, 23, and 24 April 1890; Bateman, 'The First Bristol May-Day, 1890.
70   *BM*, 7 May 1890.
71   Bateman, 'The First Bristol May-Day, 1890', p. 18.
72   Bryher, *Labour and Socialist Movement in Bristol*, II, p. 24.
73   *BM*, 5 May, 1890.
74   Ibid.
75   Ibid.; Also see Bryher, *Labour and Socialist Movement in Bristol*, II.

Louisa Street, a deputation from the National Amalgamated Sailors' and Firemen's Union, led by James Fitzpatrick, announced that Joseph Havelock Wilson, who, in 1887, founded the National Amalgamated Sailors' and Firemen's Union, was willing to offer himself as Labour candidate and that his union would bear the expenses. After a further meeting on the following day this offer was rejected. The official reason being that it was 'so near the day of the election' it was decided not to run a labour candidate on this occasion, but it would put forward one at the next General Election.[76] Dissent was shown by two members of the committee, Harold Brabham, President of the Bristol branch of Gasworkers and General Labourers' Union, and James Watts Treasure, who on their own initiative had won support for Havelock Wilson from the Bristol Trades Council and worked to get him elected as an Independent. Robert Tovey and John Gregory rallied in support.[77] Wilson was officially proposed by Samuel Pritchett and seconded by shoemaker John Wall. Without official backing, however, they were trounced at the Polls; Wilson received 602 votes, Jason Inskip (Conservative) 1,900 and Sir Joseph Weston (Liberal) 4,775. Treasure reported that on 'returning home after the declaration of the poll, the shoemakers and colliers simply buried us with turf and stones. All the glass of the cab was broken, and we were glad when we reached quieter quarters.'[78] This experience must have challenged the confident assumptions of the Bristol Socialist Society and the Clifton and Bristol Christian Socialists that the working class were to act as decisive agents for social change.

The socialists began to seek alliances. A few weeks later, at a half-full Colston Hall, Tom Mann and Ben Tillett shared a platform with Reverend J. M. Wilson, (who had vindictively berated members of the Cotton Strike Committee during the cotton operatives' dispute), Eliza Dunbar (Bristol Women's Liberal Association), Mary Talbot (Bristol Association of Working Women), Robert and John Sharland, Edward Watson, Robert Tovey, Harold Brabham and Hugh Holmes Gore. The objective of the meeting was to bring about more unity between the unions. After addresses by Mann and Tillett, the Reverend Wilson spoke in favour of organising working people into trade unions, 'the great method of combining labour into unions, working harmoniously together ... because they had shown that no class could get any benefit for itself.'[79] It was as if the attack by Reverend Wilson on the Workers' Organising Committee had never happened.

Nicol, however, still hoped the New Unionism could embody radical social and economic values. He attended the first delegate conference of the National Union of Gasworkers and General Labourers during 19-21 May 1890 as an active participant. When the time came to discuss the new rules that had been placed before the delegates, he strongly argued and won the case for adding to the Union's objectives a clause 'to obtain the same wage for women as for men,

---

76 Election Committee minutes, 5 and 6 May 1890; *BM*, 6 May 1890.

77 *BM*, 7 May 1890.

78 Bryher, *Labour and Socialist Movement in Bristol*, II, p. 27.

79 *BM*, 22 May 1890.

when doing the same work.'[80] A rider to this rule was appended:

> whenever in these Rules the word 'man', 'him', or 'his' occur, they shall be
> taken to mean 'man or woman', 'he or she', 'his or her'. Our Union is of
> men and women and our Rules apply to both.[81]

Nicol also proposed and won the principle that the Gasworkers' Union would 'not invest any funds in any company paying dividends', despite opposition from his Bristol colleague James Vickery, who argued that 'we are not here as politicians or as socialists. We are here as practical Trade Unionists'.[82] Women's participation along with a wider role for unions had featured in Nicol and Daniells' pamphlet on new trade unionism. They envisaged a new unionism as accompanied by spiritual transformation: 'Faith and Love are the Powers which alone can create and recreate.'[83]

6

By the beginning of May 1890, Daniell, Nicol and Born had moved out of Louisa Street and taken a cottage in Lower Eastville, at the back of Robert Gilliard's house — 'the two dwellings only divided by a not very high garden wall.'[84] Not only were they in close personal contact with Gilliard, whose Swedenborgian spirituality was no doubt congenial, but also with Dan Irving and William Baster, a carter, founder member of the Bristol branch of the Democratic Federation and a prominent member of the Bristol Socialist Society. All three were frequent visitors to their new home. Throughout the summer they continued to be active. Born spoke at a public meeting of the Bristol Socialist Society of around 300 people in June, on the position of women under the present system.[85] And Daniell and Nicol, with other labour movement representatives, attended meetings, on 2 and 10 July, to establish a Board of Conciliation and Arbitration.[86]

However, by the time Daniell had moved to Lower Eastville she would have realised that she was with child, and that Nicol was the father. In 1890 the implications of this pregnancy were devastating. Even though socialists were questioning convention, socialist women in particular were vulnerable to criticism about their personal lives. While some advocated 'free unions' many, including Bristol socialists Enid Stacy and Katherine St John Conway, were inclined to criticise free love ideas. While there is no indication, however, that Daniell's pregnancy became public knowledge, not even her estranged husband seemed to know judging by the reports of the divorce proceedings in 1894, once

---

80 Minutes of the First Yearly Conference of Delegates of The National Union of Gas Workers and General Labourers of Great Britain and Ireland, 19-21 May 1890, p. 5.

81 Quoted in Y. Kapp, *The Air of Freedom: The Birth of the New Unionism*, (London: Lawrence and Wishart, 1989), p. 88.

82 Minutes of the First Yearly Conference of Delegates of The National Union of Gasworkers and General Labourers of Great Britain and Ireland, 19-21 May 1890, p. 6.

83 Daniell and Nicol, *The new trade unionism; its relation to the old; and the conditions of its success*, p. 15.

84 Correspondence from Robert Gilliard, Financial Secretary of the Bristol Socialist Society, to Helen Tufts, 9 May 1901.

85 *BM*, 12 June 1890.

86 *BM*, 3 and 11 July 1890.

a child was born concealment would have been impossible.[87] An illegitimate birth would have been a political as well as a personal embarrassment and Daniell's pregnancy probably contributed to a plan to make a decisive break in the pattern of their lives. Daniell, Nicol and Born emigrated from England to America on 20 August 1890,[88] their departure leaving a serious vacuum in the Bristol labour movement. This sentiment was expressed in *The People's Press*:

> Bristol has this week lost three of its most active workers in the persons of Robert A. Nicol, Miriam Daniell, and Helena Born. They have been in the advance ranks since the formation of the Gas Workers' Union, and Mr. Nicol was the first general secretary for the Bristol district, which he filled in a most able manner until his departure. During the great cotton strike, when nearly 2,000 girls [*sic*] were out of employment for six weeks, no one toiled harder than Mrs. Daniell or Miss Born for the strikers, and they were always found leading the processions. Since then they have done yeoman service in organising the tailoresses and pipemakers of Bristol. Every Unionist in the district will regret the loss of their valuable services and join in wishing them good speed in their journey to the States. May they soon be actively engaged in the American Labour struggle as they were in the English one.[89]

However, disputes about how best to organise women workers persisted. In October 1890 it was rumoured that Clementina Black was in the process of drumming up support for a rival cotton operative's union promoted by the Women's Trade Union Association.[90] Unlike the cotton workers' Bristol branch of the Gasworkers and General Labourers' Union, the Women's Trade Union Association from its inception in 1889 had opted for a more conciliatory approach to industrial relations. Though it sought to establish independent 'self-managed and self-supporting Trade Unions', it was in favour of conciliation and arbitration to resolve disputes rather than result to strike action. It was a principle of the Association that no funds should be dedicated to aiding and abetting strikes or strikers.[91]

On 14 October, 1890, at a Bristol Association of Working Women meeting held in the Lesser Colston Hall, Clementina Black presented the case for women's trade unions recording the fact that the Bristol Association of Working Women had succeeded in getting a woman representative elected to the Bristol Board of Conciliation and Arbitration. She went on to argue that, 'Women did not want more legislation; they had their share of it, and they did not much fancy it, and when it was possible they would rather settle their own affairs themselves.' She believed there were more mature ways of resolving industrial disputes than

---

87   *BM*, 1 May 1894; *Reynolds's Newspaper*, Sunday 6 May 1894; Miriam Daniell and Robert Nicol's child, Eleanor, was born in Massachusetts, November 1890, 1900 US Census: Ward 7, Los Angeles. I am grateful to David Sachs for providing me with this reference.

88   Passenger lists leaving UK 1890-1960 reveal that they set sail from Liverpool to New York on 20 August 1890. See findmypast.co.uk. Accessed 3 September 2011.

89   *The People's Press*, 30 August 1890

90   *BM*, 16 October 1890.

91   E. Mappen, *Helping Women at Work: The Women's Industrial Council 1889-1914* (London: Hutchinson, 1985), p. 34.

resorting to strikes. Although she did not rule them out she contended that if disputes were managed properly, strikes would be less likely to occur.[92]

At this meeting she learnt about the rumour circulating that she had come to Bristol to set up a rival union to compete with the cotton workers' branch of the Gasworkers and General Labourers' Union. Instantly she delayed her return to London in order to attend a meeting of the cotton workers' union on the following day, so that she could put an end to this rumour. Vigorously and emphatically, she informed the 800 members present at this meeting that she was 'against them leaving their old organisation, and should consider them mad to do so. Her relations with the Gasworkers' Union had always been most friendly, and she trusted always would be so.'[93]

This unequivocal denial by Black that it was her intention to launch a rival union removed any doubts that she was involved in such a plan. Edward Watson welcomed her disavowal alleging that a few women shareholders of the cotton works were 'trying to sow the seeds of dissention in their midst'.[94] From differing starting points New Unionism and women's trade unions were moving towards arbitration. The cotton workers, despite the turn by their union to conducting more conciliatory industrial relations, demonstrated that they not only wanted to continue to belong to a mixed-gender trade union but also still desired to be associated with the militant spirit of New Unionism. Ironically, the socialist Dan Irving implored cotton workers' members in January 1891 'not to rush recklessly into strife, for matters could now be settled in a friendly way that previously had bitterly to be fought out.'[95] Later that month it was proposed at a Workers' Organising Committee meeting that the Women's Trade Union Association for the promotion of trade unionism amongst women, the local secretary of which was now the socialist Enid Stacy, should be united with the Workers' Organising Committee. Stacy spoke against this proposal and the matter was dropped.[96] Nevertheless, Stacy was to step into the role Daniell and Born had created for women's organising.[97]

In the early 1890s a broad consensus would emerge among Liberal and Socialist women, accepting the need for a dual strategy which combined organisation with state regulation. At the Conference of Women Workers, organised by the Bristol and Clifton Ladies' Association for the Care of Girls, held in Bristol in November 1892, and attended overwhelmingly by Liberal women, the socialist Isabella Ford 'strongly urged the appointment of women [factory] inspectors and the need for combination amongst women in trade unions'. [98]

The issue of labour representation also continued to be debated. The headline that appeared in the local press from 1890 was 'A New Labour

92   *BM*, 15 October 1890.

93   *BM*, 16 October 1890.

94   Ibid.

95   *BM*, 9 January 1891.

96   Workers' Organising Committee minutes, 28 January 1891.

97   See Chapter 5 for Stacy's role in the Sanders' 'Sweet Girls' strike in 1892.

98   *BM*, 9 November 1892; *Glasgow Herald*, 9 November 1892.

Movement in Bristol'. With Robert Tovey as Honorary Secretary and Robert Gilliard as Honorary Treasurer, the Bristol Labour Emancipation League was launched with the objective of 'the economic and political emancipation of the workers by returning to Parliament and local governing bodies, persons pledged to the programme of the League'. Its programme included Home Rule for Ireland, abolition of the House of Lords, and all hereditary authorities, free education, a 48-hour week, adult suffrage and the nationalisation of land and the commanding heights of the economy.[99] At an open air meeting of the League in the Horsefair, Bristol, in August, 2,000 people gathered to hear John Burns, prominent leader of New Unionism and executive member of the Amalgamated Engineers' Union, enthuse about organisational advances in the international labour movement in their demand for an eight-hour day. Turning to politics Burns finished with the words, 'it was a scandal and a shame' that in Bristol 'there were only two men directly representing the interests of the working classes ... he deplored the suspicions and jealousies which divided the working classes and said it was only their disunion that prevent their success.'[100] After Tovey resigned his seat in 1891, the Bristol Labour Emancipation League became inactive and was soon to be replaced by the Labour Electoral Association, a body that was to have a better relationship with the Bristol Socialist Society than its predecessor.[101]

Subsequently, the Bristol Socialist Society was to be committed to a Labour-Socialist alliance strategy rather than continue with the focus on trade union action as a means of changing workers' consciousness. There was a tendency to revert to aspects of the earlier distain for trade unions. At a Society meeting on 20 February 1891, Frank Sheppard, a new member, delivered a paper entitled 'Trade's Unionism and Socialism', arguing that socialist principles had yet to be fully understood by trade unionists, as securing increased wages 'was obtained at the expense of the general consumers.'[102] Frank Sheppard, who would go on to successfully win a council seat in 1893, considered strikes to be an antique weapon. He believed that it was much better to fight for social change through the ballot box.[103] Sheppard was later to become the first Labour Lord Mayor of Bristol and led the Labour Party in Bristol for 45 years. A decisive shift, however, had occurred. While in the 1880s socialists had imagined a transformatory revolutionary change in society, and had been prepared to back militant working class action, in January 1891 the Socialist Society was careful to make clear that it would 'not advocate the adoption of physical force as the best means of establishing a Socialistic Society.'[104]

99 *BM*, 31 July 1890; Bryher, *Labour and Socialist Movement in Bristol*, II, p. 27.

100 *BM*, 12 August 1890.

101 Atkinson, 'The Bristol Labour Movement, 1868-1906', p. 328; Bryher, *An Account of the Labour and Socialist Movement in Bristol*, II, p. 52.

102 Minutes of the Bristol Socialist Society, 20 February 1891.

103 *BM*, 16 October and 25 November 1893.

104 Minutes of the Bristol Socialist Society, 2 January 1891.

7

Before the sudden increase in strikes in the late 1880s some Bristol socialists held an ambivalent attitude toward trade unionism, while some trade unionists were equally wary of socialists. Nonetheless, the intervention of Bristol socialists in the strike wave of 1889 and 1890 was welcomed and this affected the relations between the Socialist Society and trade unionists. Participation in the momentous strikes in the city led the Bristol socialists to reflect upon workers' struggle for a better life and apply the abstract knowledge that they already possessed to formulate ways in which both short-term reforms and long-term goals could be achieved. Some socialists, including Daniell, Born and Nicol came to think that both were indeed possible. When it became clear in 1890 that despite the hard work put in and the sacrifices made, success would not always be the result, optimism turned to pessimism and unity was put under strain.

Disappointment over the failure to recruit tailoresses in sufficient numbers in the face of a fight back by employers led to doubts that the working poor could either improve their position through sustained collective effort or bring about social change. This was compounded by divisions within the organised working class, such as the tension between dockers and gasworkers. From 1890 the socialists again would come to doubt whether supporting strikes in pursuit of higher wages would help to bring about social and political change. An emphasis was placed on cooperative relations with 'enlightened' employers as opposed to the adversarial relations that were a feature of the strikes in late 1889 and early 1890. In practical terms, this involved working with the Bristol Chamber of Commerce in order to establish a Bristol Board of Conciliation and Arbitration, which, ironically, was made possible by the militant action taken by workers in the preceding period.

From the second half of 1890, Bristol socialists endeavoured to make peace with the industrial capitalists. It came to seem that workers had been deflected from seeking political power by a militant trade unionism that set economic demands (practical trade unionism) apart from politics. Bristol socialists still believed that workers should join trade unions, but they played down militancy and came closer to the views held by radical Liberals on how unions should conduct themselves. They wanted to convince workers that real and sustained social and economic change could only be brought about by securing independent labour representation both on the local council and in parliament. The Arbitration Board, created from the months of militancy, was little used during the 1890s. Apart from in a few important exceptions,[105] industrial relations would be relatively peaceful, while the socialists' strategy of political agitation, which had led to a drift back to Liberalism, met with little success at the polls.[106] In their pamphlet on trade unionism, Daniell and Nicol had asserted

---

105 See Ellen Malos, 'Bristol Women in Action, 1839-1919: The right to vote and the need to earn a living' in I. Bild (ed), *Bristol's Other History*, (Bristol: Bristol Broadsides (Co-op), 1983), for an account of the 'sweet girls" strike in 1892 and the lockout of deal-runners the same year. See also Chapter 5 below.

106 Atkinson, 'The Bristol Labour Movement 1868-1906', pp. 327-8.

that militant trade unionism was 'a potent force in the hands of capable leaders',[107] however, if they and Born had stayed in Bristol it is open to conjecture whether events would have taken a different path.

The 'days of doubt' did leave important legacies. The new militant unionism with its democratic socialist values was grafted on to the older craft traditions of Bristol's working class. Friedrich Engels' assessment of trade union action had been discovered in practice. Workplace struggles could act as 'schools of war':

> These strikes, at first skirmishes, sometimes result in weighty struggles; they decide nothing, it is true, but they are the strongest proof that the decisive battle between bourgeoisie and proletariat is approaching. They are the military school of the working-men in which they prepare themselves for the great struggle which cannot be avoided'.[108]

The concept of labour representation had also been raised and, although the Bristol political and economic elite retained their grip on power in the city, they had been forced to accommodate a socialist-influenced labour movement. Within this local labour tradition gender inequality and the importance of women's leadership started to be debated. For, while socialists in Bristol encouraged the participation of women and supported women's rights as workers, they were divided on women's political equality. A prolonged debate, covering three meetings in April 1891 on the question of the denial of the rights of women to have political power, would reveal the split. Robert Gilliard and Gertrude Dix, in particular, were critical of the stance taken by some Bristol Socialist Society members. The minutes record 'Gilliard dealing rather severely with some of the sentiments expressed' on the woman question, such as James Watts Treasure's view doubting 'whether the time had yet come for women to have political power placed in their hands, believing the tendency would be reactionary'. Drawing on the work of American socialist, Lawrence Gronlund, regarding the subjection of women outlined in his *Cooperative Commonwealth*,[109] Treasure put forward the view that women would have to wait for the establishment of a socialistic society before they could advance their cause.[110] But Bristol socialist women were not prepared to let this issue rest. Enid Stacy picked up the torch of women's emancipation which would come to the fore in the 'sweet girls' strike of 1892 in which she was heavily involved. So, while the fervent hopes aroused by the 1889-90 strike wave were not to be realised, Bristol's working class had appeared on the political, economic and social agenda as a force not to be ignored and sections of the radical middle-class had come over to their cause. It was no mean achievement.

---

107 Daniell and Nicol, *The new trade unionism; its relation to the old; and the conditions of its success*, p. 13.

108 F. Engels, *The Condition of the Working Class in England* (London: Panther, 1969), p. 251.

109 Minutes of the Bristol Socialist Society, 10 April 1891 record that Treasure had read to the meeting a chapter from L. Gronlund's, *Cooperative Commonwealth* (1884).

110 Minutes of the Bristol Socialist Society, 10, 17, 24 April 1891; Ellen Malos, 'Bristol Women in Action, 1839-1919.'

5

The Origins and an Account of Black Friday 23rd December 1892

•

Roger Ball

Introduction: 'Away with Politics, Labour to the front'[1]

The autumn of 1892 in Bristol was marked by a violent class war between employers, strike-breaking labour and police on one side and strikers and their mass of working class supporters on the other. Picketing, mass marches and public meetings of thousands of 'new' Trade Unionists were a common feature, culminating in the use of military and police by the local state to break up a pre-Christmas lantern parade to collect money for strikers and their families. Politically inspired show trials and imprisonment of Union organisers followed the event which popularly became known as 'Black Friday'.

Friday December 23rd 1892 was not only an iconic moment in the memories of Bristolians of the period, but made explicit — to both sides fighting for their class interests — the relationship of force that existed. This in turn exposed the alliances and collaboration between the state and the capitalists as well as amongst their working class adversaries. The employers were organised and intimately involved with the local and national state through their bourgeois 'comrades' in the City Council, Watch Committee,[2] police and courts. The strikers and their socialist supporters built a network of solidarity through the 'new' Industrial Unions, women's organisations and their own communities and families which not only helped sustain the strikers but also generated a series of mass demonstrations culminating in 'Black Friday'.

For the socialists and trade unionists, 'Black Friday' and the eventual defeat of the strikes, pointed towards the need for a combined economic and political strategy to fight for working class interests under capitalism. Though which political route to follow, whether reformist or revolutionary, became highly contentious as the new century began. For the bourgeoisie in business and

---

1   Taken from a poster advertising the 'Black Friday' parade (see Figure 1), BCRL Ref: B21533.

2   The Watch Committee (WC) was a sub-committee of the City Council which governed the Bristol police force and appointed the Chief Constable. Control of the police was thus effectively independent of the Home Office. The Mayor acted as Chairman and in 1892 the WC consisted of fourteen Councillors and Aldermen. B. Howell, *The Police in Late Victorian Bristol* (Bristol: Bristol Branch of the Historical Association The University, Bristol, 1989), pp. 1-2.

government in Bristol the threat of an organised and militant working class and the public relations disaster of 'Black Friday' coaxed them away from the nineteenth century tactics, marked by the use of the brute military force against strikers and those struggling for enfranchisement,[3] towards more organised policing, formal legal restraints and tactical propaganda. Their objectives to neutralise the industrial and political organisations of the working class were modified with the realisation that enfranchisement and trade union organisation were probably inevitable and in some cases provided more efficient mechanisms for social control and economic stability.

Figure 1. Original poster for the 'Black Friday' march.

---

3   Amongst many examples see in particular Peterloo (1819); Swing Riots (1830-31); Merthyr rising (1831); Newport rising (1839), and the events of 'Bloody Sunday' in London in 1887.

1. Origins of 'Black Friday': The strike wave of 1889-90

From the perspective of the Bristol working class the origins of 'Black Friday' lay in the new political and economic organisations which flourished in the wave of strikes in Bristol in 1889-90[4] and which ushered in more inclusive forms of inter and intra-workplace coordination. The phenomenal rise in membership of the 'New Unions', the most prominent of which were the Dock, Wharf, Riverside and General Labourers' Union (formed 1889), National Union of Dock Labourers (1889), the National Union of Gasworkers and General Labourers (1889) and the National Sailors' and Firemen's Union (1887), was a sign of growing confidence in the working class both locally in Bristol and nationally. These new workplace organisations differed from the old craft unions in that they were inclusive, aimed at recruiting both skilled and (crucially) unskilled workers and facilitated this with relatively minimal dues which were more attractive to low paid general workers. This 'general unionism' espoused solidarity across trades, was not divided by forms of work (as the craft unions had been) and eventually aimed at political action through the general strike. It comes as no surprise that the 'New Unions' were led by avowed socialists and communists[5] and were popularly associated with successful militant action to achieve better pay and conditions for their members. They also actively encouraged women workers to join on an equal footing to men, a fact which was to be of significant importance in Bristol in 1892. This step forward on the economic front was paralleled by the relatively new Bristol Socialist Society formed in 1885. As we have seen, this broad-based organisation provided a pole of political combination which was active in the public sphere and injected radical ideas into social life as well as the economic and political arenas. Crucially, the Socialist Society, which united anti-capitalists both working- and middle-class, male and female, was also open to backing the demands of women workers.

From the standpoint of the employers and local state, the strikes of 1889-90 in Bristol had provided some salutary lessons. Initially both had been caught unawares by the intensity and speed of the strike wave and they were unprepared and unused to the militancy of the 'New Unions'. Attempts to bring scab labour into Bristol to replace the striking gas workers had failed due to the inability or unwillingness of the police to oppose organised violent picketing.[6] As a direct result of this fiasco the striking gas workers had been victorious. The evident lack of coordination between the employers and local state in the early phases of the strike severely hampered their efforts to seize the initiative during the strike wave. However, as the winter of 1889/90 wore on the courts began to be used

---

4   See Chapters 3 and 4 above.

5   Such as Tom Mann, Ben Tillett, John Burns (Dockers) and Will Thorne (Gas Workers).

6   The Chief Constable reported in the press that, due to his resources being severely stretched during the simultaneous strikes, 'It has been very difficult to maintain discipline [amongst the police] during the present crisis'. The owners of the Barton Hill Cotton Works also complained to the Watch Committee that 'the police did not protect the company's men during the picketing of the works on Friday 25th October 1889 ... they did not afford any assistance to men wishing to get into the works stopped by men on strike'. Howell, *The Police in Late Victorian Bristol*, pp. 20-1.

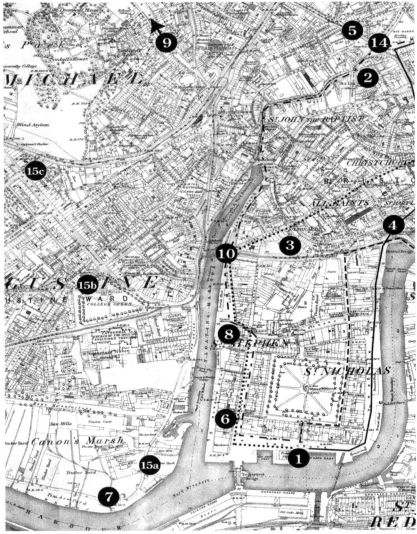

1. The Grove: Meeting point for the 'March of the Workers' on 'Black Friday' at 7.00pm 23rd December 1892.
2. Bridewell Central Police Station [Silver St]: HQ of the joint police and army operation on 'Black Friday'. Muster point for 4th Dragoon Guards.
3. Bristol Tramway Yard [Baldwin St]: A unit of the 4th Dragoon Guards was stationed here on the evening of 'Black Friday'.
4. Bridge St/St Nicholas St: Site of police cordon to prevent marchers entering the City Centre on 'Black Friday'. Police line broken by demonstrators at 8.00pm.
5. St. James Churchyard: Place of refuge for demonstrators on 'Black Friday' after cavalry broke up the rally in the Horsefair. Subsequent police charges eventually drove them out.
6. Dockers' Union Office [Prince St]: HQ of the Bristol branch of the Dock, Wharf, Riverside and General Labourers Union.
7. King Bros. Timber Yard [Canon's Marsh]: Initial workplace and billet for 'blackleg' dock labourers in November 1892.
8. Narrow Quay and Broad Quay: Common locations for mass meetings of Trade Union members. Dockers' Union leaders Ben Tillett and Tom McCarthy regularly spoke here in Nov-Dec 1892.

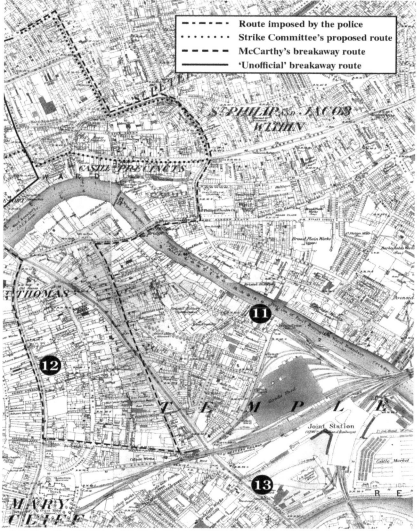

9. Highbury Chapel [St Michaels Hill]: Place of worship of the 'high and mighty' including the Sanders family owners of the Redcliff Confectionary Works. Target of regular Sunday parades by strikers October-December 1892.

10. The drawbridge between Baldwin St and St Augustin's Parade.

11. Pochin's Alum Works [Temple Back]: A strike over Union recognition began here in October 1892.

12. Redcliff Confectionary Works [Redcliff St]: Owned by Sanders & Sons, the 'Sweet Girls' strike over Union recognition began here in October 1892. Mass pickets were common on Redcliff St, the most notable being 26th October 1892.

13. Temple Meads Railway Station: The main arrival point for 'blackleg' labour. Serious violence between hundreds of strikers and police on the evening of 23rd November 1892.

14. The Haymarket/Horsefair: A common location for rallies and meetings of the strikers and their supporters. Site of Ben Tillett's 'incendiary' speech on 18th December 1892. Cavalry and police break up a mass demonstration on evening (9.30pm) of 'Black Friday' 23rd December 1892.

15a-c. Units of Hussars on 'Black Friday' were stationed at Canon's Marsh (to protect blacklegs), College Green and at the top of Park St (to protect Clifton).

more aggressively by the authorities. Strikers began to be jailed under *The Conspiracy and Protection of Property Act* (1875) which was aimed at limiting the effects of picketing. Effectively, the law was now being used to entangle both strikers and union officials, with the vague term 'conspiracy' becoming a clear threat to those who did not engage in the actual offences. This new approach was complimented by increasingly cunning manoeuvres by the employers. Rather than strict intransigence in labour disputes, they took a more flexible approach,

> intervening quickly to divide workers, taking intractable stances when they could and then conceding to arbitration which they sought to control as best they could[7].

These tactical changes were both an indication that the employers and local state were learning from their recent defeats and a portent of what was to come.

After the 1889-90 strike wave there were two additional signs that the reaction of the local state to future labour disputes would be far from benign. In February 1891 the Watch Committee assisted the South Wales police by sending fifty constables to Cardiff to help 'maintain order' during the docks and tramways strike. The local press in Bristol gleefully reported that,

> Forty seven strikers were committed for trial and nine imprisoned for violent behaviour ... the satisfactory results in stopping the strike were largely due to the loyalty, fidelity and exemplary conduct of the police force.[8]

There was little confusion in this action and its outcome concerning the role of the police. They were now principally present in industrial disputes to protect loyal 'company men' and effectively break strikes.

A couple of months after this incident, in the spring of 1891, the City Council attempted to enact bye-laws to prohibit the holding of meetings in public parks. A popular campaign to oppose the measures commenced[9] and it was clear in the public statements of the objectors that battle lines were being drawn:

> It is evident that the power which the rising democracy, and especially Trades Unionism, are obtaining, is exciting in the minds of certain sections of all governing bodies in the kingdom a desire to pass and enforce measures of a suppressive and punitive character.[10]

Although the bye-laws proposal was eventually defeated in close votes in the City Council in October 1891, it was 'the thought that counted', as was to become clear in the autumn and winter of the following year.

---

7   Chapter 4, p. 135.
8   Quoted in Howell, *The Police in Late Victorian Bristol*, p. 21.
9   According to Bryher '15,000 handbills and 500 window bills were distributed, and in all parts of the city enthusiastic public open-air meetings were held'. Bryher, *An Account of the Labour & Socialist Movement in Bristol*, II, p. 32.
10 Ibid.

2. Autumn 1892: Four strikes and a lockout

The autumn of 1892 saw the resumption of overt workplace struggle in Bristol. However, rather than demands to *increase* wages or improve *existing* conditions that in general the strikes of 1889/90 had achieved, this time the strikes were defensive and initiated by employer attempts to increase working hours, introduce piece work and, more sinisterly, to intimidate or even smash the 'New Unions' in their workplaces.

Sanders 'White Slaves': The 'Sweet Girls' strike

On September 5th 1892 at the Redcliff Confectionery Works (see Map Location 12) owned by the Sanders family and employing 300 women and girls, a one-day strike was initiated in response to the employer's attempt to increase the working day by one hour. The workers who struck were not unionised at this stage and were very low paid.[11] Many Bristol companies, especially Quaker in origin,[12] prided themselves on paternalistic relations with their workforces[13]. In the Sanders case this was definitely a Victorian form of paternalism, as Mullen noted,

> 'Their employer had enforced petty and restrictive regulations, couched in middle-class Victorian notions of the guardianship of women, which demanded that the girls should be *locked in during lunch hours* ... In this strike the women and girls were struggling not only for their right to combine but also for their independence and freedom'[14]

Following advice from the Gasworkers and General Labourers' Union (GWGLU) a group of Sanders workers formed a deputation which demanded the removal of the additional hour of work per day, the reinstatement of a 'traditional' morning break of 15 minutes and freedom of egress and access. Sanders apparently agreed to the first and last of the demands and the women returned to work.[15] Spurred on by members of the Bristol Socialist Society and the Working Women's Union,[16] over the following two weeks 80 'Sweet Girls'

---

11 Malos states: 'average pay for a 50 hour week was 4s 7¾d.' Malos, *Bristol Women in Action (1839-1919)*, p. 120. This should be judged against the national average wage in 1892 estimated at £59.74 per year, or about 14s per week (see http://www.measuringworth.com/ukearncpi/). The 'sweet girls' were thus earning about a third of the average wage. For comparative purposes a Police Constable in Bristol was earning 22-28s per week in 1878, about five times their basic earnings. Howell, *The Police in Late Victorian Bristol*, p. 8.

12 For example, J. S. Fry and Sons (Chocolate).

13 Industrial paternalism was marked by employers at an enterprise level, providing benefits, such as shares, paid holidays, sick pay, maternity payments, sports and cultural premises and even housing for employees. Richardson provides a brief assessment of the situation in Bristol in the 1890s in M. Richardson, "Trade Unionism and Industrial Conflict: A Historical Study" in *Bristol Historical Resource CD*, ed. P. Wardley (Bristol: University of West of England), Chap. 9. It is generally acknowledged that these forms of paternalism were primarily aimed at keeping Trade Unions out of their factories. As Richardson states, 'This strategy entailed placing great emphasis on personal contact with workers enabling the hierarchical distinction between owner and producer to be reinforced. This fortification of authority helped to stabilise a paternalist relationship', Ibid., Chap. 8.

14 My emphasis. Mullen, *Sweet Girls and Deal Runners*, p. 122.

15 *BM*, 12 Nov 1892.

16 The National Union of Working Women was set up in August 1874 in Bristol primarily to ensure that the Factory Act of

created the Confectioners branch of the GWGLU, which happily accepted their applications.[17] Sanders responded by informing one of the workers, Sarah Edwards, a union member and participant of the original strike delegation, who had worked there for eight years, that she had to take a pay cut or leave. After a union meeting of the confectionery workers a GWGLU official, Harold Brabham, wrote to Sanders and asked him to reconsider his decision or 'I am afraid there will be a stopping of work on the part of the workpeople'.[18] Sanders took this as a threat and subsequently issued notice to 30-40 other GWGLU members. In reaction, one month after the original stoppage on 5th October, approximately one hundred of the union members at Sanders went out on strike against employer intimidation and for 'the right to combine'.[19] Thus started a bitter 26-week long dispute where 'Sanders White Slaves', as the 'Sweet Girls' became popularly known, played an important role in the events that led to 'Black Friday'.

The Deal Runners Strike and Lockout

Exactly one month after the 'Sweet Girls' struck, on Saturday 5th November, a major labour dispute broke out on the docks. A barque, the *Revolving Light*, from Cardiff carrying a cargo of timber purchased by the Bristol firm Bancroft, Harris & Budgett was moored outside their yard on the Floating Harbour near the Cumberland Basin. Typically timber cargoes were unloaded by deal runners,[20] a specific kind of porter on the docks, who carried deal planks on his back, shoulder or head between the quay, ship or warehouse. However, in an apparently unusual step, the two companies buying and selling the cargo of timber had agreed not to use the Bristol deal runners and instead tried to get a local stevedore[21] to organise the unloading. He refused 'owing to the opposition of the local branch of the Dockers' Union to a stevedore being employed to stack the timber'.[22] During the following week the two businesses arranged to bring in a Cardiff stevedore and his team to handle the cargo at lower rates than in Bristol. This led to a strike by almost all of the 400 Bristol deal runners which effectively closed down the majority of the dockside timber warehouses in the city.[23] The Cardiff men returned home after 'seeing the feeling of the men in Bristol' and the vessel was once again left idle.[24]

The dispute appeared to be at an end after the Cardiff men left and another

---

that year, supposedly passed for the protection of women workers, did not in fact exclude them from employment. Malos, *Bristol Women in Action (1839-1919)*, p. 114.

17   *BM*, 11 Nov 1892.

18   *BM*, 12 Nov 1892.

19   Enid Stacy states in a letter to the Bristol Board of Conciliation and Arbitration, 'The majority of the girls (84 in number, since increased to 110) decided to strike work until their comrades were reinstated and the right of combination thus acknowledged'. Bryher, *An Account of the Labour & Socialist Movement in Bristol*, II, p. 34.

20   They were also generally known as *runnermen* or *carriers*.

21   Stevedores were highly skilled masters of loading gangs on the docks.

22   *BM*, 15 Nov 1892.

23   These were mostly situated on both sides of the Floating Harbour at Canon's Marsh and Redcliff.

24   *BM*, 15 Nov 1892.

Bristol stevedore was employed to move the cargo with no explicit Union opposition. However, in an unexpected move on Saturday 12th November, after a meeting of the Bristol Timber Importers Association (BTIA), the dockside timber merchants in the city refused to reopen their gates 'unless the men would agree to the discharging of all timber vessels on piece work for the future'.[25] This was effectively a red rag to a bull for the deal runners and dockers both locally and nationally as the massive London Dock strike of 1889 had specifically aimed at ending casual labour and piecework.[26] In Bristol this had also been partially achieved in the strikes of 1889.[27] Over the weeks following the lockout the BTIA refused to negotiate with the deal runners unless the principle of piecework was accepted as a given, which led both parties into a lengthy strike. Much of the local press speculated that the dispute was an unfortunate and unplanned incident. However, it appears the BTIA had secretly been making preparations since at least late August 1892[28] through the Shipping Federation[29] to acquire scab labour. This fact and the timber merchants' unified intransigence over the lockout suggest that the reintroduction of piece work was at least a semi-planned operation.

As the striking 'Sweet Girls' and locked out deal runners headed towards Christmas of 1892, they were joined by workers from two other disputes. These had broken out at the Pochin's Alum Works on Temple Back over Union recognition in October[30] and the Malago Vale Colliery[31] strike over wages had been on-going for nearly a year. Thus the events that were to follow would revolve around this diverse core of 'New Unionists': confectionery workers, dockers, chemical workers and miners.

3. Underground and over-ground: The class war in autumn 1892

The months of October, November and December 1892 were characterised by two forms of activity on the streets of Bristol. The first was a subterranean struggle between the strikers and their supporters on one side and non-strikers and scab labour brought in by the employers on the other. The second was a series of mass public meetings, parades and protests organised by the Strike Committees, the 'New Unions' and the Socialist Society and its allies. These would grow in size and frequency over the autumn culminating in a massive demonstration on 'Black Friday'.

---

25 Ibid.

26 Jim McNeill, *Ben Tillett*, Radical Pamphleteer #20, (Bristol: BRHG, 2013), pp. 5-8.

27 Atkinson, *Trade Unions in Bristol*, p. 9.

28 The evidence for this comes from a letter from the Shipping Federation agent Graeme Hunter, dated 23rd Aug 1892, to the BTIA, offering to move up to 1,500 scab labourers a week if necessary. This letter was read out to the strikers at one of the regular Sunday demonstrations on 11th December 1892. Mullen, *Sweet Girls and Deal Runners*, p. 115.

29 'The Shipping Federation was an association of employers in the shipping industry. It was formed in 1890 in response to the London Dock Strike of 1889 and the successes of the National Union of Seamen and various dockers' unions. The main function of the Federation was to co-ordinate the actions of shipowners so as to counter trade unionism and strike action' http://en.wikipedia.org/wiki/Shipping_Federation.

30 *BM*, 1 Nov 1892 and http://www.cems.uwe.ac.uk/~rstephen/livingeaston/local_history/tillett.html.

31 The Malago Vale Colliery was in Bedminster, South Bristol (Cripps Road).

Unlike the strike wave of 1889-90, the Constabulary were to have two explicit roles in the autumn of 1892, policing the demonstrations *and* protecting the strike-breakers. In October the police were unambiguously ordered by the Watch Committee to protect 'free labour' and they organised closely with the employers to achieve this.[32] This response was unsurprising, as Atkinson noted 'During the 1800-1900 period, approximately 75% of Bristol Councillors were industrialists, merchants and tradesmen'.[33] Within the Watch Committee of 1892 were major business owners and industrialists such as Sir Charles Wathen (wool), Charles Wills (clothing), Arthur Baker (corn) and Edward Robinson (paper),[34] all of whom were also magistrates. This triumvirate of Watch Committee, Police and Courts, connected by these personages and others, was crucial in linking class interest with the local and national state.

Pickets, Scabs and Beaks

> But the criminal's not he who stands on the floor,
> On the bench ye must look for the rogue.[35]

The Bristol Socialist Society reacted immediately to the 'Sweet Girls' walkout by helping set up a strike committee to provide practical and financial support to the women. Prominent Bristol socialists such as the public speaker and writer E. J. Watson and activist William Oxley were central to the activities of the organisation whose secretary was, tellingly, Enid Stacy. Stacy, had been politicised along with a number of middle-class Cliftonites during the 1889-90 strike wave, and subsequently became a tireless supporter of the cotton workers' struggle. Her experience as an activist and recent role as secretary of the Association for the Promotion of Trade Unionism Amongst Women made her a prime candidate for a leading role in the 'Sweet Girls' strike committee.[36] Stacy, in her early twenties, not only ran the routine activities of the committee but also 'fronted' the organisation in the press[37] and in face-to-face negotiations with the authorities.

Violence broke out on the picket lines at the Sanders confectionery factory the very day the Union members struck on October 5th. Long-standing striking workers were faced with colleagues who had claimed they would walk out but

---

32 Atkinson states, 'In October 1892 the Watch Committee gave policemen the responsibility of protecting blackleg 'free labourers' who had been brought into the city to take the place of the strikers'. Howell, *The Police in Late Victorian Bristol*, pp. 22-3.

33 Ibid., p. 2. Sanders the owner of the confectionery works at the centre of the 'Sweet Girls' dispute was also a City Councillor. Mullen, *Sweet Girls and Deal Runners*, p. 117.

34 *BM*, 24th Dec 1892 and http://www.davenapier.pwp.blueyonder.co.uk/mayors/history2.htm.

35 Excerpt from the poem 'To the Watch Committee – A Warning' printed on hand bills by the Bristol Socialist Society and distributed in the aftermath of 'Black Friday'. Mullen, *Sweet Girls and Deal Runners*, pp. 117-9.

36 Stacy lost her job at Redland High School as a result of her socialist politics but would go on to become a 'tireless and gifted speaker and writer for the causes of women and socialism, and a member of the ILP executive before her death in 1903 aged 35', Malos, *Bristol Women in Action (1839-1919)*, p. 119.

37 See for example Stacy's letters to *BM*, 17 Oct , 12 and 14 Nov 1892.

then took their better paid jobs in the plant.[38] Shouts of 'blackleg'[39] led to scuffles and fist fights amongst the women and drew strike supporters into melees with the police. Such violence was not new; a few months before, in January 1892 crowds of women and girls had threatened to 'kill and skin' scabs at the Malago Vale Colliery, and had been charged with common assault and bound over in the courts for throwing mud and dough laced with lime at them.[40]

In contrast, on the first day of the Sanders strike an angry 'Sweet Girl', Annie Smith, was arrested and charged with common assault and offences under the Conspiracy and Protection of Property Act which, as discussed previously, was specifically aimed at controlling picketing.[41] For employers the latter was a more useful piece of legislation precisely because of the vague terms 'conspiracy' and 'intimidation' which were open to interpretation by police and courts. However, as the previous section outlined, magistrates who tried the pickets were often serving on the Watch Committee that controlled police actions and as many were industrialists themselves they clearly shared interests with the employers involved in the disputes. The employment and interpretations of this particular Act by magistrates were thus somewhat biased to say the least.

As October wore on the Sanders strike pickets were growing in size, with hundreds of supporters turning up to back the women. On the evening of the 26th a raucous crowd estimated at 600-1,000 people gathered in Redcliff Street as 50 striking 'Sweet Girls' paraded outside the plant. As the non-striking workers left the factory protected by police, the crowd followed them shouting and jeering. The police began assaulting and arresting 'agitators' (as the prosecutors called them) and strikers alike, whilst the crowd attempted to free the captives. Eight strikers and their supporters were detained either during the events or by summonses afterwards.

The melees on the 26th led to the imprisonment and hard labour for 21 days of the French activist, Gaspard de La Croix,[42] on the dubious charges of being 'drunk and disorderly' and incitement. Socialist E. J. Watson and a GWGLU official, Harold Brabham were bound over for breaches of the peace and 'incitement to resist the police' and one other, William Johnson was fined 40s plus costs (or face 21 days in prison) for assaulting a policeman. Three strikers were charged with 'disturbing the peace': Sarah Ann Jones, Louisa Vowles and Ellen Maunders were bound over whilst a fourth, Rose Rowe, was charged with assault on a non-striker and fined 10s plus costs (or face 7 days in prison).[43]

By way of riposte and with the help of the 'people's lawyer', socialist solicitor

---

38 *BM*, 8 Oct 1892.

39 'Blackleg' referred to a strike-breaker, either those who refused to go on strike or hired labour brought in to replace striking workers. Its origins are unclear, although it may have gained racist connotations in the nineteenth century.

40 *BM*, 30 Jan 1892 and Mullen, *Sweet Girls and Deal Runners* , p.123.

41 *BM*, 8 Oct 1892.

42 In a speech at an open-air meeting on 30th October, the socialist William Oxley described his friend and comrade La Croix as 'one of the hardest workers for the girls [striking confectionery workers]', *BM*, 31 Oct 1892. Bryher stated, 'He was very excitable, but many who got to know him fell in love with his big-heartedness, and several students in Clifton thanked him for his lessons in the art of "parry and thrust". Like many of his compatriots he was an excellent swordsman', Bryher, *An Account of the Labour & Socialist Movement in Bristol*, II, pp. 45-6.

43 *BM*, 28 Oct 1892, 29 Oct 1892 and 5 Nov 1892.

Hugh Holmes Gore (who had defended all of the arrestees involved in the incidents of the 26th October), three strikers launched cases of assault against a police officer. This first legal exposure of police violence during the Sanders strike caused consternation in the court. The defence solicitor accused one of the primary witnesses, William Oxley, a member of the Sanders strike committee, of being a 'professional agitator' and insinuated he was a 'tout' who

> by his appearance it would be seen he was not one of those people who earned his living by the sweat of his brow....but went walking about the streets getting money out of these little girls...[44]

At this point, after numerous unsuccessful objections to this defamatory statement (and its veiled allusion to sexual perversion),[45] Gore grabbed his papers and, with the witnesses and strikers, walked out of the court in disgust. The case was dismissed. This moment marked the end of any attempts by the strike committees to get justice for police violence inflicted upon strikers or their supporters. Within days the violence on both sides of the class divide intensified as the docks dispute exploded.

Strike breakers, Coppers and Dockers

> ...the moment Graeme Hunter started his detective agency here, and cocked his revolver they would pick up theirs.[46]

It was 'officially' announced by the BTIA on 23rd November at a meeting with representatives of the locked out deal runners that they had contracted Graeme Hunter, the Shipping Federation agent and professional strike-breaker[47] (who they had originally contacted in August), to unload the ships lying idle in the floating harbour. This was no revelation to the strikers as they had been watching the main train station in Bristol for several nights, anticipating the arrival of scab labour from London or elsewhere. In the early hours of that very morning, after pickets had drifted away from Temple Meads station, two special trains arrived from London and Newport carrying sixty 'blackleg' labourers. Graeme Hunter, Chief Inspector Cann, several detectives and a body of Bristol Police were awaiting their arrival in a secretly organised operation. Hunter marshalled the men into a 'military' style column and marched with a police escort down to Canon's Marsh where they were billeted at a timber merchant's warehouse.[48] Having been tipped off, Tom McCarthy,[49] the Dockers Union official who had

---

44 *BM*, 17 Nov 1892.

45 Mullen, *Sweet Girls and Deal Runners*, pp. 123-4.

46 From a speech to striking deal runners by Tom McCarthy, a Docker's Union official, speaking in Bristol in December 1892: *BM*, 13 Dec 1892. This is an explicit reference to the notoriously violent strike-breaking organisation in the U.S., the Pinkerton National Detective Agency.

47 Hunter bragged in the 'August' letter to the BTIA that he had tackled 18 strikes in Scotland, Wales and Ireland and successfully broken 12 of them. Mullen, *Sweet Girls and Deal Runners*, p. 115.

48 *BTM*, 24 Nov 1892. The first group of scab labourers were billeted at the premises of King Bros. timber yards. Others were later quartered at Gefle Wharf on the Redcliffe side of the Floating Harbour.

49 Tom McCarthy was an Irishman born in Limehouse in London's Docklands who resigned in 1889 as secretary of the exclusive Stevedores' Union to become an organiser of Ben Tillett's newly formed Dockers' Union. Large and Whitfield,

been sent down from London a few days before, turned up at the station in the early hours to (unsuccessfully) remonstrate with Hunter and the 'blacklegs'. Consequently, within a few hours of the arrival of the so-called 'free labour' a large crowd of deal runners and their supporters had gathered near their billet in Canon's Marsh.

The following morning as the 'blacklegs' prepared to begin work unloading, even larger crowds, numbering thousands according to the local press,[50] gathered outside the timber yard gates, jeering and throwing mud at the strike-breakers. Whenever they needed to move to unload a vessel they were escorted by large numbers of police. During the afternoon thirteen men arrived from Cardiff in five cabs, apparently contracted by Hunter to join the 'blacklegs'. However after discussions with Union members (and being offered their fares home) they returned to Wales. At 5.00pm as the shift finished and the scabs were escorted by the police back to their billet some of the crowd made a rush for the yard gates but were blocked by a determined Constabulary.

PRESSING THE LAST PENNY OUT OF THE POOR DUPES OF DOCKERS!

Figure 3. Typically reactionary media propaganda showing 'little men' Union leaders Tillett and McCarthy squeezing dues from 'dumb' workers, as the 'hard-working', 'manly' and 'giant' strike breaker Hunter looks on. The suggestion is that the Union dues are being turned into beer!

After being surprised in the early hours of that morning, the following evening pickets and supporters not only watched the main railway station at Temple Meads but also the smaller inner-city stations of Lawrence Hill,

The Bristol Trades Council 1873-1973, p. 8.
50   *BTM*, 24 Nov 1892, *BEN*, 23 Nov 1892.

159

Stapleton Rd, Montpelier and Clifton.[51] A telegram from the Dockers Union HQ in London had arrived in the afternoon advising the strikers that 'blacklegs' were on their way to Bristol, so hundreds surrounded Temple Meads in readiness. Police attempted, without much success, to disperse these large crowds. At 11.30pm the strike-breaker Hunter accompanied by plain clothes policemen was recognised on one of the platforms and attacked by a picket. On hearing the hue and cry hundreds of strikers and their supporters invaded the station. Hunter, along with several policemen, was given a beating before being hidden from view in a Ladies waiting room with one of his now subdued assailants. After the waiting room windows were smashed by missiles, a number of policemen with drawn staves held the crowds of angry dockers at bay.[52] After literal face-to-face negotiations, the police let their prisoner go free[53] and the strikers and their supporters left the platforms. At midnight, around 800 'men, women and boys' remained at all entrances to the station singing 'Rule Britannia' and apparently up for a long night.[54] The problem remained for the police, how to get Hunter (the target of the protesting crowds) out of Temple Meads?

PROSECUTION OF
BEN + TILLETT.
(Gen. Sec. Dockers' Union.)

SPEECH DELIVERED IN HORSEFAIR, BRISTOL,
DEC. 18, 1892.

Figure 4. Tillett's supposedly 'incendiary' speech produced as a pamphlet by the Dockers' Union as a riposte to his charge of 'incitement to riot'.

The siege by the pickets was eventually broken at about 1.00am on the orders of Chief Superintendent Cann. Around 120 police[55] with drawn staves charged the milling crowds, chasing them down the concourse and into the surrounding streets, whilst Hunter was whisked away in a police van. The police violence appears to have been indiscriminate, as several eye-witnesses (including a church minister) claimed to have seen assaults on 'harmless onlookers' and 'anyone within reach'.[56] Another saw 'the police run after half a dozen women who were standing quietly by, and knock at them in all directions, and severely injured most of them'.[57] It was even suggested that 'the violence of policemen was simply wanton', 'unwarranted and brutal' and could give 'the impression that they are enemies of the labouring man and of the

---

51 *BTM*, 25 Nov 1892.

52 These lead topped staves were probably part of an arsenal of weapons (including cutlasses and firearms) held at the central police station at Bridewell (see Figure 8). Howell, *The Police in Late Victorian Bristol*, p. 10.

53 He was rearrested a few days later, tried for assault and served two months imprisonment with hard labour, *BEN*, 17 Dec 1892.

54 *BTM*, 25 Nov 1892.

55 Howell, *The Police in Late Victorian Bristol*, p. 22.

56 Letters *WDP*, 26 Nov 1892, 30 Nov 1892.

57 Letters *BM*, 29 Nov 1892.

poor'. The local press remained curiously (though perhaps unsurprisingly) silent about the police violence. However, the events at Temple Meads on the night of November 23rd had certainly bloodied both sides and shocked those bystanders who witnessed it.

A report on the serious events at the central railway station and the situation concerning the lockout was relayed to the headquarters of the Docker's Union (DWRGLU) in Mile End, London and on 25th November, Ben Tillett,[58] a representative of the Executive Council of the Union, arrived in Bristol. At 5.00pm on Broad Quay, hundreds of deal runners gathered to hear Tillett speak. It was clear that the strikers were in an uncompromising mood when the chairman, Francis Gilmore Barnett,[59] opened the mass meeting by calling for restraint:

> Mr Barnett proceeded to urge upon his hearers the necessity of being sober and prudent in their attitude towards the employers; but at this juncture a man amongst the crowd called out loudly, 'We must kill Hunter'. Mr Barnett immediately exclaimed "No"; but a large number of men shouted, "Yes, yes".[60]

Tillett responded to the threats to kill the professional strike-breaker Hunter by urging

> the men not to lose their heads. In their weakness and wilfulness the employers were relying on the violence of the men; and they should, therefore, preserve the peace, and implicitly obey the local officials, who would see full justice was done to their cause.

These were fine words, but after two weeks of the lockout,[61] the threat of more scabs on the way,[62] and organised and determined employers protected by an aggressive police force, many deal runners and their supporters were not going to take his advice.

Intimidation and attacks on 'blacklegs' and their police protectors became common over the following weeks. As Mullen related,

> the strikers were extremely hostile towards the blacklegs which aggravated the employers' difficulties in getting them to and from work, housing and feeding them. They were confronted in pubs and their shoulders 'checked' for splinters and grooves (proof of carrying timber).

---

58 For more on the Union leader Tillett see McNeill, *Ben Tillett* and J. Schneer, *Ben Tillett* (Beckenham: Croom Helm, 1982).

59 Gilmore-Barnett was a radical liberal and solicitor who had served on several strike committees in the 1889-90 strike wave; see Chapters 3 and 4 above. He is described by Bryher as giving 'valuable help to Bristol Dockers and other "new Unionists"' Bryher, *An Account of the Labour & Socialist Movement in Bristol*, II, p. 19.

60 *BTM*, 26 Nov 1892, *WDP*, 26 Nov 1892. These were not just idle threats, as according to the press 'one of the officials of the Dockers' Union called on Mr Hunter yesterday morning [25th November], and it is alleged that he informed Mr Hunter that unless he left Bristol his personal safety might be endangered'. *BEN*, 26 Nov 1892.

61 Schneer states, 'For the men on strike, no work meant little or no food, despite strike pay. The families were getting hungry and very hungry at that', one participant recalled many years later', Schneer, *Ben Tillett*, p. 82.

62 In the *BM*, 26 Nov 1892, it was stated '200 more men are to be brought into Bristol from London and elsewhere to start work on Monday [28th November]'.

The usual procedure then was a going over if the blacklegs were found guilty...[63]

Blacklegs were certainly not safe on the streets of Bristol[64] and neither was the strike-breaker Hunter who remained a primary target for the deal runners. At midday on Friday 9th December a dozen pickets spotted Hunter, Chief Superintendent Cann and two other senior police officers crossing the Floating Harbour on the Gas Works ferry. Within minutes a crowd of 50-60 deal runners had gathered to meet the party on the opposite shore. They proceeded to chase and harry Hunter and the senior policemen with threats and volleys of stones. The beleaguered strike-breaker and his 'minders' eventually found safety in the timber yards of the employers. That evening another of Hunter's 'free labourers' was hospitalised in Canon's Marsh after being exposed as a 'blackleg' in a local pub.[65] The following day a group of scab carpenters, protected by 4 or 5 policemen, were attacked by a crowd of 50-60 as they left work on the Cumberland Basin. According to the police officers present 'hundreds of stones were thrown... [and they were] struck several times'.[66] By the end of the month 22 union pickets had been found guilty of assaulting strike-breakers and their police protectors, most being jailed for several months with hard labour.[67] Reports of these court-cases of course may have only reflected the 'tip of the iceberg' in this underground war on the streets of Bristol.[68]

Processions, Parades and Solidarity

A week or so after the 'Sweet Girls' went out on strike in October, following the strategy used by the striking cotton workers in 1889, the strike committee organised a Sunday parade from Bristol Bridge to the Highbury Chapel on St. Michael's Hill in Cotham. The first procession on 16th October was headed by a brass band[69] with the strikers — ninety confectionery workers and thirty from the Pochin's Alum plant — together with a crowd of supporters following on behind. The function of the march was three fold: to popularise the two struggles, to raise money for the strikers and as in 1889 to 'morally' confront the so-called 'Christian' bourgeoisie in their places of worship.[70] The target, the

---

63 Mullen, *Sweet Girls and Deal Runners*, p. 115.

64 See for example attacks on scabs and police in *BEN*, 12 Dec 1892,

65 *BEN*, 10 Dec 1892, *BM*, 15 Dec 1892.

66 *BEN*, 12 Dec 1892.

67 Schneer, *Ben Tillett*, p. 81.

68 There is significant evidence for this supposition in a letter sent on 29th December from the Bristol Magistrates Clerk to the Director of Prosecutions which referring to cases of intimidation before the courts, stated that: 'a large number of similar offences have been reported but in which the offenders have not been brought before the magistrates although the police were assured the crimes had been committed' TNA HO 144/228/A50898A/8.

69 This was usually the Barton Hill Drum and Fife band, Mullen, *Sweet Girls and Deal Runners*, p. 122.

70 In 1889 striking cotton workers had targeted All Saints Church and the Tyndale Baptist Chapel in the same area. It was during one such intervention that members of the congregation, Katherine St John Conway and Enid Stacy, were moved to help the strikers and both eventually joined the Bristol Socialist Society. Fittingly, both women would go on to be involved in the Sanders workers' strike committee in 1892 (with Stacy as secretary) and reuse the tactic which had effectively changed their own lives a few years before. Malos, *Bristol Women in Action (1839-1919)*, p. 119.

Highbury Chapel, was chosen primarily as it was where the Sanders family (who owned the Redcliff Confectionery Works) would be on a Sunday. The strikers were accommodated in the church on the first occasion, but the atmosphere must have been excruciating for all concerned as the Reverend 'assured those present of the sympathy of that congregation with poverty and those who were in trouble'.[71] It is unclear whether Sanders and his family were present.

Such Christian 'charity' was not to last long however. Four subsequent parades which were joined by members of the Trades Council and many others through the month of November were met at the gates to the Highbury Chapel by police officers and church officials who refused them entry to the service.[72] Despite this setback, the weekly parades were very successful in uniting the strikers and their supporters. A week after the timber merchants' lockout, on 20th November, hundreds of deal runners joined the parade, and by the end of the month there were 2-3,000 people regularly participating.[73] From this point on, the marches would grow rapidly in size. On 4th December there were 4-5,000 present and Sunday 11th saw three Union marches converge at the Drawbridge in the city centre: Shoemakers from the Ropewalk, Seamen, Firemen, the 'Sweet Girls' and Gas workers from Bristol Bridge and the striking Dockers and Trades Council from the Grove. This substantial procession of 7-8,000 people, led by five brass bands then proceeded through the wealthy areas of Clifton and Cotham, with the usual ironic cheers as they passed the barred Highbury Chapel[74]. The local press described the marchers as carrying numerous banners and placards on the Sunday parades:

> some having direct reference to recent events and others inscribed with Biblical texts. Several men carried poles with a diminutive loaf and a polony or a herring and the label beneath "A docker's dinner".[75]

As the parades grew larger, typically they began to terminate with mass meetings in the Horsefair. This was an opportunity for the various strike committees to address the masses, which they did from two wagons serving as makeshift platforms at either end of the Haymarket.[76] (See Map Location 14.) These platforms were usually divided between the Unions representing the 'Sweet Girls' (GWGLU) and the deal runners (DWRGLU), though speakers from the Trades Council, the Bristol Socialist Society and sympathetic unions appeared regularly. The feeling of gathering strength must have been palpable to the thousands of marchers, especially as week by week at the Sunday rallies new unions and organisations pledged their support to the strikers. This feeling seems

---

71   *BM*, 17 Oct 1892.

72   *BM*, 7 Nov 1892, 14 Nov 1892, 21 Nov 1892, 28 Nov 1892.

73   Mullen, *Sweet Girls and Deal Runners*, p. 122. The extent of solidarity was marked by in interesting incident on 29th November 1892, when a number of dockers refused to load the Liverpool owned steamer *Jane Bacon* in Bristol Harbour as some of the packages were from the Sanders Confectionery works in Redcliff. The dockers immediately went on strike and only returned to work after receiving reassurances that steam ship owners were aware of the actions of Sanders and the strike of the 'Sweet Girls'. *WDP*, 30 Nov 1892.

74   *BEN*, 12 Dec 1892.

75   Ibid.

76   *BM*, 5 Dec 1892.

to have rubbed off on the speakers who began to be more explicitly political in their speeches. For example, at the rally on 4th December, the 'people's lawyer', Hugh Holmes Gore stated,

> the magisterial bench being packed with employers and their relations and friends, whose interests they always consult; the police being systematically used as paid hirelings of the classes, instead of impartial servants of the community, their legal advocates being paid out of our money to befoul the character of honest working men; and the authorities being deaf to appeals, the working classes are left solely without means of redress... The law, the police and the magistrates were against them.[77]

Others, particularly socialists, saw in the mass rallies the possibility of the formation of a 'labour party' to represent the political and economic interests of the working classes and spoke to the crowds on this issue. This was put most succinctly by Harold Brabham at the massive rally on 11th December who stated that the

> vast gathering showed that the working classes of Bristol were not going to be behind those in the cities in the North of England. It proved they were waking up from the apathy that had existed too long, and that they were determined to get rid of miserable party politics, and send into their local and Imperial councils men from out of their own ranks.

And Ben Tillett who moved the following resolution at the same mass meeting,

> That recent events in connection with strikes and lock-outs in the city teach the working classes the imperative necessity of forming themselves into a Labour party for the purpose of securing direct labour representation upon all public bodies, which are now systematically used in the interest of the employers against the workmen, and pledges itself in the forthcoming Parliamentary and municipal elections to secure the return of direct labour representatives on the Watch, Sanitary, and Docks Committees (applause).[78]

The effect on the bourgeoisie of thousands of angry working-class Bristolians marching through *their* hallowed avenues of privilege and then gathering for incendiary speeches at the Horsefair which increasingly exposed the nature of class power in the city must have been considerable. What had begun as a principled stand by some employers to champion 'free labour' (though actually to protect their financial interests) and to neutralise the effects and influence of the 'New Unions' appeared to be horribly backfiring. The Police and City Council were explicitly being talked about as 'class enemies' by much of the populace and the 'agitators' were talking to thousands about taking political power, albeit within the existing structures.

---

77   *BM*, 12 Dec 1892.
78   *BM*, 12 Dec 1892.

4. 'Black Friday'

> The Christmas bells are ringing, the sky is clear and bright,
> Your masters pray for peace, but are compelling you to fight.[79]

The Mayor Prepares...

The reaction was not long coming. On 12th December the Mayor of Bristol, W. R. Barker, secretly wrote to the Home Office asking for military aid to be made available.[80] Tellingly, he made reference to the 1889-90 strike wave (when Bristol had received similar assistance) as an 'analogous' situation. Barker had clearly been startled by reports on the size and content of the rally at the Horsefair on 11th December when he wrote,

> There are at present a number of unemployed through disputes in the timber and other trades. Yesterday it is computed that 7,000 men met in a public place called 'The Horsefair' and exhibited a great disposition to resort to even greater violence than what had been usual of late, if other men who are now employed in timber yards were permitted to continue to labour.

Barker then referred to several cases of intimidation coming before magistrates and continued,

> The elements of disorder are painfully apparent and it maybe (with the Police Force worn out with extra duty day and night, for the last month) that those responsible for the preservation of the peace will be unable to cope with contingencies likely to arise, unless assured that Military aid can be invoked if required.

The Mayor's real problem was not just that his police constables were 'worn out' but that he had to commit about a quarter of his available force for the whole city to constantly protect the 'blacklegs' (most of whom were billeted in the timber yards near the Cumberland basin)[81]. This severely stretched his resources, especially with the need to police ever larger demonstrations. The Home Office passed the Mayor's request onto the War Office and replied on 15th December informing him that the General Officer Commanding at Aldershot had been

> instructed to prepare to send military assistance as may be required by the Civil Authorities of Bristol as soon as possible after the receipt of a requisition from the Mayor of that city.[82]

Central government only attached one condition to this directive, that,

> before resorting to Military aid, preparation to meet any apprehended

---

79 Taken from the poster advertising the procession on 23rd December, see *Figure 1*. BCRL Ref: B21533.

80 TNA HO 144/228/A50898A/1

81 Howell estimates that of the 324 police available (69 were sick and absent), about 80 were committed to protecting the 'scabs' at any one time. Howell, *The Police in Late Victorian Bristol*, p. 22.

82 TNA HO 144/228/A50898A/3

disturbances by obtaining aid from other police forces … be made.[83]

According to Schneer, Ben Tillett's biographer, the Mayor took another step on the 12th December,

> sensing that trouble was imminent, he banned not only the weekly gathering in the Horsefair Grounds, but McCarthy's processions as well.[84]

The proscription of the workers' parades and granting of access to military assistance set the Mayor and the Watch Committee on a collision course with the growing workers' movement. The availability of military resources provided the Mayor with a feeling of strength, despite the state of his beleaguered police force. The banning of the weekly processions and mass meetings was a clear provocation as far as the demonstrators were concerned and in the circumstances, as self-proclaimed 'citizens with rights', something they were likely to ignore. It was the conjunction of these perspectives that led to the events of 'Black Friday'.

Tillett and McCarthy Up the Ante…

Figure 5. 'Chinese lanterns vs. lances': detail from a a cartoon in *The Bristol Magpie*, 1893.

A few days after the mass meeting of 11th December, the parade organisers at a meeting of the 'joint committee' consisting of delegates from the Trades Council, the Sander's workers strike committee and the Docker's Union,[85] were faced with two issues. Should they continue with Sunday morning parades and what should they do about Christmas Day, which happened to fall on a Sunday that year? They decided to go ahead with a parade and rally on Sunday 18th and decided to switch the following Sunday demonstration to the Friday night before Christmas, 23rd December.

So, despite the ban on parades, the following Sunday, the march to Clifton and Cotham and a mass meeting in the Horsefair went ahead. Several thousand people gathered in the Haymarket to hear the speeches at the two platforms which were now a regular fixture. Tom McCarthy of the Docker's Union announced to the crowds that,

it was intended to have a grand illuminated procession on Friday night, in

---

83 TNA HO 144/228/A50898A/1

84 Schneer, *Ben Tillett*, p. 82. Curiously no reference to the ban appears in the local press but it is stated in a letter, dated 30th January 1893 from the Bristol Magistrates Clerk to the Director of Prosecutions discussing the various charges against Tillett, that the gathering on the 18th December was 'unlawful'. TNA HO 144/228/A50898A/24.

85 *BM*, 24 Dec 1892.

order to enable them to raise money for the purpose of giving to the wives and children of the dockers some of the comforts of life at this season of the year.[86]

McCarthy then urged the men 'not get into more trouble with the police than they could help', before Ben Tillett rose to the platform. Tillett's (now famous) speech began with a call for solidarity in the use of force:

> he advised them — if they got into trouble — not to do so singly, "but the whole bally lot of them". If it came to a fight, they could fight too, with their fists or with clubs, and if it came to guns they could pick them up also. If it came to the point and they had got to force their demands, they would make violent physical efforts to do what was right, and he would head the first lot of men.

The crowd cheered Tillett on and in an extraordinary moment he asked the assembled mass to repeat after him the following oath,

> I will, if necessary, defend my home and wages by any means, violent or pacific.

The whole meeting chanted the oath and then cheered, with Tillett ominously rounding off his speech with 'now they [the police] could take the whole of them up if they liked'. Little did Tillett know that his words would come back to haunt him in the aftermath of 'Black Friday'.

It's Christmas Time…

The week before Christmas was marked by a game of 'cat and mouse' as the authorities tried to impede the proposed Friday night march whilst secretly organising police and military aid. As the 'joint committee' went about the city pasting up posters advertising the 'Big Lantern Parade' and 'Monstre Meeting' at the Horsefair (see *Figure 1*) correspondence was passing between them and the Chief Constable, Edwin Coathupe, who objected to both the use of flaming 'torches' and the proposed route of the march.[87] On the afternoon of 22nd December, the eve of the parade, a deputation from the 'joint committee' met Coathupe and explained that they did not propose to carry torches at all, but instead 'Chinese Lanterns' on sticks. They even produced an example for him to inspect. Despite their protestations the Chief Constable was unmoved and they reluctantly withdrew the use of lanterns on the parade. However, they refused to give a definite answer on the proposed route of the procession.[88]

That evening the Chief Constable issued a police notice referring to the

---

86 *BTM*, 19 Dec 1892.

87 There was some precedent to the Chief Constable's concern. In late November 1892 there were rumours that a midnight 'torchlight' march of the unemployed would take place through the City and West-end of London led by 'agitators'. Scotland Yard objected to the use of 'torches' and warned the organisers that the march would be attacked and dispersed by police if such items were lit. The march of several hundred actually took place on the evening of 1st December beginning on Tower Hill. Despite the fact that no torches were apparently brandished the march was violently broken up by the police in any case. TNA HO 45/9861/B13077A.

88 *BTM*, 23 Dec 1892.

parade on bills around the city and to the press. This directive to the public banned the use of torches or lanterns and threatened anyone carrying them with arrest. Even more controversially, the Chief Constable defined the route of the procession which was purposely steered away from the city-centre shopping, business and financial quarter.[89] McCarthy responded in characteristic terms with a press-released letter to the Chief Constable which conceded on the lanterns (as they had agreed) but demurred on the route,

> We are sincerely desirous of keeping the peace of the city, but cannot consent to have our line of route marked out for us, and, with all due respect, will only give way when a stronger force than our own is pitted against us, and then only under strong protest.[90]

What McCarthy and the rest of the 'joint committee' were not aware of when they made this statement was that their Christmas fund-raising procession would not just be facing the Bristol police, but a military force as well.

Having sought police reinforcements from neighbouring forces and only managing to obtain fifty or so constables from the county of Gloucestershire, the Mayor made a secret request to the Aldershot garrison for military aid on 22nd December. Three battalions of infantry were held in readiness whilst two squadrons of cavalry from the 4th Dragoon Guards and the 20th Hussars, numbering 212 men and horses were duly dispatched by special train that afternoon arriving in Bristol in the early evening. The majority were billeted for the night at Horfield army barracks in the north of Bristol, with the officers scattered amongst inns and hotels in the city centre. The presence of the military did not go unnoticed on the streets of the city, with one newspaper remarking,

> Considerable excitement was caused in the streets by the somewhat unusual sight in Bristol of the progress of mounted troops through the city, and a large crowd assembled in College street and the neighbourhood to watch the operation of telling off the billeting parties.[91]

A Press Association telegram had arrived at the offices of the *Bristol Times & Mirror* that afternoon stating ominously that

> orders had been received from the Horse Guards for two squadrons of cavalry to proceed from Aldershot to Bristol immediately in preparation, *for expected riots there.*[92]

This was met by consternation amongst the journalists as they tried to determine where and when this 'expected riot' was to occur. The only conclusion they could come to was that it must refer to the Union-organised 'lantern parade' the following night, at which they stated 'no disturbance is expected.'[93]

---

89 This was The Grove-Prince St-Thunderbolt St-Broad Quay-in front of the Tontine Warehouses to the Stone Bridge-Rupert St-terminating at the Horsefair, *BTM*, 23 Dec 1892.

90 Ibid.

91 *BM*, 24 Dec 1892.

92 *BTM*, 23 Dec 1892. My emphasis.

93 Ibid.

Friday December 23rd 1892: A Night of Infamy...

News of the arrival of the military the night before rapidly spread around the city and despite the implied threat, the 'joint committee' continued with their preparations for the march and rally that evening. Meanwhile the Chief Constable set up an operations room at Bridewell Central Police Station to act as a command centre for the supposed forthcoming 'riot'. One journalist described the scene at Bridewell as being like 'a war game in connection with a tactical society'.[94] At 4.30pm selected magistrates were called by the Clerk of Justices to a 'special meeting' at the Petty Sessional House near Bridewell.[95] The business of the meeting was to

> arrange for which part of the City you and others would be willing to attend and, on horseback, read the riot proclamation, if deemed necessary.

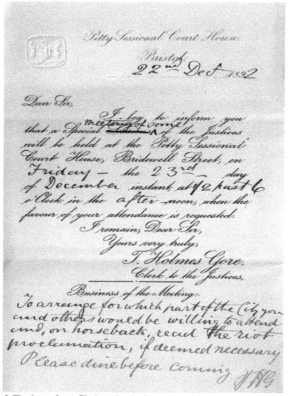

Figure 6. The letter from Clerk to the Justices to Magistrates inviting them to a meeting to organise the reading of the 'Riot Act' in advance of 'Black Friday'.

---

94   *BM*, 24 Dec 1892.
95   BRO Ref: 36269(2)a.

The invitation (see *Figure 6*) cordially advised the magistrates to 'please dine before coming' suggesting it might be a long night. Three magistrates, an aristocrat and two industrialists, were chosen to ride with the Cavalry units, Colonel Saville, Charles Wills and Arthur Baker, the latter pair being members of the Watch Committee. In case they forgot their lines in the 'heat of battle', they were provided with cards printed with the Riot Act proclamation.[96] (See *Figure 7*.) The remaining magistrates and the Mayor proceeded to the operations room at Bridewell to oversee events.[97]

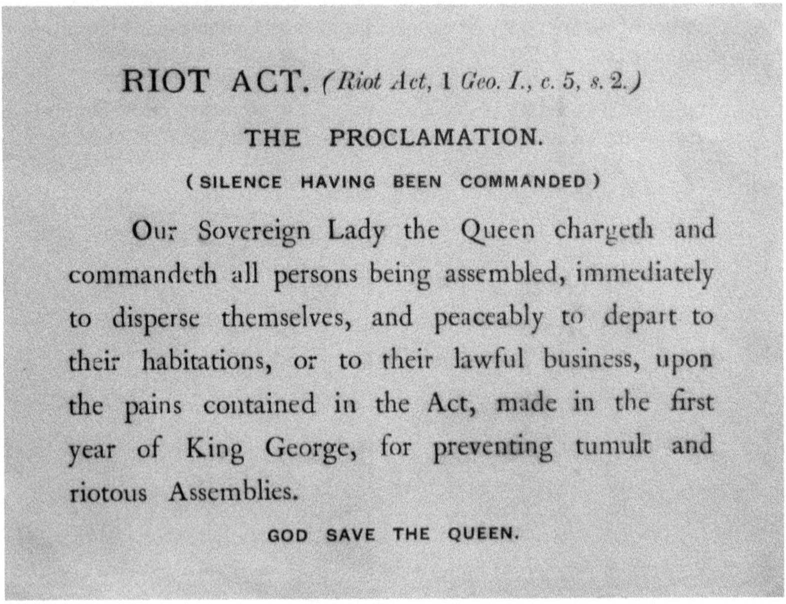

RIOT ACT. *(Riot Act, 1 Geo. I., c. 5, s. 2.)*

THE PROCLAMATION.

(SILENCE HAVING BEEN COMMANDED)

Our Sovereign Lady the Queen chargeth and commandeth all persons being assembled, immediately to disperse themselves, and peaceably to depart to their habitations, or to their lawful business, upon the pains contained in the Act, made in the first year of King George, for preventing tumult and riotous Assemblies.

GOD SAVE THE QUEEN.

Figure 7. Original card with the words of the 'Riot Act' handed to magistrates who were to marshall the cavalry units on 'Black Friday'.

The Cavalry squadrons were deployed at various strategic locations in the city. At 6.30pm fifty Hussars passed down Prince Street to Cumberland Road where they were stationed to protect the billets of the 'blacklegs' at the timber yards. The rest of the Hussars were stationed on Canon's Marsh, College Green and at the top of Park Street to 'prevent any crowd passing that way to Clifton'.[98] Twenty-five Dragoons were stationed at the Bristol Tramway Yard on Baldwin Street, close to the Drawbridge where they expected to see some 'action'.[99] The majority of the Dragoons (about seventy-five) had galloped down Gloucester Road from Horfield Barracks at 6.30pm and were then mustered at the central police station at Bridewell. A unit of mounted police was guarding Prince Street

96   BRO Ref: 36269(2)c.

97   These were Sir Charles Wathen, Herbert Thomas, C.B. Howe, Edward Robinson, J.C. Godwin and J.W. Hall. *BM*, 24 Dec 1892.

98   *WDP*, 24 Dec 1892. The magistrate Col. Saville was present with the Hussars at the top of Park Street.

99   The Drawbridge was an operational structure which crossed the floating harbour between Baldwin Street and St Augustine's Parade (see Map, Location 10, p. 150). The Drawbridge was rebuilt for the fourth and final time in 1868, but by 1893 was replaced by a fixed structure. http://en.wikipedia.org/wiki/The_Centre,_Bristol.

whilst almost the entire Bristol police force was being manoeuvred in military style formations to create cordons protecting the financial and commercial districts in the city centre.[100]

Figure 8. Bristol police practice their sabre drill without horses in the 1870s.

Around 7.00pm at The Grove (near Queen Square) thousands of demonstrators began to gather in the bitterly cold wind. At first there was some confusion as to where and when the procession was going to form up and leave. Without lanterns, the only light was provided by the new moon and the few gas lamps which made it hard to make out faces let alone marshal the masses of demonstrators. The arrival of the Dockers' Union leader, Tom McCarthy, was met by cheers. Song sheets were then distributed and soon the crowd was singing one of the deal runners' recent favourites'

> Glory, Glory, Hallelujah, Glory, Glory, Hallelujah,
> We'll hang Grammy Hunter on a sour apple tree, as we go marching on.[101]

After a few false starts, the recently released French activist Gaspard de La Croix who was waving a stick with his hat perched on top,[102] took the initiative and with a Fife and Drum band led a large contingent of the marchers out of the Grove and along the route designated by the Chief Constable.[103] Detectives and plain clothes police had infiltrated the crowds[104] and the 'troublemaker' La Croix was certainly a well-known target for surveillance. One police prosecutor later commented on this

---

100 *BM*, 24 Dec 1892.

101 Bryher, *An Account of the Labour & Socialist Movement in Bristol*, II, p. 40.

102 La Croix was probably mimicking the French revolutionaries who placed their 'liberty caps' on their pikes to celebrate victories. This was later misinterpreted in his court case.

103 *BM*, 29 Dec 1892. The routes of all three parades on the evening of December 23rd 1892 are shown on Map, p. 150-1.

104 *BM*, 24 Dec 1892.

the police followed that portion of the crowd led off by La Croix, under the impression that the whole procession would pass that way; but a ruse seemed to have been practised by those in authority amongst the processionists, because the greater portion of the crowd — La Croix having gone off, and the police having followed — went along Welsh Back towards Bristol Bridge.[105]

Having sold the police a 'pre-organised' dummy, McCarthy, some members of the 'joint committee' and a contingent of about five hundred dockers, deal runners and their supporters headed towards Bristol Bridge where they were met by a major police cordon blocking entries to the financial and shopping districts of the city centre, (see Map Location 4). Instead of attempting to break the police line, at about 7.40pm McCarthy's entourage crossed the bridge and headed down Redcliff Street.[106] This caused significant worry in the operations room at Bridewell as they feared the crowd was aiming to attack the 'blacklegs' billeted at the timber yards on the Floating Harbour.[107] Consequently twenty-five Dragoons, accompanied by the magistrate Arthur Baker were dispatched from the central police station to head them off. However, McCarthy's contingent took a circuitous route, crossing back over the river at the St. Philips Bridge and eventually making their way to the Horsefair for the mass meeting.

Just before 8.00pm a third, apparently 'leaderless', contingent of demonstrators, estimated by the police to number 5,000 or more, left The Grove and broke into a run along Welsh Back towards Bristol Bridge. The police cordon, armed with batons and staves, was concentrated at the entrances to High Street and Bridge Street, to stop the marchers entering the city centre, the most direct route to the Horsefair. Hundreds if not thousands of demonstrators and onlookers thronged the area. The crowd charging down Welsh Back however did not deviate in its aim and 'swept everything before them, Supt. Cann called upon them to stop, but the crowd rushed on, breaking the police line'.[108] The Chief Superintendent along with many other police were literally 'trampled' as the crowd smashed through their line and broke into a run along Bridge Street heading towards the Horsefair. After hundreds of demonstrators had poured through the gap, the police line reformed and constables lashed out with their staves and batons at the large crowd which confronted them. A few minutes later a party of thirty Dragoons sent from Bridewell arrived on the scene, but far too late to prevent the breach. The cavalry unit left a few minutes later making their way back along Bridge Street and Union Street to the Horsefair followed by hundreds of jeering and hooting demonstrators.[109]

---

105 *BM*, 29 Dec 1892. Conspiracy theories are not just the province of aggrieved protesters; the police often come up with such stories to explain their own failures. For example, Detective Rawle claimed in the aftermath of 'Black Friday' that 'several of the marchers had dressed as police officers and marched at the head of the procession as if to escort them. This apparently served to confuse many of the constables on duty', Howell, *The Police in Late Victorian Bristol*, pp. 23-4. However, it seems that in this particular case La Croix, by design or chance, fooled the Bristol police into following him.

106 *BM*, 24 Dec 1892.

107 There had already been earlier reports that 'there were excited crowds of dockers in the neighbourhood of the timber yard, armed with sticks'. Howell, *The Police in Late Victorian Bristol*, p. 23.

108 *BM*, 24 Dec 1892.

109 Bryher, *An Account of the Labour & Socialist Movement in Bristol*, II, pp. 40-1.

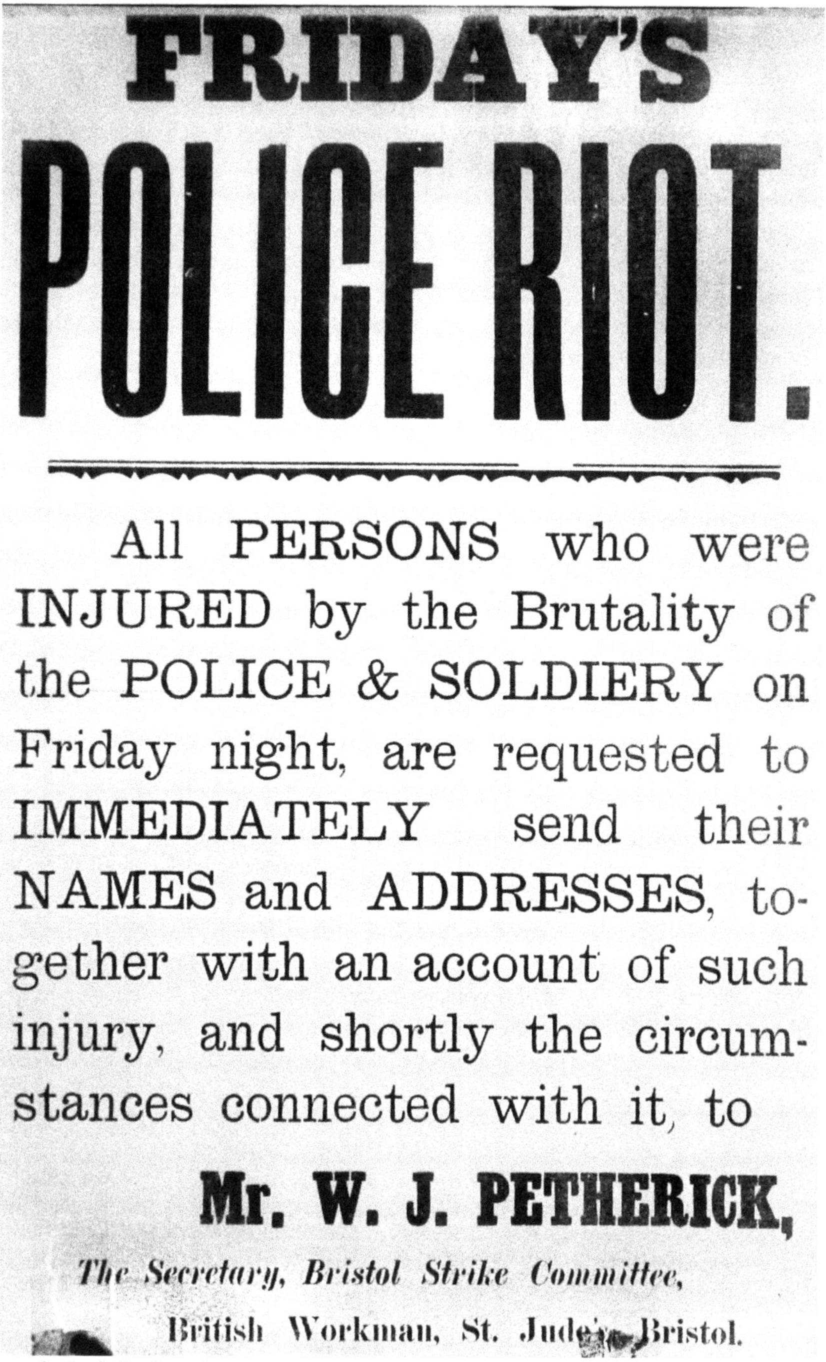

FRIDAY'S
POLICE RIOT.

All PERSONS who were INJURED by the Brutality of the POLICE & SOLDIERY on Friday night, are requested to IMMEDIATELY send their NAMES and ADDRESSES, together with an account of such injury, and shortly the circumstances connected with it, to

Mr. W. J. PETHERICK,

The Secretary, Bristol Strike Committee,

British Workman, St. Jude's, Bristol.

Figure 9. The Strike Committee poster calling for those civilians injured on 'Black Friday' to come forward.

At the Horsefair at about 8.15pm one of the bands struck up with 'See the conquering hero comes' as the first of the marchers came into view. The crowds swelled as more demonstrators arrived from different routes and others were attracted to the spectacle. One journalist described the scene: 'As far as the eye could reach, nothing could be seen but a mass of heads, reaching as far as the top of Union-street'.[110] The massive throng which packed the Haymarket and surrounding streets was estimated as being somewhere between 20,000 and 30,000 people.[111] The customary two wagons were drawn up at either end of the Haymarket to serve as platforms and speaker after speaker denounced the stupidity of the City Council, the Watch Committee and the Magistrates for calling on the military and trying to impede the parade. Francis Gilmore Barnett shouted from one platform to the crowd that they should

> not be in the least surprised if the Watch Committee ordered an ironclad
> to come into Avonmouth, gunboats to control the river, and a park of
> artillery to take up a position on Durdham down.[112]

However, most of the speakers praised the marchers for their restraint and urged them 'to maintain a peaceful and orderly demeanour', one condemned the 'men who tried to incite them' and McCarthy even praised the Chief Constable for his 'tact' in a blatant attempt to drive a wedge between the police force and the Watch Committee (who he claimed had called in the military).[113] During the speeches, detachments of cavalry ominously passed through the Horsefair soliciting groans and hoots from the crowd.

At about 9.20pm the speakers wound up the meeting but the demonstrators did not immediately disperse. At about 9.30pm, Chief Superintendent Cann, after an altercation, snatched the secretary of the Seamen and Firemen Union, Charles Jarman, out of a crowd near Silver St and arrested him for 'leading an unruly and riotous crowd at Bristol Bridge'. This act precipitated an affray as his comrades tried to retrieve the struggling Jarman from the stave-wielding constabulary. Shortly after this incident, the Chief Constable ordered a detachment of Dragoons led by their commanding officer Colonel Schwabe to leave Bridewell and assist the police. Accompanied by the Watch Committee Magistrate Charles Wills they positioned themselves in the middle of the Haymarket.[114] On the orders of Wills they then moved across the square towards

---

110 *BTM*, 24 Dec 1892.

111 Crowd estimates are given in the following secondary sources; 'at least 20,000' Bryher, *An Account of the Labour & Socialist Movement in Bristol*, II, p. 41; '30,000', Howell, *The Police in Late Victorian Bristol*, p. 23; '20,000' Kelly and Richardson, *The Shaping of the Bristol Labour Movement, 1885-1985*, p. 215; 'between 10 and 30,000' Atkinson, *Trade Unions in Bristol*, p. 12; 'about 20,000' McNeill, *Ben Tillett*, p. 11; and 'between 28,000 and 35,000' Large, *The Municipal Government of Bristol 1851-1901*, p. 88.

112 *BTM*, 24 Dec 1892. Gilmore-Barnett's remarks may have seemed fanciful in 1892, but they were actually undertaken by the British state in Liverpool only 19 years later.

113 Ibid.

114 Some sources claim that Wills read the 'Riot Act' at this point, for example 'he [Wills] attempted to read the Riot Act, stick in hand, to the crowd' Howell, *The Police in Late Victorian Bristol*, p. 24 and Large, *The Municipal Government of Bristol 1851-1901*, p. 88. Other accounts, however, specifically deny this, for example Bryher, *An Account of the Labour & Socialist Movement in Bristol*, II, p. 44, Mullen, *Sweet Girls and Deal Runners*, p. 117 and most importantly that of

Bridewell Street, scattering the crowd with the butt ends of their lances. From the opposite end of the square, the police swarmed out of Silver Street, battering all and sundry with their clubs. Stones and bottles were hurled by the crowd at police and cavalry whilst others fought them with fists and sticks.[115] The Haymarket descended into a pitched battle. A second detachment of Dragoons arrived and proceeded to chase the crowd (who responded with missiles) around the Horsefair and surrounding streets. In the confusion, many people climbed the railings into St. James Churchyard to escape the cavalry charges, but the police soon drove them out, cracking many heads in the process. Attempts to violently disperse the crowd continued for about half an hour, before the cavalry were withdrawn at 10.00pm having 'thoroughly scattered, though not dispersed the crowds'. For a further hour the police, now in the ascendency, violently broke up the remaining groups of demonstrators and bystanders, eventually leaving a silent, empty square littered with battered hats and broken placards.[116]

5. The aftermath

> Liberal fool and Tory rogue had combined together to place Bristol on the verge of destruction.[117]

The local reaction

The events of 23rd December were roundly condemned by the unions, the Socialist Society and many other organisations, including the Liberal Reform Club who railed at the 'dastardly conduct of the authorities for instructing the military and police to charge the peaceful and orderly meeting of citizens held in the Horsefair this evening'. A local newspaper, the *Bristol Mercury*, coined the term 'Black Friday' and went on to state,

> the good humour and law-abiding temper of a Bristol crowd were put to a very severe test last night, and, we rejoice to say, came successfully through the ordeal. There seems to have been plenty of Justices in readiness with the Riot Act burning in their pockets and feeling themselves major-generals at the very least. ... We feel profoundly indignant at the slur which has been passed upon the good name of Bristol by the panic-stricken and needless appeal to military force.[118]

A week after the events, a statement from the 'Strike Committee' was re-

---

Chief Superintendent Cann in TNA HO 144/228/A50898A/24. Tellingly, none of the local press mentions the reading of the Riot Act in their initial accounts of the 'Battle of the Haymarket'.

115 One knocked the Cavalry Commander Schwabe's hat off, two troopers were unseated when their horses fell and several others suffered minor injuries from missiles. TNA HO 144/228/A50898A/7.

116 This paragraph was constructed by cross referencing the following sources: *BM*, 24 Dec 1892; *BTM*, 24 Dec 1892; *CC*, 28 Dec 1892; *WDP*, 24 Dec 1892; Bryher, *An Account of the Labour & Socialist Movement in Bristol*, II, pp. 42-3; Atkinson, *Trade Unions in Bristol*, p. 12; Howell, *The Police in Late Victorian Bristol*, p. 24; Mullen, *Sweet Girls and Deal Runners*, p. 117; Malos, *Bristol Women in Action (1839-1919)*, p. 120; Large, *The Municipal Government of Bristol 1851-1901*, p. 88; and Chief Superintendent Cann's account in TNA HO 144/228/A50898A/24.

117 From a speech by Tom McCarthy at the Horsefair on 'Black Friday', Bryher, *An Account of the Labour & Socialist Movement in Bristol*, II, p. 42.

118 Ibid., p. 43.

published in the *Mercury* which claimed that 'the local press have given no adequate account of police and military brutality' and went on to state,

> the bulk of the procession reached the Horsefair (choosing their own route) with very little disorder, and the police and military, enraged at their own discomfiture, from that time and long after the meetings were over, charged the crowds up and down the main streets with batons, swords, and lances...The wonder is that Bristol men took both insult and injury so tamely, and it is hoped that by calling public attention to the outrageous action of our magistrates on this occasion you will help to prevent further scandals in the future.[119]

Initially the authorities and press played down the incident whilst (laughably) claiming that only six or eight demonstrators had been injured on 'Black Friday'. However, the *Bristol Times and Mirror* carried this interesting statement under the list of the casualties, 'Reports have been brought to our office of assaults, on the part of individual policemen, which could not have been justified by the circumstances'.[120] As a result of the official silence on this issue (other than announcing that fifty-one policemen had suffered injuries), the 'Strike Committee' published 500 posters asking injured persons to come forward. (See *Figure 9*.) As a result fifty-seven 'civilians' were confirmed as casualties of the incidents on 'Black Friday'. According to a contemporary source 'many of these claimed to be persons returning home from work or engaged in Christmas shopping, and in no way connected with the demonstrators'.[121] Despite this being almost certainly an underestimate of the number of injured civilians, this survey did demonstrate the seriousness of the event to the wider public.

The response of the Mayor and the Watch Committee to the events of 'Black Friday' was characteristically intransigent. Following on from their banning of public meetings and parades in December, the authorities proscribed all meetings of more than four persons.[122] The Mayor also appealed to central government to permanently station the requisitioned unit of the Dragoon Guards in Bristol. After a significant exchange of correspondence in which a representative of the Mayor claimed,

> Bristol bears an unfortunate reputation in connection with riots, and the Bristol Magistrates believe they know the Locality and are conscious of the requirements for dealing with the class which has been termed the "residuum", including those now designated "unemployed".[123]

Central government eventually ignored their dramatic requests and withdrew the remaining cavalry squadron in April 1893.[124] The Mayor and the Watch Committee were not finished however; someone other than themselves had to be

---

119 *BM*, 30 Dec 1892. The statement was signed by W.J.Petherick (Secretary of the Bristol Strike Committee) and Harold Brabham (Secretary of the Bristol and District Gas Workers and General Labourers Union).

120 *BTM*, 24 Dec 1892.

121 Bryher, *An Account of the Labour & Socialist Movement in Bristol*, II, p. 43.

122 Schneer, *Ben Tillett*, p. 84.

123 TNA HO 144/228/A50898A/42.

124 TNA HO 144/228/A50898A/50.

punished for the 'Black Friday' disaster.

A Public Enquiry…

Ten days after 'Black Friday' in Bristol City Council the 'people's lawyer', Hugh Holmes Gore, after receiving evasive answers from the Mayor to his questions concerning the event, proposed that the body called on the Home Office to conduct a public enquiry into the incidents. This would specifically investigate

> the cause which induced the magistrates to obtain the presence of military on the 23rd December; as to their justification in making such request; as to the conduct of the police and military on the 23rd December in relation to the disturbance on that day; and generally as to the action of the magistrates prior to and in relation to the disturbance.[125]

Unsurprisingly considering the class composition and culpability of the City Council, after a heated debate, Gore's motion was soundly defeated by 43 votes to 12.[126] This however did not stop calls for central government to act. Petitions for a public enquiry arrived at the Home Office from the Liberal Association, Trades Council, Boot & Shoe Operatives, and Cabinet Makers in Bristol and from similar organisations in Swansea, St. Helens, Birmingham, Leicester, Norwich, Nottingham, Sunderland, Bury and Glasgow.[127] However, as with Bristol City Council, central government was unmoved.

…or Some Convenient Scapegoats?

Not satisfied with precipitating the 'riot' they had predicted prior to the event, the authorities in Bristol had been working hard to find some scapegoats to justify the use of the military and absolve them of blame for 'Black Friday'. On 29th December, Charles Jarman (Secretary of the Seamen's and Firemen's Union), Gaspard de La Croix (the French activist) and James Baker (a member of the Gas Worker's Union) all appeared in court in Bristol and had the proverbial 'book thrown at them'. (See *Figure 10.*) They were indicted with 'inciting certain other persons to commit the offence of unlawful assembly to the terror of her Majesty's subjects' and with 'assaulting Police-Superintendent Cann and other members of the city force'. Jarman was also charged with inciting a 'riot' on 19th December at a public meeting.[128] In addition, they were all jointly charged with another, Charles Smith, for having participated in the offence of 'unlawful assembly'.[129] These were serious charges and in March 1893 the Judge made great play on his supposed 'leniency' in only (*sic*) sentencing Jarman, La

---

125 *BM*, 3 Jan 1893.

126 Bryher, *An Account of the Labour & Socialist Movement in Bristol*, II, pp. 43-4.

127 TNA HO 144/228/A50898A Frontispiece. This particular Home Office file was closed for many years after 'Black Friday'. Unfortunately in 1905 and 1934 the file was sifted and, for unknown reasons, all of these petitions were destroyed.

128 This was a meeting at Three Queens Lane where Jarman had allegedly 'said they were going to fight the police, Watch Committee, Council, naval and military forces'. *BM*, 25 Mar 1893.

129 *BM*, 2 Jan 1893, 25 Mar 1893.

THE LATE RIOTS. SKETCHES IN COURT.

Figure 10. 'The Late Riots. Sketches in Court' - Scenes from the 'show trial' of Jarman, Smith, Baker and La Croix for 'unlawful assembly' and 'incitement to riot' on 'Black Friday' from *The Bristol Magpie* January 1893.

Croix and Baker to three months in prison and sureties of £100 each to be of good behaviour for six months.[130]

However, the Mayor, Watch Committee and Magistrates were not satisfied with charging these 'small fry' from Bristol, they were after a much bigger fish, the national Dockers' Union leader, Ben Tillett. On 29th December, a summons was issued to Tillett to appear in court in Bristol on 9th January. Tillett was charged that on 18th December he

> unlawfully did incite certain people then and there present to unlawfully
> assemble and unlawfully commit a riot in the said city and county of

---

130 Ibid. £100 was a huge sum for each of the defendants, equal to about two years of the average wage.

Bristol on the twenty third day of December.[131]

The same day, directed by the Mayor and Magistrates, the Bristol Clerk to the Justices wrote to the Director of Public Prosecutions (DPP) in London informing him of the summons and stating,

> The prosecution of a person holding a prominent position in London and visiting Provincial Towns in which he may utter inflammatory language whereby the duties of those responsible for the preservation of the peace is rendered very difficult, is considered by the Bristol Magistrates to be one which should be undertaken by you as the Public Prosecutor and ought not be left to the Local Police.[132]

This calculated attempt by the Bristol authorities to draw Whitehall into the equation was immediately rebuffed by the DPP, who replied 'that without the express directions of the Home Secretary I must decline to take any action'.[133] This was no surprise on a legal level as it was somewhat ludicrous to attempt to charge a man for 'inciting a riot' a week previously to an event at which he was not present.[134] However, the DPP was also placing the 'ball in the court' of the Bristol Mayor and Westminster by intimating that it would be a *political* rather than *legal* decision if this case were to go ahead; effectively a show trial.

The Mayor responded on 31st December by writing to the Home Secretary asking for him to instruct the DPP to proceed.[135] The Home Secretary declined to intervene in the matter and left it in the hands of the authorities in Bristol to carry out the 'show trial' locally.[136] Tillett was no fool, the prospect of being tried by a bunch of bourgeois provincial magistrates who were directly involved in organising police and military repression of 'Black Friday' was not appealing to say the least. Tillett knew they wanted to imprison him for as long as possible to 'get them off the hook' of the debacle on 'Black Friday' and to demonstrate that the labour movement's leaders were in the firing line if working class struggles intensified. Consequently he initiated two important responses.

The first was to publish his supposedly 'incendiary speech' of 18th December in a popular pamphlet.[137] (See *Figure 4*.) This was a direct riposte to the charge of incitement being laid at his door. On the evening of Saturday 7th January 1893, Tillett arrived in Bristol ready to appear in court on the Monday to hear the charges outlined in the summons and was given a hero's welcome by crowd of 7-8,000 dockers, unionists and their supporters. He was paraded through the streets on a carriage drawn by the dockers (see *Figure 11*) and spoke briefly at a

---

131 TNA HO 144/228/A50898A/24.

132 TNA HO 144/228/A50898A/8.

133 TNA HO 144/228/A50898A/9.

134 Despite the oral history transcript from 1939 quoted in Howell, *The Police in Late Victorian Bristol*, p. 24, there is no evidence that Tillett was present on 'Black Friday' and all other sources agree with this.

135 TNA HO 144/228/A50898A/8.

136 TNA HO 144/228/A50898A/24. The Mayor complained that this 'confidential' information was leaked to the *Daily News* on 10th January, almost certainly from within Westminster. This information certainly helped Tillett as it appeared that central government did not regard the case as being legitimate.

137 *Prosecution of Ben Tillett (Gen. Sec. Dockers' Union): Speech Delivered in Horsefair, Bristol, Dec. 18th, 1892.*

rally on the Grove. The next day he spoke again at the Grove to a crowd of 5,000 in driving sleet and snow and promised,

> come what may, they would go through with the fight. The fight was not for a day, and not for a year, but for eternity … It must not finish at trades unionism — it must not finish until the workers of all grades and degrees commanded absolutely the whole machinery of the state, the whole machinery of government, of production, control and distribution.[138]

Tillett's hearing in Bristol trundled on for several weeks, until at the beginning of February 1893 he exposed his second ace. Tillett successfully applied to the Queen's Bench to transfer the trial to the Central Criminal Courts in London on the basis he would not receive a fair and impartial trial in his home city.[139]

Figure 11. Ben Tillett being drawn though the streets of Bristol by dockers on his triumphant return after being indicted for 'incitement to riot', from a detail of a cartoon in *The Bristol Magpie*, January 1893.

Having escaped the clutches of the slavering Bristol Mayor and Magistrates, Tillett was eventually tried at the Old Bailey in London in April. At this trial the Judge commended him for 'looking more innocent than anyone else in court' and he managed to cast doubt on the transcriptions of his 'incendiary speech' by police spies on 18th December 1892, which led to the jury acquitting him.[140]

Tillett's court victory effectively marked the end of the 'Black Friday' saga. However, the deal runners and 'Sweet Girls' were not so lucky. Despite a huge labour demonstration on February 9th 1893, when an estimated 30,000 Trade Unionists led by fifteen bands paraded through the streets to another rally at the

138 *The Times,* 9 Jan 1893 and Schneer, *Ben Tillett,* p. 85.
139 *The Times,* 3 Feb 1893.
140 *The Times,* 15 Apr 1893 and Ibid., pp. 85-6.

Grove,[141] both of these long-running strikes were eventually lost in the spring of 1893. The Sanders Strike Committee accepted that the Union recognition fight at the plant was over (for now) and found alternative and better paid employment for all the striking 'Sweet Girls'. After 32 weeks on strike the Deal Runners conceded defeat over the piece work issue in April 1893; though they stated confidently that the timber merchants attempt to smash the Union had failed.[142]

6. Conclusions

It is tempting to brand the disastrous events of 'Black Friday' as being merely the result of a conspiracy of corrupt local government officials. This is far from the truth. They were not corrupt, but following their own interests as members or representatives of the industrial class who 'owned' the city. Neither did they clandestinely conspire; their actions, although rooted in the overtly repressive tactics of the early nineteenth century, were merely the kind of old-school response that they would be expected to collectively organise when faced by a militant working-class active on the streets of Bristol.

If anything 'Black Friday' exposed to the ruling class of the city that less contentious (and dangerous) tactics to control disputes and demonstrations may be required. Central to this was the recognition that the 'New Unions' were a force to be reckoned with and, crucially, with which to be *negotiated*. Many liberal commentators on the 'Labour Question' argued that if the working-class joined Unions then this would actually reduce the number of unofficial 'wildcat' strikes (i.e. under their immediate control) and force them into official arbitration via their union leaderships.[143] It was also recognised that the more 'unruly' and problematic sections of the unskilled working-class, such as the deal runners, could be disciplined by these very unions, as their leaders had tried to do in the autumn of 1892.

The problem posed by the increasing enfranchisement of the working-class was to be dealt with in a similar manner. Rather than outright confrontation as had been the case earlier in the century, the 'socialist threat' had to primarily be dealt with by propaganda and sometimes compromise. The use of the military in December 1892 had clearly exacerbated a volatile situation, despite the protestations from the Mayor and City Council that they had 'saved the city' from a conflagration *a la* 1831. Consequently the police became the preferred instrument of control under normal circumstances, though of course they still had the military if they were so required.

The events leading up to and on 'Black Friday' exposed to working-class

---

141 Bryher, *An Account of the Labour & Socialist Movement in Bristol*, II, p. 47. The humour of the Bristol crowd concerning 'Black Friday' was exhibited by the marchers carrying the penny Chinese Lanterns which had so 'frightened the magistrates'.

142 Ibid., pp. 49-50.

143 For a contemporary example see the discussions in *Women Workers: Papers Read at a Conference Convened by the Bristol & Clifton Ladies Association for the Care of Ladies, in November 1892* (Bristol: J.W. Arrowsmith, 1893). See also the comments of Richardson concerning the 'problems' of arbitration for the 'New Unions' in Chapter 4 above.

Bristolians (if they did not know already) that the relatively new police force[144] were going to be ordered to protect the interests of the bosses both in labour disputes and street demonstrations. This raised the question of how to deal with this issue. At this stage the socialists and union leaders in the main saw a political route (a 'labour party'), via the existing structures (representative democracy, parliament and local government), to gain control over state bodies. This was increasingly challenged by revolutionary syndicalist ideas over the last years of the century, causing a significant schism within the labour movement. However, on a practical level, the strikes of 1889-90 and the events of autumn 1892 in Bristol demonstrated that mass solidarity between workers in many different trades, the unwaged and their communities was effective and posed a significant threat to the local bourgeoisie.[145]

This solidarity was put into effect in many diverse forms, but I shall leave the reader with one example which sums up the bravery of those Bristolians who stood up to the police and military on 'Black Friday':

> Here is a pathetic little story of Friday night's affray between the police, the troopers, and the public when the area in the Haymarket was being cleared by the aid of the Dragoons. An elderly man flying from the police only just reached the Arcade entrance when he received a blow on the head. The police were going to hit him another blow when a little girl stepped forward and begged them "not to hit her father again". The appeal was so prompt and came with such simple and touching force from the child that the man — whatever the merits or demerits of his case — escaped further truncheon visitation. His head was bound up, and the child followed him and a companion to the Infirmary, and stood beside them when the porter was taking particulars of the casualty. Seeing the ragged and scantily clothed little one of ten standing by, the porter said, "Well little girl, is this your father?" "No" replied the sharp little one; "but I saved him from another hit when the policeman was going at 'im. I asked 'im not to hit my father again, and he stopped. But he 'aint my father at all!"[146]

---

144 The police force had been formed in Bristol in June 1836. Howell, *The Police in Late Victorian Bristol*, p. 1.

145 This also solidarity extended across the country, with the Sander's workers Strike Committee reporting that 'over five hundred pounds had been subscribed from all parts of the country, in districts ranging from Scotland to Devonshire, and South Wales to the Humber ... Many of the girls actually received more as strike pay than their wages would have amounted to, so meagre was the pittance received from their late employers'. Bryher, *An Account of the Labour & Socialist Movement in Bristol*, II, p. 49.

146 *BM*, 31 Dec 1892.

BLACK FRIDAY.

(BRISTOL, December 23, 1892.)

Figure 12. The 'Black Friday' song recorded the events of 23rd December 1892.

bill up say-ing, "Oh! oh! oh!" my or-ders are to nev-er let you go, go,

go, Through Bristol's streets by night, With your lanterns all a-light, And -

1st time   *2nd time*

if you try my bob-bies will cry, "woh! woh! woh!"   "woh!"

But Labour winked its eye and said ;
    "The Chief but plays catspaw,
To those who each day sit in Court
    A-belching forth the law."
Wills, Wathen, Thomas, Baker, Low,
    And such like beaks as these,
Have sought to trap the working man,
    And bring him to his knees.

Chorus.
But they shan't stop the march we have in view,
    view, view,
With shoulder pressed to shoulder staunch and
    true, true, true ;
We'll march to the Horsefair and hold our
    meeting there,
And show the world that we can dare and do,
    do, do.

On Bristol Bridge we looked so grand
    That Cann with fright fell down ;
Across his manly chest we strode
    And marched up through the town ;
Into the Horsefair thousands poured
    With bands and flags galore,
And listened to the speeches made
    By Brabham and by Gore.

Chorus.
But Charlie Wills rode up and said, "By George,
    George, George,
This crowd like me is very fine and large, large,
    large,
A. riot *I* must make, for the law these men
    won't break,
So never mind the blessed Act, but Charge!
    Charge! Charge!"

Along the streets the soldiers rode
    Dispensing sabre cuts,
The bobbies drew their truncheons out
    And bashed in people's nuts.
And when perchance they happ'd to meet
    A fellow all alone,
They knocked him down, then ran him in,
    To save him walking home.

Chorus.
And twenty bob or fourteen days he got, got,
    got,
The beaks had sworn that they would make it
    hot, hot, hot,
For rows *they* can't abide, excepting on *their*
    side;
And justice for the working man is rot, rot,
    rot.

Intermezzo

Coffee Taverns

•

Stephen E. Hunt

While researching the radical history of Bristol in particular, we could not help but notice that much of the activity took place in the city's plentiful coffee taverns.

There are two significant links between the coffee taverns and radical traditions. First, during the in eighteenth and early nineteenth centuries, Stamp Acts were enforced to charge duty on printed matter to generate money for the government and prevent the dissemination of literature considered to be seditious. A coffee room subscription to a journal was an effective way to spread the cost to reading customers of what critics regarded as a tax on opinion.

A view of the long vanished Star Coffee House in Lower Castle Street, Bristol in the 1930s.

Second, there was a strong correlation between teetotalism and religious non-conformism. One of the first English temperance societies was set up in Bristol in 1830 and two temperance hotels opened in the city later in that decade.[1] In our period, the older tradition of teetotalism on the part of religious and radical non-conformists was acceded by a new generation of socialists and reformers such as Philip Snowden, Guy Aldred and Seebohm Rowntree who feared that alcoholism would exacerbate the burden of poverty and debt upon working-class families and neighbourhoods or undermine the class struggle.

---

1   See Andrew Davison, '"Try the Alternative": The Built Heritage of the Temperance Movement', *Brewery History* 123 (Summer 2006), pp. 92 and 101, [online]: http://breweryhistory.com/journal/archive/123/Temperance.pdf [accessed 26 January 2014].

Coal Merchants.

Ashton Vale and South Liberty Coal depot, Mead street
Beachim & Balmont, 38 Queen square
BIRD F. & CO. Station road, Montpelier
Bolt T. Prewett street, Cathay
Bristol Channel Coal Co. Temple back
Budd & Co. 18 Queen sq.—exporters
Cardiff & South Wales Co.—Bowen & Evans, props—offices, 6 Bristolbridge
Clifton Coal Co., Clifton Down station
Coalpit Heath Coal Co. Avon st, St Philip's
Cook H. 131 Hotwell road
Davies T. & Sons, St Philip's marsh
Deacon Hy. 37 Queen sq,—agent for Nixon's Navigation Co. Lim, Cardiff
Dudley and Gibson, Whiteladies road, and Merchant's parade, Hotwells
Edis & Neale, 43 York rd, Montpelier
Eyles J. Hotwell road
Foxwell T. D. & Son, Totterdown wharf
GALBRATIH W. (Poole Bros. and Co.) Hotwell road
Giles Geo. Kensington road, Lovers' walk
Hendy & Co. Kingsland pl, Batch, coal office, upper Railway wharf
Huntley & Cockram, Lawrence hill station
Jones F. W. Station road, Montpelier
Kingswood & Parkfield Collieries Co., Midland road, and Station road, Montpelier. John Henshaw, sec.
Leonard, Boult & Co. Lim., Easton colliery
Lewis Robt. 124 Newfoundland road, and Lawrence hill station
Love Wm. Philip st. Bath street
Lovell J. G. Butts wharf
Merthyr Smokeless Coal Office, A. J. Smith, 47 Queen square
Milton & Co. Station road, Montpelier
Newport Coal and Coke Company, St. Philip's bridge
Oakley & Co. Station rd, Montpelier
Paul T. & Co. Royal arcade & Clifton Down station
Peirce & Co. Station road, Montpelier
POND E. Redcliff Railway Wharf
Quin John, Temple back
Sage F. W. Upper Railway wharf, Midland road
Sharpe T. junr. Sea mills
Silvey T. & Co. coal merchants, upper Railway wharf, Midland road
Smith A. J. 47 Queen square
SNOW JOHN AND CO. Kingsland pl. St Philip's, Upper Railway wharf, Clifton down, Lawrence hill, and Fishponds stations
Stone Samuel, Upper Easton
Twining L. & Co. 91 Alma rd, Clifton
Vincent W. & Co. Commercial road, Bedminster
Wainbrook Coal Depot, Moorfields—J. Withey, proprietor
Wallis Wm. Kingsland rd siding, St Philip's, and Redcliff Railway wharf
Way & Co. 72 Queen sq—exporters
Webb Richard, Avon st. St Philip's
WILLIAMS & CO. St. Philip's, Montpelier, Clifton down & Lawrence

Coffee Dealers.
Wholesale.

Eyre Joseph and Co. Baldwin street
Polglase and Co. St. Stephen street
Poolman, and Co. St John's bridge

Coffee Houses.
See Dining and Coffee Houses.

Coffee Roasters.

Cockram Richard, Ellbroad street
Duck & Co. 2 24 Park street
Lloyd P. J. Portland pl. Clifton down
Polglase & Co. St Stephen street

Coffee Taverns.

Allen Wm. 139 Pennywell road
Bedminster Tavern Co. 68 Bdmnstr pde, John Isaac
Bishopston coffee tav. 70 Glo'ster road
Blue Star coffee tavern, Cumberland road—J. Tyler, manager
Bolwell Edward, 12 Phippen st. Redcliff
British Workman Coffee tavern Co. St George's road
Bryan John, 5 Leigh view, Ashton gte
Budd Albert, 1 East street, Bedminster
Campbell S. T. 51 Colston street
Castle coffee palace, Castle street—John H. Sprague, proprietor
Cawsey R. lower Castle street
Chapman S. 1 Temple street
Criterion Coffee tavern, Leigh view, Ashton gate—J. S. Hill, proprietor
Davey Wm. Kingsland rd. St Philip's
Elworthy T. 56 & 58 West street
Everson R. 18 Horton st, St Philip's
Fifoot E. 82 Richmond st, St Philip's
Flowers Henry, 2 St. George's road
G. W. R. Coffee Tavern, Temple gate
Giant's Castle, Philip st, Bath street
Hancock W. 51 Prince street
Harris Wm. T. 107 Thomas street
Hawker Wm. 17 Newfoundland st
Hemmings Robt. Lawrence hill
Hurford John, 22 Prince st. Queen sq
Jenkins E. 60 Milk street
Jones B. T. Welsh back
Jordan Mrs, Cumberland street
Keen George, Fishponds road
Lee Henry, 43 Broad quay
Lenthall Mrs, 81 Thomas street
Lewis John, Midland road, St. Philip's
Meecham W. Whitehouse st. Bedmnstr
Paul T. O. W. 2 Perry road
Pope J. 28 Up Somerset ter, Windml hl
Pratt Henry, Chapel street, St. Philip's
Redden T. 45 Prince street, Queen sq
Repsey Wm. 132 Newfoundland road
Rogers J. North street, Bedminster
Saunders David, Market steps
Shaftesbury coffee house, the, Kingsland road—T. J. Clevely
Short Simon, 11 & 12 High street
Star coffee house, 1 Old market street
St. John's coffee tavern, Christmas street—Jane Morley, proprietor
Suspension bridge coffee tavern, 40 Mall, Clifton
Symes A. Nelson tavern, Nelson street
Tram coffee tavern, 63 Apsley rd, Clltn
Tuplin T. 204 Easton road
Victoria Co. 4 High st. M. Phelps, propr
Wall Mrs. E. 4 Dighton st. St James's
Wallis W. J. 8 King square avenue
Williams Nathaniel, Commercial road, Bedminster bridge

Colliery & Mill Furnishers.

Smith Mrs S. W. 3 Queen's lane
Smith W. & Co. 94 Victoria street
Townsend & Young, John st, Broad st

Colliery Proprietors.

Ashton Vale Company, Long Ashton
BEDMINSTER COAL CO. Dean lane, and East st. Bedminster—proprietors of Gas, House and Steam Coal
BRISTOL COLLIERIES CO. Lintd, Malago Colliery, Bedminster
KINGSWOOD & PARKFIELD COLLIERIES CO., Midland road, St Philip's, Montpelier, and Kingswood Colliery Co. St. George's—John Henshaw, sec.
LEONARD, BOULT & CO. Limited. Head office, Easton

Colonial Brokers.
See Merchants, Brokers & Agents.

Color Manufacturers.
See also Oil Merchants.

Colthurst & Harding, Temple gate
Hare John & Co. Bath bridge
Ireland A. Cheese lane, St Philip's
Malago Vale Ochre and Color Co. Sheene lane, Bedminster
Rudman J. River street, Frome bridge
Sloman & Burge, Passage st, St Philip's
WILLS SAMUEL & Co. Paint, Colour, and Varnish Manufacturers
WILLS' HARD ENAMELS

ALBION

Castle Green, and Avonside Varnish Works, St Philip's

Commission Merchants and Agents.
See also Merchants and Agents.

Whitwill Mark & Son, Grove Avenue, Queen square

Condimental Food for Horses &c.

Chard Brothers, Bridewell street
Merritt T. Horse fair

Confectioners (Wholesale).

Barnes Jas. 62 & 72 East st, Bedminster
CHAMPION AND CO. Lewin Mead, Manufacturing Confectioners
Coates F. & L. 166 Cheltenham road
Mackay J. 61 Old Market street
SANDERS AND SONS, (late
SANDERS AND LUDLOW)
Redcliff Confectionery Works, 41 44 Redcliff st, (wholesale & export
Warbutton C. Redcross street
Wear Edward, 25 West street

Confectioners & Pastry Cook

In present-day Bristol Victorian buildings still house cafés that are true heirs of the tradition that mixed coffee and cocoa drinking with political radicalism; autonomous spaces such as Hydra Books, Café Kebele and Café Kino continue this tradition. Hydra Books and coffee shop, Old Market, Bristol.

Kebele Café, Robertson Road, Easton, Bristol.

'We can outgrow capitalism', anarchist mural at Kebele Café.

While temperance campaigners may have welcomed and sometimes initiated the development of coffee taverns, however, their appeal reached far beyond the temperance movement. We learn from the *Arrowsmith's Dictionary of Bristol* for 1884 that there were more than a hundred cocoa and coffee taverns of 'a miscellaneous character' in the city at that time. During the confectioners' strike of 1892, the Strike Committee met in the British Workman Coffee House in St Judes. The likes of the Castle Street Coffee Palace (where Edward Carpenter spoke), the Giant's Castle Coffee Tavern, the Christmas Street Coffee Shop, the Star Coffee House and the Baptist Mills Coffee House are also known to have been socialist haunts. In coffee taverns such as these, ordinary Bristolians could organise to improve their lot by fighting to seize a greater share of the commonwealth of the prosperous port and try to secure a better future for their children. Here unrest was fomented, industrial action was organised, freethinkers would challenge religious dogmas, socialists and anarchists would read, listen and debate. It is not fanciful to imagine the intrepid 'Sweet Girls', dockers, gas-workers and cotton operatives stepping out from the British Workman to join their lantern parades during Bristol's great labour unrest, or the customers of the Star Coffee House cheering on the unemployed marchers as they attempted to process down Old Market in the 1930s.

For in the cocoa and coffee taverns there were many attractions. Open to all, they were public spaces, quieter and less intimidating perhaps than alehouses, accessible, and inclusive where the closed doors of elite private clubs were not. In Gertrude Dix's *The Image Breakers*, a novel of 1900 set in Bristol, Leslie Ardent visits coffee taverns in pursuit of anarchist and socialist ideas. While middle-class women such as Leslie may have found her ventures into the poorer districts of the city edgy, such places were safer and more acceptable places for unaccompanied women to attend than drinking taverns. The kind of working-class autodidacts with a thirst for self-betterment and a curiosity about the wider world, that Anthony Iles and Tom Roberts describe, would pass the time in coffee houses reading newspapers and periodicals.[2] Invoking the era of the Stamp Acts, Marc Demarest writes that in the affordable coffee taverns 'one could go, have a drink and read a journal or magazine subscribed to "by the house" for a fee smaller than the cover price of the journal'.[3] In this environment such a culture of self-improvement was dependent not only upon private study but often grounded in mutual education as a spirit of fellowship was generated through reading literature aloud, listening to talks and debating matters of interest and concern.

Café Kino, Stokes Croft, Bristol.

---

2   Anthony Iles and Tom Roberts, *All Knees and Elbows of Susceptibility and Refusal: Reading History from Below* (London: Mute Books, 2012), Chapter 4.

3   Marc Demarest, *Controlling Dissemination Mechanisms: The Unstamped Press and the 'Net* (August 1995), http://www.noumenal.com/marc/unstamped.html [accessed 27 January 2014].

Today's Coffee Revival in Corn Street is thought to be Bristol longest existing coffee house.

We therefore include as an intermezzo some vignettes of coffee-tavern life which link and embellish the knotted tendrils of themes that hold the leaves of this book together. At a time when corporate coffee chains have outlets in every commercial street, and future historians may date images of citizens to the present day by identifying a disposable coffee cup in one hand and a smart phone in the other, Bristol today still has a few cherished spaces such as Hydra Books, Café Kino, Café Kebele and Royce Rolls whose function as radical hangouts perhaps makes them descendants of the coffee tavern of yesteryear.

A young man named Jameson, who was turning out the lights in the hall, informed [Leslie] that a special committee had been formed to consider the case of the employees in a sweet factory who had just come out on strike. Invited to attend it, she went with him through one of the meanest parts of the town to the coffee-tavern in which it was to be held. Arrived at their destination, they passed through a swing-door into a blue-washed coffee-room, with a long counter stretched across it, of which little more than the tops of its metal urns were visible. In the committee-room, where nearly a dozen men waited in silence smoking their pipes, she could see through a glass door into the apartment beyond, where the girls continually passed and repassed each other into two long streams on their way to and from a long bench at the top, at which Justin Ferrar was writing down their names. Even though the door the babble of excited tongues was confusing.[4]

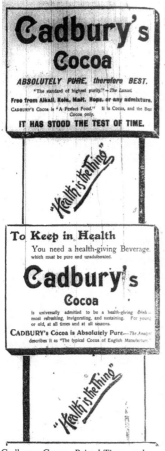

Cadburys Cocoa, *Bristol Times and Mirror* (21 February 1902). Bristol Central Reference Library.

With the prospect of two wearisome hours upon her hands, [Leslie] found herself in the near neighbourhood of the coffee-tavern in which the Socialists had held their weekly meetings. She pushed the swing-door, and, in an odour of gas and sawdust, drank a little of the tea in the large thick cup. The young woman attendant stared at her when she asked if the Socialists still met upstairs; but, on repetition of her question to the proprietor, he answered her in the affirmative, and, after a series of inquiries, vouchsafed to direct her to the shop of the gentleman who rented the room.[5]

We were few and the gospel was new. Thus in the happy virgin days of the S.D.F. [Social Democratic Federation; a socialist party led by Henry Hyndman and publisher of *Justice*], I wandered in the region of the Bristol Prison seeking a certain coffee house where the ceremony into full-blown membership of the S.D.F. was to take place. I found it at last. There was something exotic about it. The odour of saw-dust and steaming coffee, the long wooden staircase, the dimly lit small upper room with the hard penitential forms, impressed the novice with a sense of awe and expectation. That coffee shop was a cathedral, and its

---

4   Gertrude Dix, *The Image Breakers* (New York: Frederick A. Stokes, 1900), p. 22.
5   Ibid., p. 348.

odours were the smells of sacrifice which were being offered up by Demos. A paper on 'Ruskin', to a small audience, was read and thus I became a full-blown Social Democrat.[6]

Later that day, at a meeting in the Castle Street Coffee Palace, Tillett and his London colleagues, with their recent experiences in the London dock dispute still fresh, advised the locals how to form and run a strike committee, and how it might coordinate so many disparate unorganised workers into taking constructive action. Committee officers were elected there and then, and the committee met almost daily for the next month.[7]

FRY'S PURE

CONCENTRATED

COCOA.

NOT A STIMULANT MERELY FOR THE MOMENT, BUT A PERMANENT AND DELECTABLE FORM OF NOURISHMENT.

No. 8

Fry's Cocoa, *Bristol Times and Mirror*, (22 February 1902). Bristol Central Reference Library.

For singing, dramatic poetry and dancing had been a striking feature of the campaigns of the Bristol Socialist Societies in the 1880s and 1890s. Choral singing and poetry were part and parcel of every meeting, whether in the city streets, the parks, the Downs or the old meeting halls and coffee houses.

In the '80s the Socialist Union met at Elworthy's Coffee Tavern in Bedminster. Such coffee shops were popular meeting places for people of socialist and radical politics. *The Star* and *New Street* were two of the most common, the former being the Trade Council's base, and the latter the place where the Organising Committee regularly met in 1890.[8]

Carpenter's audiences were deeply moved by his addresses and several converts were made. After one given at the Castle Street Coffee Palace

---

6   Ramsay Macdonald, quoted in Samson Bryher, *An Account of the Labour and Socialist Movement in Bristol: Describing its Early Beginnings, Struggles and Growth* (Bristol: reprinted from and published by the Bristol Labour Weekly, 1929), I, p. 32.

7   *Living Easton* website, R. Stephen, 'Ben Tillett': http://www.cems.uwe.ac.uk/~rstephen/livingeaston/local_history/tillett.html [accessed 10 June 2014].

8   Sally Mullen, 'The Bristol Socialist Society 1885-1914' in *Bristol's Other History*, ed. by Ian Bild (Bristol: Bristol Broadsides, 1983), p. 36.

this most cheerful letter was received (August 1885): 'I was delighted with Mr. Carpenter's lecture on Socialism. It is the best, clearest and most sensible elucidation of true principled Socialism of any I have heard or read.'[9]

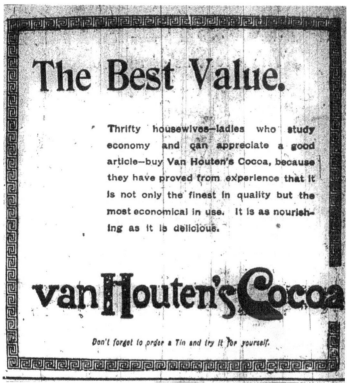

Van Houten's Cocoa, *Bristol Times and Mirror* (15 February 1902), p.11. Bristol Central Reference Library.

After the demonstration [large 1889 labour demonstration], a meeting of sympathisers was held at the Castle Street Coffee Palace. Mr F. Gilmore Barnett was voted to the chair and Messrs. Tillett, Mann and Thorne all spoke, 'urging the formation of a committee to render every possible assistance to the, at present, unorganised workers of Bristol, including the obtaining of necessary offices, the issue of posters and circulars, and by every other way to assist the workers of both sexes'. This was unanimously agreed to, and a further meeting was arranged for the following day at the same place to go into further details. At this meeting E.J. Watson presided, and on the motion of John Gregory it was decided to take a room at the British Workman Coffee Tavern (New Street).[10]

The time of this branch has hitherto been spent in fighting elections, and business has been the order of the day. Accordingly, some are sick, and

9   Robert Gilliard, quoted in Bryher, *Account of the Labour and Socialist Movement in Bristol*, I, p. 20.
10   Bryher, *Account of the Labour and Socialist Movement in Bristol*, II, p. 18.

some are sad, and some have lost the love they had. Therefore, we're going to try our hands more at education, and the general Socialistic development of our members. The first change is in the direction of a new room, which for the present is at Lee's Coffee Tavern, near Laurence [*sic*] Hill Station, where meetings for discussions, readings &c. will be held on Wednesdays, with an occasional Tuesday thrown in. – Now that there is to be a little relaxation from the stern committee work so unavoidable in the last year, it is hoped members and their friends will rally round us, and do their best for themselves and their cause.[11]

Van Houten's Cocoa, *Bristol Times and Mirror* (22 February 1902), p.11. Bristol Central Reference Library.

The following subscriptions have been received by the Relief Committee [for striking miners in South Wales] which meets at the Star Coffee House, Bristol:— Mr Pugsley 15s; Mutual Help Club, per Harrison Riley, 9s 3d; Ashton Vale Colleries, per Mr Jacobs, £1 5s 6d; Dean Lane Colliery, per Mr Clark, £2 10s 1d; Mssrs Terrell's, per Mr Hippett, 5s 6d; Mr Brown, 6s 6d; Mr Harris, 5s 9d; Mssrs Brock and Bruce, per Mr Tucker, 5s 8d; Mr Sharland, 11s 3d; amounts of 5s and under, £1 14s 5d.[12]

At a meeting of the Bristol branch of the Democratic Federation [Social

---

11 Report on Bristol East branch of Independent Labour Party, *The Clarion*, 23 November 1895.

12 '*Telegraph*', the Cardiff Correspondent, 'The Lock-Out in South Wales', *WDP*, 30 April 1875.

Democratic Federation] held at the St. Philip's Coffee Tavern, West Street, on Thursday evening, Mr C. Keene Lewis, of the Workmen's Peace Association, gave by request a lecture on 'War, its horrors and burden'. At the close of the lecture it was unanimously resolved: 'That this meeting earnestly trusts that the Government will enter into negotiation with foreign powers, seeking concurrence in the establishment of a permanent International Court of Arbitration, to which all misunderstandings between nations may be submitted for amicable arrangement, and under no pretence shall a war be undertaken without the consent of the direct representatives of the people.'[13]

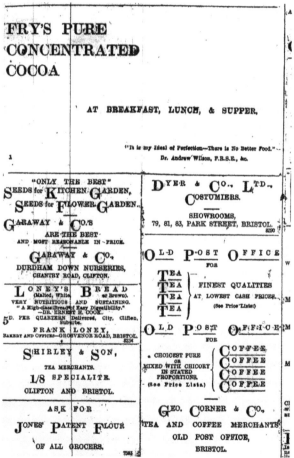

Fry's Cocoa and Old Post Office Coffee, *Bristol Times and Mirror* (24 February 1902). Bristol Central Reference Library.

---

13   *WDP*, 14 June 1884.

6

Bristol and the Labour Unrest of 1910-14

•

Mike Richardson

Introduction

1910 saw a renewed outbreak of industrial strife, as significant sections of the trade union rank-and-file began to express their frustration at the lack of progress made in their struggle for better working conditions and a new social order. Strikes reached levels not seen since the 'new unionism' upsurge of 1889-92.[1] Workers unrest combined with clashes over Home Rule for Ireland, and the militant tactics of suffrage campaigners, which added to the problems of the ruling class. Confronted by these parallel rebellions the ruling class feared their convergence and some warned of the danger of revolution.

Most accounts of the Labour Unrest have rightly focused on areas such as Liverpool, London, Manchester, Glasgow, Dublin and South Wales where labour militancy was at its most intense.[2] However, industrial conflict during this period was widespread, national and indeed international. As Dave Lyddon argues 'the energy of the strike wave of 1910-14 deserves further detailed studies',[3] and this article on Bristol's experience in the Labour Unrest is one such study. To begin, however, it is important to briefly consider the struggles and development of the labour and trade union movement in Britain in the period between the rise of new unionism in 1889 and the outbreak of social unrest in the years immediately before the First World War.

---

1   For accounts of the 1889-92 strike waves in Bristol see Chapters 3, 4 and 5 above.

2   For the Glasgow experience see M. V. Wilson, 'The Waterfront Strikes in Glasgow: Trade Unions and Rank-and-File Militancy in the Labour Unrest of 1910-1914', *International Review of Social History*, 53, (2008); For Liverpool see E. Taplin, 'The Liverpool Transport Strike, 1911', *Historical Studies in Industrial Relations*, Vol. 33 (Liverpool University Press for the Keele University Centre for Industrial Relations, 2012); For Dublin, see F. Devine (ed.) *A Capital in Conflict: Dublin City and the 1913 Lockout* (Dublin: Dublin City Council, 2013). For broader classic accounts see G. Dangerfield, *The Strange Death of Liberal England* (London: Serif, 1997; first published 1935) and H. Pelling, 'The Labour Unrest, 1911-1914', *Popular Politics and Society in Late Victorian Britain* (London: Macmillian, 1968); H. A. Clegg, *A History of British Trade Unions since 1889: Volume II, 1911-1933* (Oxford: Clarendon Press, 1987, first published 1985).

3   D. Lyddon, 'The Labour Unrest in Great Britain and Ireland, 1910-1914 – Still Uncharted Territory?', *Historical Studies in Industrial Relations*, Vol. 33 (Liverpool University Press for the Keele University Centre for Industrial Relations, 2012): 261.

The labour and trade union movement in Britain, 1892-1910: the lull before the storm

Employers regained much of the authority they lost in the course of the labour unrest of 1889-92 in their counter-offensive campaign taken against new, and indeed old, unionism during the late nineteenth and early twentieth centuries. This offensive contributed, along with the union salaried officials' desire to avoid strikes and establish peaceful relations between capital and labour, to the suppression of rank-and-file militancy. In the most damaging of industrial disputes, the lockouts of boot and shoe workers (six weeks) in 1895 and engineers (thirty weeks) in 1897/8, employers were able to dictate the terms of settlement. In these two instances, union officials endorsed national agreements that effectively conceded employers' unfettered right to manage.[4] As signatories of National Agreements full-time union leaders were committed to ensuring that their members abided by the terms of settlement including adherence to lengthy disputes procedures, which precluded official industrial action until all stages of the procedures had been exhausted. This factor had the effect of seriously weakening the voice and influence of lay members and local union bodies.

A new breed of union leaders had abandoned the militant tactics adopted by their predecessors in the general unions for 'a more cautious and conciliatory policy',[5] which harked back to the time of the mid-Victorian consensus between craft unions and employers. They welcomed the passing of the 1896 Conciliation Act which gave responsibility for conciliation to the Board of Trade, giving it more weight. Salaried officials defended their position of support arguing that 'concrete gains' had been made using conciliation machinery.[6] As Roger Davidson stressed, the Board of Trade was well suited to take on the task of taking the heat out of the relations between capital and labour through the conciliation process:

> With its fund of labour statistics and extensive knowledge of the labour movement, its labour department could readily advise its political chiefs and the cabinet as to which policy options would most effectively exploit divisions within trade unionism, reinforce the status of moderate leaders, and neutralise the influence of extremists. Similarly, the Board's permanent officials could provide an informed and realistic assessment of the threat of revolutionary movements such as syndicalism, thereby preventing the government from over-reacting to minority groups with measures that could have precipitated confrontation between labour and the state.[7]

---

4 In the case of the engineers, the consequence of union capitulation was that employers had the freedom to introduce piecework; new machinery, (with full management discretion to run machines with men and women operatives of their choice); and the right to replace skilled labour with semi-skilled or unskilled workers (dilution), see J. Haydu, *Between Craft and Class: Skilled Workers and Factory Politics in the United States and Britain, 1890-1922* (Berkeley and Los Angeles, USA: University of California Press, 1988), p. 71.

5 E. J. Hobsbawm, *Labouring Men: Studies in the History of Labour'* (London: Weidenfeld and Nicolson, 1976, first published 1964), p. 189.

6 J. H. Porter, 'Wage Bargaining under Conciliation Agreements, 1860-1914', *Economic History Review*, 23, (1970): 470.

7 R. Davidson, 'The Board of Trade and Industrial Relations 1896-1914', *The Historical Journal*, Vol. 21, No. 3. (Sep.,

By 1913 the Board of Trade along with other government departments had provided hundreds of jobs for salaried union officials.[8] Moreover, Employers' Associations offered the temptation to those officials willing to cross the class divide and work for them and against those they once represented.[9] This was not so difficult a step for some, as friendly relations between employers, civil servants and politicians were part of the day-to-day experience of salaried union officials. As one artisan quoted by Sidney and Beatrice Webb observed,

> Nowadays the salaried officer of a great Union is courted and flattered by the middle class. ... He goes to live in a little villa in a lower-middle class suburb. ... A great strike threatens to involve the Society in desperate war. Unconsciously biased by distaste for the hard and unthankful work which a strike entails, he finds himself in small sympathy with the men's demands, and eventually arranges a compromise, on terms distasteful to a large section of his members.[10]

However, the extent of dissatisfaction with salaried union officers among the general union membership is not known. And despite the employers' counter-offensive in the 1890s union membership increased between 1895 and 1910. Many firms joined the newly formed employer organisations to counter union militancy, but many of those that were dependent on a highly skilled workforce did not de-recognise unions even after scoring significant victories in major disputes. This line of action was taken in part due to the fact that skilled labour was often in short supply and therefore employers in these circumstances found it more prudent to buttress a policy of managing industrial relations through salaried union officials. This factor together with the introduction of more favourable trade union legislation in 1906 (i.e. the 1906 Trades Dispute Act) facilitated the steady growth in union membership.[11]

It was, however, the 'new' unions, such as the National Union of Gasworkers and General Labourers of Great Britain and Ireland and the Dock, Wharf, Riverside and General Labourers' Union (DWRGLU), that found it particularly hard to hold their ranks in the wake of the employers' counter-offensive, periods of depression and a plentiful supply of labour. It became a common feature of the period to replace militant workers, particularly the less skilled, such as dockers and seamen, with blackleg labour, in order to weaken industrial action and undermine trade unionism. General unions had to rely on 'a few large works branches' to carry them through.[12] Excessive haemorrhaging of their unskilled

1978): 591.

8   J. Callaghan, 'The Edwardian Crisis: The Survival of Liberal England and the Rise of a Labour Identity', *Historical Studies in Industrial Relations*, No. 33, (2012): 17.

9   Sidney and Beatrice Webb, *The History of Trade Unionism, 1666-1920* (London: Printed by the authors for the students of the Workers' Educational Association, 1919), p. 591.

10 Ibid., pp. 469-71; also quoted in B. Pearce, *Some Past Rank and File Movements* (a *Labour Review* pamphlet, November 1959), pp. 4-5.

11 For the background to and the pressures for the passing of the Trades Dispute Act see J. Saville, 'The Trades Dispute Act of 1906', *Historical Studies of Industrial Relations*, No. 1 (March 1996): 11-47.

12 Hobsbawm, *Labouring Men*, p. 188.

and semi-skilled members had occurred, especially among women and dock labourers who had contributed so much to the vibrancy, dynamism and militancy of the late 1880s.[13] In one case in 1893, several thousand non-union men, supported by police and gunboats, were introduced to break a strike at Hull docks resulting in the port becoming 'a stronghold of Free Labour'.[14]

For those employers unwilling to use gunboat diplomacy the use of conciliation and arbitration to settle disputes proved in the main fairly effective. During the 1890s and early 1900s trade union salaried officials failed either by negotiation or through conciliation and arbitration to secure wage increases sufficiently high to keep pace with inflation. The fall in the standard of living between 1906 and 1910 resulted in a widening of inequality. This, together with high unemployment and the disappointment in not achieving the eight-hour day in most industries should have sounded warning bells among the union hierarchy.[15] The level of discontent arising out of the declining influence of trade unions subscribed to the return to militancy by significant numbers of rank-and-file workers.

The interests of labour were not served particularly well on the political front either, despite the election of twenty-nine Labour Members of Parliament in the 1906 General Election. In the 1880s and 1890s, socialist organisations, which evolved out of liberal radicalism, such as the Social Democratic Federation (SDF), founded in 1884, and the Independent Labour Party (ILP), established in 1893, tended to prioritise the struggle to secure political representation for the working class rather than fixate on the day-to-day battles in the workplace. Despite some notable successes, such as the parliamentary seats won by three labour candidates in the 1892 General Election, (Keir Hardie, John Burns and Joseph Havelock Wilson), the realisation that to build a new independent labour party required trade union support was evident after all twenty-eight ILP candidates in the 1895 election failed to win a seat, including Hardie.[16] The defeat of the engineering union in 1897/8 was a major factor in shifting the Trades Union Congress (TUC) thinking on this question.

In 1899, the TUC passed a resolution calling for a special conference comprising representatives from 'all the co-operative, socialistic, trade union, and other working organisations... to devise ways and means for securing the return of an increased number of labour members to the next parliament.'[17] On

---

13   G. S. Bain and R. Price, *Profiles of Union Growth* (Oxford: Blackwell, 1988); Hobsbawm, *Labouring Men*, p. 191.

14   William Collinson, *The Apostle of Free Labour: The Life Story of William Collinson Founder and General Secretary of the National Free Labour Association*, (London: Hurst and Blackett, 1913), p. 275; Also see J. Saville, 'Trade Unions and Free Labour: The Background to the Taff Vale Decision' in A. Briggs and J. Saville (eds), *Essays in Labour History* (London: Macmillan, 1960), pp. 328-330.

15   Underground miners, however, did achieve a statutory eight-hour day in 1908. See J. Arrowsmith, 'The Struggle over Working Time in Nineteenth and Twentieth Century Britain', *Historical Studies in Industrial Relations*, No. 13, (Spring 2002): 98.

16   P. Adelman, *The Rise of the Labour Party 1880-1945* (Harlow, Essex: Longman, 1986; first published 1972), pp. 19-24. Havelock Wilson was the President of the National Sailors and Firemen's Union.

17   At the 1899 Congress, this resolution was moved by J. H. Holmes, a delegate of the Amalgamated Society of Railway Servants: see ibid., p. 28 and TUC History Online: http://www.unionhistory.info/timeline/1880_14_Narr_Display.php? Where=NarTitle+contains+'The+Labour+Party'+AND+DesPurpose+contains+' WebDisplay, [accessed 29 April,

the basis of this resolution the interested parties arranged a conference. Delegates, representing around 400,000 trade unionists, 9,000 members of the SDF, 13,000 members of ILP, and 861 members of the Fabian Society, met in February 1900 and formed the Labour Representation Committee (LRC), the forerunner of the Labour Party.

Strangled at birth, however, was the idea that this was to be a Socialist Party, rather it was to be a 'distinct Labour Group' in Parliament ready 'to cooperate with any Party which, for the time being, may be engaged in promoting legislation in the direct interests of Labour...'[18] This policy led the LRC and, after 1906, the Labour Party to accept compromises with political opponents which fuelled dissatisfaction with its performance in Parliament.[19]

Henry Pelling, the labour and trade union historian, famously challenged this assessment in *Popular Politics and Society in Late Victorian Britain*. He argued that labour unrest prior to the First World War 'owed little to feelings of disappointment with parliamentary institutions or existing political parties.'[20] He noted that there were other tangible reasons for the rise in labour militancy, such as the increase in the pace of inflation, a tight labour market, and the growth in union membership; the latter encouraged in part by the introduction of the National Insurance Scheme in 1911.[21]

Pelling did acknowledge in a later publication, however, that the disillusionment with the role of the Labour Party in parliament was indeed one of the contributory factors leading to the intensification of industrial conflict between 1911-14.[22] Notwithstanding this disillusion, a pertinent point to remember here, in regard to socialists, the TUC and labour representation in Parliament, is that the franchise before the First World War was limited. Women did not have the vote and the level of male franchise in England and Wales in 1911 was only 65.6%.[23] Casualised unskilled workers were still unrepresented, so it should have come as no surprise that workers began to vote with their feet by supporting direct action often against the advice of salaried, conservative trade union officials.

Standish Meecham summed up the difficulties of assessing this period of industrial strife by demonstrating that attitudes were far from consistent; he said that workers

> struck for wages and struck for status; they sent the TUC their money and bucked its leadership; they opposed national insurance while they collected their pensions; they voted Labour and agreed that Labour

---

2013].

18 Cited in Adelman, *The Rise of the Labour Party 1880-1945*, p. 29.

19 See Dangerfield, *The Strange Death of Liberal England*, p. 193.

20 Pelling, 'The Labour Unrest, 1911 – 1914', p. 164.

21 Ibid.

22 H. Pelling, *A History of British Trade Unionism* (Harmondsworth, Middlesex: Penguin, 1976; first published 1963), p. 139.

23 H. C. G. Matthew, R. I. McKibbin and J. A. Kay, 'The Franchise Factor in the Rise of the Labour Party', *The English Historical Review*, Vol. 91, No. 361 (Oct., 1976): 730.

accomplished almost nothing.[24]

The contradictions inherent in the labour movement at this time have proved problematic for labour historians' attempts to evaluate the significance of the influence of syndicalism.[25] This is a continuing debate; while Hugh Clegg, Henry Pelling and Keith Laybourn have played down the role of syndicalist ideas,[26] Ralph Darlington has recently reasserted its contribution to labour militancy.[27] Exploring the local history of Bristol offers a context for examining conflicting perspectives.

The experience of the labour movement in Bristol, 1892-1910

In Bristol by the turn of the century the hopes of the late 1880s and early 1890s had been quashed. Local employers, stung by the success of new unionism, 'hit back by force of military and legal might' against striking confectionery workers and deal runners.[28] After a long hard struggle these strikes ended in defeat in the spring of 1893.[29] Workers suffered the most crippling setbacks, however, in the national lockouts initiated by employers in the boot and shoe trade in 1895, and in the engineering industry in 1897/8. By the end of the 1890s, union membership on the docks, in the boot and shoe industry, and amongst women had plummeted.

Attempts to turn this situation round were met with inordinate hostility by some employers. For instance, efforts to unionise tramway workers in Bristol in 1901 were brutally crushed. Sir George White, chairman of the Bristol Tramways Company, sacked all the men in his employ who had joined the union and replaced them by non-union labour supplied by the National Free Labour Association.[30]

Workers facing attacks on their wages and conditions of work during this period turned to the unions for assistance, but in most cases the union strategy of accord with employers achieved little to prevent the deterioration in living standards. During Easter 1904, for instance, the Great Western Cotton Company imposed a wage cut of 5%, attributing such action to the depression in the cotton industry. In May the company announced a further 5% reduction. This time the

24 S. Meacham, '"The Sense of an Impending Clash": English Working-Class Unrest before the First World War', *The American Historical Review*, Vol. 77, No. 5 (Dec., 1972): 1363.

25 The Syndicalist movement's aim through direct action, rather than parliamentary means, was to abolish capitalism and replace it by a new social order, classless and free from exploitation.' See J. Spargo, *Syndicalism, Industrial Unionism and Socialism* (St Petersburg, Florida, USA: Red and Black Publishers reprint, 2009; first published B W Huebsch, 1913), pp. 16-24.

26 Clegg, *A History of British Trade Unions since 1889: Volume II, 1911–1933*; Pelling, 'The Labour Unrest, 1911-1914; K. Laybourn, *A History of British Trade Unionism c. 1770-1990* (Stroud, England: Sutton, 1997).

27 R. Darlington, *Syndicalism and the Transition to Communism: An International Comparative Analysis* (Aldershot, England: Ashgate, 2008).

28 S. Mullen, 'Sweet Girls and Deal Runners' in I. Bild (ed.) *Placards and Pin Money* (Bristol: Bristol Broadsides, 1986), p. 112.

29 For details of these disputes see S. Bryher, *An Account of the labour and Socialist movement in Bristol* (Bristol Labour Weekly, 1929) and Chapter 5 above.

30 William Collinson, *The Apostle of Free Labour*, pp. 184-89; See also the *WDP*, 2-14 August 1901.

1,000 strong workforce refused to accept this new assault on their living standards and as a result they were locked out.[31]

The Gasworkers and General Labourers' Union was called in despite the fact that it had only forty members, all men, employed at the factory. Harold Brabham, its local secretary, urged the men and women to join the union. The men signed up immediately. The women held back, although they too vehemently opposed the pay cuts. The union campaigned on the principle that if the factory were fully unionised industrial peace would likely follow. It recognised that the cotton industry was in recession and that a wage cut might be necessary, but it argued that the workforce should be consulted over the extent and terms of such a discordant measure.[32]

A compromise — based on accepting the 5% reduction provided that it would be restored on 1 September 1904 and a further 2.5% of the Easter cut returned on 1 January 1905 — was put to George Spafford, the Managing Director of Great Western Cotton Works.[33] Although this offer was rejected by the company Brabham was at pains to point out that agreement was close and that Spafford 'was not like some employers who would not see a paid secretary of the union. On the contrary he treated him [Mr Brabham] as a gentleman and he should always be prepared to treat Mr Spafford the same.'[34] This was the same George Spafford that 'was reputed to have said "that he would rather burn the mill rather than concede" to his workers' demands in the 1889 strike.[35] The lock-out ended on 1 June 1904. After a vote by the workforce, the 5% wage reduction was accepted on the company's assurance that it would be restored, provided the depression in the cotton industry eased, at the end of September.[36]

By 1900, unions were increasingly turning to of Boards of Conciliation and Arbitration to settle disputes, and while the outcomes rarely favoured workers there were some exceptions.[37] For instance, when Bristol's corn porters went on strike in June 1900 their union agreed to go to arbitration, despite opposition from some of its members. In this case, the decision seemed justified, as the arbitrator's award was favourable to the union.[38] How can this be explained? Kenneth Knowles argued, in his classic work on strikes, that 'arbitrators' judgements are based on an assessment of relative strength' with the aim of bringing about 'industrial peace rather than industrial justice'.[39] Despite the overall decline in union membership on the docks, corn porters remained solidly unionised and relative to other occupations on the docks their work was regarded as skilled. These factors along with their determined stand would have influenced the arbitrators' judgement. However, the sting in the tail was that the terms of

---

31 *WDP*, 21 May 1904.

32 *WDP*, 27 and 28 May 1904.

33 *WDP*, 28 May 1904

34 *WDP*, 30 May 1904.

35 See Chapter 3 above, p. 113.

36 *WDP*, 1 June 1904.

37 K. G. J. C. Knowles, *Strikes — A Study in Industrial Conflict: With Special Reference to British Experience Between 1911 and 1947* (Oxford: Blackwell, 1952), p. 66 n 3.

38 *WDP*, 28 June and 23 August 1900.

39 Knowles, *Strikes-A Study in Industrial Conflict*, p. 68.

arbitration formed the basis not only for the pending dispute but for all future differences arising between the parties, ruling out strikes or lock-outs.[40]

On the political front the Bristol labour movement fared little better. Despite the immense amount of work put in, little headway was made either in parliamentary or municipal elections. Labour did not win a parliamentary seat in Bristol until 1923 and the maximum number of municipal seats it held in the city before 1910 was seven in 1907 (eight if the independent socialist William Baster is included) out of 48. By 1910 the seats that Labour held had fallen to three.[41]

How much store should be placed on these results, however, is open to question, as in 1910 the parliamentary electorate of Bristol, as a percentage of its population, was only 14.5% and the municipal electorate 17.3%. Whilst women were excluded from voting in parliamentary elections before the First World War, in municipal elections after 1882, single and married women could vote provided they paid the rate qualification. And after 1907 women had the legal right to contest municipal elections.[42]

Unloading lumber at the new wharf, Portishead. By Samuel Loxton c. 1910.

40   *WDP*, 9 July 1900; Knowles, *Strikes — A Study in Industrial Conflict*, pp. 66-69.

41   K. Kelly and M. Richardson, 'The Shaping of the Bristol Labour Movement, 1885-1985', M. Dresser and P. Ollerenshaw (eds.), *The Making of Modern Bristol* (Bristol: Redcliffe Press, 1996), p. 217.

42   S. Jordan, K. Ramsey and M. Woollard, *Abstract of Bristol Historical Statistics, Part 3: Political Representation and Bristol's Elections 1700-1997* (Series Editor Peter Wardley, Bristol Historical Databases Project, Faculty of Humanities, University of the West of England, 1997), p. xiv.

Bristol and the Labour Unrest 1910-14

1910

The picture drawn above, of the travails of the Bristol labour movement, supports the view of the Bristol labour historian, Bob Whitfield, that for a decade or so before 1910 the characteristic features of trade unionism in Bristol were 'weakness, caution and moderation'.[43] It also reveals that the political representation of workers' interests in Bristol, as indeed elsewhere, had gained little traction. Yet in 1910 Bristol became one of the first areas in the country to register a resurgence of rank and file militancy not seen since 1889-90.

"Where the blow falls Bristol rate payers 'Hi! here! mind who you're hitting!'" By F G Lewin, 2nd July 1910.

On the 21 June 1910, a major unofficial strike commenced at Avonmouth docks, part of the Port of Bristol, which together with the Portishead dock and City docks were municipally owned and run by Bristol Corporation. What was significant about this industrial action was that the Avonmouth men had come out in sympathy and solidarity with their counterparts who were on strike at Newport, characteristics that, although bearing the hallmarks of syndicalism, cannot be traced to syndicalist intervention. This was a spontaneous action, self-generated, revealing the embryonic development of class-consciousness. Avonmouth men allocated to work on the Houlder Brothers & Co. steamship, *Natal Transport*, which was diverted from the Welsh port, refused to do so. Sir Frederick George Banbury, speaking in the House of Commons, described their

---

43   R. Whitfield, 'Trade Unionism in Bristol 1910-1926' in I. Bild (ed.), *Bristol's Other History* (Bristol: Bristol Broadsides (Co-op), 1983), p. 73.

action as 'malicious', which was probably why they were not given the opportunity to transfer to work on other boats.[44] As a consequence a thousand men, union and non-union, ceased work and walked out in solidarity, taking Bristol Corporation's warehousemen and grain porters with them.

The next day they formed a patrol outside the dock gates singing songs in defiance. A deputation of strikers from Newport arrived and talked to the men and their union leaders, advocating that they offer a compromise to the docks management committee along the lines that they would agree to work as usual, except on boats belonging to Houlder Brothers. Following a meeting with the docks management this was agreed. But the return to work settlement collapsed after it came to light that four officials (foremen), employed by Bristol Dock Offices and C. J. King and Sons Ltd., were sent to train and supervise strike-breakers, brought in by the Shipping Federation, to load the *Natal Transport*.[45] The men struck again demanding the sacking of these foremen.

Ben Tillett, General Secretary of the DWRGWU, intervened and extracted a promise from the dock authorities that the foremen the men objected to would be withdrawn. He addressed the strikers, who were still calling for the immediate dismissal of the said foremen, accusing them of 'acting like children and [that they] were playing into the hands of the Shipping Federation.'[46] There followed a temporary return to work between 26 June and 11 July when the foremen in question were sent on a fortnight's holiday, but on their return the strike resumed and spread to the City and Portishead docks.[47] Harry Orbell, a salaried organiser of the DWRGWU, pleaded with the men to return to work saying that they were 'playing a fool's game' but the men refused.[48] The Bristol Docks Committee, the Board responsible for the operation and control of the Port of Bristol, immediately proceeded to import Shipping Federation blackleg labour to replace the strikers.[49]

Despite the cautious approach taken by the salaried officers of the DWRGWU, workers flocked into the union from all parts of the docks. They proceeded to form their own unofficial strike committee, representing grain workers, deal runners, general labourers and cargo men, and, from their own ranks, appointed Mark Chivers, a 40 year old corn porter, as secretary and Walter Bignell, a dock labourer, as treasurer.[50] This development signified an impressive solidarity for these two men, skilled and casualised, represented opposite ends of the range of dock labour skills. It also cut through existing forms of regulation, for corn porters had been tied to the settlement of their disputes through the Corn Conciliation Board since 1900.[51] On 17 July a

44   Sir Frederick Banbury, House of Commons Debate, Hansard, June 1910, cc366-434.

45   *Aberdeen Journal*, 23 June 1910; *Hull Daily Mail* and *Derby Daily Telegraph*, 24 June 1910.

46   *Dundee Courier*, 27 June 1910.

47   W. G. Neale, *At the Port of Bristol, Vol. 2, The turn of the tide 1900-1914*, (Bristol: Port of Bristol Authority, 1970) pp. 116-124; R. Whitfield, 'The Labour Movement in Bristol 1910-1939', unpublished MLitt thesis (University of Bristol, 1979), pp. 38-45.

48   *WDP*, 14 July 1910.

49   *Evening Telegraph*, 14 July 1910.

50   *WDP*, 16 July 1910; 1911 Census, ancestry.co.uk in association with the National Archives.

51   Kelly and Richardson, 'The Shaping of the Bristol Labour Movement, 1885-1985', p. 217.

thousand dockers, comprising approximately one third permanently employed men and two thirds regularly or casually employed, marched to Clifton and Durdham Downs to hold a rally. Earnest Stinchcombe, a 40 year old cargo superintendent and a member of the unofficial strike committee, appealed to the non-permanent men 'not to make themselves the tools of the employers by offering themselves for employment and thus taking the places of men who under ordinary circumstances would get work.'[52] He need not have been concerned. The strike was solid. After the demonstration volunteers came forward to act as lookouts, participate in blockades and assemblies outside the dock gates.

The following day 'an excited crowd' greeted a dray escorted by a *posse* of mounted police on the Shirehampton to Avonmouth Road, which was the only route available to reach the dockside. It was carrying beer for the Shipping Federation men, ostensibly to quench their thirst, as dock work was physically strenuous, but understandably strikers regarded this as a perk for the blacklegs. Strikers attempted to block the way. A scuffle ensued during which a horse's harness was cut in an endeavour to stop the dray progressing further. However, mounted police forcibly pushed the crowd aside allowing the dray to continue its journey. On arriving at Avonmouth it was met by another group of strikers at the dock gates. When they noticed blood flowing from two of the horses they believed it to be caused by the rider's spurs digging into their mounts, driving them too hard in order to break the blockade. The men protested, alleging animal cruelty, but this was strongly denied by the police.[53]

The police version of events was that during the scuffle on the Shirehampton to Avonmouth road one or more persons from the crowd stabbed the horses. Orbell, the union organiser, supported this account and called for 'order and respect for the police who were only doing their job' telling Bristol dockers that they had in their midst some 'semi-hooligans'.[54] This accusation did not deter Bristol dockers from continuing their efforts to disrupt trade at Avonmouth. That night they placed a large tree trunk across the Avonmouth road to prevent traffic getting through. The horse injury incident did not inhibit the police either. On the following day, Tuesday 19 July, they escorted another consignment of drink destined for the Shipping Federation's blacklegs. A large crowd waiting in Gloucester Road, near the dock gates at Avonmouth, gave a noisy reception to the police as they approached. The local press reported two accounts of what happened next.

The first account, from police sources, maintained that mounted police went onto the pavement to break up the crowd and clear the way for the dray to continue unobstructed. The crowd panicked and 'a rush was caused into the road where the frightened folk found themselves in danger from other police horses. No case of injury was reported.'[55] The second account by eyewitnesses said that

---

52 *WDP*, 18 July 1910.

53 *WDP* 19 July 1910.

54 Ibid.

55 *WDP*, 20 July 1910.

the police charged the peaceful gathering of men, women and children, inflicting many injuries. One man remonstrated with the police pleading them to stop only to be felled by a blow to the back of the head inflicted by a mounted officer.[56] This episode and the publicity surrounding it only served to garner more support for the striking dockers. Within twenty-four hours the Bristol Socialist Society announced its continued support.[57] And more significantly on 22 July the bargemen and lightermen joined the strike.[58]

Negotiators scurried to settle the dispute on hearing news of the strike spreading. This gave rise to the striking of a return-to-work agreement on the following day, 23 July. A committee of enquiry was established to examine the circumstances of the appointment of two of the foremen, Ferguson and Scholes, that the men wanted dismissed. Pending the result of the investigation it was agreed that the two men would not supervise local labour.[59] The enquiry found that there was not enough evidence to justify pursuing the charges made against the aforesaid foremen and recommended their reappointment.[60] By this time, the end of September, the will to restart the dispute had gone.

During the period awaiting the outcome of the enquiry, local carters in Bristol, led by Ernest Bevin, were busily organising a carmen's branch of the Dockers' Union, successfully fending off competition from the Workers' Union in the process. Bevin was elected as their first chairman. He had not been directly involved in the dock strike that summer but at the request of Orbell, with the authorisation the DWRGWU, he had established and managed a strike relief fund; although it was not to be until late August before he would be officially enrolled with the dockers' union, along with the carters he had recruited.[61] By the following spring 2,050 carters had signed up to the union. The swelling of union ranks had much to do with Bevin's ability to convince Bristol employers that it was in their interests to recognise the union and negotiate a local agreement. However, the cost of union recognition to carters and other key dockside workers was 'a commitment to use the Joint Arbitration Board to settle disputes.'[62] Hence Bristol became the first major example in Britain of bringing together 'all important sections of waterside labour' into a single union.[63] Tillett recognised Bevin's organisational strength and persuasive powers and appointed him as a full-time salaried official for the Bristol area.[64]

1911

In December 1910 the National Transport Workers' Federation (NTWF) was

---

56   Ibid.; *Derby Daily Telegraph*, 19 July 1910.

57   *WDP*, 21 July 1910.

58   *Evening Telegraph*, 22 July 1910.

59   *Western Times*, 25 July 1910.

60   *Aberdeen Journal*, 28 September 1910.

61   M. Stephens, *Ernest Bevin – Unskilled Labourer and World Statesman 1881-1951* (London: TGWU publication, 1981), p. 23.

62   R. Whitfield, 'The Labour Movement in Bristol 1910-1939', (unpublished MLitt thesis), p. 45.

63   Hobsbawm, *Labouring Men*, p. 210.

64   Stephens, *Ernest Bevin – Unskilled Labourer and World Statesman 1881-1951*, pp. 24-25.

formed. Its aim was to coordinate and control disputes involving seamen, dockers and carters. It launched 'a vigorous recruiting campaign' in which Tom Mann, Britain's leading syndicalist, was heavily involved.[65] At Whitsuntide, the first week of June 1911, a three-day conference of the International Seamen's Strike Committee, in which delegates from the National Sailors and Firemen's Union (NSFU) participated, took place to consider the details of a proposed international strike.[66] Following this meeting it was announced that when preparations were completed the men would be called out. Over the next week the NSFU's President, Havelock Wilson, threatened repeatedly to declare an international seamen's strike, telling reporters eager to know when it would start to 'wait till the gun goes off'.[67] Skirmishes had already started, however, when on 9 June he learned that support from the NTWF would not be forthcoming, leaving the Sailors and Firemen's Union to fight their battle alone.[68]

Photo by Arthur Weston, Paisley, P.C.

TOM MANN, 1889

Tom Mann in 1889.

Seemingly unconcerned by the NTWF's position, that very day the crew of the White Star Ship, *Olympic*, due to set sail on her maiden voyage from Southampton on 14 June, walked off the ship.[69] A dispute between coal porters and their employer over stand-by pay and union recognition had already placed the scheduled time of the ship's maiden voyage in jeopardy.[70] The seamen had chosen an opportune moment to push parity of pay with Liverpool men working on the *Mauretania*.[71] The White Star Company capitulated. The reason that it had done so was that it was 'absolutely committed' to the *Olympic* sailing on schedule.[72] The coal porters' strike continued for another day before the employer, Rea and Company, conceded to most of their demands.

By the second week of June, however, it was plain that the Shipping Federation, representing the interests of shipowners — an organisation that was described by one contemporary newspaper as 'a body without any bowels of compassion'[73] —

---

65 Clegg, *A History of British Trade Unions Since 1889: Volume II, 1911-1933*, p. 33.

66 *Dundee Courier*, 5 June 1911.

67 *Evening Telegraph*, 6 June 1911.

68 *The Times*, 10 June 1911, cited in Wilson, 'The Waterfront Strikes in Glasgow: Trade Unions and Rank-and-File Militancy in the Labour Unrest of 1910-1914', p. 269.

69 *Evening Telegraph*, 9 June 1911.

70 *Liverpool Echo*, 10 June 1911.

71 *Liverpool Echo*, 12 June 1911.

72 *Evening Telegraph*, 15 June 1911.

73 *Dundee Courier*, 23 June 1911.

had no intention of responding to the Sailors' and Firemen's Union call for improvements in pay and conditions, and union recognition. The Federation would not tolerate the hiring of union labour and ridiculed Havelock Wilson's threat to strike as pure rhetoric. It believed he was only using the strike threat as a bargaining tool to get the employers to agree to set up a Conciliation Board, something they vehemently opposed, to deal with his members' grievances.

The international strike failed to materialise, as settlements had been reached with German, Danish and Norwegian shipowners. Thus, when it became clear to Wilson that the Federation would not budge, in what only can be described as a last throw of the dice, he called for a national strike.[74] On 14 June, the union's position was relayed to seamen and firemen at a series of meetings held in Britain's major ports, including Bristol. Much to the surprise of the union leadership, and indeed the Shipping Federation, members responded positively and the signal to cease work was given.[75]

A demonstration of 80,000 on St George's Plateau, Liverpool, on Sunday 13th August 1911, during the General Transport Strike.

On Wilson's request, Tom Mann, co-founder of the NTWF, went to Liverpool to form a strike committee.[76] Within a few days the seamen secured some significant advances in wages in Liverpool, where the White Star, Canadian Pacific, and other major shipping lines conceded the 10s a month increase the men demanded.[77] The strike spread to embrace ship's stewards, and dockers refused to unload ships employing non-union labour. Vessels were

74   M. J. Daunton, 'Inter-Union Relations on the Waterfront: Cardiff 1888-1914', *International Review of Social History*, 22 (1977): 368; Clegg, *A History of British Trade Unions Since 1889: Volume II, 1911-1933*, p. 33.

75   H. W. Lee, *The Great Strike Movement of 1911 and its Lessons* (London: Twentieth Century Press, 1911), p. 2.

76   Taplin, 'The Liverpool Transport Strike, 1911', p. 27.

77   *Liverpool Echo*, 16 and 21 June 1911; *Aberdeen Journal*, 19 June 1911.

blocked from leaving in multiple ports, including Bristol.[78]

In Bristol, the local press reported that the strike was having a significant impact. Two liners were unable to obtain crews and the Bristol Steam Navigation Company was unable to provide a service. A deal between the Sailors' and Firemen's Union and some of the large owners operating out of Bristol docks was struck for an advance in wages from 30s 4d to 32s 6d. The capitulation of some of the largest firms in Bristol and elsewhere revealed their vulnerability.

> Their overheads and fixed capital costs were high, and during the course of any dispute they incurred fines for non-compliance with the terms of their mail contracts, plus the expense of feeding and accommodating passengers. Very large numbers of substitutes were required even to form a skeleton crew for a large liner, which greatly reduced the potential for breaking strikes by importing labour.[79]

The situation was different in regard to smaller cargo boats. At Avonmouth, the Elders and Fyffes' boat, *Barranca*, left the port without a crew after negotiations between the union and the company had broken down.[80] Rather than concede to the union's demands the ship's captain arranged to pick up a blackleg crew a few miles down the coast at Walton Bay, Clevedon.[81]

"Portrait of the new manager of Bristol docks our £6,000,000 enterprise." By F G Lewin, July 30th 1910. Showing Ben Tillett and Alderman Henry Twigg.

78 *Liverpool Echo*, 19 June 1911.

79 Wilson, 'The Waterfront Strikes in Glasgow: Trade Unions and Rank-and-File Militancy in the Labour Unrest of 1910-1914', p. 278.

80 *WDP*, 20 June 1911.

81 *WDP*, 22 June 1911.

No doubt the seamen's victories spurred the coal porters at Avonmouth, Bristol to demand increases in their pay. They walked out on an unofficial strike on 21 June. Strikes by seamen, dock labourers and other waterside workers in Bristol, however, were neither as extensive nor as intensive as those in ports such as Liverpool, Hull, Glasgow and Cardiff.[82] Municipal ownership did have some impact; Bristol ratepayers were quick to express concern that trade would be lost and that the City would not reap the benefits from the capital invested in improving the docks. For example, on the completion in 1908 of the Royal Edward Dock at Avonmouth, designed specifically to take large liners, passenger and freight, the total amount the municipal authorities had invested in its docks at Avonmouth, Portishead and the City was about £6,000,000. Moreover, in 1910 the City docks lost £150,000, which represented 1s 10d in the pound on the rates.[83]

Aerial view of Avonmouth (foreground) and Royal Edward Docks (background) showing Cold Stores and Royal Edward Granary in the right of the photograph. 1913.

---

82   For accounts of the Liverpool 1911 strike see Taplin, 'The Liverpool Transport Strike, 1911'. For the 1911 Glasgow strike see Wilson, 'The Waterfront Strikes in Glasgow: Trade Unions and Rank-and-File Militancy in the Labour Unrest of 1910-1914'.

83   Arthur Strauss MP, BRISTOL CORPORATION BILL, House of Commons Debate, Hansard, 28 March 1911, cc1277-83.

Unsurprisingly then, there was pressure on the Bristol Docks Committee to bring about a resolution to the seamen's dispute. However, although the Dock Committee was the main employer of dock labour at Avonmouth, it had no jurisdiction over the hiring of seamen and there is no evidence to suggest that it acted any differently than other port employers in regard to labour relations.[84] It seems likely, therefore, that it was the potential losses that could be incurred by owners of the large shipping lines propelling them to make concessions, rather than any explicit pressure placed on them by the Docks Committee. By the end of the month, after the Canadian Northern line had conceded a 10*s* a month increase, the local press felt able to claim that the seamen's dispute at Avonmouth and Bristol docks was all but over.[85] But there was a sting in the tail, as dockers showed that they were not prepared to work on ships that had been diverted from strike bound ports.

On 3 July, the Elders and Fyffe ship, *Pacuara,* destined for Manchester with its cargo of bananas, was diverted to Bristol only to be boycotted in an act of solidarity so characteristic of dockers, not only in Avonmouth but also in all the major ports. The capacity of all sections of workers, skilled, semi-skilled and unskilled, to take class action was also evident in Bristol, as indeed elsewhere. Engineers employed by J. Jefferies and Sons and J. Sherman and Company were called upon to carry out repairs on the *Pacuara,* they refused. When their employers attempted to discipline them their colleagues walked out in support.[86]

On 13 July 1911, the Glasgow boat, *Teviot,* sailed into Bristol City docks with a non-union crew. In sympathy with Glaswegian seamen in dispute, dock labourers boycotted this vessel. Deal runners also came out, and men on the Bristol Steam Navigation Company boats stopped work in solidarity as well.[87] Bevin intervened on behalf of the dockers' union, whose official position was not to lend support to the sailors and firemen's union, despite the fact that actions such as this had greatly assisted the winning of disputes at ports around the country. He called a special meeting at which he urged his members to return to work 'to show that the union was not ruled by a mob, but by sensible men.'[88] He got his way. The men agreed to resume work.

Still in its infancy the union branch was trying to find its feet and establish its identity and independence. Just a month before, on 11 June, delegates from the Bristol branch (3) of the DWRU, in defiance of their District Committee's instruction, had voted against increasing the salaries of union officials.[89] The union hierarchy were concerned about bringing some systematic order and control over the branch, yet they had to be cautious as it was plain to see that there was a correlation between the rise in militancy and the increase in union

---

84 Kieran Kelly contends that in the inter-war years 'the experience of the Port of Bristol in the employment of dock labour was similar to that of other ports in the UK.' K. Kelly,'The Port of Bristol 1919-1939: A study of a municipally owned port' (Unpublished PhD, University of the West of England, 1999), p. 234.

85 *WDP*, 30 June 1911.

86 *WDP*, 5 July 1911.

87 *WDP*, 14 July 1911.

88 Ibid.

89 Minutes of the Dock, Wharf and Riverside Union, Branch No. 3, 11 June 1911, BRO.

membership.[90] Salaried officials viewed the spasmodic unofficial stoppages as undesirable, for they undermined their credibility with employers with whom they had struck agreements on behalf of their members. They regarded sympathy strikes with particular disfavour; their priority was to build their union and look after *their* members' interests, not the interests of members of other unions.

The seamen's union had similar issues to contend with. Havelock Wilson was not immune from his members ignoring of the leadership and taking unofficial rank-and-file action in Bristol. Much to his annoyance his members struck work at the Bristol Steam Navigation Company where the union had previously brokered an agreement. He came to Bristol and appealed to his members 'to stand by the existing agreement. They turned a deaf ear...' accusing Wilson of having 'beached them'.[91]

Despite attempts at unifying industrial action under the auspices of NTWF, the inclination of union leaderships was to resolve those disputes affecting their members directly, rather than to wage a struggle against employers on a broad united front. In this period, however, their membership's predisposition undermined this exclusivity by taking sympathy action with anyone who was involved in an industrial dispute — a consciousness of an integral connection that broadened day-to-day struggles against capitalist employers.

The seamen's strike at the Bristol Steam Navigation Company continued until 22 July when the men backed down and accepted the agreement negotiated by their union a week before.[92] Without the support of their union and local dock labourers it would have been difficult to carry on with their action.

On 15 August Avonmouth dockers once again stopped work, this time in support of goods workers on strike at the Great Western Railway Company (GWRC) in Bristol. Although Henry Geater, the district secretary of the DWRU, persuaded his members to resume work, on returning the following day they refused to touch GWR goods.[93] Consequently, food was in short supply and 'vast quantities of it were perishing'.[94] Meanwhile, the poor pay and long hours, provoking the GWRC dispute at Bristol, were also to result in a call for a national rail strike. The roots of the strike can be traced back to the establishment of a system of Conciliation Boards in 1907, which themselves had been brought into existence by the threat of a strike. Through the Boards, the union though not attaining recognition did secure a voice, as, although railway companies refused to recognise rail unions and limited the Boards to questions of wages and hours, railway companies had to listen to the unions' aspirations on these matters. However, the unions and their members soon became disillusioned in the record of these Boards. Railway unions complained about the lengthy Conciliation Board procedures, and railway workers blamed the Boards

---

90   Minutes of the Dock, Wharf and Riverside Union, Branch No. 3, 10 August 1911, noted that increasing numbers of men were joining the union.

91   *WDP*, 15 July 1911.

92   *WDP*, 24 July 1911.

93   *WDP*, 15 and 16 August 1911; *The Times*, 17 August 1911.

94   Ibid.

for allowing their pay to fall in real terms, indeed this was a key factor behind their decision to strike in the summer of 1911.[95]

On the 17 August, after talks between the government and the railway unions had broken down, the joint executive committees of the Amalgamated Society of Railway Servants (ASRS), (the largest rail union), the Associated Society of Locomotive Engineers and Firemen (ASLEF), the General Railway Workers' Union (GRWU) and the United Pointmen's and Signalmen's Society (UPSS) declared a national rail strike, although railway men had already walked out in numerous places across the country, including Bristol and Bath.[96] This declaration was wired immediately by telegram to every branch of the four unions stating, 'Your liberty is at stake. All railwaymen must strike at once. Loyalty to each other means victory.'[97]

In Bristol 2,000 railwaymen, carters, hauliers and warehousemen responded to the strike call, and 4,000 dock labourers came out in sympathy.[98] The GWR men's demands included an advance in wages, the abolition of the bonus system and a reduction in the length of the working day.[99] The dockers took advantage of their act of solidarity by reviving their outstanding claims (submitted three months previously) and insisting that unless these were met they would not return to work.[100]

The City was in turmoil. The same day, 18 August, extra troops were sent for and 'deployed at stations, goods depots and signal boxes',[101] and mounted police were called upon to escort lorries laden with goods to be taken from St Philips' goods yard to the City. Several thousand strikers and their supporters turned out and prevented 'the vehicles' progress and proceeded to do 'damage'.[102] The police sent for reinforcements, generating running battles between the police and strikers. During one such altercation 'Inspector Parfitt's horse reared at the mob who were shouting and booing'. He was unseated but saved from serious injury by falling on a passing lorry, which broke his fall.[103] The following day strikers and their supporters, including women, bombarded a signal box in Bedminster with stones, calling upon the signalman strike-breaker to leave his post. Troops were summoned and fired warning shots over their heads, and the police followed up with a baton charge, seriously injuring one of the strikers.[104]

---

95 D. Howell, 'The Contribution of Direct Action to Gradualism: The Railway Strike of 1911', *Historical Studies in Industrial Relations* Vol. 33 (2012): 65, 70; S. Davies, "Crisis? What Crisis?': The National Rail Strike of 1911 and the State Response', *Historical Studies in Industrial Relations*, Vol. 33 (2012): p. 100; Lee, *The Great Strike Movement of 1911 and its Lessons*, p. 7.

96 Ibid.

97 Cited in A. Gordon, '1911: The First National Railway Strike and the Rail Union Amalgamation Movement', *Historical Studies in Industrial Relations*, Vol. 33 (2012): 132.

98 Davies, "Crisis? What Crisis?': The National Rail Strike of 1911 and the State Response', p. 105.

99 *The Times*, 15 August 1911.

100 *WDP*, 19 August 1911.

101 Whitfield, 'Trade Unionism in Bristol 1910-1926', p. 75.

102 *WDP*, 19 August 1911.

103 Ibid.

104 *The Times*, 21 August 1911; *WDP*, 21 August 1911; Whitfield, 'Trade Unionism in Bristol 1910-1926', p. 75.

The Great Western Goods Depot, Victoria Street, Bristol. By Samuel Loxton *c.* 1910.

By Monday 21 August the rail dispute was over, 'and within a few days the dockers had achieved most of their demands.'[105] The rail strike was settled on the basis that 'the Conciliation Boards be convened for the purpose of settling forthwith the questions at present in dispute in so far as they are within the scope of such Boards.' This was a temporary settlement as a Royal Commission of Inquiry was set up to investigate the workings of the 1907 Railway Conciliation Scheme and provide recommendations thought necessary 'to the prompt and satisfactory settlement of differences.'[106] The Commission came up with recommendations that fell short of full union recognition but the longevity of settlements were reduced, and talks on wages and conditions on existing agreements were allowed to be reopened.[107]

The union membership rejected the Royal Commission's revised Railway Conciliation Scheme and voted to strike. However, the union leaders, concerned that nearly 60% of the membership did not return a vote, decided immediately to conclude the dispute. Clearly, many union members critical of the Conciliation Scheme were incensed about this decision. 'Yet while the strike vote

105 Ibid.

106 'Terms of Settlement of the National Railway Strike, 19 August 1911' cited in Howell, 'The Contribution of Direct Action to Gradualism: The Railway Strike of 1911', pp. 85-86.

107 Ibid., p. 80.

could be seen as a statement of this discontent, it offered no clear alternative to the ethos of conciliation.'[108]

The positive outcome of the 1911 strike was that railway unions in fighting as a united body bolstered the demand for the amalgamation of the rail unions. Within eighteen months, 29 March 1913, three of the five rail unions, ASRS, GRWU and UPSS, joined forces to form the National Union of Railwaymen (NUR).[109] John Marchbank, General Secretary at the time of the union's silver jubilee in 1938, reasoned that the establishment of the NUR meant the accomplishment of something more than the unification of the unions; it put a stop to that slow growth which had hitherto characterised railway trade union development. Until the NUR was formed it was never possible for any railway union to speak with the authority which goes with representative numbers.[110]

Rhondda Valleys, Tonypandy Miners in 1910. By L. Ladd.

Miners' unions too had realised the need for unity. The year long struggle that started over piecework rates for working in abnormal places on a new seam at the Ely Pit, Penygraig, one of many pits which made up the Cambrian Combine of coalfield owners in the Rhondda Valleys (1910-11), was the backdrop to the Miners' Federation of Great Britain (MFGB) eventually broadening the issue to include a call for a district minimum wage for all men and boys whether working in abnormal places or not. The MFGB, however, was hesitant because it was unsure 'whether the claims which the districts had put forward were in breach of existing Conciliation Board agreements.'[111] It decided

---

108 Howell, 'The Contribution of Direct Action to Gradualism: The Railway Strike of 1911', p. 80.

109 For a full account of the legacy of 1911 and amalgamation see Gordon, '1911: The First National Railway Strike and the Rail Union Amalgamation Movement'.

110 John Marchbank, *The Railway Review: Silver Jubilee Supplement*, 25 March 1938, p. 3, Warwick Digital Library, Modern Records Centre, University of Warwick.

111 A. Hutt, *British Trade Unionism* (London: Lawrence & Wishart, 1975; first published 1941), p. 62; Clegg, *A History of British Trade Unions Since 1889: Volume II, 1911-1933*, pp. 26-32.

at the annual conference in October, however, to continue district negotiations, which turned out not only to be painfully slow but also failed in what the MFGB set out do, which was to avoid a national strike.

Like miners in the Rhondda Valleys, dissatisfaction with wage rates, had been an on going problem in Bristol. The difficulties of hewing the coal, its relatively poor quality, and penny-pinching colliery proprietors resulted in Bristol miners, in the late nineteenth and early twentieth century, being among the poorest paid in the country.[112] At the miners' annual conference in 1910, the Bristol delegation called for an 'individual minimum daywage' for every pieceworker in order to overcome the inequity of their situation.[113] As the MFGB dragged their heels on the minimum wage, discontent over low levels of pay turned to anger. In August 1911 miners at Hanham, Speedwell and the Deep Pit at St George threatened, like the Rhondda miners had already done, to go it alone and strike for an extra 3d on the day wage for underground workers. They knew that Somerset miners had received this raise five months previously and thus felt a sense of entitlement.

Deep Pit, St George. By Samuel Loxton.

40% of the miners at these Bristol pits were unorganised and it was these men that pushed the hardest for a strike. Fully aware of this, William Whitefield, the miners' union agent, was quick to condemn the threat to strike at a meeting of the colliers held on 18 August 1911.[114] Whitefield, in his opening address, provoked hostility by stating that non-unionists present would not be allowed a voice. He went on to remind his members that in May the Bristol Colliery owners had rejected the application he had made the previous month, for them to be granted an increase of 3d a day on the highest day rate and *pro rata* on all other standard day rates. The reason given for rejection was that the pits had been working at a loss. Hence the MFGB had advised against a strike through fear of mine closures and consequent job losses. Arguing the situation had not changed Whitefield made it clear that the union would not support a strike, nor would it support a ballot for a strike. He told them he had already convinced

112 *Tamworth Herald*, 30 September 1911; Clegg, *A History of British Trade Unions Since 1889: Volume II, 1911-1933*, p. 45.

113 Ibid., p. 46.

114 *WDP*, 19 August 1911.

miners at other Bristol pits not to take industrial action.[115]

The meeting became emotional. Whitefield preyed on the feelings of the miners for their family homes. In an alarmist tone he appealed 'there were men present who loved their homes and did not want them smashed up.' In sharp response the men shouted, 'we don't get enough to keep up a home. We want 3d a day and intend to get it. We want 4s 2d a day. Somerset men have got it.'[116] Whitefield walked out because 'as far as he was concerned the meeting was closed.' George Young, a Speedwell working miner, took the chair. A resolution was then passed to give the employers a weeks notice to strike for 3d a day.[117]

The strike ballot was run, and the result announced on 23 August revealed that 1,441 were in favour of a strike, 182 against and 271 did not vote.[118] In the meantime the MFGB persuaded the coal owners to allow an arbitrator, appointed by the Board of Trade, to consider the miners' case. However, 800 men employed at the Bristol pits of Speedwell, Hanham and Deep Pit stopped work before the Board of Trade had completed its investigation.[119] In a letter published in the *Western Daily Press*, Frederick Golding, a miner employed at the Hanham pit, protested,

> After allowing them [the proprietors, the MFGB and the Board of Trade] five months they are asking another fortnight [postponement of the strike], which we think is not fair. A miner in the pit in which I am working after working a week consisting of afternoons, has 21s to take home.

He went on to say that fillers and trimmers take home pay was just a miserly 17s or 18s. And, after a long hard shift, to get home they had to trudge two miles, uphill, which taxed their already tired limbs.[120]

On the 18 September, the Board of Trade investigation found in favour of the employers, recommending that the miners' application for an advance in wages be withdrawn. While Whitefield felt vindicated, on hearing the news another 1,200 miners at Speedwell, Hanham and Deep Pit struck work to join the 800 who were already out.[121] This occurred at a time when the spirit of unrest had even spread to school children in a spate of school strikes that broke out across the country, including Bristol.[122] This spirit also extended to the general population, reflected in the widespread public support for striking miners in east Bristol, where local collections and relief concerts were held, helping miners and their families to hold out for three months without official backing before their dire financial situation forced them to concede to a settlement that

115 Ibid.
116 Ibid.
117 Ibid.
118 *WDP*, 24 August 1911.
119 *WDP*, 5 September 1911; Whitfield, 'The Labour Movement in Bristol 1910-1939', pp. 54-56.
120 F. Golding, Tower Road, Warmley, near Bristol, letter to the *WDP*, published 6 September 1911.
121 *WDP*, 18 September 1911.
122 S. Humphries, 'Radical Childhood (1889-1939)' in I. Bild (ed), *Bristol's Other History* (Bristol: Bristol Broadsides (Co-Op), 1983), p. 11.

fell well short of their initial claim.[123]

1912

In January 1912 the union conducted a national strike ballot to test the strength of feeling on establishing a minimum level of earnings for all underground workers. On the 18 January the ballot result was announced. The miners voted to strike by a majority of 445,800 to 115,271.[124] Several weeks of failed negotiations passed, and despite a last minute intervention by the Government 'suggesting the recognition of the *principal* of the minimum wage while leaving it to the local conciliation committees to establish the precise figures',[125] at the end of February the MFGB gave the go ahead for first national miners' strike to begin.

Less than a week before the national strike commenced, Whitefield had expressed severe reservations about his members' commitment to partake in a strike. He said 'they had a minimum wage agreement, and that the price they had to pay for loyalty to the Miners' Federation by bringing out their tools was almost beyond what could be expected from human nature.'[126] Bristol Colliery owners too warned their employees

> that the agreement arrived at last November settled all the points in dispute, and that the recent strike caused so much injury to the pits that even now it was impossible to find work for all the men previously employed. Further, the men knew from the Board of Trade that the collieries could pay no more, so the men should seriously consider the consequences before handing in notices.[127]

And yet Bristol miners had voted in January to strike by a majority of 1,084 to 342,[128] despite the closure of Easton (Bristol) Colliery immediately after the 1911 strike[129] and the warnings given by their local union agent, Whitefield.

Around 2,500 miners in Bristol rallied behind the strike call. Strike pay was set at 10s a man with an additional 1s for each of his children, but after a couple of weeks this amount was reduced to 7s 6d. Bristol mining communities suffered acute distress, as indeed they did in other mining areas. In Bedminster, a working class suburb near the collieries, the Salvation Army supplied hundreds of breakfasts daily for hungry children who devoured cocoa, bread and butter ('and not a crumb was left'); they also provided meals for miners and their families at the Mission Hall in New street, St Judes, and at Grafton Hall, St Philips.[130] There was one known fatality. While William Burford was rummaging for coal at Trooper's Hill, St George, the roof caved in and he was

---

123 Whitfield, 'The Labour Movement in Bristol 1910-1939', pp. 54-56.

124 Hutt, *British Trade Unionism*, p. 67.

125 T. Rothstein, *From Chartism to Labourism* (London: Lawrence and Wishart, 1983; first published 1929), p. 312.

126 *Manchester Courier and Lancashire General Advertiser*, 24 February 1912.

127 *Aberdeen Journal*, 23 February 1912.

128 *Aberdeen Journal*, 5 April 1912.

129 *Cornishman*, 26 October 1911.

130 *Bristol Observer*, 23 and 30 March 1912.

crushed to death.[131]

This was a time of heightened class tension. In January 1912, *The Syndicalist* had reprinted an open letter to British soldiers, first published in James Connolly's *Irish Worker,* calling upon them not to shoot strikers if called upon to do so, which was reproduced as a leaflet and distributed among soldiers at Aldershot. It began,

> Men! Comrades! Brothers!
> You are in the Army.
> So are We. You in the Army of Destruction. We in the Industrial, or Army of Construction.
> We work at mine, mill, forge, factory, or dock, producing and transporting all the goods, clothing, stuffs, etc. which make it possible for people to live.
> You are Working Men's Sons.
> When We go on Strike to better Our lot, which is the lot also of Your Fathers, Mothers, Brothers, and Sisters, YOU are called upon by your officers to MURDER US.
> Don't do it.[132]

At the beginning of the 1912 miners' strike, Tom Mann, then president of the Industrial Syndicalist Education League, read out the contents of the 'Don't Shoot' leaflet at a meeting at Salford. He was arrested, charged, under the incitement to Mutiny Act 1797, and jailed, a fate he shared with the editor of *The Syndicalist*, Guy Bowman; its printers, the Buck brothers; and Fred Crowsley, a railwayman.

In Bristol, during the week ending Friday 15 March, 'an inflammatory handbill' was circulated, among the striking miners. It induced them to,

> Fight for yourselves: your masters hate you: they would shoot you down like rabbits, but they need your labour for their huge profits. Don't go in till you get your minimum. No Royal Commission, no promise in the future. Leaders only want your votes; they will sell you. They lie, Parliament lies, and they will not help you, but trying to sell you. Don't touch a tool till you get your minimum. Win, win, win; it is up to all workers to support the miners.[133]

Evidence that the majority of Bristol miners were committed to 'win, win, win' came a week or so later. On the 25 March 1912 at 6am, 60 to 70 miners, driven by destitution, presented themselves for work at two of Bristol's pits, Speedwell and Deep Pit, which were in close proximity to one another. News of this disloyalty travelled quickly and by 1.30pm around 1,000 miners and their wives along with other supporters gathered to await the strike-breakers as they finished their shift. When they surfaced they 'were greeted by hissing and

---

131 This information was taken from John Lyes, *Bristol 1901-1913* (Bristol: Bristol Branch of the Historical Association: Local History Pamphlets, 2002), p. 40.

132 Cited in R. Challinor, *The Origins of British Bolshevism* (London: Croom Helm, 1977), p. 66.

133 *Hull Daily Mail,* 18 March 1912.

booing' before leaving under police escort.[134] There were, however, no reported incidents of overzealous picketing or violence.

While no sympathy was expressed for these strike-breakers, there was a grudging recognition that the forces of want driving them back were strong, as these pits had only recently endured a three-month stoppage. One sixty-nine-year-old miner, unable to find employment since the last strike, committed suicide due, it was thought, to despair brought upon by destitution.[135] The press reported it was 'well-known that the Bristol colliers only supported the [national] strike out of sympathy with the general movement, having nothing to gain but a great deal to lose.'[136] The media failed to comprehend the importance the majority of miners placed on upholding the principles of solidarity, dignity and humanity. A sense of honourable manhood bound them together.

The miners experienced intolerable working conditions in which a man's physical powers secured a higher rate of pay. However, the individuals' survival was also dependent on his work mates, and mutuality bred a strong sense of collective brotherhood. Pride in a man's ability to provide for his family, regardless of the physical exertion involved, combined with a recognition of the need for connection to other miners in a form of solidarity and dignity expressed in terms of a 'manhood', which differed from the forms of masculine control over the work process asserted among craft workers.

Dockers, like miners, were workers whose labour pre-dated industrialisation. Like the miners, Bristol dockers also competed individually, but were more mutually dependent upon one another, they articulated a consciousness of solidarity with the miners in terms of an invocation of their 'manhood'. This is not the same language of the politically-conscious leader, who wrote of a cooperative commonwealth, a society based on cooperative and socialist principles, but drew on historical memory of pride and resistance.

It is unsurprising, therefore, to find that Bristol dockers pressed their national leaders to call for a sympathetic strike in support of the miners. At a meeting of their branch of 21 March, they unanimously passed a resolution, urging

> the Transport Workers Executive to at once consider the advisability of calling upon the Transport Workers of this country to assert their manhood by at once refusing to do anymore work after a certain date until the miners' case is settled.[137]

Two weeks later the same branch carried a motion with direct reference to the charges brought against Tom Mann:

> This meeting emphatically protests against the action of the Government in encroaching upon the right of free speech and liberty of the Press when the same is undertaken on behalf of the workers and urges all workers to struggle to maintain the rights which their forefathers fought

---

134 *Bristol Observer*, 30 March 1912.
135 *Bristol Observer*, 6 April 1912.
136 Ibid.
137 Minutes of the Dock, Wharf and Riverside Union, Branch No. 3, 21 March 1912.

for and obtained believing that at the present moment a sinister attempt is being made to stifle free expression and opinions of the workers' leaders and to prevent the growth of solidarity.[138]

What became of these resolutions is not known, but once again this is an illustration of Bristol dockers' propensity to support solidarity action.

It was only a few days after the resumption of work by a small number of miners at Speedwell and Deep Pit that, in an effort to settle the national miners' dispute, the Government, supported by the Labour Party, rushed a Bill through parliament that gave the power to 'district boards to settle statutory minima for underground miners, but not for surface workers.'[139] It became law on 29 March, making the Government's previous offer, put forward at the end of February, binding on the MFGB and its members.[140] A ballot was then held on whether the men should resume work pending the settlement of district rates by the Joint Arbitration and Conciliation Boards under the new Act. Despite the fact there was a majority of 42,998 against resumption (in Bristol a majority of 446 voted for resumption),[141] on 6 April the MFGB declared the strike at an end after a special conference decided that 'a two-thirds vote for calling a strike should also apply to continuing a strike.'[142]

A series of smaller strikes also occurred in Bristol during 1912. A five-week stoppage involving 80 men at the Cooperative Wholesale Society flour mills at Avonmouth began in December 1911 and ended in the middle of January 1912, when the Executive Council of their union ordered them, against their will, to resume work and accept the terms proposed by a Joint Conciliation and Arbitration Board.[143] Similarly, in the second week of January, 60 women at a boot and shoe factory at Soundwell, Bristol who had struck work in opposition to the introduction of a piecework system to supersede the old regular weekly wage system, were instructed to return to work by their union, the Bristol Branch of the Boot Operatives' Union.[144] In May forty blind workers at the Bristol Blind Asylum workshops, supported by the National League of the Blind, withdrew their labour in an attempt to improve the poor wages and conditions at the asylum. The men demanded to be paid £1 a week and the women 13s. The strikers complained that while the asylum officials were paid well, 'blind workers, for whom the Institution is maintained, are so badly remunerated that outworkers have often to obtain parish relief to eke out their miserable doles.'[145]

Apart from the national miners' strike, however, the most significant stoppage, albeit very brief, involved around 8,000 Bristol dockers who came out on 12 June in response to a call for a national sympathy strike from their London colleagues. Bristol was one of the few ports that responded to the call but it soon

138 Minutes of the Dock, Wharf and Riverside Union, Branch No. 3, 4 April 1912.

139 Clegg, *A History of British Trade Unions Since 1889: Volume II, 1911-1933*, p. 49.

140 Rothstein, *From Chartism to Labourism*, p. 312.

141 *Aberdeen Journal*, 5 April 1912.

142 Clegg, *A History of British Trade Unions Since 1889: Volume II, 1911-1933*, p. 50.

143 *Bristol Observer*, 15 January 1912.

144 *Exeter and Plymouth Gazette*, 10 January 1912.

145 *Exeter and Plymouth Gazette*, 13 May 1912.

became clear that a national strike was not going to happen. After three days, on advice from Bevin, who said it was 'not a Dockers' union fight at all, but a Transport Federation fight', Bristol men voted to resume work.[146] London dockers, having failed to get support from workers at other key ports, such as Liverpool, soldiered on until the strike eventually collapsed at the end of July. Defeat reduced them 'to a state of disorganised casualism'.[147]

Bristol dockers, however, avoided this fate and were able to consolidate their position, despite the issue of 200 summonses to carters and warehousemen for breach of contract — as they had signed a commitment to use the Joint Arbitration Board to settle disputes — and an influx of non-union labour.[148] Their position in terms of membership actually strengthened slightly; the Bristol branch membership of DWRU increased from 932 in April to 961 in July.[149] Bristol dockers were embittered, however, about the failure of other ports to join them in support of the national strike call and rallied around their union leaders. At their meeting of 20 June they passed the following resolution:

> This meeting of members of the above branch [Bristol branch No. 3 of DWRU] have every confidence in the National officials and Executive and also their local officials and hereby call on their Executive to withdraw from the Transport Workers Federation seeing other members of the Federation did not respond to the National call.[150]

Apart from a campaign to re-establish the old Plimsoll line, as a means to protect the lives of seamen and men whose daily task was to unload and load ships,[151] dockers' militancy in Bristol seemed to have been subdued by the breakdown of solidarity in the call for a national dock strike. This quietude turned out to be a feature of relations between capital and labour in Bristol in 1913.

1913

Britain would experience a record number of strikes in 1913. It is true these were smaller than the ones that aroused such hostility from employers in the preceding three years but a wide diversity of industries was effected, including building, engineering, shipbuilding and textile trades. The Dublin lock-out proved the most notable industrial conflict of the year; and Jim Larkin, the revolutionary leader of the Irish Transport and General Workers Union (ITGWU), was to become one of the most significant and daring union leaders of the century. 'He viewed his Union as a revolutionary instrument with which he hoped to effect both economic change and social advancement.'[152]

---

146 *Bristol Observer*, 15 June 1912; *The Times* 11, 12 and 14 June 1912. For a fuller account of the 1912 London dock strike see Clegg, *A History of British Trade Unions Since 1889: Volume II, 1911-1933*, pp. 53-56.

147 Hobsbawm, *Labouring Men*, p. 216.

148 *Bristol Observer*, 15 June 1912; Minutes of the Dock, Wharf and Riverside Union, Branch No. 3, 20 June 1912.

149 Minutes of the Dock, Wharf and Riverside Union, Branch No. 3, 4 April and 4 July 1912.

150 Minutes of the Dock, Wharf and Riverside Union, Branch No. 3, 20 June 1912.

151 Minutes of the Dock, Wharf and Riverside Union, Branch No. 3, 10 October 1912.

152 Emmet Larkin, *James Larkin 1876-1947: Irish Labour Leader* (London: Routledge & Kegan Paul, 1977; first published

James Larkin. 1923.

In Bristol, however, militancy was likely to be associated more with the suffrage movement rather than with the labour and trade union movement in 1913,[153] although the year started with the continuation of a strike, over the demotion of a disgruntled foreman, of over 200 tailoresses and cutters supplying among other things police uniforms, which was eventually settled by mediation.[154] Even strikes in the nearby Black Country,[155] particularly among semi-skilled engineering workers, did not filter down into Bristol. Instead attempts to organise small engineering shops were low-key, using methods of attrition. Sometimes these did lead to minor disputes. A rule of the Bristol Operative Tin and Iron Plate, Sheet Metal Workers and Braziers Union stated that its members must not work with non-union men and must not work below the union day-work rate or piecework price. It was a continual battle to oversee this enforcement of this rule which absorbed a great deal of time and bother in

1965), p. xiv. For an account of the Dublin lock-out see Pádraig Yeates, *Lockout: Dublin 1913* (New York, USA: St Martins Press, 2000); also see John Newsinger, *Rebel City: Larkin, Connolly and the Dublin Labour Movement* (London: Merlin, 2004).

153 See L. Boyce, *The Bristol Suffragettes*, (Bristol: published by the author using Silverwood Books Empowered Publishing, 2013).

154 *Reports on Strikes and Lock-outs and on Conciliation and Arbitration Boards in the United Kingdom in 1913*, Cd 7658 (1914), p. 165. See the *WDP*, 21 December 1912, for a full account of the dispute and the corresponding court case. The strike was over the grievance of one individual foreman who, on returning to work after a long period of paid sick leave, felt that he was unfairly treated, as his foreman's role was taken away from him.

155 The Black Country is an area covering places in and around West Bromwich, Wolverhampton, Walsall, Oldbury, Blackheath, Cradley Heath, Old Hill, Bilston, Dudley, and Tipton. See R. Hyman, *The Workers' Union* (Oxford: Clarendon Press, 1971) for accounts of strikes in the Black Country during this period.

the committee meetings.

The union minutes illustrate the problems in administering this rule and against working with non-union workers. For instance, members of the Operative Tin and Iron Plate Union working for Mullets Motor Works in Coronation Road, Bristol, were ordered to cease working for this firm as it operated a 'Piece Boss' system, which turned out to be less than the union rates. Members working in the motor shop of the anti-union firm Bristol Tramways Company were struck off the books for working with non-union men.[156] Men working for Messrs Saunders, Bath Road, Bristol, came out in dispute over their union's objection to a new system of working based on sectional work, which gave the company the opportunity to use non-craft workers on some aspects of its product. The company, however, managed to replace the strikers, by offering high wages to non-union labour brought in from London and the men had to find alternative employment.[157]

Despite multiple low-key disputes involving corn porters, carters and warehousemen, dealt with through the auspices of Joint Conciliation and Arbitration Board,[158] Port of Bristol dock workers, in 1913, focused on strengthening their organisation rather than engaging in major conflicts. For instance, they were critical of their local salaried officers for not regularly turning out at Bristol and Avonmouth before 8am to carry out systematic checks to see that labour hired for dock work were paid-up union members by inspecting their union 'book'.[159] Interestingly, like dockers in London and Glasgow, they identified with political militancy. At its meeting of 14 August 1913, the Bristol branch of DWRU passed a resolution protesting against the decision to imprison the former Labour MP George Lansbury, his political associate John Scurr, and the militant suffragette Leonora Cohen for allegedly sanctioning the suffragettes' arson campaign.[160] Of the three defendants only Lansbury was sent to prison for refusing to be bound over. He went on a hunger strike and was released under the 'Cat and Mouse Act'. He was never called upon to return. It seems the government had more pressing issues than to give Lansbury the opportunity to extract more publicity. And in August it was the labour unrest throughout Ireland that demanded the British government's attention. [161]

Larkinism dominated the headlines towards the end of 1913. On 24 November, he addressed an audience of 4,000 at the Colston Hall in Bristol. Not all of the attendees were supporters of Larkin. He was acutely aware of this and singled them out. He said

---

156 Minutes of a Special Committee Meeting of the Bristol Operative Tin and Iron Plate, Sheet Metal Workers and Braziers Union, 27 August 1913 (M. Richardson private papers).

157 Minutes of Committee Meetings of the Bristol Operative Tin and Iron Plate, Sheet Metal Workers and Braziers Union, 18 September, 9 October and 16 October 1913.

158 *Reports on Strikes and Lock-outs and on Conciliation and Arbitration Boards in the United Kingdom in 1913*, Cd 7658 (1914), pp. 171- 172; *Yorkshire Gazette*, 18 January 1913.

159 Minutes of the Dock, Wharf and Riverside Union, Branch No. 3, 27 March 1913.

160 Minutes of the Dock, Wharf and Riverside Union, Branch No. 3, 14 August 1913; *Daily Herald*, 31 July 1913.

161 E. Crawford, *Women's Suffrage Movement: A Reference Guide 1866-1928* (London: University College London Press, 1999), p. 334.

He had been watching the audience during earlier proceedings, and he had seen a sneer on the face of the well fed. There were people in the hall who despised the workers, but let the workers not be humbugged. He had watched people there who had come to look at the beast, to see this new phenomenon symbolised in the person of Jim Larkin the docker. They were beyond hope of redemption.[162]

"Vote for the unionist candidate & prosperity to our Bristol Docks, prosperity & fair play for Bristol industries, own working men & safety for our country." By F G Lewin. Depicting Augustine Birrell, H Chatterton the Independent Unionist (Tory) candidate for the Bristol South seat in the 1910 election, and the incumbent Howell Davis who retained the seat.

Cheers of approval resounded around the hall. Larkin continued his speech by attacking Augustine Birrell, chief secretary for Ireland and Liberal MP for North Bristol for his conduct against Protestant and Catholic workers in Ireland since he came to office in 1906. In the 1907 Belfast dock strike, Larkin accused 'Birrell and his friends' of pouring 'on the streets of Belfast thousands of hired assassins … brought in to shoot down, at the behest of the British Government, men who were struggling to raise their miserable wages'.[163] A resolution was carried supporting locked out Dublin workers in their on-going struggle against the City's employers' attempt to crush trade unionism. It denounced the Government for 'allowing its forces to be ruthlessly used to kill, bludgeon and

---

162 *Manchester Courier and Lancashire General Advertiser*, 25 November 1913.
163 Ibid.

Avonmouth dockers leave at the end of a shift in 1903.

imprison the workers in the interests of the scoundrelly minions of capitalism.'[164]

Larkin continued his attack on Birrell calling on him 'to withdraw the police from the factories, the soldiers from blacklegging, and make a thorough investigation of the police conduct.'[165] Finally a resolution was carried unanimously summoning Birrell to accept the Bristol's Labour Party challenge to 'resign his seat and fight on this issue.'[166] Larkin, however, was soon to lose the support of the British Trades Union Congress at its special conference held on 9 December 1913. '[S]peaker after speaker condemned Larkin for his attacks on British Labour leaders.' When Larkin came to the rostrum he caused uproar when he told delegates, 'You are afraid to hear the truth. Accept the guilt if you are guilty, and don't make lying statements about me.'[167] In this highly charged atmosphere Ben Tillet's resolution was passed:

> That this Conference deplores and condemns the unfair attacks by men inside the trade union movement upon British trade union officials; it affirms its confidence in those officials who have been so unjustly assailed, and its belief in their ability to negotiate an honourable settlement if assured of effective support of all who are concerned in the Dublin dispute.[168]

This sounded the death knell for Larkin and the Dublin workers he represented. At the end of January 1914 Larkin conceded defeat.

---

164   *The Times*, 25 November 1913.
165   *Exeter and Plymouth Gazette*, 25 November 1913.
166   *The Times*, 25 November 1913.
167   Larkin, *James Larkin 1876-1947: Irish Labour Leader*, pp. 152-153.
168   Ibid., p. 152.

1914

After almost three years of industrial unrest, which was triggered in part by the fall in real wages, and in part by workers' desire to shift the pendulum of power away from capital towards labour, the most significant achievement was the growing self-awareness of workers' collective strength, although this point should not be exaggerated. Trade union membership had increased considerably from 2,477,000 at the end of 1909 to 4,135,000 at the end of 1913,[169] penetrating deep into some of the semi-skilled and unskilled trades, which is an indication of the strength of the labour revolt in this period. Expressed as a proportion of the working population, these figures show that union density had increased from around 12% to 24%. While this was a significant increase, the majority of the working population were not members of a trade union, and therefore less able to defend themselves against the worst excesses of the unscrupulous employer. However, the forward march of labour 'appeared to be a threat to the political order',[170] especially as the Labour Party had made little impact in Parliament. Moreover, this threat was given more credence by the fact that only two-thirds of men qualified for the vote, and women were still excluded. Understandably, politicians of all colours feared that workers would favour direct action rather than parliamentary politics to advance radical egalitarian change.

This was a period of economic boom so workers in some industrial sectors were in a relatively strong bargaining position. It is interesting then to see how workers in general had fared in advancing their economic situation at the end of three years of industrial unrest. In regard to workers' living standards, data compiled from trade union membership records indicates that between 1910 and 1914 unemployment, among those trade union members who paid unemployment benefit, had decreased from 6.8% in January 1910 to 2.5% in January 1914.[171] Wage rates had increased by 7% between January 1910 and July 1914. Data on the extent of price increases during this period is incomplete but what is known is that the cost of food rose about 4%, clothing increased around 7%, and the price of coal jumped as much as 10%.[172] With unemployment relatively low and wages perhaps struggling a little to track inflation it is not surprising to find that conflict continued to plague the national industrial scene in 1914.

In Bristol the breakdown in national solidarity in the 1912 London dock strike continued to have a moderating effect on dockers and some other sections of workers. On New Year's Day the dockers' union revealed that it was in talks with the Bristol Docks Committee on the formation of a Joint Conciliation Board covering all the categories of waterside labour, not just corn porters, carters and warehousemen, for settling future disputes that might arise over pay

---

169 *British Labour Statistics: Historical Abstract 1886-1968*, (Department of Employment: Her Majesty's Stationery Office, 1971), p. 395.

170 K. Middlemas, *Politics in Industrial Society: The Experience of the British System since 1911* (London: André Deutsch, 1979), p. 57.

171 *British Labour Statistics: Historical Abstract 1886-1968*, p. 305.

172 Ibid., p. 165.

and conditions.[173] It was also engaged in discussions on decasualisation. At the instigation of the Labour Alderman Frank Sheppard, Bristol Town Council had passed a resolution instructing the Docks Committee

> To take into consideration the question of decasualisation of labour and the adoption of a system of registration, and that for the purpose of such consideration, at least three other members of the Council be added to the Docks Committee, and, further, that a similar number of merchants interested and of workmen's representatives be asked to co-operate, in order that a proper solution be arrived at.[174]

The reasons Sheppard felt strongly about this issue were admirable. Under the casual system, men could be employed by the half-day, which benefited employers, as they had only to engage the number of men required to match the available work. It was demeaning for workers to present themselves at the dock-gate every morning waiting to see if they were the ones lucky enough to be hired. Those that were not called either had to wait around the docks in the hope that the odd job would become available, or they would go home until the next hiring. This routine was particularly onerous for those men who made the journey from Bristol to Avonmouth docks by train, if they could afford it, or made their way by road. Some slept on the docks overnight causing the authorities to introduce measures to stop this practice.[175]

The key concern was that those men who were regularly employed at the docks should be registered as such. These men, whose livelihoods depended on regular employment on the waterside, 'were naturally anxious to eliminate the "strapper"', which was a reference to the competition from unemployed men from other industries who acted as a reserve army of labour in times of depression.[176] However, as Bevin learned in his time as a union official in Bristol docks, 'he knew the men's resistance to any form of dramatic change.'[177] Yet this resistance had substance. Many dock workers, especially those with skills and experience, liked the freedom to be able to turn down disagreeable jobs. They often rejected time-work in the hope of securing piece-work. Short-time jobs would be rejected if they felt there was a chance of obtaining work of long-duration.[178] Moreover, the arduous nature of the work often required periods of rest to recover. If men were permanently employed they would not have the opportunity to take time off when they so desired, as they would be tied to the disciplinary and control mechanisms of their employer. '[T]hese work patterns were part of the attraction of the job; they gave the docker the freedom — highly illusory in times of great unemployment — to work as he needed to and not as his employer demanded.'[179]

---

173 *WDP*, 1 January 1914.

174 *WDP*, 17 February 1914.

175 *WDP*, 11 March 1914.

176 *WDP*, 19 February 1914.

177 D. F. Wilson, *Dockers: the impact of industrial change,* (London: Fontana, 1972), p. 79.

178 W. Hamilton Whyte, 'Decasualisation of Dock Labour at the Port of Bristol', *Economica* No. 37 (Aug., 1932): 360.

179 N. Whiteside, 'Welfare Insurance and Casual Labour: A Study of Administrative Intervention in Industrial Employment, 1906-26', *The Economic History Review*, New Series Vol. 32, No. 4 (Nov., 1979): 507-522, 518.

The major disputes in Bristol during 1914 were not to be found on the waterfront but among skilled men employed at the Bristol Tramways and Carriage Company and men working in the Bristol building trade. The dispute at the Tramway's New Motor Construction Company at Kensington Hill, Brislington, broke out, on 2 March 1914, after 200 of their employees — comprising fitters, turners, general machine hands, body makers, trimmers and painters — had refused to sign the new book of company rules. As a result they were locked out. The following morning they marched in procession to the company's headquarters at Clare Street in the City Centre. Here they confronted the company's management but failed to persuade them to back down. They quickly constructed a banner on which the words 'Bristol Tramways Company Lockout. We won't sign.' were inscribed, and proceeded to march half-a-mile to the Horsefair to publicise their plight.[180]

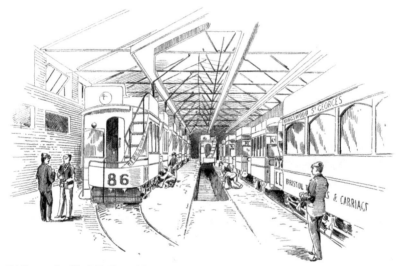

Brislington Car Shed. By Samuel Loxton.

That evening the dismissed men held a meeting at which they passed a resolution vowing not to resume work until the new book of company rules was withdrawn. This decree had the support of the President and Secretary of the Bristol Trades Council and the men's salaried union officials.[181] However, the Company, eager to undermine the men's morale, claimed that it had been inundated with applications to fill the vacancies created by the lock-out.[182] Response from the unions was painfully slow. Several weeks passed before ninety members of the Workers' Union employed at the Company's depots at Leek Lane and Brislington walked out in solidarity with their colleagues.[183] A

---

180 *WDP*, 3 March 1914.

181 Ibid.

182 *WDP*, 7 March 1914.

183 This development was announced by Charles Robert Vincent, organiser of the Workers' Union, at a meeting called in support of the men locked-out by the Tramway Company, *WDP*, 3 April 1914.

couple days later, Saturday, 4 April, at a conference of trade union delegates held at Broad Street, Bristol, two important resolutions were passed. First, it was agreed that with immediate effect members would be withdrawn from the company's employ. Second, a request was to be put out to trade union members to 'refuse to handle any diverted work of the Tramways Company, either in transit or in working or repairing'.[184] The Bristol Operative Tin and Iron Plate, Sheet Metal Workers and Braziers Union, were quick to act. It adopted the resolution 'that all members of this Society refuse to handle any work belonging to the Tramway Company.'[185]

Under the direction of the Strike Committee, the fight back gathered pace. A demonstration in support of withdrawing the labour of all union members working for the Company was held on the following day, Sunday 5 April, at the *Empire*, Old Market, Bristol. Joshua Widdicombe, president of the Bristol Trades Council, and a member of the British Socialist Party (BSP), presided. He opened the meeting by providing a history of the dispute, maintaining that the Company paid below the standard rates of wages. He assured his audience that, despite its claim to the contrary, the company had failed to recruit enough men to fill the positions of those locked out, even though, to attract applications from outside Bristol, it had offered to pay the rail fares.[186]

These same claims were made two weeks later at a further meeting of trade unionists held at the Bristol Empire. The strike was entering its eighth week but Widdicombe, who was chairing the meeting, 'complained that Bristol trade unionists had not taken up the fight as they should.'[187] And Ben Smith, organiser of the Vehicle Workers, affirmed 'the adoption of a general "down tools" policy.'[188] Picketing of the Tramway's Motor Construction Company became more vociferous as time dragged on. Walter Edward Jarrett, an employee of the Tramway Company, summoned one of the locked-out men, James Yeadon, for assault. At the court hearing it was said that the defendant, along with others, presented himself daily outside the works entrance and as the working men left the Company premises he and his fellow strikers 'followed them and called them "scabs" and "blacklegs" and other offensive names', terrorising some of the men. It was alleged that on one of these occasions, 30 April, Yeadon struck Jarrett who then re-entered the works to escape further injury. The police were summoned and provided an escort for Jarrett for his journey home. Yeadon was found guilty of ordinary assault and was bound over to keep the peace for six months.[189]

Despite the belated efforts of the Bristol Trades Council and the unions concerned, at a meeting of the Lock-Out Committee, held on 12 June, the fight to get the men reinstated, without having to sign the new rules of the Tramway's

184 *WDP* 6 April 1914.
185 Minutes of Committee Meetings of the Bristol Operative Tin and Iron Plate, Sheet Metal Workers and Braziers Union, 8 April 1914.
186 *WDP*, 6 April 1914.
187 *WDP*, 20 April 1914.
188 Ibid.
189 *WDP*, 9 May 1914.

'Bristol Tramways Strike. Scene outside Brislington Depot during dispute'. 1901.
By E. Coffin.

Motor Construction Company, was terminated. However, they pledged 'never to return to work for the Bristol Tramways Company so long as these 41 rules remained in force.' Picketing ceased 'and it was resolved to advise, and give permission to, all men whose services had been sought by other firms to accept such offers and start work immediately.'[190]

Two weeks after the folding of this dispute, Bristol's bricklayers and labourers struck work in their fight for a reduction in the length of the working day by one hour in the summer, and for a higher hourly wage rate to compensate for the loss earnings that would result from the proposed cut in hours. The employers, represented by the Bristol Master Builders, had made an offer short of the building workers' demands, which was rejected. They then offered to let the claim go to arbitration. That suggestion was spurned and, on the morning of 2 July 1914, over 2,000 men downed tools to attend a mass meeting addressed by their union officials, Frank Kennedy, national organiser of the United Builders' Labourers' Union, and George Hicks, national organiser of the Operative Bricklayers' Society and a prominent syndicalist.[191]

190 *WDP*, 15 June 1914.
191 *WDP*, 3 July 1914.

This was particularly significant because around one fifth of London's building workers, in unions affiliated to the London Building Industries' Federation (LBIF), had just rejected, (by 14,081 votes to 4,565), proposals for a settlement of their long running dispute concerning 'the right of their members to refuse to work with non-unionists'.[192] This result went against the advice of the LBIF. Dissatisfied with their union leadership, some union activists formed a new organisation called the Syndicalist Building Workers' Industrial Union, which condemned 'the ordinary trade union methods as cumbersome and out of date.'[193] And the Bristol Operative Bricklayers had at least one syndicalist member in their midst, E. Howell, who attended the First International Syndicalist Congress held in London from 27 September to 2 October 1913.[194]

Three days after the Bristol builders' strike declaration, miners, transport workers and railway men paraded from various points across Bristol to the City Centre where they 'formed one huge procession, and marched with bands and banners to [Clifton and Durdham] Downs.' They were celebrating the formation of the Triple Alliance. This was an alliance for mutual aid between the miners, railwaymen, and transport workers. Ostensibly, it had the potential to organise a general strike. Speaking at the Downs' demonstration, Robert Smillie, President of the Miners' Federation, said of the alliance that 'whilst they would not use it in every petty quarrel they wanted to strike scientifically when the need arose, and strike when least expected';[195] in reality, however, it served to deter militancy rather than promote it.[196]

Not long after this demonstration eighty spinners employed at the Great Western Cotton factory struck work for an advance in pay. Supported by the National Federation of Women Workers (NFWW), these women, who had been without union representation for several years and were among the lowest paid in the country with earnings of no more than 9s a week, secured an increase in the piece rate that 'made a difference of a couple of shillings advance in the wages of those engaged on that work.'[197] Within days 400 women had signed up with the union. Quick to build on this success the NFWW, with the assistance of Bristol Trades Council, organised a meeting to encourage more workers to join. At this meeting, held on 14 July in Redfield, Bristol, Miss Vickers, one of the union's organisers 'remarked that she did not wish them [cotton workers] to strike, because she realised that they could ill afford to lose a day's work, and she hoped there would be no further trouble, and that they would encourage all their fellow workers to come into the Union.'[198] The meeting finished with those present pledging 'to remain members of the National Federation of Women Workers,

---

192 Clegg, *A History of British Trade Unions Since 1889: Volume II, 1911-1933*, pp. 65 & 67.

193 *Western Gazette*, 3 July 1914.

194 Wayne Westergard-Thorpe, 'Revolutionary Syndicalist Internationalism, 1913-1923: The Origins of the International Working Men's Association' (unpublished PhD, The University of British Columbia, July 1979), p. 303, footnote 17.

195 *WDP*, 6 July 1914.

196 G. A. Phillips, 'The Triple Industrial Alliance in 1914', *The Economic History Review*, New Series Vol. 24, No. 1 (Feb., 1971): 63; J. Hinton, *Labour and Socialism: A History of the British Labour Movement 1867-1974* (Brighton: Harvester, 1983), p. 92.

197 *WDP*, 15 July 1914.

198 Ibid.

Workers at the Great Western Cotton factory. By Samuel Loxton.

firmly believing that only by combined efforts can our condition, both in the matter of wages and hours, be improved.'[199]

In the meantime splits began to appear between craft workers and the bricklayers and labourers over their wages and hours' dispute with their employers. Rumors spread that F. E. White, the Secretary of the Bristol and District Building Trades' Committee was about to accept terms offered by the employers that fell short of what they demanded, as they seemed to satisfy the sections of the building trade he represented, comprising plasterers, plumbers, painters, woodcutters, stonemasons and labourers belonging to the gas workers' union. On the evening of Tuesday 7 July, angry at this turn of events, thirty men accosted White on his way to a Bristol and District Building Trades' Committee meeting. Using threatening language, the men warned him against accepting the employers' offer.[200]

This incident did not deter him, however, as on 9 July White announced that he had reached an agreement with the Master Builders' Association that gave the plasterers, plumbers, painters, woodcutters and stonemasons, who were not on strike, a reduction of half-an-hour a day during the summer months and an advance of one halfpenny per hour. The builders' branch of the Gasworkers and General Labourers' Union rejected the same offer and joined those bricklayers and labourers already on strike, who were pushing for one penny an hour

199 Ibid.
200 *WDP*, 9 July 1914.

increase.[201] This left nearly 2,000 bricklayers and builders' labourers in Bristol on strike to fight their case without the support of White and those craft workers he represented.

On 7 August, just ten days before Britain declared war on Germany, the employers played the patriotic card suggesting that 'during the national crisis a temporary expedient might be employed whereby the men should return to work immediately on the same advance as that granted to the other trades, namely halfpenny an hour.' A mass meeting of the men unanimously rejected this proposal. 'They considered that the masters should have shown a patriotic spirit themselves by granting their demands.'[202] Within a few days the employers upped their offer to 'one halfpenny an hour advance in wages, to take effect immediately, and a further halfpenny advance to take effect on the 1st January next.'[203] The men accepted this offer. The official settlement to the dispute was announced the day war broke out with Germany, on 17 August.

This resistance to succumbing to the patriotic card reflected the attitude of many trade unionists towards the impending war at this time. Just two weeks before the outbreak of hostilities, Bristol Dockers passed a resolution calling on 'the Government immediately to declare its neutrality in connection with the European war'. Bevin, the dockers' organiser, in moving the resolution said he would support a national strike, if necessary, to prevent war.[204]

Conclusion

It would be too simplistic to say that the key features running through this narrative of industrial strife in Bristol between 1910 and 1914 correspond with events elsewhere in Britain, particularly in its major ports. There are of course similarities, such as the unofficial nature of many of the strikes and the solidarity across differing kinds of employment. Yet despite the plethora of solidarity strikes, in contrast to the substantial syndicalist presence in the disputes in Dublin, London, Liverpool and South Wales, there is no explicit evidence in Bristol that syndicalists played any significant part in organising strikes or that they whipped up discontent against salaried union leaders, apart from the one example of the attendance, in late September 1914, of a member of the Bristol Operative Bricklayers at the First International Syndicalist Congress.

Frustration with, and bitterness towards, salaried union leaders, who in contrast to their active members tended to be cautious and conservative, was, however, certainly present, particularly among Bristol's dock workers, miners, and building workers. This cannot, however, be equated with the ideological hostility of the syndicalists towards officials. In certain instances it is evident that the syndicalists were able to articulate complaints, which tallied with those arising from disputes in Bristol. But this does not make them the source. It was rather that they converged with discontent arising out of the actual circumstances

---

201 *WDP*, 10 July 1914.
202 *WDP*, 8 August 1914.
203 *WDP*, 12 August 1914.
204 *WDP*, 3 August 1914.

of Bristol workers. Class-consciousness among the Bristol workers was expressed in an uneven manner, even though the forms of industrial unrest at certain points closely resembled certain aspects of the syndicalist agenda. The key issue then is not whether or not their action should be labelled 'syndicalism' but specifically why they acted as they did in changing contexts.

Rejecting the strategy of accord between capital and labour, favoured by trade union leaders who had come round to accepting joint conciliation and arbitration, Bristol's dockers, seamen, miners and railway workers, often defied their leaders by adopting direct action tactics. This paid dividends. Non-unionism was reduced, union membership increased, and union organisation improved. However, the walk-out by Bristol dockers, in response to the London dockers' call for a national strike, in the summer of 1912, ended in a debacle, which had a deleterious impact on workers' confidence. The failure of London dockers, in 1912, to garner support for their strike caused Bristol's dockers to question the wisdom of taking solidarity action. As the prospect of war loomed, and the economic boom of 1911-13 stalled, they turned once again to take advice from their union leaders.

Between 1910 and 1914, industrial militancy in Bristol can be seen as uncertain and pragmatic. Regardless of some similitude there is no clear indication of a syndicalist perspective nor can it be said that the main resistance automatically generated any large scale movement for an alternative socialist society. The Labour Party, the ILP and the BSP displayed little interest in trade union struggles and remained on the sidelines.

The diffuse class-consciousness of the rank-and-file workers in Bristol, present within and between different kinds of employment, can be best understood as a broad awareness of class solidarity. Thus, although conflict during the period of the labour unrest in Bristol manifested itself in ways parallel with syndicalism, as a movement syndicalism was not able to provide the unrest in Bristol with any viable organising idea that could deepen or extend workers' resistance.

By 1914, dockers, the most highly organised workers in Bristol, had shifted away from their former militancy rooted in a broad class-consciousness. Instead they went along with talks taking place between their union and the docks committee on establishing a Joint Conciliation Board that would bring them in line with the corn porters, carters and warehousemen. The miners' union too, despite resistance from their members, continued to use Joint Conciliation Boards. For railway workers, the outcome of the 1911 strike led simply to a revision of the 1907 Railway Conciliation Scheme. This produced limited improvements, and, while these were good enough to satisfy union leaders, the membership ballot for strike action revealed strong opposition among rank-and-file members.

On the surface this adherence to Joint Conciliation Boards seems surprising, given that one of the key elements fuelling discontent, which had led to the outbreak of industrial strife between 1910 and 1914, was the failure of these Board schemes to keep wages up with the pace of inflation. Whereas militant action, backed by the growth in trade union membership, during the labour unrest squeezed significant increases in weekly wage rates out of the employers that more or less kept up with the rate of inflation.[205] However, as the impetus of spontaneous rebellion dipped the new found power began to pass over into the bureaucratic structures that had been established.

Whitfield captures this contradiction well:

> The paradox was that the outcome of a situation of open class conflict was a further institutionalisation of that conflict, for, once the officials regained control over events, their predilection for this more manageable way of conducting industrial relations asserted itself.[206]

However, this outcome should not eclipse advancements made in the strength of trade unionism in this period, fostered by both class solidarity and direct action.[207] Moreover, workers in Bristol, as indeed elsewhere, found their human dignity through collective action in the interests not only of themselves and their families but also in their awareness of being members of the working class.

The roots of Bristol's labour movement were reaching down and spreading in ways which were to shift the power dynamics within the city.

---

205 Inflation data are incomplete for this period therefore that wages kept up more or less with inflation is a rough estimate.

206 Whitfield, 'The Labour Movement in Bristol 1910-1939', unpublished MLitt thesis, p. 102.

207 As Knowles infers, a strong membership was still required if unions were to achieve satisfactory outcomes from submitting disputes to arbitration. See Knowles, *Strikes—A Study in Industrial Conflict*, p. 67.

7

Yesterday's To-morrow:
Bristol's Garden Suburbs

•

Stephen E. Hunt

To-morrow

Yesterday's approach to planning and housing does much to define the character of Bristol's residential areas today. A project such as that set out in a prospectus for a garden suburb for Shirehampton published in 1909 still has relevance for present concerns with sustainable and sociable communities more than a century later. The Bristol Garden Suburb Limited was set up to implement the ideas Ebenezer Howard popularised in *To-morrow: A Peaceful Path to Real Reform*, first published in 1898, subsequently reissued under the better known title *Garden Cities of To-morrow* (1902). A second area, nearby Sea Mills, was a much more extensive development inspired by garden-city ideas about planning. Furthermore, a huge belt of inter-war municipal housing estates around the periphery of Bristol were also planned and constructed according to garden-city principles, albeit of a diluted version, thereby substantially defining the character of many of the residential areas of the city up to the present day.

Proposed Group of Four Cottages, Passage Leaze.

Bristol Garden Suburb, Shirehampton.

Influenced by the likes of William Morris and Peter Kropotkin, garden-city idealists such as Ebenezer Howard and Raymond Unwin sought to use planning to achieve economic wellbeing, a healthy environment, robust and aesthetically appealing architectural design and an enabling infrastructure of services, thereby democratising the good life for all. Howard, a shorthand reporter and a dabbler in many things, prefigured radical ideas of dweller control far more progressive than those proposed in the early twenty-first century, such as the new generation of so-called garden-cities advocated by David Cameron's coalition government at the time of writing. In the current proposals for locations such as Ebbsfleet, the original garden-city philosophy looks to be diluted and distorted into conventional commuter-belt estates developed by volume house builders.

The approach in this essay broadly but cautiously favours the progressive nature of garden-city thinking. As we shall see, however, the impact of such ideas upon the garden suburbs of Bristol during the early twentieth century shows some of the practical deficiencies of the garden-city vision as well as its desirability. The contrasting experience of several estates indicates the necessity to take a holistic approach to urban design, so that residential zones are integrated with facilities, support services and public spaces. We also see that the attitudes of residents in the estates are not homogeneous. This raises fundamental questions about the nature of community, a slippery term which everyone across the political spectrum from greens and anarchists to conservatives professes to admire, but no one entirely trusts.

The appearance of the garden-suburb idea in Shirehampton before World War I gives a fascinating insight into early twentieth-century planning and housing reform, offering practical and utilitarian solutions to immediate social ills while attempting to advance a progressive, even utopian impulse towards social change. Howard spoke of 'the task which is before us of reconstructing anew the entire external fabric of society'.[1] The garden-city movement continued to have a defining impact on Bristol's development after the First World War. Yet while the inspiration of Howard continued during the Interwar period, the garden-cities influence was much diluted in the municipal housing schemes that circled the city by 1939 and the 'garden factory' at Keynsham. Now discussion of garden cities has returned to national planning agendas, it is an appropriate moment to look at the significant, if often overlooked, impact that the movement had on the Bristol area during the early twentieth century. It's timely to revisit Howard's ideas in the light of several recent topics of green chatter – transition towns, sustainable planning and current debates about the viability of a renaissance in garden-city style development.

Yesterday

It is fitting that garden suburbs were to have an impact on Bristol, being the site of Blaise Hamlet, an early attempt to achieve humanitarian ends through planning and architecture. After the first shock of the Industrial Revolution

---

1   Ebenezer Howard, *Garden Cities of To-Morrow* [1902] (London: Faber, 1965), p. 150.

during the Romantic period, many of the issues that the garden-city movement raised were already in place: the impact of environmental conditions and aesthetic circumstances on individual and community well-being, paternalism versus worker autonomy, the constraints of power and ownership on workers' decision making.

The Bristolian banker John Scandrett Harford (1785-1866) financed the construction of Blaise Hamlet for older residents, the architectural design being undertaken by John Nash (1752-1835) and George Repton (1786-1858). The late eighteenth-century enthusiasm for the bucolic and picturesque inspired the deliberately asymmetrical thatched dwellings near Henbury where the project was completed in 1810. The designs were intended to be aesthetically pleasing, solidly constructed and in keeping with fashionable contemporary theories about the picturesque. Rounded, thatched dwellings of this kind conform perfectly to the nest-like curvature and cosiness that the French philosopher Gaston Bachelard suggested were archetypal forms meeting primal human needs for belonging, comfort and security in his classic study *The Poetics of Space* (1958). The rustic brickwork, timbers and trellises of Blaise Hamlet were crafted not only with aesthetic considerations but also with political and religious motivations. Historian Gillian Darley records that Harford was a Quaker whose humanitarian ideas made him an energetic anti-slavery campaigner and prison reformer, making it clear that he was inspired by his faith and a desire for social improvement in the creation of Blaise Hamlet.[2]

Shirehampton

Elizabeth Sturge (1850-1944) and Eliza Walker Dunbar (1845-1925) instigated the Shirehampton garden suburb in 1907. This was planned as a modest, scaled-down version of its more ambitious cousin, the garden city, exemplified in the developments at Letchworth and Welwyn Garden City. An earlier development instigated by George White to the north of the city at Filton Park, had also been described as a 'garden suburb'.[3] In practice however, while it featured a low density of occupation, White's project reflected only a limited aspiration to implement garden-city

Elizabeth Sturge (1850-1944).

principles since it had a conventional set-up in terms of funding and ownership.[4]

2   Gillian Darley, *Villages of Vision: A Study of Strange Utopias*, revised and updated edition, (Nottingham: Five Leaves, 2007), p. 68. I have drawn upon Darley's fascinating book for the factual details about Blaise Hamlet above.

3   George White was prominent as Chair of the Bristol Tramways Company and due to his wider role in Bristol's transport and industry. For his notorious anti-union record, see Chapter 6 above, p. 202.

4   Keith J. Skilleter, 'Housing Reform, Garden Suburbs and Statutory Town Planning at Bristol, 1900-39', *Planning History*

Howard's approach more directly inspired the Shirehampton scheme as it attempted to take practical measures to provide working people with affordable, high-quality homes in a healthy environment.

Elizabeth Sturge had first-hand experience of housing poverty as an assistant to Octavia Hill in Southwark during the 1880s. Octavia Hill was already a notable figure in housing reform since John Ruskin had given her inspiration and capital to ease London housing poverty.[5] In Bristol Elizabeth Sturge's long-term commitment to improving housing conditions continued through her membership of the Bristol Committee for the Better Housing of the Poor at the beginning of the twentieth century.[6] A member of a humanitarian Quaker family, Sturge was also a prominent campaigner for votes for women, alongside her sisters Helen and Caroline. Eliza Dunbar was one of the first women to enter the exclusive medical profession as surgeon and was a member of the Bristol Association of Working Women.[7] Their intervention in the public arena of housing shows that middle-class women could be instrumental in local political reform despite being excluded from the franchise.

The Directors and Officers of the Company are as follows :—

Directors :

FRANCIS NICHOLAS COWLIN, Esq., of Messrs. William Cowlin & Son, Builders and Contractors, Stratton Street, St. Paul's, Bristol.

Miss ELIZA LOUISA WALKER DUNBAR, M.D., 9, Oakfield Road, Clifton.

FREDERICK ALLEN STURGE GOODBODY, Esq., of Messrs. J. P. Sturge & Sons, Land Agents and Surveyors, 33, Corn Street, Bristol.

HENRY HOSEGOOD, Esq., of Messrs. Henry Hosegood & Son, Corn Merchants, 3, Queen Square, Bristol.

MONTAGUE MUIR MACKENZIE, Esq., J.P., Penpole House, Shirehampton, near Bristol.

GEORGE HERBERT OATLEY, Esq., F.R.I.B.A., 25, Orchard Street, Bristol.

Miss ELIZABETH STURGE, Heathlands, Leigh Woods, Clifton.

Solicitors : PAGE & THOMPSON, 2, Bristol Chambers, Nicholas Street, Bristol.

Surveyors : J. P. STURGE & SONS, 33, Corn Street, Bristol.

Secretary and Registered Office :

A. ERNEST ASHMEAD, Chartered Accountant, Exchange Chambers, Bristol.

Resident Architect : FRANK H. BROMHEAD, A.R.I.B.A.

Officers of the Bristol Garden Suburb, Shirehampton.

Following Ebenezer Howard's inspiration, a board of seven directors was set up, including Elizabeth Sturge and Eliza Dunbar, to raise £10,000 to fund a development at Shirehampton. This was to be achieved through the sale of 10,000 £1 shares for the purchase of 26½ acres of land, from Philip Napier Miles, the last squire of the King's Weston Estate.[8] The King's Weston Action Group record philanthropist Philip Napier Miles's major impact on the

13.2 (1991): 14.

5   Elizabeth Sturge, *Reminiscences of My Life: and some account of the children of William and Charlotte Sturge and of the Sturge Family of Bristol* (Bristol: printed by J. A. Arrowsmith for private circulation, 1928), pp. 45-46.

6   Moira Martin, 'Guardians of the Poor: A Philanthropic Female Elite in Bristol', *Regional Historian* 9 (Summer 2002): 11.

7   Biographical details gleaned from Lorna Brierley and Helen Reid, *Go Home and Do the Washing! Three Centuries of Pioneering Bristol Women* (Bristol: Broadcast Books, 2000).

8   'Shirehampton Garden Suburb prospectus', 2. BRO, MS Bristol Plans Numbered/62. Ref: 07784/62.

Shirehampton area by selling land and making donations for significant community assets such as the Public Hall and Library and the King's Weston Estate Office, both designed by architect (and later Glastonbury mystic) Frederick Bligh Bond.[9] Philip Napier Miles's grandfather, Philip John Miles (1773-1845), a member of the Merchant Venturers, originally amassed much of the Miles family fortune. Steve Livings described Philip John Miles as 'Bristol's first recorded millionaire', a wealth derived through interests in shipping, sugar plantations and banking.[10] If the ethical provenance of wealth from such interests at this time is starting to sound doubtful, the King's Weston Action Group confirm that the Miles family wealth was in part derived from 'extensive plantations in Trinidad and Jamaica' — and hence was tainted by its source in both direct slave labour and the trans-Atlantic slave trade (and substantially enhanced by compensation when the trade was abolished).[11]

The financial administration was put on a firm footing by the creation of the Bristol Garden Suburb Limited, specifically founded for this purpose in 1909. The prospectus follows the meticulously costed structural model and principles set out in *Garden Cities of To-morrow*. Indeed, Howard endorsed the project personally by attending an inaugural meeting organised by Alfred Lyttleton to promote the scheme at the Victoria Rooms, Clifton in 1908.[12]

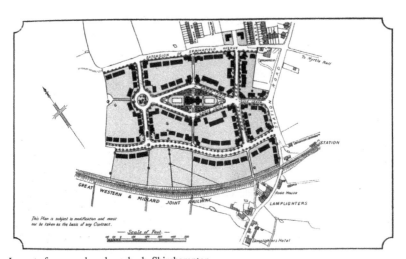

Layout of proposed garden suburb, Shirehampton.

---

9   King's Weston Action Group website, 'Philip Napier Miles: Philanthropy and Music':
      http://www.kwag.org.uk/history/philip-napier-miles/ [accessed 29 March 2014].

10   Steve Livings, 'The Miles Family and Leigh Court': http://www.abbotsleigh.org.uk/ALMiles.html [accessed 29 March 2014].

11   King's Weston Action Group website, 'The Victorian Era: The Miles Family':
      http://www.kwag.org.uk/history/the-victorian-era/ [accessed 29 March 2014]. See also UCL Department of History's Legacies of British Slave-ownership webpage for Philip John Miles: http://www.ucl.ac.uk/lbs/person/view/19118 [accessed 29 March 2014].

12   Skilleter, 'Housing Reform', p. 14.

Henrietta Barnett, wife of Bristol-born housing reformer Samuel Augustus Barnett, also spoke in Bristol the following year.[13] She was the founder of the fine Hampstead Garden Suburb which dates from 1907; based upon Howard's ideas and put into practice by planner and architect Raymond Unwin this was the immediate inspiration for the scheme in Shirehampton.

Passage Leaze, Shirehampton.

While there would be some diversity in the size and design of the dwellings, the Shirehampton prospectus promised generously adequate open spaces and a 'capital garden' for each. In anticipation of present-day initiatives for 'mixed housing', the prospectus set out the intention to build 'houses for all classes' on the site. The drive towards economic self-sufficiency is an important part of Howard's programme, which intended that residents of the garden cities would live within walking distance of their workplace. For Howard, the garden cities were to have an optimum size of 32,000 residents; above this size a second garden city would be initiated to maintain surroundings with a human scale. Howard hoped that clusters of such communities would soon emerge, linked by integrated public transport such as municipal railway systems to avoid the sense of social isolation often suffered by small-town and rural communities lacking public amenities in his own time, and to this day. It was also anticipated that the local Co-operative Societies, with their roots in Owenite socialism, would play a supportive and mutually beneficial role. The creators of the Shirehampton suburb equally looked to sub-contract the construction work to local builders, Co-operative Societies or, ideally, to a complementary building company that might be founded for the purpose. The intention that the project should combine elements of limited profit making and philanthropy is enshrined in the founding

---

13   Sarah Whittingham, *Sir George Oatley: Architect of Bristol* (Bristol: Redcliffe Press, 2011), p. 284.

SIMPLE FURNITURE.

MUCH of the effect of a well-designed house may be marred by the selection of unsuitable furniture. Where the architecture is on simple lines, the furniture should follow suit.

WE have on view in our Showrooms furniture exactly suited to the needs of the Garden Suburb House, or the Country Cottage—tasteful, dignified and eminently in keeping with the simplicity of its surroundings.

WE shall be pleased to make suggestions as to the complete furnishing of houses in the Bristol Garden Suburb, suitable colour schemes, etc., and to carry out work in accordance with the ideas of our customers

Write for full Illustrated Catalogue.

P. E. GANE (Late TRAPNELL & GANE) L^D.

House Furnishers, COLLEGE GREEN, BRISTOL.

Shirehampton Bristol Garden Suburb, advertisement from *Prospectus*.

statement: 'The rate of dividend on the Shares has been limited to 5%. in the belief that many persons will be satisfied with a moderate return in connection with a social experiment of great importance'.[14]

It is easy to be unaware of this gradualist but thoroughgoing attempt at social transformation when strolling past the houses in Passage Leaze in Shirehampton today. However, the distinctive dormer windows and cottage-style appearance, owing much to the Victorian Arts and Crafts Movement — (one is called Morris Cottage, presumably after William Morris) — unmistakeably resemble the gabled dwellings that appear in the original prospectus. The project got off to a promising start in 1907 when Thomas Adams (1871-1940) drew up plans for nearly three hundred homes. Adams was to become a significant practitioner and authority on twentieth-century planning. His mapping of the terrain at Shirehampton was complemented by the young architect Frank Harold Bromhead's (1882-1972) attractively designed houses. Sarah Whittingham records that by this date Bromhead had already worked at Letchworth and Hampstead Garden Suburb with the prominent garden-city architects Barry Parker and Raymond Unwin.[15] Unfortunately the project had only made limited progress when the work was suspended due to the outbreak of hostilities in the First World War. Ewart Culpin recorded that just 44 out of a planned 280 houses had been completed when he was writing in 1913.[16] 'It was a shame that the whole of the Shire wasn't built like it, but I suppose the Kaiser had something to do with that!', a Passage Leaze resident with an obvious affection for his home and street told me. While the existing arrangements continued after

---

14 'Shirehampton Garden Suburb prospectus', p. 2.

15 Whittingham, *Sir George Oatley*, p. 285.

16 Ewart G. Culpin, *The Garden City Movement Up-to-Date* (London: Garden Cities and Town Planning Association, 1913), p. 48.

the War, the house-building plan was not revived and the Bristol Garden Suburb Company was taken over by the Bristol Housing Company in 1923. More than 900 further houses were built in the larger estate constructed in the decade after 1920. Sadly, quality of design and planning was reduced in this larger municipal development and today 'the Shire', while retaining a strong community spirit, is an area of high deprivation with few of the amenities and opportunities enjoyed in more prosperous urban areas of Bristol or the compensations of more picturesque rural districts.[17]

Quality of life and well-being were to be a central feature of the original development at Shirehampton. Applications to set up light industry were welcomed with the proviso that 'factories are fitted with up-to-date appliances for the prevention of smoke and fumes emanating therefrom'.[18] The avoidance of overcrowding and pollution had also been understood to be a powerful and benign form of social conditioning since the pioneering work of social observers such as Henry Mayhew and Charles Booth. Howard speaks of lives being 'stunted and maimed' by the darkness and confinement of overcrowding, taking the natural metaphor of pot-bound plants who can only flourish when transplanted.[19] The environmental model for human health was in common currency in progressive discourse during the 1890s. There proved to be a persuasive evidence base for this — Gillian Darley notes that one survey of Bournville children in the early twentieth century found them to be 'two to three inches taller there than in slum areas of Birmingham'.[20]

Robert Blatchford, an influential socialist writer, was forthright on the matter, describing the present condition of workers' 'very ugly and *mean*' houses:

> The streets are too narrow. There are no gardens. There are no trees. Few working-class families have enough bedrooms, and the bathroom is a luxury not known in cottages.

> In fine, your houses are ugly, unhealthy, inconvenient, dark, ill-built, ill-fitted, and dear. [21]

Madge Dresser's study of working-class housing in Bristol reveals that many central districts, characterised by the notorious courts and tenement lodging houses, fitted Blatchford's description. At the beginning of the twentieth century many areas were blighted by overcrowding, poverty and extremely unsanitary conditions.[22] By contrast, Blatchford imagines a transformed public space if the potential for better planning could be realised:

> I would have the towns rebuilt with wide streets, with detached houses,

---

17 See Ian Bone, *Community Profile of Shirehampton* (Bristol: Shirehampton Public Hall Community Association, 2001). Viewed online at: http://www.digitalbristol.org/members/shireweb/hall/profile.htm [Accessed 8 June 2007].

18 'Shirehampton Garden Suburb prospectus', p. 2.

19 In an early manuscript entitled 'Commonsense Socialism' quoted in Robert Beevers, *The Garden City Utopia: A Critical Biography of Ebenezer Howard* (Basingstoke: Macmillan, 1988), p. 31.

20 Darley, *Villages of Vision*, p. 140.

21 Robert Blatchford, *Merrie England* (London: Clarion Office, 1894), p. 41.

22 Madge Dresser, 'People's Housing in Bristol (1870-1939)' in Ian Bild (ed.), *Bristol's Other History*, (Bristol: Bristol Broadsides, 1983), pp. 129-160.

with gardens and fountains and avenues of trees...

> I would make the houses loftier and larger, and clear them of all useless furniture. I would institute public dining halls, public baths, public wash-houses on the best plans, and so set free the hands of those slaves – our English women.[23]

In common with other socialists with temperance leanings, Blatchford regretted 'drunkenness' as one of the scourges of the working class.[24] John Roberts notes that pubs are absent from nearby Sea Mills, 'in keeping with the ethos of a garden suburb as a healthy and wholesome place to live'.[25] Indeed, pubs were notable by their absence throughout Bristol's municipal housing estates during the 1920s, a cause for complaint on the part of many corporation residents, often to be circumvented by the entrepreneurial spirit of a fleet of vans that supplied tenants with alcohol, presumably on the black market.[26]

A feature that distinguished garden cities and suburbs from their antecedents in model housing schemes created by philanthropic industrialists such as Titus Salt's Saltaire, George Cadbury's Bournville and the Lever brothers' Port Sunlight, was the degree of community ownership by the residents. Gillian Darley tellingly quotes a union official who commented, 'no man of an independent turn of mind could breathe for long in the atmosphere of Port Sunlight'.[27] Thomas Adams, involved in the Shirehampton development and Secretary of the national Garden City Association, noted the significance of this break from 'paternalism' towards an administrative structure that optimised economic autonomy and self-administration.[28] He would have had in mind intrusions such as the overbearing surveillance of Titus Salt, who had a watchtower constructed which acted as a kind of panopticon from which he could survey his employees with God-like omniscience, ever watchful for drinking or the illicit hanging of laundry on visible washing lines.

Avonmouth

Meanwhile at nearby Avonmouth plans for a major development of up to 1,200 workers' houses were drawn up under the auspices of Avonmouth Garden Suburbs Ltd. during the war years with the enthusiastic support of the Dock, Wharf, Riverside and General Workers' Union and the expertise of an equally enthusiastic Garden Cities and Town Planning Association (GCTPA). Working-

---

23 Blatchford, *Merrie England*, p. 43.

24 Ibid., p. 16.

25 John Roberts, *The Definition and Characteristics of a Post-WWI Garden Suburb with Particular Reference to Sea Mills Garden Suburb, Bristol: A Study by Save Sea Mills Garden Suburb in association with Sea Mills and Coombe Dingle Community Project* (Bristol: Save Sea Mills Garden Suburb/Sea Mills and Coombe Dingle Community Project, 2007), p. 49.

26 Madge Dresser, 'Housing Policy in Bristol, 1919-30' in M. J. Daunton (ed.), *Councillors and Tenants: Local Authority Housing in English Cities 1919-1939* (Leicester: Leicester University Press, 1984), p. 208.

27 Darley, *Villages of Vision*, p. 142.

28 Thomas Adams in collaboration with F. Longstreth Thompson, E. Maxwell Fry and James W. R. Adams, *Recent Advances in Town Planning* (London: J. & A. Churchill, 1932), p. 37.

Old Quarry Road, Penpole Housing Estate, Shirehampton [1950s].

class labour activists Frank Sheppard, Ernest Bevin and Ben Tillett, supporting the scheme, had been advocating the provision of communal kitchens and nurseries as rational time saving measures and to improve the situation of working-class women.[29] These were progressive demands, fully in keeping with the ideas of Blatchford and Howard. This promising and enlightened scheme was to be created by a co-operative but, in what was to become a familiar pattern, floundered in meeting its goals due to limited capital.[30] Only 150 houses were built in a more conventional estate for the war-time Ministry of Munitions. Despite the input of Ewart Culpin, Secretary of the GCTPA, in drawing up an advanced master plan for a much grander development at Avonmouth that was to include 'social and educational centres, several large shopping centres, swimming-baths, gymnasia and allotments', the scheme was dropped in favour of the municipal Penpole housing estate, which owed only its low-density of development and spacious gardens to the garden-city movement.[31] Richard Coates cites the 1920s Penpole Estate as including houses around The Ridge, Grumwell Close and Old Quarry Road.[32]

Sea Mills: The 'magic estate'

If the garden suburb at Shirehampton was to be thwarted by the outbreak of the First World War, then a larger development at nearby Sea Mills was to owe its

29   Dresser, 'Housing Policy in Bristol, 1919-30', p. 168.

30   Ibid., p. 160.

31   Skilleter, 'Housing Reform', p. 15.

32   Richard Coates, *The Street-Names of Shirehampton and Avonmouth* (Shirehampton: Shire Community Newspaper, 2011; rev. 2013), p. 36: http://www.shire.org.uk/content/history/streetnames.pdf [accessed 28 March 2014].

Sea Mills Square with St Edyths Church.

advent to the bid to build 'homes fit for heroes' in the form of 'village suburbs' in the aftermath of the war. Dave Backwith records that, 'before the war had ended Bristol Council had approved plans and was buying land for 5,000 houses to be built in garden suburbs at Fishponds (Hillfields), Horfield, Sea Mills, Shirehampton and Knowle'.[33] Additional developments took place at Bedminster Down, St Anne's, Southmead, Speedwell and St George.

The new development at Sea Mills delighted the poet John Betjeman. Reporting for the BBC in 1937, he described

> the new Sea Mills estate, with a surprising beauty showing off in the evening sunlight. And vistas of trees and fields and pleasant cottages that the magic estate has managed to create.[34]

The history and context of the present development at Sea Mills has been thoroughly researched by John Roberts on behalf of the campaign to protect the area's garden suburb status in association with the Sea Mills and Coombe Dingle Community Project.[35] Roberts contextualises the Sea Mills Garden Suburb as a part of the coordinated post-war building boom, following the publication of the Tudor Walters Report of 1918. This report was produced by a committee which included Raymond Unwin, the architect and planner who did much to put garden-city and garden-suburb ideas into practice before the war. The national mood of post-war reconstruction ensured more state involvement in the

---

33   Dave Backwith, *Housing not Herding? The Politics of Knowle West in the 1930s* (Unpublished thesis submitted for the degree of MA in Comparative Labour History, University of Warwick, 1990), p. 56.

34   Quoted in 'Bristol Homes Still an Inspiration', *Bristol Post* (16 September 2009): http://www.bristolpost.co.uk/Bristol-homes-inspiration/story-11281002-detail/story.html [accessed 10 April 2014].

35   Roberts, *The Definition and Characteristics of a Post-WWI Garden Suburb*.

enterprise. This fact was underlined by the presence of the President of the Local Government Board, Christopher Addison, who dug the first shovelful of sod at Sea Mills in 1919, making it integral to the national housing scheme.[36] By 1931 the plans were literally made concrete in a large geometrical development of 1,279 houses, covering the substantial area of today's Sea Mills, (previously a small outlying settlement dating back to the Roman port of Abonae).

C. F. W. Dening drew up the master plan for Sea Mills, while George Oatley designed St Edyth's Church (1926-28) and the Methodist Church (1930) in the centre of the development.[37] The involvement of George Oatley, one of the directors of the limited company set up to found the Bristol Garden Suburb in Shirehampton in 1908, establishes a direct link between these neighbouring projects.[38]

Many of the houses at Sea Mills were constructed using relatively experimental techniques involving concrete building materials; the Parkinson PRC (Pre-stressed Reinforced Concrete) and 'Dorlonco' dwellings. The use of Parkinson concrete and Dorman Long steel-frame by builders William Cowlin and Son (Francis Nicholas Cowlin of this firm was also a director of the Shirehampton scheme) was piloted at the time as an innovative attempt to provide robust housing that could be quickly constructed. Eventually, however, these materials proved vulnerable to deterioration due to so-called 'concrete cancer'. It became apparent that, over time, the concrete became susceptible to water penetration which in turn led to the corrosion of the supporting steel framework. It now appears, however, that Bristol City Council's initial assessment of the long-term damage to the concrete houses at Sea Mills was unduly pessimistic. Subsequently a programme of patching and overcladding of the affected materials and other refurbishment has temporarily addressed such deterioration, providing a solution that is anticipated to mitigate the problem for at least thirty years.[39] Therefore, while 132 of the Parkinson houses at Sea Mills were demolished during the 1980s, it was reported in 2011 that

> A survey of the remaining Council-owned Parkinsons in Sea Mills, 2009/10, revealed there to be considerably less structural deterioration than had been anticipated in the 1980s. It is now known that all the Parkinsons are repairable, an extensive programme of repair by the City Council is immanent (246 in total).[40]

36   Ibid., p. 18 and p. 40.

37   T. R. Wallis, *Sea Mills and the Battle of the Styles: Stylistic Variety in the Architecture of an Inter-War Garden Suburb and its Origins in Victorian Revivalism* (Bristol: T. R Wallis, 2004), p. 13. Keith Mallory also cites Benjamin Wakefield as the most likely designer of the Sea Mills project. Keith Mallory, *The Bristol House* (Bristol: Redcliffe Press in assoc. with Hoddell Pritchard, 1985), p. 69.

38   George Oatley was to become most renowned in Bristol as the principal architect of University of Bristol's Wills Building.

39   I am grateful to John Roberts for his technical explanation of the process of deterioration known as 'spalling'. He further commented that, 'Save Sea Mills Garden Suburb tried to persuade the Council to repair the houses more permanently using a method that had been successfully used on other PRC house types, but not yet tried on Parkinsons, with an estimated life-span of 60 years.', John Roberts, email message to the author, 9 April 2014.

40   Bristol City Council, 'Sea Mills: Character Appraisal and Management Proposals', Conservation Area 21 (January 2011), p. 22: http://www.bristol.gov.uk/sites/default/files/assets/documents/sea-mills-character-appraisal.pdf [accessed

At the time of writing in 2014, this programme of house repair is near complete.

While the use of Parkinson PRC and 'Dorlonco' templates resulted in a majority of homes that are less 'cottagey' in their design and appearance than their neighbours in Passage Leaze, Shirehampton, the use of more conventional housing materials including traditional brick, brick and render, timber and slate accounts for some diversity in the Sea Mills estate as a whole. The recent report, 'Sea Mills: Character Appraisal and Management Proposals', cites the involvement of four architectural firms in the design of the housing at Sea Mills, Benjamin Wakefield, W. H.Watkins, and Heathman & Blacker from Bristol and E.C.H. Maidman & W. A.Greener of Parkstone, in addition to the Council's architects.[41] This helped to ensure variety, while the grouping of house types helped to maintain overall compatibility of styles in the estate as a whole.

In many ways the radial pattern at Sea Mills, together with the inclusion of an abundance of features such as focal greens, avenues, cul-de-sacs, intentionally designed views and glimpses and self-contained development, epitomises the garden-suburb idea more than any other location in Bristol. The idea that each home should have a garden with either an apple or cherry tree was an appetising foretaste of the desire to create edible cities on the part of twenty-first century permaculturalists. The inclusion of facilities such as allotments, a library, local shops, grounds for sport and play, and churches also meant that the garden-suburb objective to create a well serviced and self-sufficient community was met in a way that was not fulfilled elsewhere in the city's inter-war developments. Furthermore, there were plans for light industry at Sea Mills, which, had they been actualised, would have contributed towards the kind of local economic resilience that was key to Ebenezer Howard's original garden-city objectives and aspirations. John Roberts commented,

> Dening's original plan for Sea Mills included space 'reserved for industrial development' alongside the Avon, and a separate space reserved for small holdings, although neither space was eventually used for the purpose proposed. Together with the existing railway station, the intention seemed to be to make Sea Mills Garden Suburb as self-sufficient (or, in modern terms, sustainable) as possible.[42]

Bristol City Council first designated part of Sea Mills as a 'Conservation Area' in 1981.[43] This, however, has not always allayed concerns about threats to the character of the Sea Mills estate. A campaign group, 'Save Sea Mills Garden Suburb', was set up and successfully fought Bristol City Council proposals for the demolition and compulsory redevelopment of at least a fifth of the original housing which they feared would have significantly downgraded the character of the Conservation Area. It was estimated in a Town and Country Planning report of 2008 that 20% of the Parkinson concrete dwellings in particular were prone

---

online 26 March 2014].

41   Ibid., p. 52.

42   John Roberts, email message to the author, 9 April 2014.

43   Bristol City Council, 'Sea Mills: Character Appraisal and Management Proposals', p. 7.

to defects, and, at that time, the scale of redevelopment looked to be even more extensive than this proportion.[44]

From the outset of the development, an agreement between Philip Napier Miles, the owner of the land, and Bristol Corporation afforded some legal protection for the estate at Sea Mills into perpetuity. This agreement took the form of the so-called 'Napier Miles Covenants' 1919-1921, which stipulate 'That no part of the said lands and hereditaments hereby conveyed shall be used for any purpose other than that of a Garden Suburb'.[45] In 2007, however, Bristol City Council's Legal Team were exploring options to facilitate potential redevelopment and took on expensive additional legal advice since, ominously, they were 'working on whether the Covenant can be modified or removed'.[46]

Proactive research and assessment by members of Save Sea Mills Garden Suburb, and subsequent petitioning by residents, appears to have been successful in making the case for the preservation of their estate's unique character. Indeed, in response to a petition of 1,256 signatures, a large number for such a small place, the boundary of the Conservation Area was extended in 2008, to cover the entire garden suburb. This rectified the partial nature of the protection afforded by the 1981 designation. Bristol City Council produced a sympathetic report in 2011, entitled 'Character Appraisal and Management Proposals', which recognises the requirement to preserve the holistic integrity of the garden suburb's development and identifies the kind of alterations that would undermine its character.[47]

Save Sea Mills Garden Suburb continues to put pressure upon Bristol City Council to conserve the character and original vision of the estate in the light of the assessment of the 'Character Appraisal and Management Proposals' document. In 2014 they commented,

> Save Sea Mills Garden Suburb has been unsuccessful in persuading the Council to introduce an Article 4 Direction to control incremental changes to the appearance of the Conservation Area which usually do not require planning permission. Such changes, like the grubbing up of privet hedges and front gardens to provide hardstanding for cars, painting over red brick houses, or fitting out-of-character new windows, are, in the group's view, slowly leading to a death by a thousand cuts of the character and appearance of Sea Mills.

> The group has also failed to prevent the immanent placement of a playground on one (or more) of the five greens that comprise the formal square at the heart of the Garden Suburb, known as Sea Mills Square.

---

44   Town and Country Planning Association, *Garden City Settlements and Their Future: A Project Log*, TPCA website http://www.tcpa.org.uk/downloads/20081031-GCS_Project_Log.doc [accessed online 7 Dec 2008], p. 76.

45   Roberts, *Definition and Characteristics of a Post-WWI Garden Suburb*, p. 3.

46   Alison Napper (Priority Stock Manager) to the PRC Project Consultation Group Meeting at the Council House, 26th September 2006. Bristol City Council website: http://www.bristol.gov.uk/ccm/cms-service/download/asset/?asset_id=17067004 [accessed 24 June 2007].

47   Bristol City Council, 'Sea Mills: Character Appraisal and Management Proposals'. The section on the Garden Suburb is largely based on Roberts's original analysis of the layout, and other extensive research by members of the Save Sea Mills Garden Suburb group.

This will be highly detrimental to the character and appearance of the Conservation Area, in the group's view, and runs counter to the assessment in the Council's own Conservation Area Character Assessment and Management Proposals that: "Given its function as the centrepiece to the Garden Suburb, Sea Mills Square is particularly sensitive to change. Any change to its designed layout or formal character would be highly detrimental to the Conservation Area" (Sea Mills Conservation Area Character Assessment and Management Proposals, paragraph 8.30).[48]

Maple Drive, Hillfields.

Hillfields

Another location to be included in a survey of Bristol garden suburbs is the area around Maple Avenue and The Greenway in the Hillfields ward. Hillfields was the site of the city's first municipal housing constructed under the National Housing Scheme, following the 1919 Addison Act, as can be still seen on the memorial plaque in Beecham Drive.[49] Under this legislation a funding model was set up, by which costs were split three-ways between central government, local authorities, such as the Bristol Corporation, and tenants.[50] This post-First World

---

48   John Roberts email message to the author 9 April 2014, (comment provided in conjunction with other members of the Save Sea Mills Garden Suburb group).

49   In a collection of reminiscences compiled by Jane Baker in 1988, Frederick Charles England recalled that the first houses in Beecham Drive 'were primarily to accommodate Belgian people who had been injured or left homeless in the Great War'. *Hillfields: The First Sixty Years A Local Study*, (special edition for Fishponds Library Local History File, unpaginated).

50   Peter Malpass and Jennie Walmsley, *100 Years of Council Housing in Bristol* (Bristol: Faculty of the Built Environment, University of the West of England, 2005), p. 4.

War development features some of the characteristics of the garden-city movement, such as relatively low-density housing set among green parkland and solidly designed houses. The houses at Maple Avenue were built in 1922 for the benefit of employees at the nearby E. S. and A. Robinson paper company,[51] a firm inspired by the non-conformist faith and paternalism of its Baptist founders, Elisha Smith Robinson (a Liberal Lord Mayor of Bristol in 1866) and Alfred Robinson.[52] John Bartlett describes tenure arrangements under which houses 'could be purchased from the company by payments stopped from the workers' wage packets. As the Bristol Corporation owned the land, ground rents were paid directly to them'.[53] To this day Maple Avenue boasts a strikingly wide avenue lined with the still healthy maple trees, now venerable nonagenarians, which were specially imported from Canada as saplings. It retains plentiful green spaces above, towards Hillfields Avenue, and below, at Quadrant West. Such developments reflect the public demand to provide 'Homes Fit for Heroes' after the First World War — many war veterans moved into the newly constructed homes at Hillfields.[54] Despite poverty at Hillfields, the estate was regarded as a desirable place to live during the inter-war period, due to factors like its spirited sense of community and, in keeping with Sea Mills, the provision of gardens and green spaces. An older Hillfields resident spoke of such features fondly when recalling her childhood on the estate in the 1920s,

> This was supposed to be one of the best council estates ever built and it was lovely because the builders put a tree in everybody's garden, you had an apple tree or a pear tree ... at the time it was lovely. People had hedges, trees in their gardens, the trees up the road.[55]

However, while the layout and construction of the housing and generous open spaces may have been influenced by Howard's ideas, more far reaching aspects of his social and economic objectives were not carried through. Other parts of Hillfields continued to suffer from extreme poverty. Dresser documents claims of 'actual starvation' by members of a tenant's association in the ward in 1922 – any limited improvements were gains made due to tenant organisation and activism.[56] One of the key objectives of Howard's programme, that garden cities should be built on community-leased land, was not met. Occupancy has been determined by a combination of finance from private paternalism such as Robinson's, municipal control, and later sell-offs to owner occupiers by 'right to buy' legislation. A recent survey found that 67% of homes in the Hillfields ward have owner occupation, while 19% are rented from Bristol City Council. Only 7% are rented from private landlords — the area is not considered a 'desirable' part of

51 http://en.wikipedia.org/wiki/Hillfields,_Bristol: [Accessed 15 Nov 2008].

52 http://www.benrff.org/documents/Philip%20Robinson.pdf: [accessed 15 Nov 2008].

53 John Bartlett, *Fishponds* (Stroud: Tempus, 2004), p. 126.

54 Paul Hoggett, *et al*, *Class, Race and Community Cohesion: A Profile of Hillfields, Bristol*. Report of research conducted for the Community Cohesion Unit of Bristol City Council by the University of the West of England and Community Resolve (Bristol: University of the West of England, 2008) [online]: http://www.uwe.ac.uk/hlss/research/cpss/research_reports/Hillfields.pdf [accessed 1 May 2014] p. 6.

55 Ibid., p. 6.

56 See Dresser, 'Housing Policy in Bristol, 1919-30', pp. 194, 199.

the property market, so few homes have fallen prey to 'buy to let' speculators.[57]

It is vital to remember that in Howard's vision a garden city encompassed not merely suburban houses with attractive gardens considered in isolation, but an entire supporting economic and community infrastructure, rich in what today might be termed 'social capital'. When Hillfields was first developed, a tenant's association called the Hillfields Park Community Association campaigned hard for facilities and public spaces because, it was reported, 'there were no corner public houses, no theatres or cinemas, in fact no public meeting place at all apart from the local Baptist chapel.'[58] The situation was to persist for many years during which the school at Hillfields was used as a venue to host local events. After much lobbying, the Community Association was finally granted some land for a Community Centre following the Second World War; but no funding to build it! The outcome was an impressive feat of community participation. In a section of a local history of the Hillfields estate compiled by Jane Baker it is recorded that

> It had been decided that the centre would be built by voluntary labour, a remarkable decision, and Hillfields is the only Community Centre in the country to enjoy the distinction of having been built by the people who were to use it. While the men laboured at digging the foundations the wives were no less active providing teas and lunch and much encouragement. Work started out in 1950 on the site and over 40 men were involved in carrying out the necessary work.[59]

In most working-class suburbs non-profit making community ventures and amenities have fared poorly in recent decades. In Hillfields, for example, Beeching's axe severed Staple Hill Railway Station in 1966, Robinson's factory closed in 1996, and the local swimming pool and community centre have also been lost.[60] Without genuine community control and ownership local facilities have proved to be vulnerable to council cuts or sell-off and privatisation. Too often such areas have suffered from trickle-up economics in which 'wealth creation' and economic growth have increased alongside an erosion of local amenities. Bristol City Council's halt to support for the Woodland Way garden development has caused controversy strongly relevant to the area's garden-suburb past. Local volunteers and young offenders on community service orders transformed a small area of disused land into a community nature reserve which was to be used as a sensory garden for disabled children. Early in 2008 the voluntary groups that had established the site, the Fishponds Locality Action Group and Hillfields Futures, were unexpectedly given notice to quit so that a

---

57   Bristol City Council, *Hillfields: 2006 Ward Profile*, accessed online at:
      http://www.bristol.gov.uk/WardFinder/pdfs/hillfields-profile.pdf [accessed 6 Dec 2008], p. 11.

58   *Hillfields: The First Sixty Years A Local Study*, special edition for Fishponds Library Local History File, unpaginated.

59   Ibid. Unfortunately later newspaper cuttings record that the Community Centre closed during the late 1990s, after
      running into substantial debt and regular incidents of vandalism which inflicted extensive damage to the premises. The
      claim that this was the only self-built community centre in the country may not be tenable as Lockleaze could also boast
      a self-built community centre constructed in the aftermath of the Second World War.

60   Hoggett, *et al*, *Class, Race and Community Cohesion*, p. 4.

social housing development could take place.[61] Such policy shifts fuel the suspicion that environmental initiatives in working-class districts are less valued than those in more prosperous neighbourhoods.

Selby Road, Speedwell.

Speedwell

Near to Hillfields a direct labour scheme was used to construct a further 170 council houses at Ridgeway Road, Fishponds in the early 1930s.[62] Also between the Hillfields Ward and St George Ward is the former mining area known as Speedwell where a separate municipal housing estate was constructed on a 33 acre site between 1924 and 1931. Speedwell Estate has retained its identity as an inter-war housing estate to this day with characteristic cul-de-sacs, privet hedges and a mix of gabled and non-gabled houses in the area around Selby Road and Meadow Vale that counters the homogenous appearance of many developments from this era. The gross density of 10.30 houses per acre is comfortably in keeping with the Tudor Walters recommendation that there should be twelve houses per acre.[63] The area was enhanced by the art-deco style Speedwell Baths nearby. This pool was funded by the Bristol Corporation and opened in 1937 and is now sadly missed following its closure in 2005.

61   'Homes Blow for Sensory Garden Site', *BEP* 8 February 2008, p. 7. See also Hoggett, *et al*, *Class, Race and Community Cohesion*, p. 10.

62   John Lyes, *Bristol 1927-1933* (Bristol: Bristol Branch of the Historical Association, 2004), p. 9.

63   Rosamond Jevons and John Madge, *Housing Estates: A Study of Bristol Corporation Policy and Practice Between the Wars* (Bristol: Pub. for the University of Bristol by J. A. Arrowsmith, 1946), p. 17.

257

Glyn Vale, Knowle West.

Knowle West

By far the largest of the post-war municipal housing estates was developed at Knowle West and Bedminster from 1920 to 1939, numbering more than 6,000 houses, together with a further 442 at nearby Bedminster Down.[64] The Knowle West development is a textbook example of a garden-suburb approach, in its most diluted sense, being lost in a massive housing programme. As Rosamond Jevons and John Madge noted, by 1939 Knowle West, with a population of 27,000, was twice the size of Welwyn Garden City.[65] Many of the sociological and demographic facts we have about Bristol's inter-war housing estates are due to Jevons and Madge's detailed survey of the estates from the 1940s, published as *Housing Estates* (1946) — we know the occupations of the residents, how they travelled to work and what was for sale in the local shops. Again like the developments at Sea Mills and Hillfields, Knowle West was a part of the 1920s housing boom that followed the passage of the *Housing and Town Planning Act 1919* (the 'Addison Act') and the first Labour government's *Housing (Financial Provisions) Act 1924* (the 'Wheatley Act').

By the mid-1930s there was already considerable demoralisation and discontent at Knowle West, so much so that the local authorities attempted, unsuccessfully, to re-brand it as 'Filwood Park'.[66] Dissatisfaction with the solid new housing on the purpose-built estate perplexed middle-class support workers such as May Bolt, an 'Almoner at the Bristol Homeoepathic [*sic*] Hospital'. Bolt, who moved onto the estate as a warden in 1936 and had a great affection for the Knowle Westers, wrote:

---

64 Ibid.

65 Ibid., p. 20.

66 Martin J. Powell, 'From Bemmy Down to Bishopsworth', in James Belsey *et al, Bristol: The Growing City: Life in the Suburbs – from the 18th Century to Today* (Bristol: Redcliffe, 1986), p. 110.

> When I visited some of them and saw the pleasant little houses with the wide streets and the gardens and compared them with the awful slums of my other visits, I marvelled at the contrast and at the discontent.[67]

While some of the initial lack of facilities and services started to be addressed from the late 1930s onwards, progress was stopped by the outbreak of the Second World War. There was a sense that the mass programme of rehousing lacked opportunities for positive community relations to evolve and for neighbourhoods to bond. The geographical isolation from the rest of the city was an important factor and, as Martin J. Powell argued, although partly mitigated by bicycles.

> Many of the men in the slums were on casual work. — 15 per cent on the new estates earned their living in this way. It was harder for these men now they were further away from the city centre and the docks. People who had previously lived by such things as hawking for furniture removal work in the new central area now found it impossible on the outskirts and the resentment built up.[68]

Filwood Broadway, Knowle West.

The story of Knowle West is largely one of unfulfilled promise – Filwood Broadway, for example, was intended to be a 'fine boulevard well lighted and lined with trees.'[69] It would be difficult to disagree with Dave Backwith's assessment that, while there were marked health benefits following slum clearance in the area, the improvement of the environment and the provision of lower-density housing, 'generally the houses and their gardens were seen as the most, if not the only positive feature of the estate'.[70] Madge Dresser may be justifiably sceptical about the popularity of gardens among low-income workers

67   Unpublished, hand-typed account by Mary Bolt (warden 1936-1947) and Phyllis Bazeley (warden 1950-1960), *The Story of Corner Cottage Settlement. Knowle West 1936-1961* [1961?] (Bristol Central Library manuscript 08041199), p. 1.

68   Powell, 'From Bemmy Down to Bishopsworth', p. 112.

69   Backwith, *Housing not Herding?*, p. 85.

70   Ibid., p. 79.

employed in manual labour, suspecting that gardening was partly imposed by municipal overseers as a means to make tenants more virtuous. However, other evidence suggests that a vast new urban population had voluntarily taken to vegetable gardening during the lean post-war years when there were well over a million allotment holders.[71] Certainly since at least the time of William Cobbett's *The English Gardener* (1829) there has been support for the working-class garden as a space that created opportunities to supplement diet, provide recreation, enjoy hobbies and socialise. Surveys carried out by Jevons and Madge found that the residents were attracted to the 'pleasures of a new home with a garden, of the fresh and healthy atmosphere of the estate' which were chief among the compensations of living on the new schemes — two thirds of families interviewed were 'either very pleased or quite satisfied with the environment on the estates' — and claim that 'the great majority of gardens admirably reflect the care taken of them.'[72]

Filwood Broadway Cinema, Knowle West.

Unfortunately, even such infrastructure and services that did exist were lost towards the end of the twentieth century. The pool at Filwood Broadway which opened in 1962 was a victim of the same cuts to swimming pools such as Speedwell, closing in 2005. Most symbolic, however, is the sad spectacle of the Broadway cinema in Filwood Park, opened in 1938 and once a cultural hub, as it hosted not only film but concerts, boxing and bingo, but now boarded up for the last quarter of a century.[73]

---

71 Dresser, 'Housing Policy in Bristol, 1919-30', p. 207. David Crouch and Colin Ward, *The Allotment: Its Landscape and Culture* [1988], (Nottingham: Mushroom, 1994), pp. 71-76.

72 Jevons and Madge, *Housing Estates*, pp. 66-67, 78.

73 Dave Stephenson and Jill Willmott, *Bristol Cinemas* (Stroud: Tempus Publishing, 2005), p. 17. At the time of writing Bristol City Council hope to tempt a large supermarket chain to develop the building while maintaining the 'Metroland'-style façade. See City Design Group, Neighbourhoods and City Development, Bristol City Council, *Filwood Broadway*

Trowbridge Road, Southmead.

Southmead

The slightly later Bristol Corporation estate, started at Southmead at the end of the 1920s, was one of the larger developments with up to a thousand houses built between the wars on land purchased by the Housing Committee in 1928.[74] By the time the initial Southmead and Knowle West schemes were completed after the war, Jevons and Madge estimated that around a third of all working-class Bristolian children lived on the Corporation estates. They also claimed that of these, 28% of under 14 year-olds lived in poverty (7% more than the city average).[75]

Similarly to Knowle West, the development at Southmead was used to re-house many families following slum clearance. The distance from the city centre meant that isolation and lack of opportunities often contributed to continued deprivation on the new estate.[76] Therefore, also in common with Knowle West, some residents considered the supply of well constructed and spacious houses with gardens as a poor substitute for the kind of close knit neighbourhoods that they felt they had experienced previously. A further aggravating grievance was a

---

Framework: Final Report (Bristol: Bristol City Council, 2012), p. 10 and p. 21:
http://www.bristol.gov.uk/sites/default/files/documents/planning_and_building_regulations/urban_design/
urban_design_projects/Filwood%20Broadway%20Framework%20Final_1.pdf [accessed 21 April 2014].

74 Lyes, *Bristol 1927-1933*, p. 7.

75 Jevons and Madge, *Housing Estates*, pp. 31-32.

76 Ibid., p. 61.

sense that such redevelopments were something done *to* residents by municipal authorities for their own good without their participation in the decision-making process. In one Southmead resident's objection, the garden ironically signified a kind of uprooting:

> I didn't ask to be moved from my so-called slum — it was nice there. The people were nice, always in and out. The rats didn't particularly bother us, either. Now what do I want with a garden and a box-hedge and all this respectability? Can you blame me for not caring? I want my comfortable slum, so I let the garden go.[77]

'Pride of Southmead', Southmead Youth Centre.

While as we have seen other residents of the Bristol's inter-war council estates often spoke of their gardens with pride and pleasure, such contrasting comments indicate the complex and often contradictory expressions of community in such neighbourhoods. In this respect it is relevant that Jeremy Brent, a youth worker at Southmead for 25 years before his untimely death in 2006, based his analysis of the unstable and conflicting notions of the idea of 'community' on the estate at Southmead in his excellent study *Searching for Community*. Bristol City Council figures still identify parts of Southmead as among the 10% most deprived areas in England and Southmead Central as the most deprived area of the city for older people and in terms of income

---

77   Quoted in Roger Wilson, *Difficult Housing Estates* (London: Tavistock, 1963), p. 12. Jeremy Brent, in *Searching for Community: Representation, Power and Action on an Urban Estate* (Bristol: Policy Press, 2009), confirms that the Bristolian estate of Upfield described in Wilson's study is in fact based upon research undertaken in Southmead.

deprivation.[78]

Upper Horfield

Like Sea Mills, the estate at Upper Horfield made use of experimental housing using Parkinson pre-stressed reinforced concrete. The Upper Horfield scheme was a municipal housing estate, built 1926/1927, that has now been substantially redeveloped due to widespread structural damage caused by concrete cancer and damp, which led to the demolition of the houses in 2005 (although as we have seen in the case of similar houses at Sea Mills, it is now known that such deterioration can be prevented and addressed by patching and overcladding). The abandonment of the more wholesome stone and clay bricks of earlier garden-suburb style dwellings denoted a shift from the Arts and Crafts tradition and is likely to have been motivated by factors that were pragmatic rather than aesthetic. Dresser records that a shortage of bricks during the post-war period was a consideration in the search for practical alternatives.[79] This said, developments could have been much worse. Backwith records the (rejected) proposal by Ernest Savory, the Conservative Chairman of the Housing Committee during the post-war era, for the construction of 1,500 "Chalets' made of corrugated iron and breeze blocks'.[80]

The regeneration scheme at Upper Horfield was completed in late 2008. The programme for mixed-tenure housing has, predictably, been developed with the higher density of 1,000 units (half of which are to be 'affordable') replacing the 600 homes on the former garden-suburb influenced estate.[81] The following comment from a correspondent who calls him or herself 'Sea Mills gardener' indicates that Bristolians that are affected by such redevelopment are aware of their garden-suburb heritage and the links between districts:

> If the Council's recent development at Horfield is anything to go by, 'Sea' Mills will be a 'sea' of tarmac and flesh-pink concrete brickettes, instead of a 'sea' of the flowers, garden produce and tree-lined avenues we love to live with'.[82]

So far the verdict on the future of the Upper Horfield estate has been more upbeat for most tenants, who are pleased to have escaped the increasingly dilapidated concrete housing. Nevertheless, in an essay published in 2010, lecturers on the built environment, Henry Shaftoe and Andrew Tallon, had already noted the apparent trend for property speculators to buy up the houses,

---

78 Bristol City Council, *Southmead: 2008 Ward Profile*: http://www.bristol.gov.uk/WardFinder/pdfs/southmead-profile.pdf [accessed online 18 Dec 2008], p. 8.

79 Dresser, 'Housing Policy in Bristol, 1919-30', p. 188.

80 Backwith, *Housing not Herding?*, pp. 56-59.

81 Bristol Community Housing Foundation report, 'Regeneration of Upper Horfield Estate, Bristol', accessed online at: http://www.southwesthousing.co.uk/pdfs/SWHI%20BP%20Regeneration%20of%20Upper%20Horfield%20Estate.pdf [accessed 7 Dec 2008], pp. 1-2.

82 Letter to *The Community Voice: Newsletter of the Sea Mills and Coombe Dingle Community Project* (2006), accessed online at: http://community-voice.org.uk/cvoice/cvoice_21_5.pdf [accessed 16 Nov 2008], p. 5.

which they describe as 'fairly bland in design', for rent.[83]

As well as patterns of tenure, future conditions will be determined by the quality of local amenities and opportunities, conspicuous by their absence on many of Bristol's inter-war corporation estates. Dresser details the lack of social provision and the failure of coordination in terms of basic infrastructure such as transport, medical facilities, electricity and telephones. In Horfield, for example, a school, library and pub were only just available at the end of the 1920s, several years after the housing was constructed. There was still no evidence of shops, a crèche, a surgery, churches, social centres, sports grounds or a cinema by 1930.[84]

St Anne's

The council estate at St Anne's, built between 1928 and 1933 was similarly a product of the 1919 Housing Act. Again the houses were well designed and laid out, under the coordinating eye of C. F. W. Dening.[85] Several streets in the development are named after cathedrals, including Ripon Road, Guildford Road, St Davids Crescent and Lichfield Road, this ecclesiastical theme intriguingly being underpinned by their layout in a circled cross. Within this circular development, inset with smaller cul-de-sacs, many of the houses have characteristically prominent gables. While the homes were built with more traditional materials, and have proved to be more durable than the estate at Upper Horfield, in common with other Bristol Corporation schemes, there has a lack of social amenities, exacerbated by the loss of St Anne's Park Station in 1970.

Lockleaze

The Bristol Corporation council housing at Lockleaze in north Bristol, although conceived during the inter-war period, was built later than the city's other garden-suburb inspired estates, not being developed until 1946-1950, and marking perhaps the final episode in a four decade experiment. Noting that some of the first residents of the large new estate (numbering 1,164 houses) had lost their former homes during the Blitz, Gerry Brookes writes of Lockleaze that,

> The rather utopian idea was to create a garden suburb — a spacious, modern, self-sustaining place for all ages with its own schools, shops and recreation areas.[86]

Ian Haddrell describes the construction of the Lockleaze estate:

> The original material palette used in Lockleaze comprised a simple set of

---

83   Henry Shaftoe and Andrew Tallon, 'Bristol: Not a Design-Led Urban Renaissance', in *Urban Design and the British Urban Renaissance*, ed. by John Punter (London: Routledge, 2010), p. 124.

84   Dresser, 'Housing Policy in Bristol, 1919-30', pp. 194-96.

85   I am grateful to Andy Foyle, architectural historian and member of the Brislington Conservation and History Society who lives in the Brislington/St Anne's ward, for information about this development. Andy Foyle, email message to the author, 16 December 2008.

86   Gerry Brooke, 'Distinct lack of community a worrying reality in "lost" suburb', *Bristol Post*, 29 November 2011.

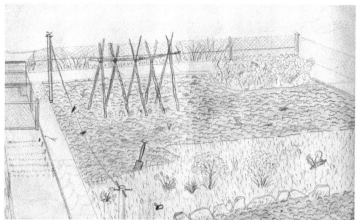

View of rear garden 4 Haydon Gardens, Lockleaze, 1961.

complimentary [*sic*] materials. These generally included a mixture of rendered concrete and precast sections and red/brown concrete tiles, or brown brickwork and brown concrete roof tiles.[87]

Regularly cycling down Romney Avenue in the present day I see that in many cases brightly painted exterior walls render the distinctive flat-topped houses less monotone, that village green spaces have been retained and that arrays of recently installed solar panels indicate local attempts at environmental and economic sustainability. Haddrell further points out that the street nomenclature is entirely derived from the names of artists from the Romantic era and their neo-Romantic successors.[88] Consistent with recollections from other garden suburbs such as Hillfields and Upper Horfield, one-time Lockleaze resident Joyce Storey expressed her appreciation for the estate's prolific greenery:

> [...] in the spring sunshine, the avenue was a delight with the misty-pink blossom of the newly planted Japanese cherry trees. The pastel pinks, greens and greys of the painted houses blended with the foliage and clustered blossom of these trees. Every so often along the avenue there were cul-de-sacs, in front of which were grassland play areas, which had been planted by the Council with young saplings that looked as though they had been retained from the original meadow.[89]

Despite this early promise, Lockleaze has shared some of the endemic problems of deprivation and lack of services with other Bristolian council estates. According to a 2008 Ward Profile for Lockleaze compiled by Bristol City Council, three Lockleaze wards are ranked as among the 10% most deprived areas in both Bristol and England.[90] Nevertheless, the area has an

---

87 Ian Haddrell, *Lockleaze Schools* (Stroud: History Press, 2008), p. 7.

88 Ibid., pp. 8-9.

89 Quoted in ibid., pp. 7-8, from *The House in South Road*.

90 Bristol City Council, *Lockleaze: 2008 Ward Profile*, online:
    https://www.bristol.gov.uk/WardFinder/pdfs/lockleaze-profile.pdf [accessed 30 April 2014].

established tradition of community activism with Lockleaze Voice and Lockleaze Environment Group campaigning to preserve something of the low-density character of the estate and opposing council sell-offs of green spaces.

Chocolate factory at Keynsham after closure.

Life is Sweet at Somerdale

Another significant example of the influence of the garden-city movement locally is at nearby Keynsham where Fry's, the Quaker chocolate manufacturers, developed the 'Somerdale Garden Village' for their workers at the factory in 1925.[91] Quaker families such as Fry, Cadbury and Rowntree were prominent in chocolate manufacture and enjoyed a reputation for philanthropic attempts to raise the conditions of their workforce at production centres such as Bournville, New Earswick and Somerdale. As nonconformists, Quakers were excluded from public office in the government, church and military until the repeal of the Test and Corporation Acts in 1829, so often found a professional outlet in business; chocolate production was particularly fitting given their affinity with the temperance movement.

The location of Somerdale on the banks of the River Avon at Keynsham Hams was chosen not only for its transport connections using rail, road and water but also for the ample development space and attractive surroundings. The site was carefully selected and it took nearly fifteen years to landscape and construct the factory for production. The factory was named Somerdale following a national competition in 1923. It was consciously planned with the inspiration of the garden-city movement. Peter Roberts of Keynsham Heritage Trust said

---

91   Skilleter, 'Housing Reform', p. 18. Former employee Eric Miles produced a 300-page photographic history of the factory's construction and operation on the eve of its closure – *Somerdale Story 1921 to 2009* (2009).

Somerdale was really in part conceived as 'a garden factory'.[92] This is confirmed by the inclusion of lines from the July 1928 edition of *The Quiver* in the *Fry's Works Magazine*:

> We have brought the people from the rural areas to the factories of the town: let us take back our industries to the wide spaces and purer air of the countryside: that way lies content and happiness.[93]

Such lines posit the idea that the industrial revolution could enter a new enlightened phase, ushering a reconciliation of industrialism with Romanticism — the magazine is interspersed with quotes from William Wordsworth, John Keats and other Romantic-era poets, thus soothing the age-old antagonisms between the country and the city that Raymond Williams documented, and solving both lack of rural opportunity and urban pollution.[94] In meeting the preconditions for human happiness, health and well-being the idealism of Fry's approach at Somerdale is far-reaching and chimes with a key aspect of Howard's programme to reconcile the town/country split by creating intentional communities without rural isolation or the squalor of city slums and heavy industry. Despite the pastoral elements in the Garden-City Movement, as Frederick Aalen points out, Howard's enthusiasm for the socially emancipatory potential of the latest technology distinguished his ideas from those that were 'harking back to a pre-industrial age'.[95]

The playing fields and other recreational facilities and the Fry Club and Conference Centre were a key part of the employee benefits on offer.[96] The housing estate adjacent to the factory was constructed during the mid-1920s along garden-suburb principles, with soundly built houses and immediately available employment for key factory employees — as well as permanently hanging with sickly sweet wafts of chocolate. However, the housing estate that was eventually built was considerably smaller than that first projected. In an unpublished dissertation based upon Fry's internal publications, Tim Clench notes that only 64 of the initially projected 176 houses were completed and that a much larger programme to build up to 500 houses was shelved.[97]

Following the merger with Cadbury's in 1919, much of the paternalist ethos of the Fry family, who operated under the motto 'Happiness in Industry', was carried over to the new factory at Keynsham when production was shifted from central Bristol in 1935. A Fry's mission statement dating from this time stated the aim to give 'the workpeople the best facilities for recreation and happiness.'[98] Despite the generosity of Fry and its reputation as a model employer, from the

---

92 Personal conversation at 'Remembering Somerdale' event, 4 November 2008.

93 *Fry's Works Magazine 1728-1928* (Bi-Centenary Number) ed. by W. T. Pearce (Bristol: J. S. Fry & Sons Ltd, 1928), p. 67.

94 Raymond Williams. *The Country and the City* (London: Chatto & Windus, 1973).

95 Frederick H. A. Aalen, 'English Origins' in Stephen V. Ward (ed.), *The Garden City: Past, Present and Future* (London: E & FN Spon, 1992), p. 32

96 The Fry Club and facilities remain in operation in 2014, despite the closure of the Cadbury factory.

97 Tim Clench, "Happiness in Industry' - Working for J. S. Fry & Sons, Cocoa and Chocolate Manufacturers, Bristol (1865-1971)', [Unpublished Final Project Report for Open University course DA301 2001], p. 7.

98 Quoted by Paul Chrystal, *Cadbury and Fry Through Time* (Stroud: Amberley Publishing, 2012), p. 20.

outset there had been a regime in which prayer and scripture were mandatory at work, while chat between women and men was prohibited and pubs were off limits even outside of working hours, both offences which numbered among misdemeanours which could result in financial penalties or dismissal.[99] At Fry's female workers had been known as 'angels' and male workers as 'devils'. A former resident from Greenbank, site of the former Packer's chocolate factory (later Elizabeth Shaw), also told me that her mother quipped about 'Fry's angels and Packer's devils', to point up the contrast in attitudes towards local employers on the part of their workers. At Fry's employees were expected to be 'clean, sober and of good character' and stoppages and wage deductions could be made for talking on the shop floor.[100]

When Fry's became a subsidiary of Cadbury's, Somerdale employees continued to be rewarded with a package of benefits, including hospital funds, pensions, and sick benefits that were generous given the economic climate in the years following the Depression. Despite the inherent tedium involved in producing standardised confectionery on production lines with a rigid division of labour, many young working-class people aspired to work in the factory in order to take advantage of the preferred working conditions on offer. Women outnumbered men by a ratio of 2:1. Even after the war, if they lacked qualifications they might demonstrate good character by taking along their Sunday school book and an example of some embroidery. Given this continuation of the old Fry's paternalism, there was very little agency for workers within Somerdale although industrial disputes were not unknown later in the twentieth century. Shop floor activism during the 1930s finally made some inroads into the entrenched paternalism. At this time Ernest Bevin, then General Secretary of the Transport and General Workers' Union, negotiated a deal with Egbert Cadbury to recognise trade union representation at the garden factory.

Mostly, however, worker loyalty to the amenities at Somerdale was maintained, as was reflected in the high-profile and spirited fight to save the plant, then run by Cadburys, when its phased closure was announced in October 2007.[101] Film director Ken Loach joined a protest march against the relocation of production to Poland to save labour costs. The tensions between the tradition of paternalism at the site and the imperative to turn increasing profits were long-standing. Somerdale's precarious situation was revealed in Cadbury's announcement that confirmed the company's intention to close the Keynsham factory by 2010, despite continued profit making and the fact that most of the production at the site is for the home market. The economic conflict of interests between confectionery workers and their bosses could only be partially glossed over by the aspiration to 'Happiness in Industry' and has perhaps sharpened the sense of betrayal at Cadbury's imminent relocation. Decades of rationalisation and job losses from the 1960s onwards seem to have only delayed the perhaps inevitable capitulation to the operations of the global market.

---

99   Ibid., pp. 22-23.

100   According to interviewee in 1978 BBC documentary on Somerdale presented by Gwyn Richards.

101   Campaign website: http://wwwsaveoursomerdale.co.uk/ [accessed 22 Jan 2008, now unavailable].

This sense of betrayal was to be sharpened when the giant American food producer Kraft bought out Cadbury in a hostile takeover in 2010. The predatory corporation's promises to reconsider and save the Somerdale factory were swiftly broken; renewed hope for the remaining 400 workers was dashed when Kraft reneged on its promises — within a week of its takeover![102] The factory closed on 31 March 2011. At the time of writing in 2014 work has started on demolishing the garden factory and volume-house builders Taylor Wimpey have been granted planning permission to build up to 700 houses and accompanying development on the site.[103]

Real Reform?

Those influenced by Ebenezer Howard's ideas sought to accommodate housing schemes within state capitalist or private industrial enterprises. Inevitably, obstacles confronted his *Peaceful Path to Real Reform* when attempting to transform the conditions of working-class communities within a capitalist infrastructure. Fundamental conflicts of interest between the need for a residential community to flourish in an environment with well-designed architecture, pleasant surroundings, adjacent social amenities and the means to make a living were not easily reconciled with the demand to balance budgets and accumulate profits. Such tensions were to become particularly pronounced during the inter-war period as the different aspirations of capitalist sponsors and those like Raymond Unwin, a leading architect of garden cities and suburbs, who looked to the uplifting and progressive aspects of the projects. Working in the tradition of William Morris, Unwin sought to transform the quality of human life by beautifying surroundings. Mark Swenarton writes,

> For socialists such as Raymond Unwin, the garden city movement was the way to make an unparalleled improvement in the lives of the people; for capitalists such as Lever, it offered a way of making the workforce more contented (and thereby more productive) without affecting the basic relationships of capitalist production.[104]

Employers hoped that satisfying employees' basic needs would help to nurture a quiescent workforce, while local government housing and planning administrators believed that the provision of municipal housing could head off the potential for revolutionary aspirations, as the mass demand for decent homes helped to fuel labour militancy after the First World War. However, the provision of the inter-war municipal housing schemes influenced by the garden-city movement coincided with the turbulent years of the General Strike, the Depression and the Hungry Thirties. This created an environment in which the chief imperative was to be cost effective. The result was a dilution of quality in municipal housing, due to pecuniary incentives on the part of local authorities

---

102 'Kraft job row earns firm a city rebuke', *The Bristol Post*, 27 May 2010, p. 3.

103 'Permission for 770 homes on old Cadbury's site', *The Bristol Post*, 28 February 2014, p. 16.

104 Mark Swenarton. *Homes Fit for Heroes: The Politics and Architecture of Early State Housing in Britain* (London: Heinemann Educational, 1981), pp. 6-7.

operating in the context of an economic downturn, and understandable pressure from slum dwellers, homeless families and others on waiting lists who were desperate for housing sooner rather than later.[105] While the low density of twelve houses per acre under the 1924 Housing Act was adhered to, Jevons and Madge regarded the higher percentage of the more ample houses with parlours built immediately after the war as a critical difference to the non-parlour houses of later municipal developments.[106]

Furthermore, Swenarton convincingly argues that Raymond Unwin and Alexander Harvey (the chief architect at Bournville) were also eventually complicit in taking an approach to upscaling projects from small model villages to large council estates that prioritized the 'simplification of design and the standardisation of building components'.[107] This was rational enough given the demands of the moment and the incentive to make economies of scale, but was to lead inexorably to the stultifying conformity and monotony of later twentieth-century housing schemes, in which aesthetic priorities came a poor second to budgetary considerations. A report on Bristol's Southmead estate, for example, speaks of the 'monotonous consistency of building type and streetscape which emphasizes its separation from surrounding areas'.[108] As we have also seen in Bristol, the scale — though not the quality — of garden-city influenced planning exceeded that of its 'official' representation in Letchworth and Welwyn Garden City. The history of Bristolian inter-war planning in the 1920s and 1930s, as told in studies such as those by Dresser and Backwith, is one of deteriorating standards, with economies in the quality of housing construction and increasing standardisation of design.[109] This was accompanied by cost-cutting in the provision of public amenities and community infrastructure. Commenting on the pitiful absence of amenities at Knowle West and throughout the municipal housing estates of Bristol's working-class suburbs, Backwith writes,

> This situation flowed from the Post-War Government's conception of municipal housing which, despite the inspiration of the Garden City movement, was of housing estates rather than integrated, 'reconstructed' communities. Given the numbers of houses promised in the 'Homes fit for Heroes' rhetoric it seems, with hindsight, an amazing oversight that the need to furnish estates with the social institutions which were [an] essential, if taken for granted, part of the working class life was simply not considered.[110]

---

105 In the mid-1930s the health department conducted about 1,400 housing inspections annually, with a yearly average of 980 houses found unfit for habitation,' *City and county of Bristol Annual Report of the Medical Officer of Health,* Bristol: 1934-1938, *passim.* Findings reported by Martin Gorsky, 'Public Health in Interwar England and Wales: Did it fail?', *Dynamis* 28 (2008) Section 4.

106 Jevons and Madge, *Housing Estates,* pp. 20-21.

107 Swenarton, *Homes Fit for Heroes,* p. 24.

108 Safe Neighbourhoods Unit, *The Southmead Survey 1991* (Bristol: Bristol City Council / Bristol Safer Cities Project, 1991), p. 3, quoted in Jeremy Brent, *Searching for Community: Representation, Power and Action on an Urban Estate* (Bristol: Policy Press, 2009), p. 77.

109 Dresser, 'Housing Policy in Bristol, 1919-30', p. 191.

110 Backwith, *Housing not Herding?,* p. 124.

The result was that few vestiges of the Garden-City movement survived into the brave new world of Bristol's post-war reconstruction from the late 1940s onwards. Planning influenced by the Tudor Walters report emerged because of concerns about the poor quality of working-class housing; garden-city principles that had been extremely diluted by the outbreak of the Second World War were effectively lost altogether in the tower block housing that was to follow. This was partly explained by the even more onerous demands of reconstruction facing post-war administrations in the aftermath of the Blitz. It should also be remembered that many lives were lost and much housing stock was destroyed in the garden-suburbs influenced municipal estates, particularly at Horfield and Southmead due to their proximity to the Bristol Aeroplane Company at Filton, but casualties were also recorded in all of the city's municipal council estates.[111]

There was also a radical contrast in the defining ethos of the kind of modernism influenced by Le Corbusier, whose conception of houses as machines for living in came to predominate in many more urban schemes after 1945. As I have shown, under the inspiration of Howard, English town planning had been imbued with garden-city ideas — the Town and Country Planning Association began life as the Garden Cities Association at the end of the nineteenth century. Howard had a holistic vision of planning in which there were several key elements that helped to define the garden-city project — strong housing design creating dwellings that are durable, comfortable and aesthetically appealing; a rejection of urban sprawl so homes are situated in environmentally attractive surroundings which have accompanying gardens, green spaces nearby and are free from pollution; a variety of social amenities to encourage community cohesion and avoid alienation, opportunities for creative work within walking distance so that the gap between workplace and home is minimal. In this sense garden cities were in fact an antidote to today's leafy suburbia in their explicit rejection of the separation of work and home. The Edwardian idea of the garden city and garden suburb may enjoy a new relevance as critics posit the idea of an 'End of Suburbia' in the title of Gregory Green's film documenting the social consequences of rapidly depleting oil reserves.[112] One of these consequences could be an end to the kind of urban developments in which the priorities of through traffic by private cars have over-ridden the needs of local neighbourhoods.

Another radical ingredient of Howard's conception of the garden city was that the development should be community owned. Once the capital had been raised to plan and construct the infrastructure, homes should be leased from the community constituted as a democratic entity. Rather than mortgage payments or rent to a private owner or municipal authority a regular payment is made to a community fund, thus the intention was to build up a sense of direct responsibility for the locality on the part of the residents, and to create an

---

111 'The Bristol & District Blitz War Memorial: A Register of those who Lost their Lives due to Enemy Action and Surrounding Districts, 1940-1944', compiled by John Penny: http://fishponds.org.uk/bristolmem.html [accessed 21 April 2014].

112 *The End of Suburbia Oil Depletion and the Collapse of the American Dream* (2004).

alternative to interference and profiteering on the part of outside agencies, whether state or private. Proponents of the garden-city idea went to considerable lengths to create stable communities in line with what nineteenth-century German sociologist Ferdinand Tönnies characterized as *Gemeinschaft*, a social structure based upon face-to-face communication, though without wishing to return to the more exclusive and static societies of a pre-industrial past.

There was a conscious intention to implement environmental conditioning in this, through attempts to bring about the preconditions in which mutual aid and self-help would flourish. Partly to this end cul-de-sacs were created, such as those at Sea Mills, so that micro-communities would emerge, neighbours would be encouraged to cooperate and enjoy a degree of collectivity rather than being divided by individualism. Some planners were reluctant to incorporate hedges and fences as they presented physical barriers between households. The environmental approach was associated with early sociologists such as Seebohm Rowntree, who was influential in supporting model industrial villages, the experimental settlements that were to be the forerunners of garden cities. Gillian Darley writes that, 'with industrial interests [Seebohm Rowntree] placed particular emphasis on root causes, recognising that change of environment was 100% more worthwhile than charity meted out later; the model village versus the dosshouse. He gave people independence and the best possible means with which to achieve it'.[113]

The lack of pubs was motivated by concern for alcoholism's role in undermining social ties and perpetuating poverty. The reluctance to provide public houses in garden suburbs was based on links between alcohol and poverty in studies by reforming social thinkers such as Henry Mayhew, Charles Booth and Seebohm Rowntree as much as a puritanical distaste for pleasure. However, while there were established temperance leanings in the Chartist, co-operative and labour movements, it was also recognised that in practice it was notoriously difficult to determine the extent to which alcohol was the cause or effect of deprivation. Some socialist critics regarded temperance as an attempt to blame disadvantaged individuals for systemic failures and anticipated the futility of prohibition. Even a teetotaller such as Philip Snowden wrote in 1908 that 'alcoholism cannot be completely solved apart from the treatment of the whole problem of the economic and social condition of the people', noting the correlation with bad housing and acknowledging that 'the public house has become the centre of social intercourse'.[114] Regardless of objections to alcohol consumption, public houses were (and obviously remain) cherished public spaces and the lack of them on moral grounds was a thin excuse for the failure to provide social spaces — Jevons and Madge objected, 'Why are there no billiard saloons or milk bars?'[115] The reason, it seems, was that the Housing Committee was extremely cautious about the presence of licensed premises on the new municipal estates. John Lyes records that in 1931 the Committee agreed that

---

113 Darley, *Villages of Vision*, pp. 188-89.

114 Philip Snowden, *Socialism and the Drink Question* (London: Independent Labour Party, 1908), p. 3, pp. 57-59, 82.

115 Jevons and Madge, *Housing Estates*, p. 86.

premises could only be opened if it could be demonstrated that a majority of tenants were in favour, although some members preferred an outright ban.[116] This nervousness on the part of local authorities may have been motivated by considerations beyond public health and order. Alison Ravetz suspected that the 'weakness of the public realm on estates, were disincentives to engage in union or political activity'.[117]

Garden-city advocates hoped to create a society of empowered citizens rather than simply consumers or employees. In this they anticipated key components of Murray Bookchin's creation of a reinvigorated *polis* which would incorporate the positive features of Athenian democracy — conviviality, direct democracy, creativity, ecologically sustainability, locally committed yet internationalist in its embrace through libertarian municipalism — and also present-day New Urbanist initiatives in the United States.[118] Jevons and Madge identified the lack of a culture of self-government and opportunities for direct democracy through community-run social centres on Bristol's municipal estates as a problem to be remedied back in the 1940s.[119]

Howard did not, however, challenge the context of the vast inequality of wealth, and hence power, in which such social relationships already exist. A thoroughgoing improvement in human physical conditions and the physical environment is largely unobtainable in isolation from wider social and cultural transformation. Political questions of power and ownership will continue to provide challenges to contemporary initiatives like Transition Towns which will need to be 'savvy' and learn some hard historical lessons if their good intentions are not to be compromised by accommodating entrenched economic interests. The achievements at Letchworth and Welwyn Garden City were undoubtedly diluted as a consequence of the heavy reliance of the garden-city programme upon wealthy sponsors, such as George Cadbury and William Lever, for advice and financial backing.[120]

It seems that there are strong parallels here with the common accusation that has become almost *cliché* in discussions about the Arts and Crafts Movement — that finely crafted goods were produced at a cost that could only be afforded by the better off patrons. In any discussion about the Arts and Crafts Movement it is customary for detractors to point out that, 'Ah, such beautiful work, but for all their lofty principles, these socialist artists could only sell to the rich'. There is some truth in this. Yet, if it is ironic, it is not the crushing irony that it may seem. Socialists such as William Morris and Charles Robert Ashbee did not overlook the all-embracing reality of capitalism and the wealthy elite's grip upon the means of production, which they knew could not be simply sidestepped. It

---

116 Lyes, *Bristol 1927-1933*, p. 19.

117 Alison Ravetz, *Council Housing and Culture: The History of a Social Experiment* (London: Routledge, 2001), p. 167.

118 Discussed in works such as *From Urbanization to Cities: Towards a New Politics of Citizenship* [1992], (London: Cassell, revised edition, 1995).

119 Jevons and Madge, *Housing Estates*, p. 70. Backwith, however, demonstrates that the Knowle Westers could be far from politically apathetic when the need arose, citing the spirited rout of fascist blackshirts in Melvin Square six weeks before the celebrated 'Battle of Cable Street' in 1936, *Housing Not Herding*, pp. 98-99, 137.

120 Darley, *Villages of Vision*, p. 184.

was their awareness that mass-production in factories had largely concentrated the control of the production in the hands of a few wealthy capitalists and exacerbated alienation of producers through the division of labour that prompted the Arts and Crafts approach. The principles and practice of the almost contemporaneous Arts and Crafts and the Garden-City movements were sound ones which floundered on the massive inequalities of wealth and power in the society within which they found themselves. The practical consequences of this context were all too apparent. In Knowle West, for example, tenants suffered from the damp despite having new homes because they could not afford to the heat the houses that they rented.[121] Howard maintained his commitment to far-reaching social change despite the conflicting demands and compromises that led to the curtailment and watering down of key aspects of his programme.

For the Garden-City Movement confidence that improved material circumstances could positively influence social outlooks and structures fed into a belief that that social gains could be made through benign planning and design, hence paving the way to ongoing transformation. Influential urban theorists, such as Patrick Geddes, later shared this environmentalist premise, in part derived from nineteenth-century thinkers such as John Ruskin and William Morris. The ecological imperatives of the great Austrian utopian artist and designer Friedensreich Hundertwasser were at once strikingly original yet strongly in this earlier Romantic tradition. His belief that all urban dwellers had an obligation to plant trees — a 'tree duty' — was part of a declaration that a revolutionary transformation towards a new urban mode of living was necessary, in which planning and design should be assessed by both its life-enhancing and aesthetic qualities and ecological consequences.

While the Garden-City Movement did not anticipate the radical environmental trajectory of Hundertwasser with his extravagant material constructions, it was characterised by prevailing planning assumptions about the well-being of individuals and communities that contrasted substantially with those that predominated after the Second World War. A functional, utilitarian approach began to emerge with demands for mass provision of municipal housing as quantitative measurements — the 'felicific calculus' of the greatest happiness of the greatest number — replaced more qualitative estimations of community well being. This is evident in the starkly contrasting, and contested, versions of modernity represented by the Garden City or made concrete in the tower block estates of the post-war era. One telling change of direction in the philosophy of well-being was brought about by the democratisation of private transport through mass production so that urban life was held to benefit by easy transit by accommodating cars. This was a strategic decision too often made at the expense of localities such as Bristol's Baptist Mills and Eastville, severed by major roads. The potential for communities integrated with places of work becomes an impossible dream in such a context and has yet to be reversed by the predicted trend towards internet home working. Garden-suburb planning also represents an optimistic view of the motivations and impulses of intended

---

121 Backwith, *Housing not Herding?*, p. 80.

residents. This is clear from efforts to design in consideration of well-being, hoping to achieve a change in housing conditions with an improved physical and natural environment and aspirations to greater community autonomy, which would in turn bring about a change for the better in society. This was surely lost in planning strategies that presumed certain urban populations to be dysfunctional, an attitude which seemed to cause the authorities to regard inner-city populations primarily as a problem to be policed and contained by the time riots erupted in the city (including Southmead and Knowle West) during the 1980s.

Today schemes closest to the garden-city influence such as the early Shirehampton housing have endured and held their value more than tower blocks, such as those already disused at Barton Hill and more 'identikit' estates such as those at Southmead and Upper Horfield. On the one hand the inter-war municipal housing programme was relatively successful in the construction of 9,000 dwellings by 1931 and 15,000 in the inter-war period as a whole.[122] However, the undoubted quantitative achievements in terms of bulk provision were not matched by qualitative improvements in community well-being. At the same time the vision and idealism of the Garden-City Movement was lost in a climate of economic expediency and, consequently, many of the areas loosely influenced by Howard's ideas through the Tudor Walters report are now deprived areas, such as Knowle West, Southmead, Hillfields and parts of Shirehampton. Passing through the city suburbs to arrive at Temple Meads Station from any direction today it is easy to imagine that the social and environmental legacy of the twentieth century could have been so much better.

Today

Peter Hall and Colin Ward argue that the mass production of the motor car and the post-War baby boom were both critical factors in undermining the possibility of a revival of the garden cities in the second half of the twentieth century.[123] This analysis has proved to be accurate, with the result that, despite a rhetorical revival in the use of the term 'garden city', presently proposed garden cities turn out to be blueprints for new town developments, lacking many of the characteristics that inspired Ebenezer Howard and other pioneers of the idea more than a century before.

Garden suburbs were intended as developments to support what — according to prevailing Edwardian notions — were the deserving poor. In the long run, however, it was perhaps inevitable that, in more desirable areas, market forces would ensure that such homes would be unlikely to stay affordable and would deprive even these sectors of the working class of the quality of design and spaciousness that they achieved. In the Hampstead Garden Suburb much surrounding woodland has long since been cut down and developed while the homes are the preserve of the super-rich — the larger houses currently being

---

122 Dresser, 'Housing Policy in Bristol, 1919-30', p. 161. Jevons and Madge, *Housing Estates*, p. 9.

123 Peter Hall and Colin Ward, *Sociable Cities: The Legacy of Ebenezer Howard* (Chichester: Wiley, 1998), Chapter 7.

offered on the market for several million pounds. Murray Bookchin was right to observe that the central shortcoming in Howard's proposal for social change was that visionary design is only one element of the profound transformation that he sought. In his brave attempt to construct a bridge linking pragmatism and utopia,Bookchin suggests, Howard was to leave 'undefined the nature of work, the control of the means of production, the problem of distributing goods and services equitably, and conflicting social interests that collect around these issues'

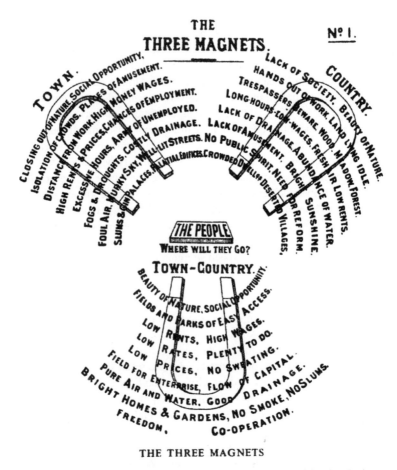

THE THREE MAGNETS

Ebenezer Howard's 'Three Magnets' illustration from *Tomorrow: A Peaceful Path to Real Reform* (1898).

— in short, the other materials of which community is forged.[124] Today's predominance of empty dwellings and office blocks, second homes and demographic factors, such as a sharp rise in single-occupancy households, indicates that the housing shortage is as much about distortions in capital flows

124 Murray Bookchin, *The Limits of the City* (New York: Harper Colophon, 1974), p. 119.

(locally and globally) and social power, expressed through the hugely inequitable distribution of land and housing, as the problem of a deficient supply of buildings.

There has been a resurgence of interest in the idea of garden-city principles in recent years. In 2008 Gordon Brown (Prime Minister 2007-2010) proposed a series of new 'eco-towns' based on his admiration for the housing innovations he had seen on a visit to Hammarby Sjöstad in Sweden.[125] Even pre-dating this initiative, Housing Minister Yvette Cooper had announced in June 2007 that the Bristol area was to be the site of a test development, Hanham Hall, a pilot for Gordon Brown's plans to create five of these 'eco-towns', which were ultimately intended to house up to 100,000 people in homes with zero-carbon emissions.[126] This development is now underway, with some residents already living in the eco-village, and completion scheduled for 2015. The final project will consist of around 180 homes, of which approximately a third will be designated as affordable while others will be shared ownership. This is undoubtedly a useful experimental site with environmental features that are a significant advance on other estates by volume house builders. While this is to be welcomed, it seems that we have to go back to the Garden-City Movement and its influence — albeit diluted — on the construction of inter-war estates, and post-war new towns, to look at what actually constitutes the collective provision of intentional community planning for social and environmental ends. A slow build movement that gets it right in terms of combining attractive design (a subjective quality of course) with local distinctiveness and ecological innovation would surely, in the long run, be more effective in meeting human housing and economic needs than the perpetual regeneration of urban areas. This benefits today's corporate construction industry but does nothing for the social fabric of city life or the environment.

If there were limitations in the eco-villages of the Brown administration, divergence from the radical aspirations of the garden-city pioneers has become even more evident in the proposals of the succeeding government. When Brown's political opponents in the Conservative/Liberal coalition government gained power in 2010, the idea of a new generation of garden cities emerged and gained leverage in planning discussions once more. The right-wing think-tank Policy Exchange saw them as a way for the construction industry to make profits in the context of a worsening housing crisis. It is also believed, however, that Prime Minister David Cameron will approach such initiatives with caution, given that the demand would be chiefly in South-East England where available land is difficult to identify and where such proposals would risk stiff opposition from Tory-voting constituents in the Home Counties.[127]

At the time of writing in 2014, the coalition's Deputy Prime Minister, Nick Clegg, has announced the government's intention to initiate three new schemes,

---

125 'Brown "inspired" by Swedish eco-town', *Building Design*, 1 June 2007, p. 5.

126 'Eco-villages challenge launch by minister', *WDP*, 4 June 2007, p. 4.

127 Jonathan Brown, 'Cameron accused of dropping support for garden cities for fear of a backlash from "nimbys"', *The Independent*, 30 December 2013.

explicitly called 'garden cities', of 15,000 houses each.[128] There is currently no stated start date for these developments, which are major projects, although significantly smaller in scope than the Brown administration's aspirations. Everyone likes gardens so there is a danger that the term 'garden cities' is used as a favourable, cuddly expression and a sweetener to reduce opposition to large conventional developments with little in keeping with Howard's origin vision. As we have seen, to be truly congruent with the philosophy and practical application of Howard's notion of a garden city, a development would encompass the following characteristics:

> Robust housing design, combining ergonomic and aesthetic features;
>
> Low density, with ample gardens and accessible green spaces held in common;
>
> Tenures based on community leasing as a safeguard against speculation, or at least embrace affordable pricing;
>
> Provision of self-contained opportunities for work, services and community facilities which are integrated within easy reach of residential zones, rather than a reliance upon commuter-based employment;
>
> In the twenty-first century it would also be reasonable to ensure that carbon-zero features and other sustainability-features are also factored into the architectural design, such as the use of passivhaus technology.

None of these characteristics is apparent from the early announcements about a new generation of garden cities at Ebbsfleet in Kent and at other yet to be specified locations. For example, it has already been conceded that there would be no obligation upon developers to include any allocation of affordable housing, and that a chief attraction of Ebbsfleet is the availability of motorways and rail links into London. We are then left to hope that the greater quantity of houses will itself 'trickle down' to the wider benefit, an unconvincing restatement of the conventional Conservative argument that economic benefits for the better off will 'trickle down' to all.[129]

So, despite these fresh developments, the initial misgivings about the character of the kinds of new eco-cities, or garden cities, or suburbs now proposed remain. Their largely technocratic approach may fall short of the broader social vision that Howard projected. The non-separation of workplace and home to forge living, working, integrated environments would also be crucial in any new proposals. The Garden-City Movement favoured the decentralization of self-sufficient communities with amenities and opportunities for creative work nearby, rather than the marginalisation of populations in

---

128 'Nick Clegg to Promise up to Three New Garden Cities with 15,000 Homes Each', *The Guardian*, 14 April 2014: http://www.theguardian.com/society/2014/apr/14/nick-clegg-garden-cities-homes [accessed 21 April 2014].

129 Internationally, an even more controversial example of the government's 'trickle-down' approach has been the inclusion in the foreign aid programme funding for such mega-developments for the wealthy as the 'Garden City Village' in Nairobi, Kenya. See Claire Provost, 'Hotels, shopping malls, luxury property, Is this the best use of UK aid funding?', *The Guardian*, 3 May 2014, p. 5.

alienated zones between city and country. Howard's ideas embraced a creative synthesis, as he holistically concerned himself with aesthetic and functional aspects of housing design and planning. He gave considerable thought to the social and economic context and the mental and physical health of their occupiers as well as the neighbourhoods and communities in which they lived and broader ecological considerations. His proposal for community leasing, offered a late-Victorian version of a 'third way' beyond municipal or private control, as a self-governing exercise in direct democracy. This owed much to the ideas of thinkers such as Peter Kropotkin and looked forward, via Lewis Mumford and others, to a tradition kept alive in social ecologist ideas about creating a more urbane urbanism, through radically devolved democracy in human-scale communities, theorised in such works as Murray Bookchin's *From Urbanism to Cities.* Kropotkin, in particular, alongside Edward Bellamy, Herbert Spencer and Edward Carpenter, was to influence garden-city ideas, as he urged a more holistic approach to economics, calling for the 'decentralisation of industries' and regretted that 'under the pretext of division of labour, we have sharply separated the brain worker from the manual worker', an approach that had later echoes in E. F. Schumacher's ideas.[130]

This essay is largely sympathetic to the aspirations of the garden-city idealists in creating benign environmental conditions and strong design and believes that the model still has potential benefits for more sustainable living in the future. In the present day, however, the opportunities for coordinated community-based, rather than top-down developments are few. I am also cognisant of Jane Jacobs's misgivings about the garden-city's movement and her shrewd observations about the shortcomings of areas that are planned rather than evolve according to the desires of the community itself.[131] It is frequently true that successful neighbourhoods, those that are diverse and intensive, evolve and regenerate from within. In this respect older parts of cities, lived in and endlessly adapted by people's needs and desires, are the most resilient and accommodating; qualities reflected in the fact that older houses and buildings often command the highest prices.

In this respect, reclaiming urban land not used for the commonweal and retrofitting existing housing stock for sustainability will be as necessary for sustainability in the coming decades as sprouting entirely new garden suburbs and eco-villages. A grassroots present-day initiative to make communities more ecologically viable, neighbourly and socially just, is that of the Transition Towns network.[132] Again, Bristol has been a pioneer as one of the first cities to participate in the process of identifying practical community-based strategies for making localities sustainable and integrated for the coming decades, challenged by climate change and constraints upon the use of fossil fuels. As more localised

---

130 Peter Kropotkin, *Fields, Factories and Workshops Tomorrow*, ed., introduced and with additional material by Colin Ward (first pub. as book in 1899 from articles written 1888-90; London: Freedom Press, 1985), pp. 23, 169.

131 In her classic 1960s study, *The Death and Life of Great American Cities: The Failure of Town Planning* [1961] (London: Penguin, 1965).

132 See Rob Hopkins, *The Transition Handbook: From Oil Dependency to Local Resilience* (Bideford: Green Books, 2008) and the website at: http://www.transitionnetwork.org/ [accessed 3 May 2014].

economies re-emerge and the mass commute to work by private car becomes outmoded, Howard's *To-Morrow* may appear less anachronistic. Howard's legacy and impact remains controversial. When considering what might constitute socially viable and ecologically sustainable developments today, however, it would be wise to look again at its most prominent historical prototypes in the theory of Ebenezer Howard and its practical implementation by Raymond Unwin, Thomas Adams and others in the Garden-City Movement.

8

Bread or Batons?
Unemployed Workers' Struggles in
Bristol in the 1930s

•

Dave Backwith & Roger Ball

1. Unemployment, Protests and the Slump

In December 1920 there were nearly 700,000 insured[1] workers unemployed in Britain. Three months later the total had doubled and by June 1921 had trebled to 2,171,000 insured unemployed.[2] The slump of 1921-22 set the tone for the inter-war years when the average annual rate of unemployment was over 14% of the insured workforce.[3] The collapse of the post-war boom reflected Britain's decline as 'Workshop of the World'. The industries on which Britain's export trade was based suffered most. By December 1922 insured unemployment in ship building was 35.6% of the workforce and in engineering was 20.6%, while the average for all industries was 12.2%.[4] As these heavy industries were often concentrated in particular locations there were regions and towns where unemployment was far higher than the national average. In Scotland and Northern Ireland unemployment was over 20% and in the Midlands and North-East of England over 18%. Heavily dependent on ship building, unemployment in Barrow-in-Furness was 49% and in Jarrow 43% in August 1922.[5]

This uneven distribution of mass unemployment, which was further accentuated in the 1930s, had two consequences relevant to unemployed protests. One was the sharp geographical polarisation of employment patterns. In December 1932, the worst year for inter-war unemployment, the level of insured unemployment in Wales (37.2%) was nearly three times that in London (12.9%).[6] The other significant feature was the very high level of long-term (i.e. more than six months) unemployment. Thus in coal-mining, where

---

1   Insured workers were those who paid Unemployment Insurance and so qualified for Unemployment Benefits. Because not all workers were insured the actual number of unemployed was higher than these figures show.

2   C. L. Mowat, *Britain Between the Wars, 1918-1940* (London: Methuen, 1955), p. 126.

3   S. Glynn & J. Oxborrow, *Interwar Britain* (London: Allen & Unwin, 1976), pp. 144-5, Table 5:1.

4   Mowat, *Britain Between the Wars*, p. 126.

5   Ibid.

6   *The Ministry of Labour Gazette* (HMSO, January 1933), p. 15.

unemployment stood at 22.6%, over one third (36%) of out of work colliers had been unemployed for over one year in 1936.[7]

The 1930s have been described as 'The Dawn of Affluence' with improved living standards accompanying the restructuring of the British economy. Growing average incomes contributed to better health and increased life expectancy among the population.[8] Although the many social surveys of the time support this view, high levels of poverty remained. Rowntree, for instance, found that in York nearly one third of the working class were poor (as defined by a revised 'basic needs' standard) in 1935/6, with approximately half of all children in poverty.[9] Although working class poverty in York was particularly high, the average level found by such surveys was over 20%, with about one third of poverty caused by unemployment. Of the hardships associated with poverty, ill health, malnutrition, etc., it was, as ever, 'the wives of the unemployed ... who bore the brunt'.[10] Poverty was more likely to strike the longer unemployment continued as any savings were exhausted and the means test loomed.

> By the late 1930s almost four out of every five clients of the Unemployed
> Assistance Board (UAB) — who by definition had been out of work for
> at least six months were in poverty.[11]

The living standards of the unemployed were dependent on access to, and the level of unemployment benefits. Unemployment Insurance had been extended to cover 12 million workers in 1920. Up until 1931 the real value of Unemployment Insurance Benefits (UIBs) rose — by 240% for a man with a dependant wife and two children.[12] Such increases reflected the changing role of UIBs which were originally intended to supplement the resources of workers during brief spells out of work. They were not designed to support the 'undeserving', chronic unemployed. No sooner was unemployment insurance coverage extended than mass unemployment set in. When the 1920 Unemployment Insurance Act came into effect the unemployment rate was 3.7% in the insured industries, barely six months later (June 1921) it was 22.4%.[13] The persistence of high levels of unemployment undermined the insurance principle of the scheme that claimants received UIBs as a right for a limited period having previously paid contributions towards their benefits.

In the 1920s the alternative for people not entitled to UIBs had been the means tested outdoor relief of the Poor Law, something working class people were at pains to avoid. Successive governments in the 1920s were obliged to introduce Extended or Transitional Benefits to allow insured workers who had exhausted their right to UIBs to continue drawing benefits. The political

---

7   W. H. Beveridge, *Full Employment in a Free Society* (London: Allen & Unwin, 1944), p. 83, Table 15.

8   J. Stevenson & C. Cook, *The Slump: Society & Politics During the Depression* (London: Quartet, 1979), Ch. 2.

9   Ibid., pp. 33-6

10   N. Whiteside, 'The Social Consequences of Unemployment'; in, S. Glynn & A. Booth (eds.), *The Road to Full Employment* (London: Allen & Unwin, 1987), p. 19.

11   Ibid.

12   A. Booth, 'Systems of Interwar Relief', in Glynn & Booth, *The Road*, pp. 33-4.

13   Ibid.

imperative was that insured workers (often male, skilled and unionised) could not be reduced to pauperism without incurring the threat of political unrest. There were over twenty amendments to the insurance scheme to this effect in the 1920s such that,

> At any time after 1921 over half those drawing benefits would not have qualified under the 1920 Act.[14]

The consequences of this compromise were that, despite efforts to restrict their costs, UIBs became a financial burden on the state. By September 1931 the National Insurance Fund had a deficit of £116 million.[15] This became the central issue in the political crisis of 1931, the upshot of which was a 10% cut in the UIB rates, their restriction to workers who had paid 30 contributions in the previous two years, and entitlement to UIBs was limited to 26 weeks.[16] Those unemployed no longer eligible for UIBs had to apply for Transitional Payments, paid to meet needs as assessed by a Household Means Test. The means test was operated by the Public Assistance Committees (PACs) local Poor Law administrators, on the assumption that the resources of an entire household were available to support its unemployed members. Thus, say, an unemployed skilled worker might find himself having to survive on the wages of his wife, children or even the lodger. To the strictures of poverty was added the public shame of Poor Law scrutiny and familial loss of status.

An unforeseen result of the introduction of Transitional Payments was the projection of PACs as obvious targets of unemployed protest. As PACs were sub-committees of elected local authorities they were susceptible to political pressure as the unemployed still retained the right to vote. Thus in areas where the local authority was sympathetic to the unemployed, or where the unemployed made the loudest protests, scales of relief were likely to be higher and/or the means test likely to be less severely applied. In Durham and Glamorgan, for example, virtually all other household income was disregarded in means test assessments.[17]

Unemployed protests developed first among ex-servicemen frustrated that the promised 'Land fit for Heroes' did not materialize. Originally their local organisations lacked 'any clear working class policy',[18] sometimes amounting to little more than organised begging. When the recession came many of the trade union militants who had participated in the Shop Stewards Movement during WWI were shaken out of industry. To these people working class struggle was second nature and their gravitation towards the unemployed organisations was inevitable. With their organisational skills these militants also brought socialist politics to the unemployed. Simultaneously official indifference to their plight and police baton charges were awakening the ex-servicemen to the realities of class divisions in post-war Britain. As the unemployed became more receptive to

---

14   Ibid.

15   A. Deacon & J. Bradshaw, *Reserved For The Poor* (Oxford: Blackwell & Robertson, 1983), p. 15.

16   Ibid., p. 16.

17   A. Booth, 'Systems of Interwar Relief', in Glynn & Booth, *The Road*, p. 38.

18   W. Hannington, *Unemployed Struggles, 1919-1939* (London: Lawrence & Wishart, 1979 edn.), p. 13.

the Marxist ideas of the former shop stewards the impetus for the unification of the various unemployed groups grew and culminated in the creation of the National Unemployed Workers' Committee Movement (NUW(C)M, became the NUWM in 1929) in 1921.[19]

The majority of the trade union militants who, in most cases, became the branch and national leadership of the NUWM also joined the Communist Party of Great Britain (CP/CPGB) which was formed at the same time. Having a Communist leadership, the NUWM generally followed the line of CP policy but it was never merely a CP 'front'. The NUWM never received funding from the CP or from the Communist International (Comintern) and always maintained a degree of autonomy.[20] One example of this is the NUWM's refusal to curtail its advisory and representative work for unemployed claimants despite incurring the wrath of the CP and the Comintern for this 'legalism'. The burden of this work greatly increased after 1929 and the NUWM was aware that it threatened to detract from their main objective of building a revolutionary mass movement, but they also saw it as essential to keeping the support of the unemployed[21] as it, 'meant that the workers viewed the unemployed movement as an asset'.[22]

From the outset the main policies of the NUWM included the traditional labour demand for 'Work or Full Pay' and a commitment to struggle for a socialist society.[23] The organisation also adopted a detailed programme of reforms for the unemployed.[24] The intervention of socialists and Communists was sufficient to orientate the NUWM towards the official labour movement, overcoming some anger at Labour's passive response to unemployment.[25] The NUWM also employed spectacular and uncompromising forms of direct action, most famously the 'Hunger Marches'.

At first the attitude of Labour officialdom towards the NUWM was ambivalent. While the TUC refused to accept the NUWM as an affiliate they did participate in a Joint Advisory Committee (JAC) from 1924. But while the NUWM always retained some support among Labour movement activists, the leadership was always wary of the Movement's Communist links. When Labour politics moved to the right following the 1926 General Strike the NUWM, like the CP, was ostracised. In 1927 the TUC abruptly closed down the JAC and later even refused to correspond with the NUWM.[26] The NUWM also contributed to its own isolation by following the Comintern's 'Third Period' policy. This characterised reformist labour leaders and organisations as props to the capitalist system and therefore to be attacked as 'social fascists'. The CPGB and the NUWM adhered to this line from 1929 well into the 1930s[27] resulting in

---

19   R. Hayburn, 'The National Unemployed Workers' Movement, 1921-36: A Re-appraisal', in *International Review of Social History*, Vol.28 (1983): 286.

20   Ibid.

21   R. Croucher, *We Refuse to Starve in Silence* (London: Lawrence & Wishart, 1987), pp. 113-7.

22   May Berry (former Bristol NUWM member) in interview, 18 Nov 1988.

23   Stevenson & Cook, *The Slump*, p. 147.

24   Hannington, *Unemployed Struggles*, p. 44.

25   W. Hannington, *Never On Our Knees* (London: Lawrence & Wishart, 1967), p. 119.

26   Hannington, *Unemployed Struggles*, pp. 79, 92, 140, 303.

27   A. Howkins, 'Class Against Class: The Political Culture of the Communist Party of Great Britain, 1930-35' in F.

their alienation from the established labour movement at precisely the time the unemployment crisis was most acute.

Labour formed a minority government in June 1929 having given an 'unqualified pledge to deal immediately and practically with ... unemployment'.[28] At the time there were 1,164,000 insured unemployed.[29] Five months later the Wall Street Crash precipitated 'immeasurably the worst slump ever known' in the international economy.[30] The value of British exports fell by 45% in two years.[31] Unemployment leapt to 2 million in 1930 and by 1932 nearly 3.5 million people were 'on the stones'.[32] The dismal record of this second Labour Government on unemployment policy was typical of its adherence to political orthodoxy. The only significant concession to the unemployed was the relaxation of the 'genuinely seeking work' regulations. The effect of this was to make benefits easier to claim just as unemployment began to increase.

The crisis of August 1931 apparently centred on the need to cut public expenditure. In the context of Britain's long-term economic decline the fundamental political issue was capitalism's efforts to put the burden of the crisis on the working class. The editor of *The Economist* confirmed this:

> We must ... bring about as smoothly ... as possible, a general fall in wages.[33]

As unemployment grew so too did the insolvency of the National Insurance fund which, by March 1931 had a debt of £75.5 million.[34] The government-appointed 'May Committee' on public expenditure recommended cuts of £97 million, most of which was to come from unemployment insurance, principally by a 20% reduction in benefit rates.[35] For Labour this was unthinkable, but the Cabinet did consider a 10% cut in benefits. This proposal brought the government down.

To secure loans from international banks the government required all-party support for its economic measures. Both Conservative and Liberal leaders made such support conditional on the cut in benefits. At the decisive meeting on 23 August the Cabinet, irrevocably split when a large minority opposed the 10% cut, resigned. Within 24 hours the Labour Prime Minister, Ramsay MacDonald was returned to office, leading a Tory dominated 'National Government'.[36] With similar speed the vital credits from New York and Paris were granted, even before the new Cabinet had decided on any economies.[37]

Gloversmith (ed.), *Class, Culture & Social Change* (Brighton: Harvester Wheatsheaf, 1980), p. 241.

28   R. Miliband, *Parliamentary Socialism* (London: Merlin, 2nd Edn., 1972), pp. 159-61.

29   Mowat, *Britain Between the Wars*, p. 357.

30   N. Branson & M. Heinemann, *Britain in the Nineteen Thirties* (London: Panther, 1973), p. 11.

31   i.e. from £839 million in 1929 to £491 million in 1931, Mowat, *Britain Between the Wars*, p. 358.

32   C. A. Feinstein, *National Income, Expenditure & Output of the United Kingdom, 1855-1965* (Cambridge: Cambridge University Press, 1972) T 128, Table 58.

33   Branson & Heinemann, *Britain in the Nineteen Thirties*, pp. 32-33.

34   B. Gilbert, *British Social Policy, 1914-1939* (London: Batsford, 1970), pp. 162, 164.

35   R. Skidelsky, *Politicians and the Slump* (London: Macmillan, 1967), p. 345.

36   Mowat, *Britain Between the Wars*, p. 393.

37   Gilbert, *British Social Policy*, p. 175.

Much is often made of the King's (George V) role in persuading MacDonald to continue as prime minister. The purpose of this is revealed in the Liberal Sir Herbert Samuel's advice to the King:

> In view of the fact that the necessary economies would prove unpalatable to the working classes, it would be to the general interest if they could be imposed by a Labour Government ... [failing this] ... It would be preferable that Mr MacDonald should remain Prime Minister ... in a National Government.[38]

In the subsequent general election this strategy paid off handsomely. The National Government was returned with 556 seats (including 472 Tories), while Labour, divided, demoralised and not a little discredited, was reduced to only 46 MPs.[39]

Even before the election the National Government introduced the 10% reduction in UIBs. This was followed by tightened 'Anomalies' regulations which excluded 134,000 married women from claiming benefits by the end of 1931.[40] Finally, means tested Transitional Payments replaced uncovenanted benefits. In the first two months of the operation of Transitional Payments, of the more than 800,000 claims made 20% were disallowed, over 33% had payments reduced and some '440,000 claimants were made wholly or partially dependent on the people they lived with'.[41] That the National Government were able to impose this 'most resented inquisition the British working class was ever to suffer',[42] is testimony to the extent that the labour militancy of the early 1920s had been tamed. Loud as the unemployed might protest, they did so alone.

2. Bristol between the Wars

Writing in 1922, A. J. Pugsley defined diversity as the 'chief feature' of the economic development of Bristol:

> Practically every phase of industry is represented ... in Bristol ... [and, crucially] ... its economic life is not bound up with the prosperity of one or two trades as is the case of most of our large towns.[43]

Labour market statistics confirm this diversity and also reveal the employment trends in the inter-war economy.[44] As might be expected, the staple industries of the industrial revolution were all in decline in Bristol. Shipbuilding and textiles both virtually disappeared at this time. The small Bristol coalfield, long in decline, shrunk from six pits employing 1,800 men in 1910 to only one mine, Coalpit Heath, in 1939.[45] Employment in the Port of Bristol also fell. In

---

38 Miliband, *Parliamentary Socialism*, pp. 176-7.

39 Mowat, *Britain Between the Wars*, pp. 411-2, 404.

40 Branson & Heinemann, *Britain in the Nineteen Thirties*, p. 32.

41 Deacon & Bradshaw, *Reserved For The Poor*, p. 17.

42 R. Blythe, *The Age of Illusion* (London: Hamilton, 1963), p. 159.

43 Cited in R. Whitfield, *The Labour Movement in Bristol 1910-1939* (M. Litt. Thesis, University of Bristol, 1979), p. 5.

44 Ibid. p. 393; *The Ministry of Labour Gazette* (HMSO, Vol. 31 (1922)–Vol. 48 (1940)).

45 Whitfield, *The Labour Movement in Bristol*, pp. 7, 259.

the decade 1923-33 the daily employment rate of dockers dropped from 2,134 to 1,138, with a similar proportionate decline in the number of registered dockers.[46] The reasons for this were twofold; first the slump in trade, and also increasing mechanisation.[47]

In Bristol's manufacturing industries there was a division by scale of operation and degree of mechanisation and concentration. On one side there were the big, monopolistic employers such as Fry's (confectionery), Wills (tobacco) and Robinsons (printing and packaging). All of these companies, using modern mass production techniques, fared relatively well in the inter-war years. Indeed, Robinsons expanded even at the depth of the slump. These companies were also typical of the local tradition of paternalistic employers. Wills, for example, although using a high proportion of unskilled, female labour, had a reputation for paying high wages and had a policy of not dismissing workers when sales fell off.[48] The other area of large scale production was in engineering, where aircraft production came to dominate. Here, too, diversity played a part, so that in 1932 when airframe production was almost halted a night shift was being run in the aero-engine shops. By 1935 there were 8,000 Bristol Aeroplane Company workers at Filton.[49]

On the other hand production of shoes, furniture and clothing seems to have been widespread but in small units using a low level of technology. A union organiser in the furniture trade described Bristol in 1923 as being 'honeycombed with a large number of small shops'.[50] These industries produced for working class customers in South Wales and locally. The priority, therefore, was with cost rather than quality. Consequently, low pay and insecure employment were endemic. (The boot and shoe industry employed a large number of out-workers.) The depression in the South Wales coalfield badly effected these industries with closures, wage reductions and redundancies resulting.[51] Finally, there was also an increase of white collar employment in Bristol; from 11,500 workers in 1911 to 50,000 by 1931.[52]

Notwithstanding the resilience of its economy Bristol also had distinct social problems. In the summer of 1937 a survey of local living standards confirmed that,

> ... the Bristol working classes on the whole are distinctly better off than those of London, and probably of other towns.[53]

Nonetheless, Tout's survey also found that 21% of working class families were 'hard put to make a decent home' and a further 11% were in poverty. This last figure represented 11,000 families or about 40,000 people out of a population of

---

46   G. Phillips & N. Whiteside, *Casual Labour* (Oxford: Clarendon Press, 1985), pp. 178 & 215.

47   W. H. White 'Decasualisation of Dock Labour at the Port of Bristol' in *Economica* (August 1932): 358-9.

48   Whitfield, *The Labour Movement in Bristol*, pp. 260-1.

49   B. Little, *The City & County of Bristol* (London: Wernar Laurie, 1954), pp. 296-7.

50   Whitfield, *The Labour Movement in Bristol*, p. 8.

51   Ibid., pp. 9, 25.

52   Ibid., Appendix II, p. 393.

53   H. Tout, *The Standard of Living in Bristol* (London: Arrowsmith, 1938) p. 51.

452,000. Because large families are more prone to poverty approximately 20% of working class children did not have 'a fair start in life'. These findings were obtained by measuring incomes against a minimum needs standard which was harsh in that it made no allowances for sickness, holidays, furniture, tobacco, newspapers or postage, etc. The three main causes of poverty were old age (15.2%), low wages (21.3%) and, above all, unemployment (32.1%).[54]

While Tout's survey does give a revealing glimpse of working class living conditions, it is important to note that it was conducted at the peak of the recovery from the Great Depression. At the time most immediately relevant here (c. 1932) poverty must have been considerably greater. When the survey was carried out unemployment reached its lowest point of the inter-war era, a total of 11,651 insured unemployed in September 1937. At its worst point, May 1932, the equivalent figure was 27,432 and at this time the means test and anomalies regulations were in full force and benefits had been cut. As unemployment was the main cause of poverty it is likely that in 1932 not only would there have been greater numbers in poverty but that also the experience of poverty would have been more severe.

In July 1932 Bristol PAC were spurred to implement cuts in relief scales by a letter from the Ministry of Health which, referring to local wage rates, suggested that, '... there may be very little financial inducement to a man to seek independent employment ...' if relief were not cut.[55] At the time the average wage for unskilled labour in Bristol was about 47s, while unemployment relief was cut from a maximum, including full rent allowance, of 35s to 30s for a family of four. The equivalent UIB payment would have been 27s 3d plus rent allowance.[56] In August 1932 there were about 7,000 people receiving unemployment relief from Bristol PAC. It is a revealing statement on the 'political economy' of Bristol that despite this level of hardship and a revised budget for unemployment relief (increased from £35,000 to £53,000 in 1932/3), the Citizen Party (the majority party on the City Council) was able to make a 6d reduction in the rates. This brought the rates down to 12s in the pound, compared to 17s in socialist boroughs in London.[57]

Although 13,000 council houses, for some 65,000 people, were built in the inter-war period in Bristol[58] there were still concentrations of slum housing in central Bristol in the early 1930s. In 1927 a feature in *The Times* estimated that there were at least 25,000 people in Bristol living in unfit accommodation and commented that,

> Within a short distance of the central streets of Bristol dwellings may be seen which could without exaggeration, be described as hovels.[59]

Council rents could, in general, only be afforded by better off sections of the

---

54 Ibid., pp. 28, 22, 11, 19, 46.

55 *WDP*, 30 July 1932.

56 City & County of Bristol, *Council Minutes*, (hereafter CCB minutes), 23 August 1932, pp. 295-7.

57 *WDP*, 30 July 1932, 27 August 1932, 1 November 1932.

58 Little, *The City & County of Bristol*, p. 299.

59 Whitfield, *The Labour Movement in Bristol*, p. 229.

working class (e.g. skilled workers). Thus, as the new estates were populated, the 'residual' of the poorest working class families were concentrated in the central slums. This is one reason why areas such as Welsh Back and Queen's Square were the sites of frequent NUWM meetings.[60]

The Labour Party won increasing support in this period. Bristol's first Labour MPs were elected in 1923 (for Bristol North and Bristol East) and in 1929 Labour won four of the five parliamentary seats. Stafford Cripps, in Bristol East, was the only Labour candidate to win in the debacle of 1931.[61] By 1937 Labour had sufficiently recovered to hold a majority on the City Council for the first time.[62] It is interesting that in Bristol East, the safest Labour seat in the city, the Labour Party was well to the left of the Bristol Labour movement generally. Certainly Bristol East was much the readier to support the NUWM in 1932 although even this was guarded. Perhaps because of the relative prominence of an organised Left in Bristol, in the form of the Independent Labour Party (ILP), the CP seems to have been fairly weak in Bristol in the 1920s.[63]

Possibly because social inequalities are more apparent in a prosperous city Bristol seems to have had a turbulent history of unemployed protest. After WWI these were led by various ex-servicemen's organisations whose politics were fairly reactionary. This was demonstrated in April 1920 when the International Union of Ex-Servicemen demanded that the Bristol Tramways Company dismiss all their female labour within a week. To enforce their demand the unemployed attacked the Company offices, burnt tramcars and assaulted conductresses. This earned them the condemnation of the women's trade union but persuaded the Company to concede. As unemployment among trade unionists grew things began to change. Another wave of protest came in September 1921; this time the target was the Board of Guardians, who felt obliged to raise the relief scales. On this occasion the leadership appears to have been in the hands of unemployed militants, mostly engineers, including a W. Hayman, probably the founder of the Bristol CP branch in 1922. These later demonstrations were large, angry events of thousands of unemployed workers, who were subjected to several police baton charges.[64]

The development of an NUWM branch in Bristol at this stage seems to have been pre-empted by the intervention of the official Labour movement. W. H. Ayles (a Labour councillor) and E. H. Parker (full-time secretary of Bristol Trades and Labour Council) led the unemployed deputation received by the City Council on 13 September 1921. Perhaps because they had access to the authorities, Parker and Ayles were able to direct the protests along more moderate lines. This was not an easy process as they were both subjected to bitter criticisms at a conference of the unemployed called by the Trades Council that October. Despite this Parker was able to set up the Bristol Unemployed

---

60   Bill Nicholas (ILP and later CP member), interview 24 November 1988.

61   F. W. S. Craig, *British Parliamentary Election Results, 1918-1939* (London: Macmillan, Revised edition, 1977), pp. 98-102.

62   Whitfield, *The Labour Movement in Bristol*, p. 340.

63   Ibid.

64   Ibid., pp. 216-22; *WDP*, 1-14 September 1921; Hannington, *Unemployed Struggles*, pp. 34-5.

Committee (later the Bristol Unemployed Association — BUA) as an affiliate of the Trades Council.[65] As unemployed protest subsided in the later 1920s the BUA emerged as a substantial organisation. Its main function was to maintain contact between the unemployed and the unions. Between 1927 and 1932 at least 700 BUA members were passed on to local union branches on finding employment. By 1927 the BUA had four area-based branches and two womens' branches. The following year the TUC commended the BUA as a model for organising the unemployed.[66]

A non-political organisation like the BUA was ill-suited to the upheavals of 1931-32. In May 1931 the Trades Council severed its links with the BUA and Parker was replaced as secretary by F. Berriman, a prominent local ILP member.[67] It may be that, under pressure from the NUWM, the BUA was moving to the left at this stage. However, relations between the BUA and NUWM were not good. Berriman denounced the NUWM's lobby of the 1931 TUC as a 'Communist stunt'.[68] While in May 1931, G. Cocking (Bristol NUWM) reassured the NUWM's National Administrative Council (NAC) that the 'scab organisation ... exists today in name only'.[69]

When precisely the NUWM first established a presence in Bristol is not clear but it was probably not before the late 1920s.[70] Jack Potter (Bristol CP member), who participated in the unemployed protests in Bristol of the early 1920s, was very clear that the NUWM were not involved.[71] However in the summer of 1931 the Bristol NUWM was gathering momentum having set up new branches in Bristol East and Bristol Central.[72] On 7 September 1931, 150 unemployed Welsh marchers arrived in Bristol to lobby the TUC, in session at the Victoria Rooms in Clifton. This led to the first serious clashes between the NUWM and the Bristol police. As the Hunger marchers were leaving from an evening meeting at the Haymarket (Horsefair) the police baton charged them, 'knocking down men and women at the bottom of Union Street'.[73] Will Paynter, (leading South Wales Communist and future General Secretary of the National Union of Mineworkers), was among the eight protesters arrested and fined. Two days later the Welsh Hunger marchers and their supporters made their way to the Victoria Rooms to press for a deputation to be heard at the congress:

> A powerful police cordon was drawn up to prevent them from reaching
> their objective, but a small deputation of six...were permitted to go

---

65 Whitfield, *The Labour Movement in Bristol*, pp. 223-9.

66 D. Large & R. Whitfield, *The Bristol Trades Council 1873-1973* (Bristol: Bristol Historical Association, 1973), pp. 23-5.

67 Whitfield, *The Labour Movement in Bristol*, pp. 321-2.

68 Ibid., p. 322. The animosity between the two organisations (BUA and NUWM) reflected the general hostility between the Communist Party and the more reformist labour movement which developed after the defeat of the 1926 General Strike.

69 NUWM National Administrative Council Report (NAC) 7-8 May 1932.

70 Croucher, *We Refuse to Starve in Silence*, pp. 200-21, cites Whitfield, *The Labour Movement in Bristol*, as source for references to Bristol NUWM in 1923-24. This is incorrect. Whitfield's (p. 332) first mention of the Bristol NUWM is at the 1931 TUC.

71 Jack Potter, (unemployed ex-serviceman early 1920s later CP member), interviewed 25 November 1988.

72 NAC 11-12 July 1931.

73 International Labour Defence (Bristol) (ILD), *Bread or Batons?* (1932), p. 4.

through the cordon. When we reached the entrance to the congress hall we found our way barred by another force of police and hefty stewards. An altercation arose, and although there were only six of us we attempted to force an entry; a fierce fight took place at the top of the high steps, whilst the main body of marchers, 300 yards away, were being held back and threatened by the main police cordon. Our small deputation were finally overpowered by police and stewards.[74]

Among those injured was Wal Hannington (the author of the above excerpt) who claimed that 20,000 Bristol workers turned out to prevent a second baton charge on the NUWM that same night.[75] This show of working class solidarity won the leadership of the Bristol unemployed for the NUWM.

Figure 1. Western Daily Press February 10th 1932. "Police in conflict — A striking picture of the scene in Old Market Street, Bristol yesterday when the conflict between police and unemployed was at its height. Banners similar to that on the right were broken up and used as missiles"

3. Bread or Batons in Bristol: 1931-32

On 29th January 1932, with 26,561 registered unemployed in Bristol,[76] the PAC

---

74 Hannington, *Unemployed Struggles*, pp. 219-20.

75 Hannington, *Never On Our Knees*, pp. 235-6; Hannington, *Unemployed Struggles*, p. 220; W. Paynter, *My Generation* (London: Allen & Unwin, 1972), pp. 86-7; *WDP*, 8, 10, 11 September 1931.

76 *WDP*, 7 January 1932.

decided to reduce unemployment relief scales by about 10%. The reasons given for this were that relief scales were too high in relation to both wages and UIBs. A more compelling reason might have been the upsurge in relief applications since the introduction of Transitional Payments. In October 1931 2,235 persons were receiving unemployment relief from the Bristol PAC, three months later this had increased to 7,230 people. The reductions announced were to become effective in March.[77] This sharp increase in the number of people on means tested relief, the cuts in benefits and the arrival of the NUWM as the militant leadership of the Bristol unemployed combined in a potentially explosive mixture. All that was needed was the spark of police repression to set Bristol alight. This is precisely what happened.

Tuesday 9th February 1932: 'We Want Power Not Pancakes!'[78]

Disregarding the prior refusal of the Mayor to receive a deputation, within ten days of the cuts being announced, the NUWM led 2,000-3,000 unemployed protesters to lobby the Council which was in session on the afternoon of Shrove Tuesday, 1932. The violence that followed is described by various sources, including newspapers, eye witness accounts and the Chief Constable in a letter to the Home Office.[79] The police had apparently agreed to allow the NUWM to march on a route dictated by them, but not to approach the Council House (then in Corn Street), though it is unclear where they expected the march to terminate.

The events began with a mass meeting called by the NUWM at the Haymarket (Horsefair) at 2.00pm where according to local journalists,

> One speaker threatened that if there was another Imperialist War it might be followed by one in which the workers would take part and we should have a civil war.[80]

One protester remembered,

> We formed up four abreast, police escort. Back on the roof of Bridewell Police station, which was within sight, they had binoculars and telescopes on us to see that we formed up in an orderly procession, police either side of us…some of us had banners … and we set out.[81]

The unemployed then marched, 'singing popular wartime songs', to Old Market Street where they were 'met by men from other parts of the city', swelling the crowd to several thousand.[82] Awaiting the protesters was a cordon of policemen blocking access to Castle Street the route to the Council House (see *Figure 1*). As the procession approached the line 'policemen attempted to divert

77   *WDP*, 30 January 1932.

78   Written on a placard on the march. Interview with Bill Curtis 11 November 1998. British Library Shelf Mark C900/00510 http://sounds.bl.uk/Accents-and-dialects/Millenium-memory-bank/021M-C0900X00510X-2600V1.

79   BRO, File 34908(46)D Letter, 10 February 1932, Chief Constable to Home Office.

80   *BEW*, 9 February 1932.

81   Interview with Bill Curtis 11/11/1998. British Library Shelf Mark C900/00510 http://sounds.bl.uk/Accents-and-dialects/Millenium-memory-bank/021M-C0900X00510X-2600V1.

82   *WDP*, 10 February 1932.

the marchers down Carey's Lane'[83] (a side street) away from their intended destination. This inflamed the demonstrators and,

> Policemen were jostled and bustled and eventually the order was given [by the Chief Constable] for them to draw batons and charge the demonstrators. In the general melee that followed, banners and placards were broken and the pieces and poles were used by the unemployed against the police.[84]

As the hand-to-hand fighting intensified, 'women in the procession cheered the marchers on … trams and motorcars were held up and thousands of people blocked the streets'. It was estimated that 4,000 people were present at the height of the disturbance.[85] The Chief Constable quickly deployed mounted police and reinforcements from nearby vans, who proceeded to charge the crowds, breaking up the procession. An unemployed man from St. Philips recounted the police attack,

> The police on mounted horses and the other police with batons, charged us and drove us back into Old Market Street. Oh yes people got hurt, people who weren't even in the scuffle. I can remember … a little lady there, there was a man and a woman there, they was clubbed down. They said they had just come from the pictures. And they had nothing to do with it. Well of course the police didn't know who they were. I know what I done. I run across Old Market street and jumped on a tram, got on top of a tram so that the copper couldn't follow on horseback. Cause he was chasing them and hitting them as he was going. To break up the demonstration.[86]

One policeman and several demonstrators (including leaders of the NUWM) were seriously injured though, conspicuously, there were no arrests.

After the melee in Old Market Street, the police attempted to stop the scattered procession from recombining by keeping the crowds on the move. However, later in the afternoon 700-800 protesters, shadowed by large numbers of foot and mounted police, managed to meet at the Horsefair (the Haymarket park) where speeches were delivered by NUWM leaders. One journalist commented,

> At the close of the meeting the men, among whom it was apparent feeling was running high, crowded behind the park railings booing and hurling comments at the police who lined the surrounding streets.[87]

At this point a motorcar burst into flames and the arriving fire brigade were jeered by the crowd. According to local journalists some of the demonstrators used this diversion to hurl stones and assault the police encircling them. A hundred reinforcements rushed from central police station less than 150 metres

83   Ibid.
84   Ibid.
85   *BEW*, 9 February 1932.
86   Bristol Central Reference Library Oral History Transcriptions R005 p. 6.
87   *WDP*, 10 February 1932.

away at Bridewell and set about dispersing the crowd by force. During the 'disorder' the police (finally) made two arrests, which led to a stormy court case the following morning as protesters were ejected from the public gallery. Both men were sentenced to two weeks in prison for disorderly conduct and assaulting police officers.[88] The judge remarked, 'It is impossible for us to allow mob law to become the condition of the day',[89] though for the thousands that participated on the demonstration the police had certainly executed 'mob law' to brutal effect.

Figure 2. Bristol Guardian & Gazette, 27th February 1932. "Bristol police preparing for the baton charge during the disturbance on Old Market, Bristol. Some of the officers already have their batons drawn."

Tuesday 23rd February 1932: Old Market Riot

Two weeks later a similar sequence of events occurred, this time attitudes seemed to have hardened and the fighting more prolonged and bitter. On this occasion the Chief Constable refused permission for the NUWM to march on the grounds that they had 'broken faith' with him a fortnight earlier and because disorder was likely to ensue if they did march. Undeterred, the NUWM marched anyway, meeting once again at the Haymarket (Horsefair) where,

> Fiery speeches were delivered to an enormous crowd of men, who finally banded together and marched off with a red banner waving at their head.[90]

Via a winding route, the procession headed towards Old Market Street, the scene of the previous confrontation and the route to the Council House where

---

88   BRO, File 34908(46)D Letter 10 February 1932, *WDP*, 10 February 1932 & 11 February 1932, *BEW*, 9 February 1932 & 10 February 1932.

89   *BEW*, 10 February 1932, *WDP*, 11 February 1932.

90   *WDP*, 24 February 1932.

the NUWM deputation hoped to gain an audience.[91] According to one local journalist, some demonstrators armed themselves with half bricks from a passing lorry on Milk Street.[92] The crowds swelled as they marched, until thousands of protesters (including 'many women carrying red flags') arrived in Old Market Street (see *Figures 2* and *4*).[93] Another local journalist stated,

> At the unemployed headquarters at Shepherds Hall, over which continually floats the Red flag, a posse of police barred the way. For a time the crowd halted, but eventually, urged on from the back, it advanced again, and the police drew batons in readiness. Immediately came a shower of missiles, half-bricks, coke, gas-piping and iron bars, all of which had been collected by the procession on route. Immediately the police charged and in a moment the demonstrators were scattering in all directions, those who stood their ground being speedily dealt with. Again and again the police swept through their ranks and two ambulances were soon busy carrying casualties to the Infirmary.[94]

Many eye-witness accounts of the 'flashpoint' in Old Market contradict this press version and put the responsibility for the violence with the police. Bill Nicholas (then a member of the Labour League of Youth) saw the marchers enter Old Market Street and the police form a double cordon across the street. Then,

> The first rank stopped then ... they tried to push them [the marchers] back but it was so big that the people behind didn't know what was going on, and the pressure and pressure — and what they did, they [the police] pushed them back. And then, suddenly, there was a row behind them, and the ones that were pushing them back parted and the row behind came in with batons and beat them down.[95]

Another participant, Bill Curtis, remembered that Chief Constable Maby was present on a horse, directing affairs and had organised an 'ambush' well in advance:

> To the right hand side as we faced Castle Street...in the annex to the Empire Theatre...he [the Chief Constable] had two more motor coach loads of police there in reserve ... hiding in the annex and the theory was if they came out from the annex and took the first dozen rows from behind they'd have the ring leaders and the all the march would break up into disorder ... which he wasn't very far wrong...these other police piled out from the annex and took us from behind...and of course right away a punch up started, people was getting whacked with the batons ... we was getting a right licking.

---

91 The route of the march was from the Horsefair, via Milk Street, Leek Lane, Rosemary Street, Wellington Street, West Street, Waterloo Street and Midland Road to Old Market Street, *WDP*, 24 February 1932.

92 Ibid.

93 Estimates of the numbers of demonstrators vary with the *WDP* stating 3,000 (24 February 1932), the *Bristol Guardian and Gazette* 10,000 (27 February 1932) and the NUWM 15,000 (Hannington, *Unemployed Struggles*, p. 230).

94 *South Gloucester Gazette*, 27 February 1932 .

95 Bill Nicholas, interview 24 November 1988.

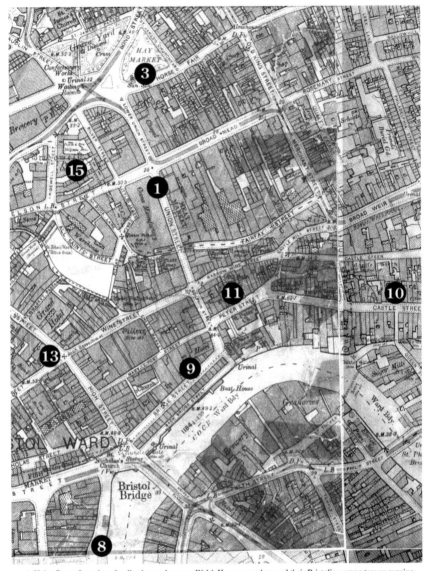

1. Union Street: Location of police baton charge on Welsh Hunger marchers and their Bristolian supporters on evening of September 7th 1931.
2. Old Market Street/Carey's Lane: Site of police cordon diverting NUWM from marching to the Council House on February 9th 1932. Followed by police baton chage.
3. The Haymarket: Known these days as the Horsefair this park was a regular assembly point for NUWM marches. Scene of disturbance on the evening of February 9th 1932.
4. Castle Street/Old Market Street: Site of the police cordon and flashpoint on NUWM demonstration February 23rd 1932.
5. Empire Cinema, Carey's Lane: Ambush from behind on NUWM marchers by police secreted in the annex on February 23rd 1932.
6. Old Market Street: Police baton charge on NUWM marchers on afternoon of February 23rd 1932 immortalised in the photograph on the front cover of this book.
7. Lawfords Gate: Centre of serious 'rioting' on afternoon of February 23rd 1932 which spread into St. Judes and St. Phillips.

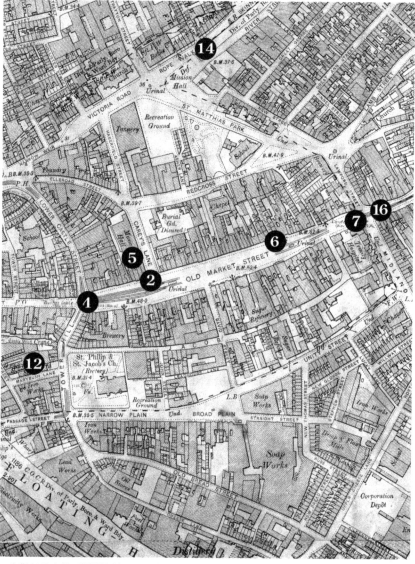

8. Welsh Back: The NUWM held many evening rallies here including February 23rd 1932.

9. Bridge Street: Stampede by hundreds of Bristolians supporting the NUWM marchers on evening of February 23rd 1932.

10. Castle Street: Major shopping street, scene of disturbance on the evening of February 23rd 1932 and location of the police ambush on east Bristol NUWM demonstrators returning home on the night of June 9th 1932 (79 injured).

11. Peter Street: Site of the Public Assistance Committee Office, scene of many NUWM pickets and demonstrations.

12. Marybush Lane: The NUWM held their weekly meetings in the School Room.

13. Corn Street: Location of the City Council building.

14. The Ropewalk: Common meeting point for NUWM demonstrations.

15. Central Police Station, Bridewell.

16. West Street: The NUWM office was at No. 78.

Figure 4. Western Daily Press 24th February 1932. 'A graphic picture of the encounter between Bristol police and unemployed in Old Market. It clearly shows the line of police, with drawn batons, parting the crowd and pressing them

Danny Price, a member of the ILP Guild of Youth, was on the demonstration with a visiting student from Hamburg. To the student the police violence was such that he identified it with the methods of the Nazi Brown Shirts.[96] However, despite the violence initially unleashed by the Constabulary on the front ranks of the procession, many of the marchers were unbowed. As the protesters were driven up Old Market Street by the police 'some of the crowds dispersed down the side-streets … come back with half-bricks and nuts and bolts from scrap yards and pelted the police' whilst others raided the fruit and vegetable stalls and carts lining the street; 'they were stripped … they was throwing cabbages and potatoes and anything they … [could get their hands on at the police]'.[97]

As the crowds were driven towards the junction of Lawford Street, West Street and Midland Road, the marchers raided coal wagons and flung the contents at their pursuers; 'the bags were tipped and lumps of coal were flying across the road at the police … it was a right old set to'.[98] Baton charge after baton charge was met with a hail of missiles whilst six mounted police tried to take control of West Street.[99] The battle continued for an hour and a half and appears to have spread to neighbouring areas as 'the entire of St. Judes and St. Philips districts were finally combed out by the police and all groups dispersed'.[100] Rumours spread around the city of numerous casualties, (at least thirty people had been injured during the first police assault), and that a woman had been killed by the police. There were once again, and tellingly, no arrests.

Despite the efforts of the police, a NUWM deputation of three people finally reached the Council House, only to be turned away by a further cordon of fifty police officers.[101] In a rather pathetic gesture the Councillors decided to 'defer the reception of a deputation until the next meeting in March'.[102] The NUWM were neither deterred by the police attempts to violently drive them off the streets of Bristol nor the supposed conciliation offered by the Councillors. They called a mass meeting on the same evening in Welsh Back whilst 'thousands of people gathered across Bristol Bridge, along Baldwin Street and Bridge Street'. Huge numbers of police failed to disperse the crowds who waited expectantly for the demonstrators to make their move and at 10.00pm,

> The meeting finished with cries of 'Are we downhearted?' — 'No' and the singing of the 'Red Flag'[103]

The protesters then moved off *en bloc* along Bridge Street followed by the police who were booed and jeered at by the gathered crowds who were blocking

---

96   Danny Price, interview 20 December 1988.
97   Interview with Bill Curtis 11 November 1998. British Library Shelf Mark C900/00510 http://sounds.bl.uk/Accents-and-dialects/Millenium-memory-bank/021M-C0900X00510X-2600V1.
98   Ibid.
99   *WDP*, 24 February 1932.
100 Ibid.
101 Ibid.
102 Ibid.
103 Ibid.

the roads. As arguments broke out between the police and groups of onlookers a stampede began. Hundreds of people charged along Bridge Street towards Peter Street and Castle Street, breaking shop windows and wrecking and molesting motor cars caught in the traffic. Police vehicular reinforcements were rushed to the scene to disperse the crowds, though this time, without baton charges. Once again there were no arrests.

Figure 5. Police baton charge unemployed workers' march on Old Market Street, February 23rd 1932.

Following the events of February 23rd, Chief Constable Maby gave a press conference, (which appears not to have happened after earlier incidents), and displayed a selection of the 'murderous weapons' used by the unemployed for the uncritical eyes of local journalists (see *Figure 6*). Given the weapons the police claimed they were attacked with, it seems fortunate that none of them were killed. Maby also played down the size of the police operation, suggesting that the Constabulary felt the need to justify their actions. He (laughably) claimed 'not more than 50 police were engaged in dispersing demonstrators', while the *Bristol Evening World* reported that 'nearly 300 police took part'.[104]

The Aftermath

If the police intended to intimidate the unemployed with violence then they clearly failed. A CID report of the 20 February 1932 records that in three weeks

---

104 *WDP*, 25 February 1932; *BEW*, 24 February 1932.

the average attendance at the Tuesday NUWM meetings, (in the School Room, Marybush Lane, near Castle Park), had increased from 200 to between 350 and 400. Average attendance at BUA meetings was 200, which was doubled when the NUWM turned up at open meetings on Thursdays. Letters to the police asking permission to hold street activities (meetings, marches, collections, etc.) suggest there were at least four NUWM branches in Bristol in early 1932.[105] At this stage the Bristol NUWM was apparently thriving.

Despite heavy rain 'a procession of more than 5,000 unemployed demonstrators', with a large police escort, again made for the Council House on 8 March.[106] The Council now saw fit to grant a hearing to deputations from the NUWM, the BUA and the National Federation of Building Trades Operatives.[107] Charlie Webber argued the case for the NUWM, calling for a programme of public works for slum clearance and the building of 5,000 homes for cheap rental.[108] In typical style Webber also told the Council that,

> ... on the hands of every member of this council is the blood of the men and women battered down in Old Market Street, and you can only wash it off by refusing to operate these vicious cuts in the scale of relief.[109]

Figure 6. Bristol Guardian & Gazette. 27th February 1932. "Weighty Evidence! — A selection of the weapons taken by police from the rioters in Old Market, Bristol, on Tuesday. The Chief Constable had a collection in his room at Central Police Station."

Unmoved the Council threw out a Labour Party motion calling for an inquiry into the operation of the means test and the suspension of the pending cuts in relief scales.[110]

The demonstration on 8 March and another on 13 April 1932 appear to have passed without serious trouble. However, following four arrests on the later march the first of several major trials of local NUWM members was held on 20th April. Alongside those facing public order charges were five NUWM leaders with thirteen summonses against them for 'disorderly conduct by statements made when addressing various meetings'. All of the accused denied the charges but were found

---

105 BRO, File 34908(46)D Letter 10 February 1932, *WDP*, 10 February 1932 & 11 February 1932, *BEW*, 9 February 1932 & 10 February 1932.

106 *BEW*, 9 March 1932.

107 In December 1931 the Council had reduced its target of building 1,500 homes in 1932 by one third. *WDP*, 8 December 1931.

108 CCB minutes, 8 March 1932, p. 146.

109 *WDP*, 9 March 1932 (These remarks are not recorded in the Council minutes).

110 CCB minutes, 8 March 1932, p. 154.

guilty and either bound over or fined.[111] Similar charges were later to be brought against local NUWM leaders with telling effect.

That the activities of the police probably helped the NUWM win wider support is shown by a conference held on 17 May 1932 to launch united front action in defence of the unemployed. Participating with the NUWM and the CP was the Cooperative Women's Guild, the ILP Guild of Youth and a number of trade union branches. The conference agreed to campaign for a Town's Meeting by presenting a petition demanding higher relief etc., to the Mayor after a demonstration on 5 July. 13,000 signatures were collected and 5,000-10,000 strong demonstration, including 2,000 striking building workers, delivered the petition to the Council House.[112] The support of the Trades and Labour Council was noticeably lacking. Although, also in May, the Trades Council officers did meet the Lord Mayor to ask him to reopen his Christmas Dinner Fund as 'unemployment was still great'.[113]

Although the call for a Town's Meeting was refused, the unremitting pressure the NUWM was bringing to bear on the local authorities was having an effect. Demonstrations and pickets of the Council and PAC offices were frequent events. Twice more, in April and May 1932, the PAC postponed the implementation of the cuts in relief originally agreed in December 1931.[114]

Thursday 9th June 1932: Police Ambush

To maintain this pressure more protests were held on June 9th. These began with a mass meeting of 2,000 unemployed at the Ropewalk.[115] This meeting was followed by a march to the nearby PAC in Peter Street,[116] where a deputation was refused entrance. An evening rally was then held in Welsh Back.

At about 10.00p.m. when the meeting ended those protesters who lived in east Bristol made their way home singing songs and carrying their banners and placards. A crowd of 600-700 people were half-way along Castle Street when they were suddenly attacked by baton wielding police and then scattered by charges of a mounted squadron. As the fighting erupted the audience of the Regent Cinema emptied out of the theatre straight into the melee. A description of the scene given by one of the (presumably respectable) film-goers speaks of the police action as being unprovoked and recklessly violent. The *Evening Post* stated,

> ... the street looked like a battlefield. Men lay prone in every direction and blood ran on the pavements.

Seventy people were reported to be injured, twenty-nine of them seriously. No

---

111 *WDP*, 21 April 1932.

112 Whitfield, *The Labour Movement in Bristol*, p. 325; NAC Report, 17-18 September 1932; International Labour Defence (Bristol) (ILD), *Bread or Batons?* (1932), p. 17.

113 *WDP*, 12 May 1932.

114 *WDP*, 30 April 1932, 28 May 1932.

115 Now the site of Champion Square adjacent to Cabot Circus. A nearby block of flats is named 'Ropewalk House'.

116 Peter Street, since demolished, was situated on the current Castle Park.

policemen were injured and there were no arrests.[117]

This premeditated 'ambush' united the Bristol Labour movement in protest against the policing of the unemployed demonstrations. Condemnation of the police by the Labour group caused pandemonium at the Council meeting on 14th June.[118] Later in the month a special Council meeting was held to discuss Labour's call for a public inquiry, although this motion was defeated in favour of an amendment expressing confidence in the police. The Trades Council also took up the demand for an independent inquiry.[119] Support for the NUWM was less than wholehearted, however. *Bristol Labour Weekly*, for instance, felt that 'it would have been far better for the police to have made arrests' than to bludgeon the unemployed!'[120]

Show Trials

Arising out of the Castle Street ambush was the most important trial of Bristol NUWM leaders. Summonsed to appear on 17 June, Ernest Parker, Archibald Bailey and Charlie Webber were all accused of incitement to assault the police by remarks made in various at meetings from 9 to 12 June. Other than this trial there are no references to Bailey's role in the NUWM. But, (with Bill Fairman), Parker and Webber were the most prominent local leaders. Parker had been prominent in the earlier trial in April wearing his WWI medals in court. When the case came to full trial on 27 June, in the dock were at least two key figures in the Bristol NUWM.[121]

At both hearings the court was heavily guarded by police and the NUWM staged large protest demonstrations outside.[122] Ignoring this, the prosecution emphasised that the proceedings 'had no political significance whatever'.[123] As the accused made clear when conducting their defence the NUWM did not share this view. Charlie Webber explained their assessment of the significance of the case in his closing speech:

> The police had deliberately planned to murderously attack the unemployed on the night of June 9th ... The whole city is indignant because it is obvious to all that the baton charge was unprovoked... So the police have launched their prosecutions in an attempt to justify their diabolical work, and try to put the responsibility for their attack on the backs of the NUWM and members of the Communist Party.[124]

Webber convincingly denied the more inflammatory remarks attributed to him and pointed out that the theme of his statements was the unemployed

---

117 *WDP*, 10 June 1932; *BEP*, 10 June 1932, ILD *Bread or Batons?*, pp. 5, 6.

118 *WDP*, 15 June 1932.

119 *BEP*, 29 June 1932.

120 Quoted in ILD, *Bread or Batons?*, p. 8.

121 *WDP*, 21 April 1932, 18 June 1932, 28 June 1932.

122 *BEP*, 17 June 1932; *BEW*, 27 & 28 June 1932.

123 *WDP*, 28 June 1932.

124 ILD, *Bread or Batons?*, p. 15.

workers organising to defend themselves against police brutality.[125]

The judge preferred the non-political line, telling the jury to disregard allegations of police violence. In response to Parker's claim that when getting up after being hit by the police people were struck a second time, the judge merely observed, 'It appears the police did not strike hard enough the first time'.[126] All three accused were found guilty and despite the jury recommending leniency, Webber and Bailey were given six months imprisonment and Parker twelve months.[127] These sentences were far more severe than any previously given to Bristol NUWM members.

The NUWM in Bristol

Although the Bristol NUWM continued to lead mass demonstrations, June 1932 does mark a turning point, certainly in their relations with the police. This is a useful moment to consider some aspects of the NUWM's organisation in Bristol. As mentioned previously, they had at least four branches in the area as well as a District Council and one, possibly two, women's sections.[128] There is no precise evidence of the NUWM membership figures, though they had weekly meetings in a room with a capacity of 400 people. In February 1932 their support was such that they were having overflow meetings in the lane outside.[129] At the May 1932 NAC meeting the militancy of women on NUWM demonstrations in Bristol was noted but the Bristol comrades were rebuked for not drawing the women into the movement. The new branch in Avonmouth, where four women were on the executive committee, was an exception to this. Later in the year successful work among women on a housing estate in Kingswood was executed.[130] The NUWM does not appear to have attracted many black members although one of their youngest activists, T. H. 'Darkie' Lawrence, aged 17, was black.[131]

The Bristol NUWM was closely tied to the local CP branch. Virtually all the 20-30 CP members in Bristol were then unemployed.[132] Bill Fairman was, according to Angela Tuckett (a Bristol CP member), secretary of both the local NUWM and CP branches and Gilbert Hitchings, the CP Chairman, became more prominent in NUWM activities in the autumn of 1932.[133] I have been informed, by his son, that Charlie Webber also held the offices that Fairman occupied.[134] The general impression is that most of the activists who shouldered the burden of organising the Bristol NUWM were communists.

On the other hand, the Bristol leaders do not fit the stereotype NUWM

---

125 Ibid., pp. 7,8,13, 14; *WDP*, 19 June 1932.

126 ILD, *Bread or Batons?*, p. 15.

127 *WDP*, 28 June 1932.

128 NAC reports, 11-12 July 1931, 3-4 October 1931, 7-8 May 1932, 17-18 September 1932.

129 BRO, File 34908(46) D, letter from Chief Constable to Town Clerk, 26 February 1932.

130 NAC reports 7-8 May 1932, 17-18 September 1932.

131 *WDP*, 30 August 1932.

132 Harry Pollitt, Letter to Angela Tuckett, 15 January 1956; Angela Tuckett interview, 20 December 1988.

133 Angela Tuckett, *Angela's Anecdotage unpublished memoirs*, pp. 38-9.

134 Ray Webber in conversation June 1988.

activist of unemployed skilled workers and shop stewards. Hitchings was an engineer but Webber was a warehouseman, and Parker and Bailey were labourers.[135] Len Berry (CP member) was sure that the local leaders had not had much experience as trade union organisers before joining the NUWM.[136] Another significant feature is the close proximity of Bristol to South Wales, one of the NUWM's strongest areas in the 1930s. As well as benefiting from the visits of South Wales Hunger Marchers, Bristol also received frequent visits from leading Welsh Communists such as Lewis Jones, an unemployed Rhondda miner with national standing in the NUWM. In the CP organisational structure, Bristol was then in the same regional unit as South Wales.[137]

As the protests, violence and arrests continued, the NUWM was gaining increasing support from the official labour movement. There were two sides to this response. One was that labour representatives were obliged to be more vocal in their support for the unemployed. Thus, on several occasions in 1932, particularly after the Castle Street incident in June, normally respectful Labour members caused angry scenes in the Council Chamber. The Labour group also forced three special Council meetings (in June, August and September) on issues related to the unemployed.[138] Also, after a long debate in the Bristol Labour Party, Labour members of the PAC staged a boycott when it was finally decided to implement the cuts in unemployment relief on 29 July 1932.[139]

The Bristol Labour movement was also drawn into cautious cooperation with the NUWM. Bristol East Labour Party had led the way (as they had with the boycott of the PAC)[140] holding at least two public meetings with NUWM speakers protesting against the police tactics in Old Market in February.[141] After 9 June the wider labour movement began to follow suit. The fragile unity reached its height on Saturday 10 September when the Trades and Labour Council, the BUA and NUWM organised a joint demonstration against the means test and the cuts in benefits. Some 5,000 people marched in separate contingents from each of the Bristol constituencies to Queen Square. The limits to this unity were shown by the NUWM speakers, Fairman and Hitchings, who felt compelled to verbally attack the Labour Party.[142]

A similar ambivalence is apparent in the NUWM's attitude to the BUA. More than once they denounced it as a scab organisation whose leaders represented nobody but themselves.[143] Likewise when the BUA hosted a conference to found a National Federation of Unemployed Associations the intervention of the NUWM came close to wrecking the Council.[144] On other

135 *WDP*, 28 June 1932.

136 Len Berry, interview, 18 November 1988.

137 Tuckett, *Angela's Anecdotage unpublished memoirs*, pp. 39, 42, interview, 20 December 1988; Len Berry, interview, 18 November 1988.

138 *WDP*, 29 June 1932; *BEP*, 23 & 24 August 1932; *WDP*, 28 September 1932.

139 *WDP*, 30 July 1932; Whitfield, *The Labour Movement in Bristol*, pp. 329-32.

140 Ibid., p. 329.

141 BRO file 34908(46) D, reports of meetings on 27 February 1932 & 2 March 1932.

142 Whitfield, *The Labour Movement in Bristol*, p. 326; *WDP*, 12 September 1932.

143 *WDP*, 9 March 1932.

144 *WDP*, 15 February 1932.

occasions the NUWM and BUA lobbied the same authorities on the same day, which suggests a degree of cooperation. But, again, at other times, the two organisations refused to associate with each other; on the 28 October 1932, for instance, when the PAC would only agree to see a joint deputation.[145]

The activities of the Bristol NUWM reached their climax in the autumn of 1932. The area reports at the September NAC show that activity in Bristol more than equalled that in any other area in August and early September.[146] However, with the approach of the National Hunger March against the Means Test there are indications that NUWM activity in Bristol was tailing off. Police reports on the NUWM's preparations to receive the South Wales contingent of the March (which arrived in Bristol on 16 October 1932) show their meetings were significantly smaller than they had been earlier in the year. For example, two days before the marchers arrived only about 150 people attended a meeting at Welsh Back, the next evening only 60 were present. Confirmation that all was not well can be found in the speeches of NUWM organisers. Chairing a meeting at Barton Hill on 7 October 'Farmer' (possibly Fairman) is reported to have said,

> Well comrades, no doubt you have been wondering what is wrong with the NUWM. Well things have been going back and we have not been having your support.[147]

References to small turnouts and the apathy of the rank-and-file were made at other meetings by Fairman and Cocking. (Cocking was to lead the 32 strong Bristol contingent on the 1932 Hunger March).[148] This picture of decline is supported by the scant press coverage given to the passage of the Hunger March through Bristol.[149] Although this can partly be explained by there being no clashes with the police.

When interviewed, former NUWM or CP members have consistently said that the effect of police repression was to increase the support of the Bristol working class for the NUWM. However, it seems that while this was the case to begin with, as time went on the toll of arrests began to tell on the NUWM. The apparent decline in late 1932 cannot, for instance, be attributed to falling unemployment. In December 1932 there remained nearly 25,000 insured unemployed in Bristol, only a marginal decline on the highest level of 27,500 in May. A year later, in December 1933, there were still over 24,000 unemployed in Bristol.[150]

After the imprisonment of Webber, Parker and Bailey there were three more trials which resulted in NUWM members being gaoled in 1932. That August eight NUWM supporters were charged with public order offences after incidents at the Council House on 24 August. All were convicted and three were sent to

---

145 *WDP*, 29 October 1932.

146 NAC report, 17-18 September 1932.

147 BRO, file 34908(46)F, Bristol Constabulary, Administration Department, Subject; Hunger Marchers (1932); D: Division report NUWM meeting, 7 October 1932.

148 Ibid.

149 e.g. see *WDP*, 17 October 1932.

150 *Ministry of Labour Gazette* June 1932, p. 219; January 1933, p. 23; January 1934, p. 21.

prison for 2-3 months.[151] At the end of October five people were found guilty of disorderly conduct at a lobby of the PAC and all were imprisoned for up to four months.[152] Most importantly on 9th November Bill Fairman[153] and J. C. Lloyd were both gaoled, for four and three months respectively, for incitement to assault the police.[154]

Thus by mid-November 1932 eighteen NUWM members or supporters had been imprisoned and several others were bound over to keep the peace. The gaoling of many of the leading organisers inevitably had an adverse effect on an organisation committed to as hectic a level of activity as the NUWM. Fairman's remarks in his defence before being gaoled in November 1932 alluded directly to the intentions of the prosecutions. After arguing that the charges against Lloyd and himself were brought with the object of suppressing the working class Fairman warned,

> I may go to prison — it may put the movement back for a short time, but the workers will never go under.[155]

That the Bristol NUWM was all but finished as a mass movement by 1933 is confirmed by the NAC reports. From the December 1932 meeting onwards no Bristol representative attended and, whereas the 1932 NAC reports are full of references to successful campaigning in Bristol, the few subsequent mentions point to the weakness of the Bristol NUWM. In May 1933, for example, the NAC received a report on the 'bad situation in Bristol'.[156] However the NUWM did retain a presence in Bristol for some time. In 1933 the NUWM was involved with the BUA and the Trades Council in organising a strike of 700 task workers.[157] Charlie Webber was on the 1934 Hunger March and, on reaching London, was a member of a NUWM delegation to the House of Commons.[158] Finally, in the national wave of protest that greeted the creation of the Unemployed Assistance Board (UAB) in February 1935, the NUWM and BUA held a joint demonstration to the local UAB office. This passed off 'perfectly orderly and with very few police in attendance'.[159] Led by the two former rivals, Webber and Jack Linton (BUA), the organisations could only muster 300 protesters between them.[160] Several years had passed since the propertied classes of Bristol had felt directly threatened by the organised unemployed.

---

151 *WDP*, 25 & 30 August 1932.

152 *WDP*, 21 October 1932, 1 November 1932.

153 Fairman appears to have come in for particular attention from the police. He was among those arrested during the September 1931 match to the TUC offices in Bristol. In July 1932 he was acquitted of a charge of sedition and later police harassment drove him to leave Bristol. A. Tuckett, interview, 20 December 1988.

154 *WDP*, 10 November 1932.

155 Ibid.

156 NAC reports.

157 Large & Whitfield, *The Bristol Trades Council*, p. 27.

158 Claude Stanfield, *1934 Hunger March Diary*, unpublished MS. University of Swansea.

159 *WDP*, 8 February 1935.

160 Ibid.

4. Politics, Police and the NUWM

The unemployed struggles of 1931-32 were a response to the economic measures introduced in autumn 1931. The National Government also provoked wider unrest by cutting the pay of public employees. At the centre of these protests was a two-day strike by sailors which paralysed the Royal Navy's Atlantic Fleet. Faced with this opposition the Government limited pay reductions to 10% and went on to a landslide victory at the general election.[161] Only the unemployed continued to protest against the emergency measures. Far from accepting the situation the NUWM set out to

> ... rouse and rally the whole of the working class to mass and stormy activity against the attacks of the National Government.[162]

But this challenge was mounted in the most difficult circumstances.

The electoral rout of the Labour Party in 1931 was the last of a series of defeats which had quelled the potentially revolutionary workers' movement of the post-war years. Clear confirmation of this was the imposition of the household means test on the uncovenanted unemployed just as unemployment approached its highest level of the inter-war period. Unemployment in the 1920s was mainly a structural problem of the declining export industries. The collapse of world trade in the Great Depression dealt a particularly harsh blow to these already struggling industries. In shipbuilding insured unemployment leapt from 24.3% in 1929 to 62.1% in 1932, while in coal-mining it rose from 16.0% to 38.9% in the same period.[163] Yet, in the 1920s it was workers in industries like these who had 'constantly exerted their organised strength to avoid being subjected to'[164] the inquisitional and stigmatised means test. But by January 1932 nearly one million unemployed workers were being means tested.[165]

It has been said of the household means test that, 'Nothing was more perfectly designed to goad otherwise peaceful men to revolution'.[166] If the state faced a revolutionary challenge in 1931/32 it was against the NUWM which it had to deploy its defences. But to what extent were the leaders of the NUWM building a revolutionary rather than a protest movement? As we have seen the organisation was built around a core of communists and socialists, many of them former trade unionists. Yet by submitting to the dictates of the Comintern's 'Third Period' the NUWM was in practice isolating itself from the employed workers whose active support was essential to their revolutionary goals. Belfast was the only area where trade unions took major strike action in support of the NUWM in 1932.[167]

---

161 Branson & Heinemann, *Britain in the Nineteen Thirties*, pp. 22-29.

162 NAC, 3-4 October 1931.

163 Beveridge, *Full Employment*.

164 F. M. Miller, 'National Assistance or Unemployment Assistance? The British Cabinet and Relief Police, 1932-33', *Journal of Contemporary History* Vol. 9 No 2 (1974): 163.

165 Stevenson & Cook, *The Slump*, p. 69.

166 Blythe, *The Age of Illusion*, p. 160.

167 Croucher, *We Refuse to Starve in Silence*, pp. 136-9.

In a sense the CP *cadres* who led the NUWM can be seen as being torn between two conflicting tasks. On the one hand they were obliged to acknowledge the exhortations to revolution from the Comintern. Equally they had to accept that as a 'trade union of the unemployed' the NUWM was not an adequate vehicle to spearhead the socialist transformation.[168] The disputes over the NUWM's legal and advisory work were a symptom of this tension. The pressures towards reformism are also manifest in the NUWM's campaigns. The agitation of 1932 culminated in nothing more radical than a mass lobby of Parliament to petition against the means test. This reflected the reality that the majority of NUWM members, not to mention the wider unemployed, continued to give their political allegiance to the Labour Party.[169] The NUWM put their demand for 'Work or Full-Maintenance' on the back burner and engaged in a defensive campaign for the amelioration of the worst privations of the unemployed.

While the NUWM never endangered the social order, they did cause the government grave concern. In October 1932 the Minister of Labour informed the Cabinet that if protests continued the means test might have to be abandoned.[170] To avoid this, a Cabinet Committee was set up to find ways of dealing with the Hunger Marches, even going so far as to draft a bill banning them.[171] In fact, since the first Hunger March in 1922 government efforts to undermine the NUWM had involved increasing co-ordination of the state apparatus and manipulation of the media. In 1922 the prime minister fed details of the communist leanings of the NUWM leaders to the press, with allegations of a plot against the Crown. Simultaneously the Ministry of Labour refused to pay insurance benefits to Hunger Marchers while the Ministry of Health ordered that poor law relief be given in accordance with casual regulations, (i.e. that 'paupers' be searched, be set task work and be detained for two days). Despite this, Hunger Marchers were usually able to persuade local Boards of Guardians to give them food and shelter on more favourable terms.[172]

In 1932 these efforts were stepped up. The Ministry of Health circulated Chief Constables and PACs hoping that this time,

> ... local Poor Law authorities may be less inclined to weakness of action. Their close connection with the police may be of assistance in this regard.[173]

When the Hunger Marchers converged on London news cameras were prevented from filming the rally in Hyde Park.[174] But above all the attempts to control the

---

168 Ibid. p. 110.

169 R. Hayburn, 'The Police & The Hunger Marchers', *International Review of Social History* Vol. 17 (1972): 626.

170 Miller, 'National Assistance or Unemployment Assistance?', p. 171.

171 M. Turnbull, 'Attitude of Government and Administration towards the 'Hunger Marches' of the 1920s and 1930s', *Journal of Social Policy* Vol. 2, No 2 (1973): 137.

172 Ibid. pp. 133-4.

173 BRO file 34908(46)F, Home Office to Chief Constable, 653 963/2, undated, with Ministry of Health memo dated 26 September 1932.

174 Stevenson & Cook, *The Slump*, p. 223.

unemployed protests of 1932 were based on intensive policing of the NUWM. In this respect the parallels between the experiences of the NUWM nationally and in Bristol are illuminating.

From their earliest emergence radical working class movements have been the subject of police scrutiny. The infiltration of spies and the manipulation of informers was a prominent feature of the policing of the Luddites and other movements during the social upheavals which followed the Napoleonic Wars. Such methods were vital to

> ... the extraordinary skill with which the Government succeeded in forestalling serious revolutionary developments.[175]

In the case of the NUWM the police seem to have taken these methods to the extreme. Metropolitan police files reveal the extent to which police agents 'swarmed all over' the NUWM's national leadership and London organisation as well as infiltrating the contingents of Hunger Marches.[176] The records which are available in Bristol, only a fraction of the extensive documentation which must have been compiled, also provide ample evidence of spying and well placed informers.

In February 1932, Sergeant Bond, Bristol CID, reported on a NUWM meeting in the Horsefair, stating that while the public meeting was in progress the NUWM Committee was meeting at their West Street Office to plan a forthcoming demonstration. At the Horsefair meeting Parker, one of the NUWM speakers, said that holding the two meetings simultaneously was a deliberate ploy to prevent the police learning of their plans. Despite this, Bond's report concludes, 'copy of plan and arrangements made are in the hands of Supt. Barnes'.[177] This suggests that there was an informer in the inner circle of the Bristol NUWM. Parker's statements also confirm that the NUWM leaders knew they were under surveillance, even if they were unaware how close this surveillance was.

An indication of the problems of relying on informers, and the thin line that distinguishes a spy from a *provocateur*, lies in an anonymous letter to 'Mr Bond' which remains in the Bristol police files. The letter was written days before the South Wales contingent of the 1932 Hunger March arrived in Bristol, with the apparent aim of persuading the police that they are mistaken in 'not expecting trouble' from the March. Instead the informant warns that instructions have been issued 'to give the police all the trouble possible' and names two Bristol NUWM leaders as likely troublemakers.[178] This is reminiscent of the nature of police spying more than a hundred years earlier as pointed out by E. P. Thompson:

---

175 E. P. Thompson, *The Making of the English Working Class* (London: Victor Gollancz, 1965), p. 439.

176 See Hayburn, 'The Police & The Hunger Marchers'; R. Harrison, 'New Light on The Police & the Hunger Marchers', *Society for the Study of Labour History*, Bulletin 37 (Autumn 1978): 17-47; P. W. Kingsford, 'The Police and the Hunger Marchers', *Society for the Study of Labour History*, Bulletin 38 (Spring 1979): 21-2; J. Stevenson, 'The Police and the 1932 Hunger March', *Society for the Study of Labour History*, Bulletin 38 (Spring 1979): 24-34.

177 BRO file 34908(46)D, 1932, CID report, 25 February 1932.

178 Ibid., file 34908(46)F, 1932, anonymous to Mr Bond, undated.

> The informer was paid by piece-rate; the more alarmist his information, the more-lucrative his trade.[179]

As it turned out, the Hunger March passed through Bristol without incident, but had the police acted on their informant's letter this might not have been the case.

It was a more open type of surveillance that provided the evidence to prosecute and imprison NUWM leaders nationally and in Bristol. The police appear to have had a policy of arresting leaders at time likely to cause maximum disruption to NUWM activities. (Their surveillance would have told the police when these times were.) Wal Hannington was arrested on the morning of 1 November, the day the 1932 Hunger March was to climax with a mass lobby of Parliament. The police were determined to prevent this taking place and did so, aided no doubt by Hannington's enforced absence. The evidence offered against Hannington was the notes made by police officers of his speech in Trafalgar Square the previous day.[180]

The imprisonment of the NUWM leadership nationally must have contributed to subduing their protests. By December 1932 Maud Brown (Women's Organiser) was the only member of the NUWM's 'most formidable headquarters team' not in prison. Even Tom Mann, the veteran workers' leader, was incarcerated in Brixton prison at the age of 78.[181] From the formation of the National Government until the end of 1932, police action against the NUWM included over 100 baton charges, 1,300 arrests and 421 convictions.[182] That the NUWM should need a respite after more than a year of intense campaigning and equally intensive policing was inevitable. It has to be remembered that for a mass movement of 50,000 members, in this its most active period,[183] the NUWM was very dependent on a small centralised leadership composed mostly of communists. (In January 1932 the CP had 9,000 members, 60% of whom were unemployed).[184] This made the movement especially vulnerable to this type of police strategy.

With regard to Bristol there are two points about the policing of the NUWM that need explaining. The first is to ask why the local NUWM was much more severely weakened by the imprisonment of its leaders than was the case nationally. It is possible to detect a clear change in police tactics in the summer of 1932. Control and confrontation on the streets seems to have given way to a more subtle tactic of targeted arrests. This change of emphasis has to be seen in relation to the objectives of police policy. Was Chief Constable Maby simply concerned to maintain order on the streets of Bristol or were his intentions more overtly political?

A clue to the causes of the rapid demise of the Bristol NUWM lies, paradoxically, in its achievements. Although the protests in Bristol never reached

---

179 Thompson, *The Making of the English Working Class*, p. 485.

180 J. Stevenson, 'The Politics of Violence' in G. Peele & C. Cook (eds.), *The Politics of Reappraisal, 1918-1939* (London: Macmillan, 1975), pp. 155-6.

181 Croucher, *We Refuse to Starve in Silence*, pp. 119, 141-3.

182 G. Allen Hutt (1933) cited in Stevenson & Cook, *The Slump*, p. 229.

183 Stevenson & Cook, *The Slump*, p. 158.

184 Ibid., p. 136.

the level of those in Birkenhead or Belfast, the Bristol NUWM earned the right in 1932 to consider itself *'a leading NUWM branch'*,[185] compared to many more traditional areas of labour militancy. One of the problems inherent in organising the unemployed lies in the division that separates them from employed workers. In Bristol this would have been particularly acute given the relatively high pay and secure employment enjoyed by the employees, especially skilled workers, in the large factories. It is likely that the Bristol unemployed comprised a disproportionate number of low paid, unskilled and casual workers, relatively unaccustomed to trade union organisation. Thus the unemployed would have been more isolated than in the more traditionally strong NUWM areas; centres of the engineering industry such as the Clyde, Manchester and Coventry and the South Wales coalfield.[186]

This isolation was intensified by the divisions in the labour movement. Here the sectarianism of the CP served only to make them more vulnerable to police oppression. Even when the labour movement voiced its opposition to the batoning of the unemployed it did not go so far as to speak up for the NUWM. Bristol East MP, Stafford Cripps, made his reservations plain as late as October 1932:

> Many members of the Labour Party have been doing their utmost to keep the unemployed away from the influence of the Communists. ... Only a few weeks ago I was asked by the unemployed of Bristol to lead a deputation, and I refused because I was not going to associate myself with the rioting which I knew would probably result.[187]

In fact there had not been a 'riot' in Bristol for four months. But this public rebuttal from a leader of the Labour left indicates how beyond the pale the NUWM was in 1932.

All these difficulties were accentuated by the weak position of the CP in Bristol. Not only was the local CP branch small, it also had little influence among the organised working class as 'practically every member was unemployed'.[188] The secretary of Bristol Trades Council was a fierce opponent of the NUWM but the CP had hardly any voice within the official movement to oppose him. Furthermore the limited resources of the CP/NUWM in Bristol meant that once their frontline leaders were removed there were not sufficient reserves to replace them. Mass unemployment in Bristol persevered well beyond 1932 but the NUWM did not.

The early part of the history of the Bristol NUWM described here is characterised by a series of violent clashes with the police. After 9th June 1932 this ends and instead relations with the police are highlighted by the trials of NUWM activists. A similar change occurred nationally but only at a much later date. When the 1932 Hunger Marchers reached London they became embroiled

---

185 G. Cocking at Bristol NUWM meeting in Barton Hill, 6 October 1932, BRO file 34908(46)F, report, 7 October 1932.

186 Hayburn, 'The National Unemployed Workers' Movement', p. 286.

187 Quoted in Whitfield, *The Labour Movement in Bristol*, p. 330.

188 H. Pollitt to A. Tuckett, 15 January 1956.

in a week long battle with the police.[189] But when the South Wales contingent had earlier passed through Bristol there was no hint of trouble as the Chief Constable's report confirms.[190] The most plausible explanation for this change in police strategy is simply that violent confrontation was proving counter-productive. As we have seen, police baton charges on the NUWM in September 1931 and February 1932 had provoked increased support for the NUWM from Bristol workers. After the February events the labour movement began to protest against the (perceived) police brutality.

The violence in Castle Street on 9 June brought this first phase of policing to a conclusion. An examination of accounts of this incident points to a well laid ambush by the police, presumably intended to intimidate NUWM supporters. None of the press reports offer any evidence of behaviour by the unemployed to provoke the police attack. These reports describe baton wielding police springing from nowhere, rapidly followed by a charge of mounted police; indeed, the very speed of events suggests the police were lying in wait. (On other occasions the police had to call for reinforcements even when they knew the route of marches beforehand.)[191] Even the *Western Daily Press* coverage, which as usual assumed the police to be in the right, conveys the impression of a carefully prepared trap with the street in darkness (it was after 10.00pm) and then, when the rout is nearly completed, the scene is 'flooded with light as the street lights came on'.[192] The fact that there is not a single mention of this incident in the police files in the Bristol Record Office does suggest that the files have been 'weeded'; any incriminating evidence having been removed.

The importance of the Castle Street ambush is not just that it was an unprovoked, premeditated attack, but that it was seen to be so; not least by the Bristol film-goers who came out of the cinema to find themselves in the middle of a violent assault on defenceless families. When a local paper carried the accounts of these shocked witnesses the police could only have been embarrassed.[193] NUWM leader Charlie Webber's claim from the dock that 'the whole city is indignant at the unprovoked baton charge'[194] was probably near the mark. As we have seen, the labour movement was stirred and so probably was public opinion generally. That violent state repression of the working class can be counter-productive in this way is not particularly novel. E. P. Thompson notes other incidents (especially the Peterloo Massacre of 1819) when violent attacks by the authorities extended the protests they were supposed to quash:

> Indignation provoked Radical organisation where it had never before existed, and open-air demonstrations were held in regions hitherto under the spell of the 'loyalists'. ... The Yeomanry rode down their meeting and the right of public meeting was gained.[195]

---

189 Kingsford, 'The Police and the Hunger Marchers'.
190 BRO file 34908(46)F, Chief Constable to Sir Vernon Kell, 17 October 1932.
191 BRO file 34908(46)D, Chief Constable to Home Office, 10 & 24 February 1932.
192 *WDP*, 10 June 1932.
193 *BEP*, 10 June 1932.
194 ILD, *Bread or Batons?*, p. 12.
195 Thompson, *The Making of the English Working Class*, pp. 690, 831.

Having made this strategic error, the Bristol police were obliged to revise their tactics. They now set out to portray the NUWM as the perpetrators of violence against the police. There is some evidence that they were helped in this by the local authorities and the press. The centrepiece of what amounted to a public relations campaign was the 'show trial' of Parker, Bailey and Webber on 27th June 1932. The prosecution in this case was acting on the instructions of the Town Clerk.[196] A further suggestion of collusion is a curious report in a local newspaper only two days before the trial. Here the Director of the PAC complained of attempted intimidation of relief officers by demonstrations outside their homes by an unnamed organisation — by implication the NUWM.[197] The trial itself, at which a plethora of police allegations of NUWM incitement to violence against the police were aired amid great publicity, was held the day before the Special Council meeting demanded by the Labour Group to call for an inquiry into the Castle Street incident, a call which was lost.

The NUWM Chairman, Parker, had been convicted of similar offences that April and could probably have expected to be sent to prison. But for Bailey and Webber the six months sentences seem particularly harsh given that these were their first appearances in court and that the jury recommended leniency.[198] None of those convicted of incitement in April had been gaoled. The conclusion must be that this trial was a calculated response to the Castle Street ambush where the police attempt to break the NUWM badly backfired. It was also the first of several trials which were to put most of the Bristol NUWM leaders behind bars in the later part of 1932, all on similar charges. In the charge of incitement to violence against the police, Chief Constable Maby had found an effective weapon with which to fight the NUWM. Maby discovered this approach being used by the Manchester police, with whom he corresponded in April 1932, writing that the time had come for the NUWM demonstrations to be 'stopped'.[199]

A former Commissioner of the Metropolitan Police has pointedly remarked that 'The real art of policing a free society or a democracy is to win by appearing to lose'.[200] The Bristol Police manifestly won the physical battle in Castle Street but by being caught in the act of such a victory they were in danger of losing the wider struggle for public support which they were contesting with the NUWM. To acknowledge this is to affirm that the police were locked in a political struggle with the NUWM. The police, of course, are generally at great pains to deny that they are anything other than politically neutral, or at least are not politically partisan. As Reiner has argued, law enforcement in a society stratified on class and other lines is inevitably partisan. Even if laws were made on universal and impartial principles they would still reinforce and reproduce-social inequalities:[201]

---

196 *WDP*, 18 June 1932.

197 *WDP*, 25 June 1932.

198 *WDP*, 28 June 1932, *BEP*, 28 June 1932.

199 F. M. Miller, 'National Assistance or Unemployment Assistance?', p. 163.

200 Sir Robert Mark quoted in R. Reiner, *The Politics of the Police* (London: Harvester Wheatsheaf, 1985), p. 54.

201 Ibid., p. 2.

> The law in its majestic equality, forbids the rich as well as the poor to
> sleep under bridges, to beg in the streets and to steal bread.[202]

This is the point behind the NUWM challenge, 'Bread or Batons?' By
demanding bread the unemployed were pointing up the vast inequalities of inter-
war Britain. Accordingly they received batons — in defence of a concept as non-
partisan as public order.

The gist of Reiner's thesis is that being a social organisation in an unequal
society the police, in carrying out their duties, cannot but be politically partisan
in impact. But this does not mean the police are intentionally partisan. It is the
intention that the police are denying when they proclaim their political
neutrality. Studies of the policing of the NUWM tend to concur with this
analysis. Royden Harrison's examination of Metropolitan Police files relating to
the 1934 Hunger March leads him to conclude that,

> ... at least 90% of the material ... is confirmatory of a comfortable,
> orthodox liberal view of the State. The police emerge as functionaries
> who have an overriding interest in protecting persons and property. *Their
> aim is to avoid public disturbance not to provoke it.*[203]

More generally Stevenson and Cook's discussion of the threats to public order in
the 1930s finds that, while the police were a good deal less even handed with the
NUWM than they were with the British Union of Fascists, they,

> ... reacted less in political terms than in response to the challenge to
> public order and to their own position as the custodians of law and
> order.[204]

Such 'comfortable' findings may be tenable in relation to the later 1930s but
not to the tense months of 1932. Then there was quite clearly an orchestrated
attempt by the police and the state generally to paint a picture of the NUWM as
little more than a gang of subversives predisposed to violence. As the police's
own surveillance of the NUWM must have told them, this was a
misrepresentation of a disciplined body which eschewed 'the politics of
violence'. In part this false impression was created simply for public
consumption but it also served a more sinister purpose. Such was the level of this
distortion that the police must have been influenced by their own propaganda
with the result that, 'the police received orders which permitted extraordinary
violence...' against the NUWM.[205]

When this happened, as it did in Castle Street on 9th June 1932, the police
were provoking public disturbance, not avoiding it. Neither were they 'protecting
persons and property'. These methods failed only when the police were found
out and thus jeopardised their 'secret weapon' of public sympathy.[206] Then a

---

202 Anatole France (1894) quoted in ibid., p. 3.

203 My emphasis. Harrison, 'New Light on The Police & the Hunger Marchers', p. 19.

204 Stevenson & Cook, *The Slump*, p. 243.

205 Kingsford, 'The Police and the Hunger Marchers', p. 22.

206 Reiner, *The Politics of the Police*, p. 54.

new, less belligerent strategy was called for but the ends, the intention, remained the same; to 'stop at all costs' the NUWM, a legitimate movement of the unemployed.

Bibliography

Books and Pamphlets

ADAMS, T. WITH THOMPSON, F. L., FRY, E. M. AND ADAMS, J. W. R., *Recent Advances in Town Planning* J. & A. Churchill, London, 1932.

ADELMAN, P., *The Rise of the Labour Party 1880-1945*, Longman, Harlow, Essex, 1986; first published 1972.

ALDCROFT, D. H. AND RICHARDSON, H. W., *The British Economy 1870-1939*, Macmillan, London, 1969.

ALDRED, G. A., *At Grips with War*, Bakunin Press, Glasgow, 1929.

ALFORD, B. W. E., *W. D. & H. O. Wills and the Development of the U.K. Tobacco Industry, 1786-1965*, Methuen, London, 1973.

[ANON.], *Bye-Laws, Rules & Orders, for the Conduct, Management & Government of all Pilots and others within the Port of Bristol*, Bryan, Bristol, 1809.

[ANON.], *The Lysaght Century, 1857-1957*, J. Lysaght, Bristol, 1957.

[ANON.], *Women Workers: Papers Read at a Conference Convened by the Bristol & Clifton Ladies Association for the Care of Ladies, in November 1892*. Papers Read at a Conference Convened by the Bristol & Clifton Ladies Association for the Care of Ladies, in November 1892, J.W. Arrowsmith, Bristol, 1893.

[ANON.], *British Labour Statistics: Historical Abstract 1886-1968*, Her Majesty's Stationery Office, Department of Employment, 1971.

[ANON.], *International Labour Defence Bristol. Bread or Batons?*, Bristol, 1932.

ARCHER, I., JORDAN, S. AND RAMSEY, K., *Abstract of Bristol Historical Statistics part 4: Health Statistics 1838-1985*, University of the West of England, Bristol, 1997.

ATKINSON, B., *Trade Unions in Bristol*, Bristol Branch of the Historical Association, The University, Bristol, 1982.

BAIN, G. S. AND PRICE, R., *Profiles of Union Growth*, Blackwell, Oxford, 1988.

BALL, R, *Tolpuddle And Swing – The Flea And The Elephant*, Bristol Radical History Group, Bristol, 2010.

_____, *The origins and an account of Black Friday – 23rd December 1892*

Bristol Radical History Group, Bristol, 2013.

BARRETT, G., *The Anarchist Revolution*, Freedom Press, London, 1915.

_____, *The Last War: A Collection of Three Essays by George Barrett*, Pirate Press, Sheffield, 1990.

BARTLETT, J., *Fishponds*, Tempus, Stroud, 2004.

BEEVERS, R., *The Garden City Utopia: A Critical Biography of Ebenezer Howard*, Macmillan, Basingstoke, 1988.

BELSEY, J. [*et al*], *Bristol: The Growing City: Life in the Suburbs – from the 18th Century to Today*, Redcliffe, Bristol, 1986.

BENHAM, P., *The Avalonians*, Gothic Image, Glastonbury, 2006.

BEVERIDGE, W. H., *Full Employment in a Free Society*, Allen & Unwin, London, 1944.

BILD, I., (ed), *Bristol's Other History*, Bristol Broadsides, Bristol, 1983.

_____, *Placards and Pin Money*, Bristol Broadsides, Bristol, 1986.

BLATCHFORD, R., *Merrie England*, Clarion Office, London, 1894.

BLYTHE, R., *The Age of Illusion*, Hamilton, London, 1963.

BOOKCHIN, M., *The Limits of the City*, Harper Colophon, New York, 1974.

_____, *From Urbanization to Cities: Towards a New Politics of Citizenship*, rev. edn. 1995, Cassell, London, 1992.

BOSTON, S., *Women Workers and Trade Unions*, Lawrence and Wishart, London, 1987.

BOYCE, L., *The Bristol Suffragettes*, Silverwood Books, Bristol, 2013.

BRANSON, N. AND HEINEMANN, M., *Britain in the Nineteen Thirties*, Panther, London, 1973.

BRENT, J., *Searching for Community: Representation, Power and Action on an Urban Estate*, Policy Press, Bristol, 2009.

BRIERLEY L. AND REID, H., *Go Home and Do the Washing! Three Centuries of Pioneering Bristol Women*, Broadcast Books, Bristol, 2000.

BRIGGS, A. AND SAVILLE, J. (eds), *Essays in Labour History*, Macmillan, London, 1960.

BROWN, T. (ed), *Edward Carpenter and Late Victorian Radicalism*, Frank Cass, London, 1990.

BRYHER, S., *An Account of the Labour & Socialist Movement in Bristol*, Bristol Labour Weekly, Bristol, 1929.

BULLEY, A. A. AND WHITLEY, M., *Women's Work*, Kessinger Legacy Reprints, Montana, USA, first published Methuen, London, 1894.

BUSH, G., *Bristol and its Municipal Government 1820-1851*, Bristol Record Society, Bristol, 1976.

CARPENTER, E., *Never Again: A Protest and a Warning Addressed to the Peoples of Europe*, National Labour Press, Manchester, 1916.

CHALLINOR, R., *The Origins of British Bolshevism* London: Croom Helm, 1977.

CHARKE, C., *A Narrative of the Life of Mrs Charlotte Charke, written by herself*, Whittaker, Treacher and Arnot, London, 1755.

CHRYSTAL, P., *Cadbury and Fry Through Time*, Amberley Publishing, Stroud, 2012.

CLARKSON, L. (ed), *British Trade Union and Labour History: A Compendium*, Humanities Press International, Atlantic Highlands, New Jersey, USA, 1990.

CLAYWORTH, A., *Oscar Wilde: Selected Journalism*, Oxford University Press, Oxford, 2004.

CLEGG, H. A., *A History of British Trade Unions since 1889: Volume 2 1911–1933*, Clarendon Press, Oxford, 1987, first published 1985.

COATES, R., *The Street-Names of Shirehampton and Avonmouth*, Shire Community Newspaper, Shirehampton, 2011; rev. 2013

COLLINSON, W., *The Apostle of Free Labour: The Life Story of William Collinson Founder and General Secretary of the National Free Labour Association*, Hurst and Blackett, London, 1913.

COLVILE, H. C. A., *Thomas William Harvey, Prophet and Priest*, J. W. Arrowsmith, Bristol, 1918.

COSTLEY, N., *West Country Rebels*, Breviary Stuff, London, 2012.

CRAIG, F. W. S., *British Parliamentary Election Results, 1918-1939*, MacMillan, Revised edition, London, 1977.

CRAWFORD, E., *Women's Suffrage Movement: A Reference Guide 1866-1928*, University College London Press, London, 1999.

———, *The Women's Suffrage Movement in Britain and Ireland: A Regional Survey*, Routledge, Abingdon, 2006.

CRICK, M., *A History of the Social Democratic Federation*, Ryburn Publishing/Keele University Press, Wakefield, Yorkshire, UK, 1994.

CROUCH, D. AND WARD, C., *The Allotment: Its Landscape and Culture*, [1988] Mushroom, Nottingham, 1994.

CROUCHER, R., *We Refuse to Starve in Silence*, Lawrence & Wishart, London, 1987.

CULPIN, E. G., *The Garden City Movement Up-to-Date*, Garden Cities and Town

Planning Association, London, 1913.

DANGERFIELD, G., *The Strange Death of Liberal England*, London: Serif, 1997; first published 1935.

DANIELL, M. AND NICOL R. A., *The Truth about Chocolate Factories or Modern White Slavery*, G.H. Wood Collection, Huddersfield University, 1889.

_____, *The New Trade Unionism: Its Relation to the Old; and the Conditions of its Success*, A. Jenkins, Bristol, 1890.

DARLEY, G., *Villages of Vision: A Study of Strange Utopias*, rev. and updated edn., Five Leaves, Nottingham, 2007.

DARLINGTON, R., *Syndicalism and the Transition to Communism: An International Comparative Analysis*, Ashgate, Aldershot, England, 2008.

DAUNTON, M. J. (ed), *Councillors and Tenants: Local Authority Housing in English Cities 1919-1939*, Leicester University Press, Leicester, 1984.

DEACON, A. AND BRADSHAW J., *Reserved For The Poor*, Blackwell & Robertson, Oxford, 1983.

DEVINE, F. (ed), *A Capital in Conflict: Dublin City and the 1913 Lockout*, Dublin City Council, Dublin, 1913.

DIX, G., *The Image Breakers*, Frederick A. Stokes, New York, 1900.

DRESSER, M. AND OLLERENSHAW P. (eds), *The Making of Modern Bristol*, Redcliffe Press, Tiverton, 1996.

ENGELS, F., *The Condition of the Working Class in England*, Panther, London, 1969.

FEINSTEIN, C. A., *National Income, Expenditure & Output of the United Kingdom, 1855-1965*, Cambridge University Press, Cambridge, 1972.

GAY, K. AND GAY, M. K. (eds), *Encyclopedia of Political Anarchy*, ABC-CLIO, Santa Barbara, Calif., 1999.

GERMAN, L. AND REES J., *A People's History of London*, Verso, London, 2012.

GILBERT, B., *British Social Policy, 1914-1939*, Batsford, London, 1970.

GIRDLESTONE, E. D., *Christian Socialism in England, The Dawn*, Andover–Harvard Theological Library, first published in Cambridge, Massachusetts: Progress Publishing Company, May 1890.

GLAGE, L., *Clementina Black: A Study in Social History and Literature*, Carl Winter, Heidelberg, 1981.

GLOVERSMITH, F. (ed), *Class, Culture & Social Change*, Harvester Wheatsheaf, Brighton, 1980.

GLYNN, S. AND OXBORROW J., *Interwar Britain*, Allen & Unwin, London, 1976.

GLYNN, S. AND BOOTH A. (eds), *The Road to Full Employment*, Allen & Unwin,

London, 1987.

GOLDMAN, E., *Living My Life*, [1931] in 2 vols. Dover, New York, 1970.

GOULD, P., *Early Green Politics: Back to Nature, Back to the Land, and Socialism in Britain 1880-1900*, Harvester Press, Brighton, 1988.

GRAVES, R., *Goodbye to all that*, [1929], rev. ed. Penguin, Harmondsworth, 1960.

HADDRELL, I., *Lockleaze Schools* Stroud: History Press, 2008.

HALL, P. AND WARD C., *Sociable Cities: The Legacy of Ebenezer Howard*, Wiley, Chichester, 1998.

HARDY, D., *Alternative Communities in Nineteenth Century England*, Longman, London, 1979.

HANNINGTON, W., *Never On Our Knees*, Lawrence & Wishart, London, 1967.

———, *Unemployed Struggles, 1919-1939*, Lawrence & Wishart, London, 1979.

HARVEY, C. AND PRESS J. (eds), *Studies in the Business History of Bristol*, Bristol Academic Press, Bristol, 1988.

HAYDU, J., *Between Craft and Class: Skilled Workers and Factory Politics in the United States and Britain, 1890-1922*, University of California Press, Berkeley and Los Angeles, USA, 1988.

HILL, C., *Reformation to Industrial Revolution: A Social and Economic History of Britain 1530-1780*,Weidenfeld & Nicolson, London, 1967.

HINTON, J., *Labour and Socialism: A History of the British Labour Movement 1867-1974*, Harvester, Brighton, 1983.

HOBSBAWM, E. J. (ed), *Labour's Turning Point: Nineteenth Century Vol. 111 1880-1900*, Lawrence and Wishart, London, 1948.

———, *Labouring Men: Studies in the History of Labour*, Weidenfeld and Nicolson, London, 1968.

HOGGETT, P. [*et al*], *Class, Race and Community Cohesion: A Profile of Hillfields, Bristol.* Report of research conducted for the Community Cohesion Unit of Bristol City Council by the University of the West of England and Community Resolve, University of the West of England, Bristol, 2008.

HOLTON, B., *British Syndicalism 1900-1914: Myths and Realities*, Pluto, London, 1976.

HOPKINS, R., *The Transition Handbook: From Oil Dependency to Local Resilience*, Green Books, Bideford, 2008.

HOWARD, E., *Garden Cities of To-Morrow*, Faber, London, 1965; first published 1902.

HOWELL, B., *The Police in Late Victorian Bristol*, Bristol Branch of the Historical Association, The University, Bristol, 1989.

HUNT, S., *Anarchism in Bristol and the West Country to 1950*, Bristol Radical History Group, Bristol, 2010.

HUTCHINSON, J. R., *The Press-Gang Afloat and Ashore*, Kessinger Publishing, Montana, USA, 2004, first published in Dutton & Co, New York, 1914.

HUTT, A., *British Trade Unionism*, Lawrence & Wishart, London, 1975; first published 1941.

HYDE, D., *I Believed: The Autobiography of a Former British Communist*, William Heinemann, Melbourne, 1951.

HYMAN, R., *The Workers' Union*, Clarendon Press, Oxford, 1971.

INGLIS, K. S., *Churches and the Working Classes in Victorian England*, Routledge, London, 1963.

ISLES, A. AND ROBERTS, T., *All Knees and Elbows of Susceptibility and Refusal: Reading History From Below*, Mute Books, The Strickland Distribution, Transmission Gallery, 2012.

JACOBS, J., *The Death and Life of Great American Cities: The Failure of Town Planning*, Penguin, London, 1965; first published 1961.

JEVONS, R. AND MADGE J., *Housing Estates: A Study of Bristol Corporation Policy and Practice Between the Wars*, Pub. for the University of Bristol by J. A. Arrowsmith, Bristol, 1946.

JOINT ADVISORY COMMITTEE FOR CONSCIENTIOUS OBJECTORS, *What Every Bristol Man Should Know*, Joint Advisory Committee for Conscientious Objectors, Bristol, 1916.

_____, *Conscientious Objectors at Horfield*, Joint Advisory Committee for Conscientious Objectors, Bristol, [c.1916-c.1917].

JORDAN, S., RAMSEY, K. AND WOOLLARD M., *Abstract of Bristol Historical Statistics, Part 3: Political Representation and Bristol's Elections 1700-1997*, Series Editor Peter Wardley, Bristol Historical Databases Project, Faculty of Humanities, University of the West of England, 1997.

KAPP, Y., *The Air of Freedom: The Birth of the New Unionism*, Lawrence and Wishart, London, 1989.

KELLY, K. AND RICHARDSON M., 'The Shaping of the Bristol Labour Movement, 1885-1985', in *The Making of Modern Bristol*, edited by M. Dresser and P. Ollerenshaw, Redcliffe Press, Tiverton, 1996.

KNABB, K. (ed), *Situationist International Anthology*, Bureau of Public Secrets,

Berkeley, CA, 1981.

KNOWLES, K. G. J. C., *Strikes—A Study in Industrial Conflict: With Special Reference to British Experience Between 1911 and 1947*, Blackwell, Oxford, 1952.

KROPOTKIN, P., *Fields, Factories and Workshops Tomorrow*, Colin Ward ed. first pub. as book in 1899 from articles written 1888-90; Freedom Press, London, 1985.

_____, *Mutual Aid: A Factor of Evolution*, Freedom Press, London, 1993; first pub. 1902.

_____, *Wars and Capitalism*, Freedom Press, London, 1916.

LAMB, P., *Electricity in Bristol 1863-1948*, Bristol Branch of the Historical Association, Bristol, 1981.

LARGE, D., *The Municipal Government of Bristol 1851-1901*, Bristol Record Society, Bristol, 1999.

_____, *Radicalism in Bristol in the Nineteenth Century*, Bristol Record Society, University of Bristol, Bristol, 1981.

_____ AND R. WHITFIELD, *The Bristol Trades Council 1873-1973*, Bristol Branch of the Historical Association The University, Bristol, 1973.

LARKIN, E., *James Larkin 1876-1947: Irish Labour Leader*, Routledge & Kegan Paul, London, 1977; first published 1965.

LATIMER, J., *The Annals of Bristol in the Nineteenth Century: 1887-1900*, George's sons, Bristol, 1902.

_____, *Sixteenth Century Bristol*, J. W. Arrowsmith, Bristol, 1908.

LAURENT, J. (ed), *Tom Mann: Social and Economic Writings: A pre-Syndicalist selection*, Spokesman, Nottingham, 1988.

LAYBOURN, K., *A History of British Trade Unionism c.1770-1990*, Alan Sutton, Stroud, England, 1992.

LEDGER, S., *The New Woman: Fiction and Feminism at the fin de siècle*, Manchester University Press, Manchester, 1997.

LEE, H. W., *The Great Strike Movement of 1911 and its Lessons*, Twentieth Century Press, London, 1911.

LEVINE, P., *Victorian Feminism 1850-1900*, Hutchinson Education, London, 1987.

LEWENHAK, S., *Women and Trade Unions: An Outline History of Women in the British Trade Union Movement*, Ernest Benn, London, 1977.

LITTLE, B., *The City & County of Bristol*, Wernar Laurie, London, 1954.

LYES, J., *Bristol 1901-1913*, Bristol Branch of the Historical Association: Local History Pamphlets, Bristol, 2002.

MALLORY, K., *The Bristol House*, Redcliffe Press in assoc. with Hoddell Pritchard, Bristol, 1985.

MALOS, E., 'Bristol Women in Action (1839-1919)', in *Bristol's Other History*, edited by I. Bild, Bristol Broadsides, Bristol, 1983.

MALPASS, P. AND WALMSLEY, J., *100 Years of Council Housing in Bristol*, Faculty of the Built Environment, University of the West of England, Bristol, 2005.

MANN, T., *Tom Mann's Memoirs*, Macgibbon and Kee, London, 1967; first pub. 1923.

MANN, T AND TILLET, B., *The "New" Trades Unionism: a reply to Mr George Shipton*, Green and McAllan, London, 1890.

MANSON, M., *Bristol: Beyond the Bridge*, 2nd ed., Past & Present Press, Bristol, 2000.

MAPPEN, E., *Helping Women at Work: The Women's Industrial Council 1889-1914*, Hutchinson, London, 1985.

MARSHALL, P., *Demanding the Impossible: A History of Anarchism*, Fontana/Harper Collins, London, 1993.

McGRATH, P. (ed), *Bristol in the Eighteenth Century*, David and Charles, Newton Abbot, 1972.

_____, *The Merchant Venturers of Bristol: a History of the Society of Merchant Venturers of the City of Bristol from its Origin to the Present Day*, American Society of Civil Engineers, Greensboro, NC, USA, 1975.

_____ and J. Cannon (eds), *Essays in Bristol and Gloucestershire History*, Bristol and Gloucestershire Archaeological Society, Bristol, 1976.

McNEILL, J., *Ben Tillett*, Bristol Radical History Group, Bristol, 2012.

MELLER, H. E., *Patrick Geddes: Social Evolutionist and City Planner*, Routledge, London, 1990.

MIDDLEMAS, K., *Politics in Industrial Society: The Experience of the British System since 1911*, André Deutch, London, 1979.

MILIBAND, R., *Parliamentary Socialism*, Merlin, London, 2nd edn., 1972.

MILLS, S., *A Barbarous And Ungovernable People – A Short History Of The Miners Of The Kingswood Forest*, Bristol Radical History Group, Bristol, 2010.

MOWAT, C. L., *Britain Between the Wars, 1918-1940*, Methuen, London, 1955.

MULLEN, S., 'Sweet Girls and Deal Runners', in *Placards and Pin Money*, edited by I. Bild, Bristol Broadsides, Bristol, 1986.

NABB, H., *The Bristol Gas Industry 1815-1949*, Bristol Branch of the Historical Association, The University of Bristol, Bristol, 1987.

NEALE, W. G., *At the Port of Bristol, Vol. 1: Members and Problems 1848-1899*, Port of Bristol Authority, Bristol, 1968.

_____, *At the Port of Bristol, Vol. 2: The turn of the tide 1900-1914*, Port of Bristol Authority, Bristol, 1970.

NEWSINGER, J., *Rebel City: Larkin, Connolly and the Dublin Labour Movement*, Merlin, London, 2004.

NICHOLLS, F. J. AND TAYLOR, J., *Bristol Past and Present*, Arrowsmith, Bristol, 1882.

PEACE PLEDGE UNION, *Refusing to Kill: Conscientious Objection and Human Rights in the First World War*, Peace Pledge Union, London, 2006.

PEARCE, B., *Some Past Rank and File Movements* a *Labour Review*, pamphlet, November 1959.

PEARCE, W. T. (ed), *Fry's Works Magazine 1728-1928*, Bi-Centenary Number J. S. Fry & Sons Ltd, Bristol, 1928.

PEELE G. AND COOK, C. (eds), *The Politics of Reappraisal, 1918-1939*, MacMillan, London, 1975.

PELLING, H., *A History of British Trade Unionism*, Penguin, Harmondsworth 1976; first published 1963.

_____, *Popular Politics and Society in Late Victorian Britain*, Macmillian, London, 1968.

PHILLIPS, G. AND WHITESIDE, N., *Casual Labour*, Clarendon Press, Oxford, 1985.

POWYS, J. C., *Letters of John Cowper Powys to Louis Wilkinson 1935-1956*, Macdonald, London, 1958.

PRICE, R., *Labour in British Society*, Croom Helm, Beckenham, Kent, 1988.

PROTHERO, I. J., *Artisans and Politics in Early Nineteenth-Century London: John Gast and His Times*, Dawson, Folkestone, 1978.

PUNTER, J. (ed), *Urban Design and the British Urban Renaissance*, Routledge, London, 2010.

PYE, D., *Fellowship is Life: The Story of the Clarion Cycling Club,* 2nd ed., Clarion Publishing, Bolton, 2004.

ORWELL, G., *The Road to Wigan Pier* [1937], Penguin, Harmondsworth, 1962.

QUAIL, J., *The Slow Burning Fuse: The Lost History of the British Anarchists*, Paladin, London, 1978.

RAVETZ, A., *Council Housing and Culture: The History of a Social Experiment*, Routledge, London, 2001.

RAW, L., *Striking a Light: The Bryant and May Matchwomen and their Place in History*, Continuum, London, 2009.

REINER, R., *The Politics of the Police*, Harvester Wheatsheaf, London, 1985.

RICH, J., *The Bristol Pilots: A Treatise on the Bristol Pilots, from Their Origination, to Their Amalgamation: Including a List of Pilots' Names, Dates and Some of the Boats, for Almost 500 Years*, Atlantis 33, Pill, England, 1996.

RICHARDSON, M., *The Bristol Strike Wave of 1889-1890: Socialists, New Unionists and New Women: Part 1: Days of Hope*, Bristol Radical History Group, Bristol, 2012.

_____, *The Bristol Strike Wave of 1889-1890: Socialists, New Unionists and New Women: Part 2: Days of Doubt*, Bristol Radical History Group, Bristol, 2012.

_____, 'Trade Unionism and Industrial Conflict: A Historical Study' in *Bristol Historical Resource CD*, edited by P. Wardley Bristol: University of West of England.

ROBERTS, J., *The Definition and Characteristics of a Post-WWI Garden Suburb with Particular Reference to Sea Mills Garden Suburb, Bristol: A Study by Save Sea Mills Garden Suburb in association with Sea Mills and Coombe Dingle Community Project*, Save Sea Mills Garden Suburb/Sea Mills and Coombe Dingle Community Project, Bristol, 2007.

ROTHSTEIN, T., *From Chartism to Labourism*, Lawrence and Wishart, London, 1983; first published 1929.

ROWBOTHAM, S., *Edward Carpenter: A Life of Love and Liberty*, Verso, London, 2008.

_____ and Weeks, J., *Socialism and the New Life: The Personal and Sexual Politics of Edward Carpenter and Havelock Ellis*, Pluto, London, 1977.

RUDÉ, G., *The Crowd in History: A study of popular disturbances in France and England, 1730-1848*, Serif, London, 1995.

SCHNEER, J., *Ben Tillett*, Croom Helm, Beckenham, 1982.

SKIDELSKY, R., *Politicians and the Slump*, MacMillan, London, 1967.

SNOWDEN, P., *Socialism and the Drink Question*, Independent Labour Party, London, 1908.

SPARGO, J., *Syndicalism, Industrial Unionism and Socialism*, Red and Black Publishers, St Petersburg, Florida, USA, reprint; first published B W Huebsch, 1913.

STEPHENS, M., *Ernest Bevin – Unskilled Labourer and World Statesman 1881-1951*, TGWU publication, London, 1981.

STEPHENSON, D. AND WILLMOTT, J., *Bristol Cinemas*, Tempus Publishing, Stroud,

2005.

STEVENSON, J. AND COOK, C., *The Slump: Society & Politics During the Depression*, Quartet, London, 1979.

STUCKEY, P. J., *The Sailing Boats of the Bristol Channel*, David and Charles, Newton Abbot, England, 1977.

STURGE, E., *Reminiscences of My Life: and some account of the children of William and Charlotte Sturge and of the Sturge Family of Bristol*, printed by J. A. Arrowsmith, Bristol, for private circulation, 1928.

SWENARTON, M., *Homes Fit for Heroes: The Politics and Architecture of Early State Housing in Britain*, Heinemann Educational, London, 1981.

TALBOT, M., *A Plea for Women's Trade Unions*, Pamphlet, Bristol, 1892.

THACKER, J., *Whiteway Colony: The Social History of a Tolstoyan Community* Alan Sutton, Stroud, 1993.

THOMAS, E., *Shirehampton Story* Avonmouth, Ethel Thomas, Bristol, 1983.

THOMAS, S., *The Bristol Riots*, Bristol Branch of the Historical Association, Bristol University, Bristol, Reprint, 1999.

THOMPSON, E. P., *The Making of the English Working Class*, Penguin, Harmondsworth, 1982, first published by Victor Gollancz, 1963.

_____, *Customs in Common*, Merlin, London, 1991.

TIDWELL, S. C., *Pill Methodist Church 1757-1982*, Pamphlet, Bristol, July 1982.

TORR, D., *Tom Mann and his Times*, *Vol. 1 1856-1890*, Lawrence and Wishart, London, 1956.

TOTHILL, M. C., *Toleration or Persecution*, Joint Advisory Committee for Conscientious Objectors, Bristol, 1916.

TOUT, H., *The Standard of Living in Bristol*, Arrowsmith, London, 1938.

TUCKETT, A., *The People's Theatre in Bristol 1930-45*, Our History pamphlet 72 History Group of the Communist Party, London, 1979.

TUFTS, H., *Whitman's Ideal Democracy and other Writings*, Everett Press, Boston, MA., 1902.

WALLIS, T. R., *Sea Mills and the Battle of the Styles: Stylistic Variety in the Architecture of an Inter-War Garden Suburb and its Origins in Victorian Revivalism*, T. R Wallis, Bristol, 2004.

WALTER, N., *Damned Fools in Utopia and Other Writings on Anarchism and War Resistance*, PM Press, Oakland, Calif., 2011.

WARD, S. V. (ed), *The Garden City: Past, Present and Future*, E & FN Spon, London, 1992.

WEBB, S. AND WEBB B., *The History of Trade Unionism, 1666-1920*, Printed by the authors for the students of the Workers' Educational Association, London, 1919.

WELLS, C., *A Short History of the Port of Bristol*, J. W. Arrowsmith, Bristol, 1909.

WHITTINGHAM, S., *Sir George Oatley: Architect of Bristol*, Redcliffe Press, Bristol, 2011.

WILLIAMS, R., *The Country and the City* Chatto & Windus, London, 1973.

WILSON, D. F., *Dockers: the impact of industrial change*, Fontana, London, 1972.

WILSON, R., *Difficult Housing Estates*, Tavistock, London, 1963.

WOODCOCK, G. AND AVAKUMOVIĆ, IVAN, *The Anarchist Prince: A Biographical Study of Peter Kropotkin*, T. V. Boardman, London, 1950.

WRIGHT J. & CO.'S, *Mathew's Bristol and Clifton Directory*, 1889.

YEATES, P., *Lockout: Dublin 1913*, St Martins Press, New York, USA, 2000.

Papers and Articles

ALLEN, V. L., 'The Origins of Industrial Conciliation and Arbitration', *International Review of Social History* Vol. 9:2 (1964).

[ANON.], *The Ministry of Labour Gazette* HMSO, January (1933).

ARROWSMITH, J., 'The Struggle over Working Time in Nineteenth and Twentieth Century Britain', *Historical Studies in Industrial Relations*, No. 13, Spring (2002).

BEVIR, M., 'British Socialism and American Romanticism', *The English Historical Review*, Vol. 110, No. 438 September (1995).

CALLAGHAN, J., 'The Edwardian Crisis: The Survival of Liberal England and the Rise of a Labour Identity', *Historical Studies in Industrial Relations*, No. 33 (2012).

DAUNTON, M. J., 'Inter-Union Relations on the Waterfront: Cardiff 1888-1914', *International Review of Social History*, 22 (1977).

DAVIDSON, R., 'The Board of Trade and Industrial Relations 1896-1914', *The Historical Journal*, Vol. 21, No. 3. Sep. (1978).

DAVIES, S., "Crisis? What Crisis?': The National Rail Strike of 1911 and the State Response', *Historical Studies in Industrial Relations*, Vol. 33 (2012).

DAVISON, A., '"Try the Alternative": The Built Heritage of the Temperance Movement', *Brewery History* 123, Summer (2006).

DUFFY, A. E. P., 'New Unionism in Britain, 1889-1890: A Reappraisal', *The Economic History Review*, Vol. 14, No. 2 (1961).

FARR, G., 'Bristol Channel pilotage: historical notes on its administration and craft', *Mariner's Mirror*, XXXIX (1953).

GORDON, A., '1911: The First National Railway Strike and the Rail Union Amalgamation Movement', *Historical Studies in Industrial Relations*, Vol. 33 (2012).

GORSKY, M., 'Mutual aid and civil society: friendly societies in nineteenth-century Bristol', *Urban History*, 25, 3 (1998).

_____, 'Public Health in Interwar England and Wales: Did it fail?', *Dynamis* 28 (2008).

GREENWAY, J., 'No Place for Women? Anti-Utopianism and the Utopian Politics of the 1890s', *Geografiska Annaler* Series B, Human Geography, Vol. 84, No. 3-4.

HARRISON, R., 'New Light on The Police and the Hunger Marchers', *Society for the Study of Labour History* Bulletin 37, Autumn (1978).

HAYBURN, R., 'The Police and The Hunger Marchers', *International Review of Social History* Vol. 17, (1972).

_____, 'The National Unemployed Workers' Movement, 1921-36: A Re-appraisal', *International Review of Social History* Vol. 28, (1983).

HIGNETT, H., 'Pilotage History', *The Pilot: The Official Journal of the United Kingdom Maritime Pilots' Association UKMPA*, No. 278, July (2004).

HOWELL, D., 'The Contribution of Direct Action to Gradualism: The Railway Strike of 1911', *Historical Studies in Industrial Relations*, Vol. 33 (2012).

JONES, E. T., 'Illicit Business: Accounting for Smuggling in Mid-Sixteenth-Century Bristol', *The Economic History Review*, New Series, Vol. 54, No. 1 Feb. (2001).

KINGSFORD, P. W., 'The Police and the Hunger Marchers', *Society for the Study of Labour History* Bulletin 38, Spring (1979).

LYDDON, D., 'The Labour Unrest in Great Britain and Ireland, 1910-1914 – Still Uncharted Territory?', *Historical Studies in Industrial Relations*, Vol. 33 Liverpool University Press for the Keele University Centre for Industrial Relations (2012).

MALTZ, D., 'Ardent Service: Female Eroticism and New Life Ethics in Gertrude Dix's The Image Breakers 1900', *Journal of Victorian Culture* 17.2 (2012).

MARCHBANK, J., *The Railway Review: Silver Jubilee Supplement*, Warwick Digital Library, Modern Records Centre, University of Warwick, 25 March (1938).

MARTIN, M., 'Guardians of the Poor: A Philanthropic Female Elite in Bristol', *Regional Historian* 9, Summer (2002).

MATTHEW, H. C. G., McKIBBIN, R. I., AND KAY J. A., 'The Franchise Factor in the Rise of the Labour Party', *The English Historical Review*, Vol. 91, No. 361

Oct. (1976).

MEACHAM, S., '"The Sense of an Impending Clash": English Working-Class Unrest before the First World War', *The American Historical Review*, Vol. 77, No. 5 Dec. (1972).

MILLER, F. M., 'National Assistance or Unemployment Assistance? The British Cabinet and Relief Police, 1932-33', *Journal of Contemporary History* Vol. 9, No 2 (1974).

PHILLIPS, G. A., 'The Triple Industrial Alliance in 1914', *The Economic History Review*, New Series Vol. 24, No. 1 Feb. (1971).

PORTER, J. H., 'Wage bargaining under conciliation agreements, 1860-1914', *The Economic History Review*, 23 (1970).

SABLES, G., 'John Gregory and William Morris: Two Socialist Poets', *William Morris Society Newsletter*, Summer (2008).

SAVILLE, J., 'The Trades Dispute Act of 1906', *Historical Studies of Industrial Relations*, No. 1 March (1996).

SAYWELL, R. J., 'The Unitarian Meeting 1691-1774' in *Notes on Bristol History* No. 8 University of Bristol (1968).

SKILLETER, K. J., 'Housing Reform, Garden Suburbs and Statutory Town Planning at Bristol, 1900-39', *Planning History* 13.2 (1991).

STEVENSON, J., 'The Police and the 1932 Hunger March', *Society for the Study of Labour History* Bulletin 38, Spring (1979).

TAPLIN, E., 'The Liverpool Transport Strike, 1911', *Historical Studies in Industrial Relations*, Vol. 33 Liverpool University Press for the Keele University Centre for Industrial Relations (2012).

TURNBULL, M., 'Attitude of Government and Administration towards the 'Hunger Marches' of the 1920s and 1930s', *Journal of Social Policy* Vol. 2, no. 2 (1973).

WESTERGARD-THORPE, W., 'Towards a Syndicalist International: The 1913 London Congress', *International Review of Social History* 23 (1978).

WHITE, W. H., 'Decasualisation of Dock Labour at the Port of Bristol', *Economica* August (1932).

WHITESIDE, N., 'Welfare Insurance and Casual Labour: A Study of Administrative Intervention in Industrial Employment, 1906-26', *The Economic History Review*, New Series Vol. 32, No. 4 Nov. (1979).

WHYTE, W. H., 'Decasualisation of Dock Labour at the Port of Bristol', *Economica* No. 37, Aug. (1932).

WILSON, M. V., 'The Waterfront Strikes in Glasgow: Trade Unions and Rank-and-File Militancy in the Labour Unrest of 1910–1914', *International Review of Social History*, 53 (2008).

WILSON, R. AND HEATHERTON, C., 'Lore Turned Upside Down', *Mute Magazine*, 8 February 2007 Metamute.org accessed 27 August 2012.

Websites and blogs

ANNARKY'S BLOG, *Enemy of God and Foe of Kings*:
http://radicalglasgowblog.blogspot.co.uk/2013/04/enemy-of-god-and-foe-of-kings.html [accessed 29 December 2013].

BBC LIVERPOOL WEBPAGE, *Liverpool's Fatal 1911 Riot's Remembered*:
http://www.bbc.co.uk/news/uk-england-merseyside-14529243 [accessed 15 December 2013].

BONE, I., *Remembrance Sunday November 8th'*, Anarchist in the UK:
http://ianbone.wordpress.com/2009/10/27/remembrance-sunday-november-8th/ [accessed 27 October 2013].

_____, *Community Profile of Shirehampton* Bristol: Shirehampton Public Hall Community Association, (2001):
http://www.digitalbristol.org/members/shireweb/hall/profile.htm [accessed 8 June 2007].

BRISTOL CITY COUNCIL, *Southmead: 2008 Ward Profile*:
http://www.bristol.gov.uk/WardFinder/pdfs/southmead-profile.pdf [accessed 18 Dec 2008].

_____, *Lockleaze: 2008 Ward Profile*:
https://www.bristol.gov.uk/WardFinder/pdfs/lockleaze-profile.pdf [accessed 30 April 2014].

_____, *Sea Mills: Character Appraisal and Management Proposals*, Conservation Area 21 January (2011):
http://www.bristol.gov.uk/sites/default/files/assets/documents/sea-mills-character-appraisal.pdf [accessed online 26 March 2014].

_____, *Filwood Broadway Framework: Final Report*. City Design Group, Neighbourhoods and City Development. Bristol: Bristol City Council (2012):
http://www.bristol.gov.uk/sites/default/files/documents/planning_and_building_regulations/urban_design/urban_design_projects/Filwood%20Broadway%20Framework%20Final_1.pdf [accessed 21 April 2014].

_____, Napper, A. (Priority Stock Manager) to the PRC Project Consultation

Group Meeting at the Council House, 26th September 2006. Bristol City
Council website:
http://www.bristol.gov.uk/ccm/cms-service/download/asset/?
asset_id=17067004 [accessed 24 June 2007].

BRISTOL MAYORS & SHERIFFS - a collection of historical data:
http://www.davenapier.pwp.blueyonder.co.uk/mayors/history2.htm

BRISTOL COMMUNITY HOUSING FOUNDATION REPORT, *Regeneration of Upper Horfield
Estate, Bristol*: http://www.southwesthousing.co.uk/pdfs/SWHI%20BP
%20Regeneration%20of%20Upper%20Horfield%20Estate.pdf [accessed 7
Dec 2008].

BUSH, H., *Bristol Town Duties - A collection of original and interesting documents*,
British History online, Chapter 4, Wharfage, Cranage and Pilotage (1828):
http://www.british-history.ac.uk/report.aspx?compid=108166 [accessed 20
July 2012].

BUCK, R., http://www.lifestoriesandmemories.co.uk/37/1/story/Ray-Buck.asp
[accessed 14 September 2012]

CHRONOLOGY OF EMMA GOLDMAN WEBSITE, http://anarcho.tripod.com/emma3.html
[accessed 12 July 2010].

COATES, R., *The Street-Names of Shirehampton and Avonmouth* Shirehampton:
Shire Community Newspaper, 2011; rev. 2013:
http://www.shire.org.uk/content/history/streetnames.pdf [accessed 28 March
2014].

COMMUNITY VOICE: NEWSLETTER OF THE SEA MILLS AND COOMBE DINGLE COMMUNITY
PROJECT (2006), http://community-voice.org.uk/cvoice/cvoice_21_5.pdf
[accessed 16 Nov 2008].

CURTIS, B., Interview 11 November 1998. British Library Shelf Mark
C900/00510: http://sounds.bl.uk/Accents-and-dialects/Millenium-memory-
bank/021M-C0900X00510X-2600V1.

GOLDMAN, E. AND J. COLTON LETTERS, http://libcom.org/history/letters-emma-
goldman-james-colton [accessed 20 April 2010].

GLASGOW CALEDONIAN UNIVERSITY, RADICAL GLASGOW WEBPAGES, *Guy Aldred*:
http://www.gcu.ac.uk/radicalglasgow/chapters/aldred.html [accessed 25
November 2013].

HEATH, N., *Kavanagh, Mat (1876-1954)*, Libcom.org website:
https://libcom.org/history/kavanagh-mat-1876-1954 [accessed 17 May
2014].

_____, *Anarchists Against World War One: Two Little Known Events –*
Abertillery and Stockport. Libcom.org website:
http://libcom.org/history/anarchists-against-world-war-one-two-little-known-
events-abertillery-stockport [accessed 27 October 2013].

_____, *Barrett, George 1888-1917*. Libcom.org website:
http://libcom.org/history/barrett-george-1888-1917   [accessed 29 October
2013].

Hoggett, P. [*et al*], *Class, Race and Community Cohesion: A Profile of Hillfields,*
Bristol. Report of research conducted for the Community Cohesion Unit of
Bristol City Council by the University of the West of England and
Community Resolve Bristol: University of the West of England (2008)
http://www.uwe.ac.uk/hlss/research/cpss/research_reports/Hillfields.pdf
[accessed 1 May 2014].

Hopkins, R., *The Transition Handbook: From Oil Dependency to Local Resilience*
Bideford: Green Books (2008), website at: http://www.transitionnetwork.org/
[accessed 3 May 2014].

Jenkins, T., *Bristol Borough: The History of Parliament: the House of Commons*
1820-1832, ed. D.R. Fisher, Cambridge University Press, 2009:
http://www.historyofparliamentonline.org/volume/1820-
1832/constituencies/bristol

King's Weston Action Group website, http://www.kwag.org.uk/history/philip-
napier-miles/ [accessed 29 March 2014].

_____, *The Victorian Era: The Miles Family*:
http://www.kwag.org.uk/history/the-victorian-era/ [accessed 29 March
2014].

Living Easton website,
http://www.cems.uwe.ac.uk/~rstephen/livingeaston/local_history/tillett.html

Livings, S., *The Miles Family and Leigh Court*:
http://www.abbotsleigh.org.uk/ALMiles.html [accessed 29 March 2014].

Penny, J. (ed.), *The Bristol & District Blitz War Memorial: A Register of those*
who Lost their Lives due to Enemy Action and Surrounding Districts, 1940-
1944: http://fishponds.org.uk/bristolmem.html [accessed 21 April 2014].

Pill Churches, http://www.pillchurches.org.uk [accessed 15 September 2012]

Rich, J., *The Parish of Easton-in-Gordano*: http://www.easton-in-
gordano.org.uk/Pages/History.html accessed 14 September 2012.

Sea Mills and Coombe Dingle Community Project webpage, *How we got here*:

http://community-voice.org.uk/l2_how.php [accessed 7 Dec 2008].

SELFED COLLECTIVE, *History of Anarcho-Syndicalism*, Unit 6: 'Revolutionary Syndicalism in Britain and Ireland 1910-1917': http://www.selfed.org.uk/docs/units/2001/pdfs/06.pdf [accessed 10 Apr 2010].

SOMERDALE CAMPAIGN WEBSITE, http://wwwsaveoursomerdale.co.uk/ [accessed 22 Jan 2008, now unavailable].

STONE, W. A., *A History of Gloucester Harbour Trustees: Part 1 1890 – 1966*: http://www.gloucesterharbourtrustees.org.uk [accessed 14 September 2012].

TOWN AND COUNTRY PLANNING ASSOCIATION, *Garden City Settlements and Their Future: A Project Log*, TPCA website: http://www.tcpa.org.uk/downloads/20081031-GCS_Project_Log.doc [accessed 7 Dec 2008]

TSUZUKI, C., *Carpenter, Edward (1844-1929). Oxford Dictionary of National Biography*: http://www.oxforddnb.com/view/article/32300?docPos=1 [accessed 29 December 2013].

TUC HISTORY ONLINE, http://www.unionhistory.info/timeline/1880_14_Narr_Display.php? Where=NarTitle+contains+'The+Labour+Party'+AND+DesPurpose+contains+WebDisplay [accessed 29 April, 2013].

UCL DEPARTMENT OF HISTORY'S LEGACIES OF BRITISH SLAVE-OWNERSHIP WEBPAGE FOR PHILIP JOHN MILES, http://www.ucl.ac.uk/lbs/person/view/19118 [accessed 29 March 2014].

WELLER, K., *The London Transport Women Workers' Strike 1918*, Libcom.org website: https://libcom.org/history/london-transport-women-workers-strike-1918 [accessed 17 May 2014].

WEST OF ENGLAND BAPTIST ASSOCIATION, http://www.webassoc.org.uk/ChurchDetail.aspx?id=77 [accessed 15 September 2012].

Unpublished works

ATKINSON, B., *The Bristol Labour Movement 1868-1906*, D.Phil., Oxford University, 1969.

BACKWITH, D., *Housing not Herding? The Politics of Knowle West in the 1930s*, Unpublished thesis submitted for the degree of MA in Comparative Labour History, University of Warwick, 1990.

BATEMAN, D., *The First Bristol May-Day, 1890: Eleanor Marx-Aveling on the Downs*, Unpublished paper, no date.

CLENCH, T., *'Happiness in Industry' – Working for J. S. Fry & Sons, Cocoa and Chocolate Manufacturers, Bristol 1865-1971*, Unpublished Final Project Report for Open University course DA301, 2001.

KELLY, K., *The Port of Bristol 1919-1939: A Study of a Municipally Owned Port*, Unpublished PhD, University of the West of England, 1999.

STANFIELD, C., *1934 Hunger March Diary*, Unpublished Ms., University of Swansea.

WESTERGARD-THORPE, W., *Revolutionary Syndicalist Internationalism, 1913-1923: The Origins of the International Working Men's Association*, Unpublished PhD, The University of British Columbia, 1979.

WHITFIELD, R., *The Labour Movement in Bristol 1910-1939*, Unpublished MLitt. Thesis, University of Bristol, 1979.

Reports

SAFE NEIGHBOURHOODS UNIT, *The Southmead Survey 1991*, Bristol City Council/Bristol Safer Cities Project, Bristol, (1991).

Newspapers and Periodicals

Aberdeen Journal
Bristol Evening News
Bristol Evening Post
Bristol Evening World
Bristol Guardian and Gazette
Bristol Mercury
Bristol Observer
Bristol Post
Bristol Times and Mirror
Building Design
Clifton Chronicle
Cornishman
Daily Express
Daily News
Derby Daily Telegraph
Dundee Courier
Evening Telegraph
Exeter and Plymouth Gazette
Freedom: A Journal of Anarchist Communism

Glasgow Herald
Hull Daily Mail
Justice
Liverpool Echo
London Gazette
Manchester Courier and Lancashire General Advertiser
Reynold's Newspaper
Social Democrat
South Gloucester Gazette
Tamworth Herald
The Clarion
The Commonweal
The Felix Farley Bristol Journal
The Guardian
The Independent
The People's Press
The Powys Review
The Raven
The Times
The Tribunal
Western Daily Press
Western Gazette
Western Times
Women's Penny Paper
Women's Union Journal
Yorkshire Gazette

Miscellaneous

GREENE, G., (dir) *The End of Suburbia Oil Depletion and the Collapse of the American Dream*, 2004.

HURD, M., 1983, sleeve notes to *The Immortal Hour*, performed by the Geoffrey Mitchell Choir and the English Chamber Orchestra and conducted by Alan G. Melville London: Hyperion Records, 1998.

INDEX

INDEX

INDEX

INDEX

INDEX

INDEX

INDEX

Paul, F., 138
Paynter, Will, 290
Peace Pledge Union, 41
Pelling, Henry, 201-2
Perry, J. H., 138
Petherick, W. J. 27, 176
Pill Friendly Society, 73
Pilots, 4, 65-90
Plimsoll, Samuel, 82
Pochin's Alum Works, 155. 162
Police and policing:
    ambush, 302, 313;
    attacks upon, 9-10, 157, 160, 162, 172, 207, 215, 293-4, 299-300, 302, 307;
    bans, 33;
    baton charges, 283, 289-90, 311, 313;
    breaking up meetings, 33, 38, 56, 160;
    Bristol, 158, 168, 171, 290, 310, 314;
    'class enemies', 164;
    condemnation, 303;
    conspiracy, 157;
    cordon, 172, 290, 292, 295, 299;
    court, 88;
    demonstrations, 156, 303;
    inner-city, 275;
    Manchester, 314;
    Metropolitan, 314-15;
    mounted, 170, 207-8, 215, 293, 299, 313;
    notice, 167;
    NUWM, 310-11;
    papers, 54;
    parades, 114, 163;
    plain clothes, 171;
    protecting 'blacklegs', 159-61
    raids, 36;
    records, 11-12;
    reinforcements, 168, 313;
    reports, 306;
    repression, 179, 292, 306;
    'riot', 10, 294;
    role, 152;
    routes of marches, 292;
    South Wales, 152;
    spies, 180, 310-11;
    station (Bridewell), 169-70, 172, 293;
    strategy, 148, 313-5;
    strike breakers, 39, 133, 147, 156-7, 200;
    surveillance, 315;
    sympathetic, 105, 107, 149;
    tactics, 311;
    Temple Meads, 160;
    threats to, 167;
    Tonypandy, 43;
    uniforms, 225;
    violence, 157-8, 160-1, 175-6, 207-8, 215, 293, 295, 299, 304, 312-13, 315;
    Watch Committee 147, 156-7, 174;
    water, 84-5;
    'worn out', 165-6;
Port of Bristol, 65-8, 70, 75-6, 83, 85, 109, 205-6, 213, 226, 230, 286
Port Sunlight, (Merseyside), 248
Portishead, 39, 74-5, 204-6, 212
Portsmouth, 40, 58
Potter, Jack, 290
Powell, Martin J., 259
Powys, John Cowper, 4, 30, 60-1
    A Glastonbury Romance, 30
Press-gangs, 69
Price, Danny, 299
Priestman, Anna, 115
Pritchett, Samuel, 140
Proudhon, Pierre-Joseph, 15
Psycho-geography, 6
Public Assistance Committees, 283, 288, 291-2, 302, 305-9, 314
Public houses, 6, 38, 81, 161, 248, 256, 264, 268, 272
Pugsley, A. J., 286

Quail, John, 21, 38, 42
Quakers and Quakerism, 17, 97, 104, 106, 108, 153, 242-3, 266

Radstock, 4
Railway Conciliation Scheme, 216, 237
Rawle, Frank, 102, 104, 112-4, 132-3
Ray, Thomas, 80, 85
Reddie, Cecil, 19
Reed, George, 83-5
Reiner, R., 314
Repton, George, 242
Rhondda Valley, 217-8, 305
Riley, William (John) Harrison, 18-9, 100, 194
Riots, 8, 43, 75, 168, 176, 275
Roberts, John, 248, 250, 252
Roberts, Peter, 266
Robinson, Alfred, 255
Robinson, Edward, 156 170
Robinson, Elisha Smith, 255
Rogers, Henry, 112
Rowbotham, Sheila, 18, 24-5, 97-100, 115
Rowe, Rose, 157
Rowntree, Seebohm, 185, 266, 272, 282
Rumley, Charles, 75-6
Rumley, John, 76
Ruskin, John, 30, 62, 243, 274

INDEX

INDEX

INDEX

Also from
BREVIARY STUFF PUBLICATIONS

Ralph Anstis, Warren James and the Dean Forest Riots, *The Disturbances of 1831*
£14.00 • 242pp *paperback* • 191x235mm • ISBN 978-0-9564827-7-8

John E. Archer, 'By a Flash and a Scare', *Arson, Animal Maiming, and Poaching in East Anglia 1815-1870*
£12.00 • 206pp *paperback* • 191x235mm • ISBN 978-0-9564827-1-6

Victor Bailey, Charles Booth's Policemen, *Crime, Police and Community in Jack-the-Ripper's London*
£17.00 • 162pp *paperback* • *2 colour and 8 b/w images* • 140x216mm • ISBN 978-0-9564827-6-1

Victor Bailey, Order and Disorder in Modern Britain, *Essays on Riot, Crime, Policing and Punishment*
£15.00 • 214pp *paperback* • *5 b/w images* • 191x235mm • ISBN 978-0-9570005-5-1

Alastair Bonnett & Keith Armstrong (eds.), Thomas Spence: The Poor Man's Revolutionary
£15.00 • 214pp *paperback* • 156x234mm • ISBN 978-0-9570005-9-9

John Belchem, 'Orator' Hunt, *Henry Hunt and English Working Class Radicalism*
£14.00 • 248pp *paperback* • 191x235mm • ISBN 978-0-9564827-8-5

Bob Bushaway, By Rite, *Custom, Ceremony and Community in England 1700-1880*
£14.00 • 206pp *paperback* • 191x235mm • ISBN 978-0-9564827-6-1

Malcolm Chase, The People's Farm, *English Radical Agrarianism 1775-1840*
£12.00 • 212pp *paperback* • 152x229mm • ISBN 978-0-9564827-5-4

Malcolm Chase, Early Trade Unionism, *Fraternity, Skill and the Politics of Labour*
£14.00 • 248pp *paperback* • 191x235mm • ISBN 978-0-9570005-2-0

Nigel Costley, West Country Rebels
£20.00 • 220pp *full colour illustrated paperback* • 216x216mm • ISBN 978-0-9570005-4-4

James Epstein, The Lion of Freedom, *Feargus O'Connor and the Chartist Movement, 1832-1842*
£17.00 • 296pp *paperback* • 156x234mm • ISBN 978-0-9929466-1-6

James Epstein, Radical Expression, *Political Language, Ritual, and Symbol in England, 1790-1850*
£15.00 • 220pp *paperback* • 156x234mm • ISBN 978-0-9929466-2-3

Catherine Howe, Halifax 1842, *A Year of Crisis*
£14.50 • 202pp *paperback* • 156x234mm • ISBN 978-0-9570005-8-2

Barry Reay, The Last Rising of the Agricultural Labourers, *Rural Life and Protest in Nineteenth-Century England*
£12.00 • 192pp *paperback* • 191x235mm • ISBN 978-0-9564827-2-3

Buchanan Sharp, In Contempt of All Authority, *Rural Artisans and Riot in the West of England, 1586-1660*
£12.00 • 204pp *paperback* • 191x235mm • ISBN 978-0-9564827-0-9

Dorothy Thompson, The Chartists, *Popular Politics in the Industrial Revolution*
£16.00 • 280pp *paperback* • 191x235mm • ISBN 978-0-9570005-3-7

E. P. Thompson, Whigs and Hunters, *The Origin of the Black Act*
£16.00 • 278pp *paperback* • 156x234mm • ISBN 978-0-9570005-2-0

David Walsh, Making Angels in Marble, *The Conservatives, the Early Industrial Working Class and Attempts at Political Incorporation*
£15.00 • 268pp *paperback* • 191x235mm • ISBN 978-0-9570005-0-6

Roger Wells, Insurrection, *The British Experience 1795-1803*
£17.50 • 372pp *paperback* • 191x235mm • ISBN 978-0-9564827-3-0

Roger Wells, Wretched Faces, *Famine in Wartime England 1793-1801*
£18.00 • 412pp *paperback* • 191x235mm • ISBN 978-0-9564827-4-7

Lightning Source UK Ltd.
Milton Keynes UK
UKHW010605180419
341232UK00002B/49/P